'*The Uncivil Wars* differs from most other books written on Northern Ireland. It is not a 'history' of the conflict since 1968 (for that has been done often before), but an attempt to construct a framework that will accommodate a range of alternative settlements. This attempt, however, is not made until the final chapters, and the core of the book is devoted to detailed analyses of lengthy interviews with key political figures in Northern Ireland, the Republic and Britain. The author's technique is to encourage the principal protagonists – Molyneaux, Paisley, Hume, Morrison, Tyrie, Prior, Haughey and FitzGerald – to discuss the main issues at considerable length, then to submit their views to the most rigorous and penetrating examination. It is done brilliantly, and there can scarcely be a politician on either side of the great divide who will not be infuriated to find his prejudices and self-delusions exposed in this unmerciful way. . . . *The Uncivil Wars* contains the best analysis we have had so far of the Troubles and of the policies of the leading political figures. . . a real tour-de-force.' – Jack Magee, *Irish News*

Padraig O'Malley is Senior Policy Analyst at the John W. McCormack Institute of Public Affairs at the University of Massachusetts, Boston.

The Uncivil Wars

Ireland Today

Padraig O'Malley

The Blackstaff Press

To Gina

First published in the United States of America by
Houghton Mifflin Company
2 Park Street, Boston, Massachusetts 02108

First UK edition published in 1983
by The Blackstaff Press Limited
3 Galway Park, Dundonald, Belfast BT16 0AN
Reprinted 1984

Printed in Northern Ireland by The Universities Press Limited

British Library Cataloguing in Publication Data

O'Malley, Padraig
The uncivil wars.
1. Ireland – Politics and government –
1949-
I. Title
941.508214 DA963

ISBN 0-85640-301-6

Where jargon turns living issues into abstractions, and where jargon ends up competing with jargon, people don't have causes. They only have enemies. Only the enemies are real.

—V. S. Naipaul
"The Return of Eva Peron"

Acknowledgments

My sincere thanks to Professor Dan Aaron, Professor Bruce Logan, Professor Bernard McCabe, Professor Shaun O'Connell, Professor Catherine Shannon, Jim Carroll, and Arthur Green for having read all or part of the manuscript and for the helpful and insightful criticisms they provided. Responsibility for the faults that remain is, of course, entirely mine. My special thanks to Professor Franklin Patterson, Director of the Center for Studies in Policy and the Public Interest at the University of Massachusetts at Boston, for his constant encouragement and support and for always insisting in his gentle way that I could do better. Also thanks to those who helped me with my research in Boston —Jennifer Togher, Sheila Murphy, Ellis Robertson, and Una O'Brien — and in Dublin — Dr. Kieran Kennedy, Dr. Richard Sinnott, and above all Geraldine Keough; thanks again to my editors at Houghton Mifflin, Robie Macauley and Sarah Flynn, and to two wonderful and patient typists, Arlene Boumel and Audrey Megquier, who deciphered an almost indecipherable handscript. My gratitude and love to my brother Peter, publisher of *Ploughshares,* who in many ways made this project possible, and to my dear friends Ellis, Gail, and Elaine for taking my various and on occasion none too pleasing humors in stride. And finally, but by no means least, my best wishes and deepest care for all those in Ireland, North and South, Protestant, Catholic, and Dissenter, who gave so freely of their time and their thoughts. I will remember you always.

Padraig O'Malley
University of Massachusetts, Boston
May 1983

Contents

The Players

Following is a list of the players in the Republic of Ireland, Northern Ireland, and Britain who were interviewed by the author for this book. They are arranged according to party affiliation.

In the Republic

From Fine Gael

Garret FitzGerald: Taoiseach (Prime Minister) and leader of Fine Gael. Member of Dáil Éireann (Irish Parliament) since 1969; Minister for Foreign Affairs in the Fine Gael–Labour coalition from 1973 to 1977. Became leader of Fine Gael in 1977. Served as Taoiseach for nine months in 1981–82 before his coalition government with Labour fell. However, the Fianna Fáil government that took over lasted less than six months. After the November 1982 election he formed a new coalition government with Labour.

Fine Gael originated in the pro-treaty (that is, the Anglo-Irish Treaty of 1921) wing of the old Sinn Féin. It has never been able to sustain a government from its own ranks. Since the mid-1970s it has moved somewhat to the left of Fianna Fáil (see below) — not that the concept of "left" has much meaning in the context of Irish politics. It is regarded as being less "Republican" than Fianna Fáil.

Paddy Harte: Former Minister of State for Posts and Telegraphs (1981–82) and former spokesman for Fine Gael on Northern Ireland. Member of Dáil Éireann for County Donegal since 1961. Maintains close contacts with a wide variety of parties in Northern Ireland, including paramilitaries.

From Fianna Fáil

Charles Haughey: Leader of Fianna Fáil and Leader of the Opposition in Dáil Éireann (Irish Parliament). Member of the Dáil since 1957.

Minister for Justice, 1961–64; Minister for Agriculture, 1964–66; Minister for Finance, 1966–70; Minister for Health and Social Welfare, 1977–79. Taoiseach, 1979–81 and again in 1982 for six months.

Fianna Fáil is the largest political party in the Irish Republic. It originated in the Republican wing of Sinn Féin, which opposed the Anglo-Irish Treaty of 1921. It came to power in 1932 and has ruled the country for most of the period since, except for 1948–51, 1954–57, 1973–77, mid-1981 to March 1982, and beginning in December 1982, when coalition governments headed by Fine Gael governed in its place. Fianna Fáil is a staunchly Republican party. At the moment it is divided—badly, in the eyes of many—between those who support Charles Haughey and those who do not.

Martin Mansergh: Director of Research for Fianna Fáil and Charles Haughey's special adviser on Northern Ireland; a Protestant, a graduate of Trinity College, Dublin, and son of the celebrated historian Nicholas Mansergh, whose book *The Government of Northern Ireland: A Study in Devolution* (London, 1936) is regarded as a classic in its field.

From Provisional Sinn Féin

Daithi O'Conaill: Believed to have been Chief of Staff of the Provisional IRA in 1973. Vice President of Provisional Sinn Féin. Credited with the invention of the car bomb. O'Conaill was among the IRA officials the British government flew to London in 1972 for talks with William Whitelaw, then Secretary of State for Northern Ireland. He also took part in the secret meeting with Protestant clergymen at Feakle, County Clare, which led to the 1975 IRA cease-fire

The Provisional IRA and the political wing, Provisional Sinn Féin, came into being in January 1970 after the IRA Army Council voted to give token recognition to the parliaments in London, Dublin, and Belfast. The Provisional IRA (PIRA) has sustained a thirteen-year military campaign to end what it terms the British "occupation" of Ireland.

From the Workers' Party

Thomas MacGiolla: President of Official Sinn Féin (now the Workers' Party) since January 1970, and President of Sinn Féin, before the split, from 1962 to 1970. Elected to Dáil Éireann in November 1982.

In Northern Ireland

From the Social Democratic and Labour Party

John Hume: Leader of the Social Democratic and Labour Party (SDLP). Member of the European Parliament since 1979. A member of the Assembly (1973–74) for Londonderry, head of the Commerce Department in the 1974 power-sharing Executive, and member of the Constitutional Convention (1975–76).

The SDLP speaks for the majority of Catholics in Northern Ireland. Founded in 1970 by a group of ex-civil rights activists, it was an umbrella party. It brought together the remnants of the old Nationalist Party, which stood for unity with the rest of Ireland and little else, the National Democratic Party, and the Republican Labour Party. Its long-term goals are a socialist state, in the European social democratic tradition, and Irish unity based on the consent of a majority of the people of Northern Ireland. It is now split between those who hew to a strictly nationalist line — the "Greens" — and those who do not. It demands power sharing as a right and, in the short term, an institutional link with the South — the so-called Irish Dimension.

Hume was elected to the Northern Ireland Assembly (October 1982), but did not take his seat.

Seamus Mallon: Deputy leader of the SDLP. Represented Armagh in both the Assembly (1973–74) and the Constitutional Convention (1975–76). Adheres to the nationalist line; among the most "Green" in the SDLP. Appointed to the Irish Senate (Seanad Éireann) by Charles Haughey in May 1982. Served in the Senate until the fall of Haughey's government in November 1982. Elected to the Northern Ireland Assembly (October 1982), but did not take his seat.

From the Official Unionist Party

James Molyneaux: Leader of the Official Unionist Party (OUP) and Member of Parliament at Westminster for South Antrim since 1970.

The OUP traces its origins to the Ulster Unionist Party, which was founded in 1892 and remained the sole voice of the Protestant population of Northern Ireland until the late 1960s. The monolith, however, collapsed during the divisions that ensued over civil rights, the fall of Stormont, and power sharing with the minority community. The OUP remains the largest Unionist party in the province. It is split between the integrationists — those who want full integration with Great Britain — and the devolutionists — those who want a return to devolved government in Northern Ireland. Officially, the OUP supports devolution. It opposes power sharing and an Irish Dimension.

Despite his position as party leader, Molyneaux remains an integrationist. He was elected to the Assembly (October 1982).

Harold McCusker: Deputy leader of the OUP. Member of Parliament at Westminster for County Armagh since 1974. Often talked of as a successor to Molyneaux. A former integrationist, now the party's foremost proponent of devolved government. Elected to the Assembly (October 1982).

Rev. Martin Smyth: Senior member of the OUP. Member of Parliament at Westminster for South Belfast since March 1982, when he was elected in place of the murdered Robert Bradford. Minister in Irish Presbyterian Church. Member of the Constitutional Convention (1975–76).

Since 1973 Smyth has been Imperial Grand Master of the Orange Order, the largest Protestant organization in Northern Ireland, with some eighty thousand to one hundred thousand members. About one Protestant adult in three is a member. In religious terms the Order stands for "good, Protestant clean living, fundamental sabbatarianism . . . and vehement opposition to the Catholic Church." In political terms the Order is pledged to "support and maintain the laws and constitution of the U.K. and Protestant succession to the throne."[1]

Smyth was elected to the Assembly (October 1982).

Robert McCartney: Queen's Counsel. "Liberal" Unionist. Calls himself a Unionist with a small "u." Prominent member of the OUP. Elected to the Assembly (October 1982).

From the Democratic Unionist Party

Rev. Ian Paisley: Member of Parliament at Westminster for North Antrim since 1970. Member of the European Parliament since 1979. Moderator of the Free Presbyterian Church and leader of the Democratic Unionist Party (DUP). Member of the Assembly (1973–74) and the Constitutional Convention (1975–76).

Founded in 1971, the DUP regards itself as being "right wing in terms of being strong on the Constitution but to the left on social policies."[2] It represents hard-line Unionism and political Protestantism. It opposes power sharing and an Irish Dimension. There are no divisions: it wants Northern Ireland's Parliament returned to Northern Ireland. It is engaged in a bitter struggle with the OUP to establish itself as the dominant voice of Unionism in Northern Ireland.

Paisley was elected to the Assembly (October 1982).

Jim Allister: Barrister-at-law. Press Officer for the DUP. Elected to the Assembly (October 1982) and appointed chief whip of DUP delegation in Assembly.

From the Alliance Party

Oliver Napier: Leader of the Alliance Party. Elected in East Belfast to both the Assembly (1973–74) and the Constitutional Convention (1975–76). Became head of the Office of Law Reform in the 1974 power-sharing Executive.

Founded in 1970, the Alliance Party campaigns on a strictly nonsectarian platform. It supports power sharing and the continuation of the U.K. link.

Napier was elected to the Assembly (October 1982).

From the Workers' Party's Republican Clubs

Seamus Lynch: Regional Chairman of the Workers' Party's Republican Clubs in Northern Ireland.

When the split in the IRA developed in 1970, the Republican Clubs became the political counterpart of the Official IRA in Northern Ireland. The Official IRA brought a halt to its military operations in 1972. In 1976 the Official Sinn Féin movement split, the more radical and militaristic wing forming the Irish Republican Socialist Party (IRSP) and its military counterpart the Irish National Liberation Army (INLA). Today, the Republican Clubs are the Northern wing of the Workers' Party. They disavow violence, contest elections, and support majority-rule devolved government in Northern Ireland as a first step toward an all-Ireland Workers' Republic.

Lynch was elected to the Workers' Party Ard Comhairle (ruling body) in April 1982. He stood for the Assembly but was defeated.

From Provisional Sinn Féin

Danny Morrison: Editor, *An Phoblacht,* Provisional Sinn Féin's weekly newspaper. National Director of Publicity for Sinn Féin. Elected to the Assembly (October 1982), but did not take his seat.

From the Ulster Defence Association

Andy Tyrie: A founding member of the Ulster Defence Association (UDA) and its Supreme Commander (later Chairman) since 1973. The UDA is the province's largest Protestant paramilitary organization.

John McMichael: Senior member of the UDA and Chairman of the Ulster Loyalist Democratic Party (ULDP), the political wing of the UDA. Former Secretary of the New Ulster Political Research Group (NUPRG), the organization set up by the UDA in 1978 to produce plans for an independent Northern Ireland.

Tommy Lyttle: A founding member of the UDA. Former Public Relations Officer for NUPRG.

Others

Mairead Corrigan Maguire: One of the three founders of the Peace People. Joint recipient with Betty Williams of the Nobel Peace Prize for 1977. Today the Peace People mainly concerns itself with social work and social justice, especially in the areas of prison reform and the curtailment of abuses under the emergency security laws. Maguire stood down from the movement's Executive in 1978 but remains active with the organization.

Sir Jack Hermon: Chief Constable, Royal Ulster Constabulary (RUC), the province's police force, since January 1980.

Des Wilson: Priest and a community activist in the Ballymurphy area of West Belfast. Outspoken and often radical, he is frequently at odds with the Catholic hierarchy.

In Britain

From the Conservative Party

James Prior: Secretary of State for Northern Ireland since September 1981. M.P. for Lowestoft (East Anglia). Minister for Employment, 1979–81.

Nicholas Scott: Parliamentary Under-Secretary of State for Northern Ireland since September 1981. M.P. for Chelsea (London). Served as Parliamentary Under-Secretary of State for Employment under Prior.

From the Social Democratic Party

James Dunn: Social Democratic Party (SDP) M.P. for Kirkdale (Liverpool) and party spokesman for Northern Ireland. Former Labour

M.P. for Kirkdale. Parliamentary Under-Secretary in Northern Ireland Office, 1976–79.

From the Labour Party

Don Concannon: M.P. for Mansfield (Nottinghamshire) and Labour Party spokesman on Northern Ireland. Minister of State in Northern Ireland Office, 1976–79; Parliamentary Under-Secretary in Northern Ireland Office, 1974–76. Longest-serving Minister ever in Northern Ireland Office.

Introduction

The Housing Executive is to build a "peacekeeper" wall in East Belfast to keep Protestants and Catholics apart in new housing developments.

— *The Belfast Newsletter*
17 August 1981

ALMOST FIFTEEN YEARS have elapsed since the bloody civil strife in Northern Ireland first made world headlines, and though many things there have changed during the intervening years, some even for the better, the divisions between the Catholic and Protestant communities are deeper, wider, more bitter, and seemingly more irresoluble than ever before.

The British Army continues to maintain a presence — an army of occupation to some, and to others a safeguard against civil war. The constitutional political parties are either unwilling or unable to agree upon a workable constitutional framework to resolve their differences. Protestants continue to oppose vehemently anything that would weaken the province's ties to Britain, while Catholics continue to dream dreams of unification. The paramilitaries on both sides continue to traffic assiduously in the marketplace of death. A life is cheaper now, a killing on one side less an occasion for outrage than for casual retaliation. Like any other business, the business of murder has its own learning curve: repetition enhances productivity. The IRA survives, a symbol of implacable resistance to British rule, its will to drive the "Brits" out unwavering and seemingly unshakable. And the Protestant paramilitaries survive, symbols of implacable resistance to a united Ireland, their will not to be driven into an all-Ireland state also unwavering and seemingly as unshakable. Meanwhile, successive governments in the Republic continue to articulate ambiguous and equivocal policies that insist on unification as the only long-term solution but are uncertain and inconsistent about the short term.

But, above all, the human cost continues: random deaths, mutilating injuries, the constancy of uncertainty, the destruction of property and the debilitation of the public interest, the deterioration of the economic and social fabric, the exacerbation of difference, the suppression of human rights, individual liberties, and due process in the name of order and security, and the legacy of a generation of children who from infancy — in Belfast child psychiatrist Morris Frazer's memorable phrase — "have lived with fear, have been taught to hate and who now aspire to kill."[1]

As the need for a political solution grows more urgent, the constitutional political parties have abandoned all attempts to compromise their differences. There is a perverse fatalism at work, a reluctant but nevertheless gratuitously smug assumption that events somehow are out of control. It is a dangerous assumption with tragic implications, nudging the prospect of civil war to the foreground.

Proposed solutions vary, depending upon which of the protagonists is doing the proposing, the only agreement being the extent of the disagreement.

The Provisional IRA, which for a long time had advocated one federal parliament and regional assemblies along the lines of state governments in the United States for each of Ireland's four historic provinces, has abandoned that goal in favor of a unitary state.

The constitutional political parties continue to wrangle about power sharing, which means one thing to the Catholic minority and quite another to the Protestant majority. Positions have hardened. On the Protestant side, the slogans "no surrender" and "not an inch" mean just that. Protestants find any suggestion of even an institutional link with the South an anathema, and some speak of the possibility of an independent Northern Ireland. Protestants want either the restoration of a simple majority-rule parliament or full integration with the United Kingdom. The former is unacceptable to the British government and more unacceptable still to the Catholic minority; the latter is improbable to the point of being unthinkable. On the Catholic side, the calls for a parliament in which Catholics would have a guaranteed share of power and for an institutional link between the two parts of Ireland as a precursor to the unification of Ireland in the long term have become more insistent as advocates of the constitutional route find themselves increasingly isolated and frustrated — with nothing to show for twelve years of patient adherence to the rule of law.

The Republic shows no overwhelming enthusiasm for unification. The people are for it, of course, but only in the abstract. They will hear of no financial, social, or political cost — and all the while they painstakingly avoid the very changes that would at least reassure the Protestant majority in the North that its rights as a Protestant minority in an all-Ireland state would be protected.

And after ten years of stalemate, owing in large measure to intractable Protestant intransigence on the question of power sharing, the British public has grown increasingly disillusioned with Northern Ireland and increasingly receptive to thinking of it in terms of "Ireland's Irish problem" rather than "Britain's Irish problem." In times of austerity and record unemployment levels, the financial cost to the British taxpayer is becoming both enormous and unbearable.

Seamus Heaney captures the undercurrents of fright lurking beneath the passivity of despair:

The ground we kept our ear to for so long
Is flayed or calloused, and its entrails
Tented by an impious augury.
Our island is full of comfortless noises.[2]

• • •

There is not, of course, a Northern Ireland problem per se but rather three interrelated problems: first is the question of the external relations between Britain and Ireland; second, the question of the internal relations between Catholics and Protestants in Northern Ireland; and third, the question of the relations between the two parts of Ireland.

The first question was ostensibly settled in 1920 when the Government of Ireland Act set up Northern Ireland as a political entity in its own right, and in 1921 when the Anglo-Irish Treaty brought the Irish Free State into being.

Under the Government of Ireland Act, the six northeastern counties of Ireland were given their own parliament at Stormont, on the outskirts of Belfast. The Stormont government had authority over domestic matters, including the maintenance of internal law and order. The U.K. government, however, continued to exercise full authority with regard to foreign affairs, income taxes, and the postal services. Nevertheless, despite its formal status as a subordinate government and the limitations on its powers, Northern Ireland was, for all intents and purposes, an independent state within the United Kingdom for the next fifty years, and an entirely Protestant one at that, given the fact that Protestant voters outnumbered Catholic voters by a two-to-one margin. The minority had no voice in the government of the state, and evinced no interest in having one until the late 1960s.

But by that point events were assuming a momentum of their own. The Stormont government itself came to an abrupt and inglorious end in March 1972 when the British government, acting decisively for once, invoked the authority vested in it under the 1920 Act to suspend Northern Ireland's Parliament after Brian Faulkner, the province's Prime Minister, balked at handing over all security powers to Westminster. The British government took full charge of Northern Ireland's affairs: Direct Rule had come, and though it was conceived of only as a temporary measure, it remains to this day the mode of government, the least unacceptable alternative.

The political settlements of 1920 and 1921 were a failure. The resulting partition of the island reinforced cultural and political separatism, making the development of parallel confessional states inevitable. This, in turn, has made the resolution of the other two problems more difficult, perhaps even impossible, within existing nation-state frameworks. The corollaries of this dilemma are the cornerstone of the conflict in Northern Ireland, and once again they bring into sharp question the nature of the basic relationship between Britain and Ireland.

It will, of course, always be an unequal relationship: a small, relatively underdeveloped island of less than five million people and a powerful economic and political giant, even if a pitiful one in the eyes of some, of fifty-four million people. The need of Ireland to assert herself in order to preclude her individual identity from being submerged into the larger entity will always exist — even if the vexing problem of Northern Ireland were to vanish.

Historically, Ireland has had two political traditions: the one constitutional and nonviolent; the other, unconstitutional and violent. And historically the proponents of the constitutional proved themselves uncannily adept at using either the threat or the fact of the unconstitutional to gain their own particular ends. Both Daniel O'Connell and Charles Stuart Parnell owed much of their success to their facility at the art, and the Unionist Sir Edward Carson took matters one step further in 1912 when he mobilized the Protestant community in Ulster to fight Home Rule, thus making the threat of treason the ultimate act of patriotism.

The quasi acceptance of the unconstitutional has given Irish politics its easy toleration of violence. Hard-line nationalists will follow the teachings of the Catholic Church in all matters except one — where they address the use of violence for political ends. The IRA was formally condemned by the Catholic Church in 1931 and again in 1956. The condemnations since 1972 have been frequent and harsh. But they make no difference. Otherwise devout Catholics continue to ignore the Church's denunciations — the national question transcends questions of faith and morals. When the righteousness of fanatical nationalism and papal claims to being infallibly right collide, the latter give way to the former. Thus the IRA's brusque response to Pope John Paul II's impassioned plea during his visit to Ireland in September 1979 for an end to the violence. Their cause was right: they would deal with God in their own way.

Implicit toleration of political violence is also made easier for many because "the unconstitutional" prevailed in 1921. Moreover, the terrorist of today has a disconcerting propensity for turning up as the statesman of tomorrow. Examples abound of what were once widely condemned as "terrorist" organizations that were transformed by victory into movements wrapped in the mantle of "benign respectability" — the Irgun in Israel, the Mau Mau in Kenya, EOKA in Cyprus, the FLN in Algeria, the NLF in Vietnam, MPLA in Angola, Frelimo in Mozambique, and in more recent years Robert Mugabee's Patriotic Front in Zimbabwe. The Palestine Liberation Organization, of course, now sits in the councils of the United Nations.

Thus, many see the Dublin government's professed repugnance at the tactics of the IRA as at best self-serving and at worst hypocritical. For it was these very tactics — the clandestine bomb, assassination on the street, murder from a ditch, destruction of property, and random terror — that shaped the struggle between the IRA and the British in the years 1918 through 1921, and that led to the independence of the Twenty-Six Counties and the foundation of the Irish Free State.

Historically, Ireland has had three cultures: a Gaelic Catholic one, an Anglo-Protestant one, and a Scots-Presbyterian one. The Presbyterian culture broke down into two traditions: the tradition of the "New Light," with its emphasis on individual freedom and tolerance; and the tradition of the "Old Light," with its emphasis on strict, uncompromising Calvinism. However, the Anglo-Protestant and Scots-Presbyterian cultures were confined almost exclusively to Ulster, thus giving the province the characteristics that set it aside from the rest of Ireland. The latter is homogeneous, the former diverse. But the diversity has not produced either a synthesis or even a toleration of difference. On the contrary, the clash of the three cultures and the divergent national allegiances they inspire are at the root of the conflict in Northern Ireland.

And, historically, Ireland has had two sets of starting points. The Catholic starting point is 1170, when Norman warriors speaking Norman-French crossed to Ireland from England with the approval of Henry II, and at the invitation of the Irish chief Dermot MacMurrough. The Protestant starting point is 1641, when the remnants of the old Gaelic Catholic aristocracy rose up to reclaim their confiscated lands. The uprising confirmed the worst expectations of the Protestant minority. It gave birth to the myth of massacre, and the myth of massacre reinforced the myth of siege.

But there are two myths of siege in Northern Ireland, two psychological preconceptions of suppression: Protestants, who account for a little more than one quarter of the island's population, see themselves as a minority in all of Ireland; Catholics, who account for a little more than one third of Northern Ireland's population, see themselves as a minority in Northern Ireland.

And there are two sets of perspectives: the Protestant perspective is essentially religious. Protestants fear Catholicism and absorption by what they see as the Catholic state on their frontiers. The Catholic perspective, on the other hand, is essentially political. Catholics want more political power in Northern Ireland and some form of association with the rest of Ireland.

Out of the conflicting myths, the conflicting cultures, and the conflicting perspectives come the conflicting contradictions. Robert Kee, in his fine book *The Most Distressful Country,* points out just a few:[3]

- Between 1845 and 1919 the British garrison "holding" Ireland consisted of twelve thousand Catholic Irish, members of the Royal Irish Constabulary.
- Patrick Pearse, Commander in Chief of the Irish forces in the rebellion of 1916, was the son of an Englishman from Birmingham.
- Erskine Childers, one of the most unswerving supporters of the Republican cause in 1918, was an Englishman. And he was shot by an Irish firing squad.
- Cathal Brugha, another hero of the 1918–21 struggle, was born Charles Burgess. And he, too, was shot to death by uniformed Irish soldiers for his loyalty to an Irish republic.
- Sir Henry Wilson, British Chief of the Imperial General Staff

in 1918, was born and raised in the South of Ireland. And he was shot by fellow Irishmen on the doorstep of his home in London in 1922.

- Sir Edward Carson, founder of the Ulster Volunteers and guiding light of Unionism, who vowed in 1912 to fight England to remain part of England, was born in Dublin.
- But Eoin MacNeill, one of the founders of the Irish Volunteers, who vowed to fight England to get Ireland out of England, was born in Northern Ireland.
- Between 1919 and 1921 the British government executed in cold blood or hanged twenty-four Irishmen who bore arms on behalf of an independent Irish republic. Between 1922 and 1923, however, the new Irish government executed more than three times that number just as cold-bloodedly for continuing to bear arms on behalf of the same cause.

And there are other ironies:

- In 1916, fewer than three thousand rallied behind the Republican cause, yet more than a hundred thousand Irishmen from the South fought on behalf of Britain on the battlefields of Europe during World War I.
- Sean McStiofain, Chief of Staff of the Provisional IRA during the 1970s, was born plain John Stephenson in England.
- And Lord Gowrie, the British government's Minister of State for Northern Ireland since September 1981, was born in the South of Ireland and has maintained a home there.

Ireland cannot escape either the "British influence" or the cultural interrelationships that are the hallmark of an era of mass communications. Nor does it appear that she is particularly eager to. I remember arriving in Dublin on December 21, 1980, three days after the first hunger strikes were called off. Everyone, of course, was immensely relieved. But the relief didn't prompt much soul-searching. In a matter of days the issue had ceased to command national attention. Indeed, the burning topic of discussion in the mass media that particular Christmas was whether Prince Charles would pop the question to his Lady Di.

A mass age, of course, demands mass distractions. Both parts of Ireland are adjuncts of the British media market, the appurtenances of mass culture now comfortably familiar to both. The historian F.S.L. Lyons asks:

> Is it possible that while we have been elaborating on political differences, while Northern Ireland has been torn apart by desperados from both sides of the cultural divide, the filthy modern tide has been washing us closer and closer together? Do we not share the same exposure to the same media, the same obsessive cult of sport as a substitute religion, the same sleazy seductions of the consumer society?[4]

The answer, he concludes, is both yes and no — yes in the sense that "Anglo-Americanism" is rampant, and no in the sense that it "has not yet obliterated differences that are centuries deep."[5]

Time may take care of the "yet."

• • •

Religion is the badge of identity, and identity the key to allegiance. The million Protestants of Northern Ireland are for the most part "Unionists" or "Loyalists." They support the Union of Great Britain and Northern Ireland, they regard themselves as ethnically British, they fly the Union Jack or the flag of Ulster, their national anthem is "God Save the Queen," their strongest cultural links are with Scotland, and their allegiance is primarily to the British Crown rather than to the British Parliament. Indeed, many are deeply resentful of the intrusion of the British Parliament into "their" affairs. Thus one of the ironies of the conflict: rabid Loyalists are often more anti-English in their invective than rabid Republicans. Hence their periodic mumblings about "going it alone," about taking matters into their own hands.

On the other hand, the half a million Catholics in Northern Ireland are, for the most part, ethnically Irish. They regard themselves as part of a historic Irish nation artificially divided by the partition of the island in 1921. They are called "nationalists" or "Republicans" because they support, by and large, the historical nationalist aim of an all-Ireland republic; they fly the Tricolour, and their national anthem is the "Soldier's Song." Thus the labels, according to historian Desmond Fennell:

> Due to the absence of any language difference between the two communities, the preponderance within them of Catholics and Protestants respectively, and the self-defined Protestantism of the British community, the two communities are conventionally referred to as "Protestants" and "Catholics." In this conventional usage, therefore, these denominational names are ethnic terms with cultural and political connotations, analogous to "Greeks" and "Turks" in Cyprus . . .[6]

At its most basic level, therefore, the conflict pits one million-plus Protestants who believe "the maintenance of the Union with Great Britain is the only means of securing their future"[7] against the one half million Catholics who believe "they can only secure their future within a united Ireland."[8]

And thus the arithmetic of the impasse: the number of Catholics in Northern Ireland is too great for Protestants to impose their will unilaterally within a stable political structure in Northern Ireland, while the number of Protestants in Ireland as a whole is too great for Catholics to impose their will within a stable political framework in Ireland as a whole. Either situation is subject to the tyranny of the minority.

The smallness of it all adds to both the intensity and the poignancy of the conflict. In terms of physical size, Northern Ireland is just slightly less than one fifth of the area of Ireland, which itself would almost fit into Lake Superior. Northern Ireland's land area is 5451 square miles, the Republic's 27,073; the greatest length of the island as a whole is a mere 302 miles from north to south, and its greatest width 189 miles from east to west. But the geographic strictures add to the claustrophobia of the violence: some 2300 have died. Between 1971 and 1982, there were over 28,500 shooting incidents in Northern Ireland, over 7200 bomb explosions and another 3100–plus bombs neutralized, over 9600 armed robberies, and over 17,000 civilian injuries — an injury or death in one out of every twenty households. Which means that in the tight-knit community that is Northern Ireland there is hardly a family that does not personally know at least one other family that has sustained at least an injury as a result of the violence of the last decade. And behind every injury there is a personal story — of random victims, luckless scapegoats, and innocent pawns caught in the vise of the extreme. You get an idea of the scale of the violence if you multiply the figures by a factor of 150 to arrive at comparable figures for the U.S. population. Thus, the number of dead would stand at 345,000 — almost as many as the number of people who died in the American Civil War — and the number of civilians injured at 2,550,000.

Adding to the climate of intensity is the fact that for the most part the violence is compressed into the Catholic and Protestant working-class areas of Belfast and some other towns, and into certain Border areas. Memories are constant, fixed in time, set in some immutable dialectic, immune from change, impervious to reason. In 1922 Winston Churchill wrote:

> The whole map of Europe has been changed . . . The modes of thought of men, the whole outlook on affairs, the grouping of parties, all have encountered violent and tremendous changes in the deluge of the world. But as the deluge subsides and the waters fall short we see the dreary steeples of Fermanagh and Tyrone emerging once again. The integrity of their quarrel is one of the few institutions that has been unaltered in the cataclysm which has swept the world.[9]

Other cataclysms have followed and doubtless more are yet to come. But the quarrel persists, its integrity pristine, the steeples of Fermanagh and Tyrone as dreary, ugly props in what one disillusioned commentator calls "a tragedy in endless acts."[10]

• • •

It is much written about and lends itself to a continued outpouring of publications. In 1976 the same eminent scholar noted that for "historians and sociologists and political scientists, for specialists in conflict bargaining or ethnic perception, Ulster has practically become an essential case study."[11]

There is no lack of theories, interpretations, hypotheses, and "newly trained people with novel means and novel results."[12] The academic penchant to quantify, to isolate a single factor as primarily causative, is obsessional, as though the delineation of a clear-cut cause-and-effect relationship would open the way to a miracle solution. Some observers stress the anthropological, some the cultural, some the economic, some the religious, some the political. The precise mix, however, is not important. Elements of each have contributed, although in moments of particular crisis some elements may appear to have more significance than others. But the mix is fluid, and what may appear to be the "right" balance today is often irrelevant tomorrow.

This book is not a "history" of the conflict, nor even of the last few years. The interviews, which form its core, took place between August 1981 and October 1982—a period of great turmoil in both parts of Ireland. The hunger strikes, the British government's political initiatives, and a precipitous increase in the level of violence gave a precarious momentum to events in Northern Ireland not evident since 1974. Meanwhile, in the South, a succession of general elections, minority governments, and the perilous state of the country's finances gave an urgency to events there that brought into question the capacity of the state's institutions to respond to crisis. The two summit meetings between British Prime Minister Margaret Thatcher and the South's Taoiseach (Prime Minister) of the day seemed to jolt Anglo-Irish relations onto a new level, to the dismay of Northern Ireland's Protestants. But the war in the Falklands soured Anglo-Irish relations, and the elections for a new Assembly in Northern Ireland opened divisions not only between Catholic and Protestant but also between Catholic and Catholic and Protestant and Protestant: the center would not hold.

But even as the key political players wrestled with events over which they often had little or no control, they graciously consented to be interviewed. Their words, more than anything else, tell the extent of the impasse. All were sincere, and open to the point politicians are wont to be, or, in the case of Northern Ireland, can afford to be. All were utterly convinced of the righteousness of their own positions and invariably at a puzzled loss to understand "the other side's" failure to follow what to them was the simple, compelling logic of their own arguments. Few talked of the future, fewer of their children, and none of hope. Most thought of the problem only in terms of their own existence. All were hostages, albeit on occasion willing ones, to the more irredentist elements within their own party ranks. There are memories:

- John Hume, tired and drawn, recounting how neighbors he had known for years in Derry had turned on him during the hunger strikes because he would not endorse the prisoners' demand for political status. John Hume, eager for the Provisionals' challenge for the Catholic vote, confident of turning it aside. And in Provisional Sinn Féin's headquarters in Dublin, the poster with an ugly, forbidding picture of Hume, and the caption "Dump This Traitor."
- Andy Tyrie's vast amusement at his own story of the dilemma two ever-so-uncompromising Presbyterian parents found themselves in when they learned that the one person who could "deprogram" their errant son who had taken up with the Hare Krishnas was a Catholic priest. Andy Tyrie matter-of-factly admitting that, yes, the Ulster Defence Association did indeed randomly kill hundreds of Catholics in the bad old days but that these were "emotional" rather than criminal acts, and that anyway Republicans were no less guilty, only less honest.
- Daithi O'Conaill's interest in American politics; his almost pedagogical way of making a point, his statements cautious and measured, more typical of a middle-level bureaucrat than of a former IRA Chief of Staff who had, allegedly, invented the car bomb; his request, on the last occasion we talked, that we no longer use a tape recorder. Some of the issues, he said, were sensitive, and they were. And he was on the losing side of many.
- Harold McCusker's insistence that there was an Irish Dimension but that he could not speak of it. But when could he? He did not know. His intense, emotional description of how his constituents in the more remote Border areas of Armagh were being murdered at will by the IRA; his bewilderment

at the British Army's unwillingness to ferret out the perpetrators. His despair.

- James Molyneaux's gleeful assertion that heads would roll at the Foreign Office in the wake of Argentina's invasion of the Falklands; the enemies from within — and they were Ulster's too — would be exposed and routed.
- Charles Haughey's suspiciousness, his enigmatic remark to his aide, Dr. Martin Mansergh, that I had made "a strategic mistake" by asking him first for his reaction to Garret FitzGerald's "Constitutional Crusade"; his dismissing both my question and FitzGerald's efforts, and his off-the-cuff insistence that constitutional issues and alternatives had come up during his meeting with Mrs. Thatcher.
- Martin Mansergh's savoring how nonplused Protestant labor union officials at Harland and Wolff were when he met with them at the shipyards and they discovered that Haughey's adviser on Northern Ireland was a Protestant who spoke with an upper-class British accent.
- Garret FitzGerald, patient to a fault, almost apologetically accommodating one morning when the results of a crucial by-election were coming in. FitzGerald lost in a bewildering sequence of subordinate clauses, oblivious to verbs and his own untied shoelaces.
- Ian Paisley, huge and hearty, a row of his constituents sitting quietly, literally cap in hand, waiting to see him; the plush and carpeted antechamber in contrast to the restrained shabbiness of the places in which the other political parties conducted their business.
- James Prior's assurance and fatalism: what would be would be; his less-than-disguised irritation at the Social Democratic and Labour Party for failing to see that more emphasis on an Irish Dimension in the government's White Paper on Northern Ireland would have led to a Protestant boycott of the Assembly elections.
- Danny Morrison's obvious excitement when he talked of what he saw as a "first" for a revolutionary organization — the marriage of the constitutional and the unconstitutional, the Armalite in the service of the ballot box. And the sense of change

he conveyed. The enemy was no longer just "the Brits" but Loyalism. There was no more pretense about Loyalists being Irish. If a British Army withdrawal meant civil war, then better to get the inevitable over with. There would be no more "sops." *Sop* was a much-used word.

- Seamus Lynch lashing out at the Provisionals, unsparing in his condemnation of their actions, ridiculing their socialism, accusing them of being as unequivocally sectarian as the dregs of militant Loyalism.
- Seamus Mallon, only in his early forties but with one heart attack behind him, puffing furiously on one cigarette after another, dismissing suggestions that he should, perhaps, cut down. He, too, was fatalistic: what would be would be.
- Belfast, ugly and sore to the eye, the will to go on gone, the signs of departure everywhere. In ten years it has lost one quarter of its population. Buildings are boarded up. There is little construction, and no skyline. Business is desultory, pace lacking, energy absent, burned-out housing estates a vivid reminder of the sectarian tensions that mark the quiet expression of passion in private places. The tall, silent cranes of the Harland and Wolff shipyards look down on a modern wasteland, on what is perhaps the first real-life laboratory of urban guerrilla warfare. A dead industry presides over a dead city. Only the ghettos have their own vitality. By early evening Belfast is abandoned. The military presence is pervasive yet somehow unobtrusive. Or perhaps so visible that it has become ordinary, part of the ebb and flow of traffic and people. You get used to the body searches, the detours, the polite requests for identification, and the watching helicopters. At night you don't travel much.
- The soldiers, small and boylike, out of place in their oversized uniforms and flak jackets; their weapons appear to intimidate them, and so do the children who routinely harass them. Many are from the far outposts of the Commonwealth. Do they know why they are there? Do they understand any of it?
- The countryside, green and undulating, the fields for the most part empty, the cottages modern, detached, and vulnerable. Do the occupants listen for sounds in the night? Are they

watchful during the day? Do neighbors look each other in the eye?

- A phrase: "at the end of the day." Everyone I interviewed, whether Catholic, Protestant, Loyalist, Republican, constitutional politician, paramilitary operator, British, Irish, working class, or ruling class, used it at some point during our conversations. And invariably everyone was referring to the reckoning to come when the ledgers of hate would be balanced and the accounts of history finally settled. Only a phrase binds them together, a phrase suggesting impending doom and their own rather detached anticipation of the cataclysm they feel they are inexorably heading toward. The prospect chills most. But some are looking forward to it. And they are in a special hurry.

Nor is this book about "solutions." On the contrary, it argues that tendencies to think in terms of solutions aggravate the problems. Rather, my purpose is to question the assumptions each side brings to its position, to find the "logic," if any, that forms the basis of its assumptions, to indicate how its preconceptions of its protagonists' positions influence its own, especially when these preconceptions are based on cherished myths rather than actual facts, and to examine the strategies it employs to achieve its ends.

But above all, my purpose is to stir debate, to have people on every side reexamine their own assumptions and attitudes, and, perhaps, to have them inch forward by having them agree not to what *is* possible but to what is *not* possible.

Part I

1

The Anglo-Irish Process: A Question of Consent

. . . a single purpose can be founded on
A jumble of opposites

— Louis MacNeice
"Autumn Journal"

SHORTLY AFTER the second Anglo-Irish summit, in November 1981, John Hume, leader of the Social Democratic and Labour Party (SDLP), addressed his party's annual conference in Newcastle, County Down. He used the occasion to attempt, once more, to assuage the fears of Unionist politicians whose condemnations of the newly established Anglo-Irish Intergovernmental Council bordered on the hysterical, even among the "moderates." The Anglo-Irish strategy, he explained, was originally designed by the SDLP "not to further SDLP or Irish nationalist priorities but to accommodate, to an extent that some would view as a gratuitous excess, the fears and anxieties expressed by those very Unionist politicians of whom I despair. The purpose of the concept was to meet — comprehensively and transparently — all the Unionist objections to any dialogue with their neighbors in Ireland."[1]

Some weeks later, the Taoiseach, Dr. Garret FitzGerald, also went to great lengths to reassure the Protestant community in the North. The new Anglo-Irish structures were "an arrangement that would make it easier to bring Northern Unionists into a process of dialogue." They were intended to "reassure Unionists about the position of Northern Ireland within the U.K. through involvement of Northern Ireland in the Anglo-Irish dialogue as a constituent of the U.K. side." Indeed, the structures could even be construed as being "inimical to nationalists' interests inasmuch as they could result in the Republic involving itself in an intimate bilateral institutional relationship with Britain."[2]

Given these intentions and possibilities and the often repeated commitment of every political party in the Republic to the aspiration of "unity by consent and only by consent," FitzGerald found it difficult to understand how any "reasonable person in Ireland, North or South, could object to consultations between the Irish and British Attorneys General with a view to seeking to overcome the enormous difficulties which we face on the problem of fugitive offenders." Nor did he see how any reasonable person could object to "our proposal to extend our franchise to British citizens resident in our State." Or to "the proposals that Kinsale gas should be shared with some centres in Northern Ireland," or to reestablishing "the North-South electricity interconnector . . . with a view to saving jobs in Northern Ireland and making economic savings in our own State, or that there should be an interconnector between Wales and ourselves which would link us into the Continental European grid."

But something had gone wrong. The reassurances did not reassure, the men of reason were wanting or quiet or disillusioned. Indeed, as Dr. FitzGerald himself probably well knew, reasonableness was often a measure of irrelevance in the politics of Northern Ireland. Political behavior followed a simple imperative: if anything could be misinterpreted it would be misinterpreted.

• • •

From the beginning, the Anglo-Irish process was extraordinarily vulnerable to misinterpretation. The very fact that it was the brain child of the SDLP — or Fine Gael or Fianna Fáil, depending on who was doing the talking (although both Southern parties paid their respects to the SDLP's policy document, "An Agreed Ireland") — in itself suggested to Unionists that the British government had accepted the nationalist line of reasoning, and hence the desired nationalist outcome, unification. Moreover, despite prior intentions, the concept of an Anglo-Irish dialogue meant one thing to Fianna Fáil, another to Fine Gael, yet another to the SDLP, something entirely different to Unionists, and only the British knew for sure what it meant to the British. Thus, the absence of common political and psychological perspectives created an ambience of uncertainty that added immeasurably to the possibilities for misinterpretation.

Other factors would also have a deleterious impact on the process. First, the manner in which it came into being damaged the prospects for progress. Indeed, the fact that the word *progress* was used over and over again to describe its activities begged the obvious question: progress toward what? Unfortunately, some politicians in the South, for domestic political considerations, were only too quick to suggest the answer, and some politicians in the North, also for domestic political considerations, were only too quick to exploit these suggestions as a confirmation of the worst. Second, the demands of the media, their propensity to exaggerate minutiae, to find significance in the trivial and nuance in the obvious, created perceptions of the events being covered that altered the nature of the events themselves. Events were choreographed, given direction, a touch of emphasis, and placed in the context of future possibilities. In short, events were distorted. It was a variation of the Heisenberg uncertainty principle: the act of examination transformed the object under examination. Third, in order to succeed, the Anglo-Irish dialogue not only had to be nonthreatening to Unionists, it had to be seen to be nonthreatening. At the very least this meant that Northern Ireland policy had to be taken out of the realm of party politics in the South: a nonpartisan approach was imperative. This did not happen for a number of reasons, some having to do with crude scrambling for political advantage, and some with very real philosophic and political differences on the issue. Fourth, the process itself was a catalyst forcing Northern Ireland into the national consciousness, inducing, almost inevitably, a long overdue debate on strategies, alternatives, and intentions, exposing and magnifying the differences between the major political parties, and making bipartisan agreement more difficult. The inherent dynamics of the process itself created a set of tensions that undermined the working of the process. Fifth, the concept of an Anglo-Irish framework was never adequately reconciled with the concept of unity by consent. As a result there was an appearance of contradiction; contradiction, of course, was seen as deviousness.

• • •

Charles J. Haughey was elected Taoiseach on 11 December 1979. It was a stunning, almost miraculous comeback for a politician who had spent the better part of the previous decade in the political wilderness after having been fired from the government in 1970, arrested, and tried for conspiracy to import arms illegally for shipment to Northern Ireland. He is the most controversial figure in Irish politics — a private entrepreneur of seemingly great astuteness who has amassed a considerable fortune while holding down public office, a man of the people with a penchant for high living, good horses, and fine art, an imperious administrator who holds only to his own counsel.* He reveals little, yet rumors about his doings and undoings fill to overflowing the vacuum of his silence. To the people he is "Charlie," to associates "CJ," but the suggestion of familiarity is misleading. He is remote: that rare political phenomenon, a leader who is not trusted, or for that matter trusting. And he trusts the media least of all.

Both his parents were from the vicinity of Swatragh in County Derry, Northern Ireland.[3] His father was an IRA man who joined the Free State Army and fought in its behalf during the Civil War. His mother was also involved with the IRA during the War of Independence. One of Haughey's uncles on his mother's

* Haughey owns a 280-acre estate at Kinsealy, County Dublin, where he breeds racehorses (one of his horses is named Aristocrat), and an island, Inishvickillane, off the coast of West Kerry.

side was interned by the authorities in Northern Ireland during World War II.

Haughey was born in Castlebar, County Mayo, in 1925. Three years later, the family moved to County Meath, and some years later to Dublin. He was educated at St. Joseph's Christian Brothers' School, University College, Dublin, and the King's Inns. On V-E day in 1945 he and a friend caused what has been described as a "minor riot" outside Trinity College when they burned a Union Jack to protest the flying of that flag on the college roof.

He joined Fianna Fáil in the late 1940s and married Maureen Lemass, daughter of Sean Lemass, who succeeded Eamon de Valera as leader of Fianna Fáil and Taoiseach in 1959. Elected to Dáil Éireann in 1954, he advanced rapidly, becoming Parliamentary Secretary to the Minister for Justice in 1960, Minister for Justice in 1961, Minister for Agriculture in 1964, and Minister for Finance in 1966. He was highly regarded as Minister for Justice, less highly regarded in Agriculture, and most successful in his later days in Finance when the buoyant economy allowed him to initiate far-reaching social and economic welfare programs. All the while he was becoming rich; how, even to this day, remains largely a mystery.

Haughey was widely backed as a successor to Lemass, who retired in 1966, but his rivalry with the choice of the establishment wing of the party, George Colley, threatened to split Fianna Fáil. Jack Lynch was chosen as the compromise leader and Haughey became his senior minister. Two serious accidents — a car accident in 1968 that left him nearly dead, and a horse-riding accident in 1970 that caused him severe injuries — seemed to erode his self-confidence, making him more diffident, less assertive, and definitely less decisive.

The Arms Crisis came in 1970.* Although he was acquitted

* In early May, Charles Haughey and Neil Blaney, the two most powerful members of the government, were abruptly fired, ostensibly for their failure to subscribe fully to government policy on Northern Ireland. Three weeks later, they were arrested along with three others and charged with conspiracy to import arms illegally. Two other Ministers resigned their Cabinet posts — one in protest and one on request — and in the ensuing confusion and disarray the collapse of the government seemed inevitable. But the Fianna Fáil government prevailed

of the charge of conspiring to illegally import arms — arms that were to be shipped to the Provisional IRA in Belfast — there is considerable evidence that Haughey lied under oath about his involvement in the affair.†

When it also emerged that substantial sums of money from a fund for the relief of distress in Northern Ireland, administered by Mr. Haughey as Finance Minister, had found their way to the two wings of the IRA in Belfast, Haughey again denied any knowledge of how it had happened. For five years he was excluded from the circles of power in Fianna Fáil. Had the party been returned to power in 1973, he almost certainly would have been finished as a political force. But that was not to be. During the years of his exclusion he traveled the constituencies, working on behalf of back-bench members. Finally, Lynch had to acknowledge his popularity: he was returned to the front benches in 1975 and given the brief on Health. Two years later, when Fianna Fáil again came to power, Haughey became Minister for Health and Social Welfare. His Family Planning Act of 1979, a denominational piece of legislation confirming once again to Northern Protestants the enormous clout of the Catholic hierarchy, made contraceptives available in the South for the first time under certain rigidly prescribed conditions, but only, of course, to married couples. When the backbenchers rebelled against Jack

---

because it was intent on holding on to power no matter what the cost. All other considerations, especially the considerations of truth, were subordinated to that one overriding imperative. Whether the Cabinet either knew or implicitly approved of Haughey's activities remains to this day a less than satisfactorily answered question. But the intrigues and cabals the crisis spawned, as individuals scrambled to either protect or promote their own self-interests, set faction against faction, reinforcing the divisions that had been papered over since Lynch's accession. For a comprehensive account of the controversial details see "The Arms Crisis 1970," *Magill*, May 1980, pp. 17–28; "The Berry File," *Magill*, June 1980, pp. 39–73; and "The Misconduct of the Arms Trial," *Magill*, July 1980, pp. 17–28. The three articles were written by Vincent Browne, *Magill*'s editor at the time. Also see Conor Cruise O'Brien, *States of Ireland*, pp. 248–58. [Note: When author and short title alone are given in footnotes, the full reference will be found in the Bibliography. — Ed.]

† Vincent Browne concludes that ". . . it is difficult to see how the jury could have believed Mr. Haughey, for to do so would have meant that they would have had to reject the evidence of four witnesses, including the evidence of Mr. Haughey's codefendant, Captain Kelly." See *Magill*, July 1980, p. 19.

Lynch's leadership in December 1979 because of their disenchantment with his handling of the economy, they turned to Haughey. He defeated Colley, who was once again the choice of the establishment wing of the party, by a vote of 48 to 38, and became party leader, a victory all the more remarkable since Colley had the support of twenty out of twenty-five government ministers. It was a moment of great irony: ultimately Haughey achieved what he had always aspired to, but he himself had little to do with it.[4]

Northern Protestants had no illusions about Mr. Haughey. He was the hard man of Irish politics, the most Republican, the most cunning, the most insistent on one Ireland for one island.

It took Mr. Haughey just two months to let all and sundry know where he stood on the Northern issue.

Northern Ireland, he declared at the Fianna Fáil Ard Fheis (its annual conference) in February 1980, was a failed political entity "artificially sustained." Thus, violence and repression were inevitable. He called for "a declaration by the British government of their interest in encouraging the unity of Ireland," and foresaw "some new, fair and open arrangement in which Irishmen and women, on their own, without a British presence but with active British goodwill, [would] manage the affairs of the whole of Ireland."[5] Northern Ireland was the major national issue, its solution his first priority.

Three months later, Mr. Haughey, as Taoiseach, met with the British Prime Minister, Margaret Thatcher, for the first time. They agreed to have regular meetings on a continuing basis in order to develop "new and closer political cooperation between our two countries."[6]

Mr. Haughey affirmed yet again the wish of the Irish people "to secure the unity of Ireland by agreement and in peace," and Mrs. Thatcher affirmed yet again that "any change in the constitutional status of Northern Ireland would only come about with the consent of a majority of the people of Northern Ireland."[7]

In July Mr. Haughey elaborated on the Anglo-Irish framework he envisaged. A settlement should take into account "relations between North and South in Ireland, between Ireland and Britain, and between both parts of the community in Northern Ireland." The British government should take the first step by declaring "their interest in Irish unity by consent and in peace, and their readiness to participate in the process for achieving it."[8]

The stage was set for the Dublin summit.

• • •

It took place on Monday, 8 December 1980, the forty-fourth day the seven hunger strikers in the Maze Prison had gone without food in their quest for special-category status as political prisoners, and two days after an estimated twenty thousand people had marched on the British embassy in Dublin to protest the British government's inflexibility on the prison issue.*

It had all the trappings of a historic occasion: the imposing setting of Dublin Castle, heads of governments meeting alone behind closed and highly guarded doors, senior ministers and their advisers, and teams of lesser officials. The presence of Lord Carrington added to the atmosphere of expectation. Had he not already achieved the impossible in Zimbabwe? And had he not, in the process, persuaded Mrs. Thatcher to reverse her position on fundamental issues?

Afterward, Mr. Haughey was cautiously euphoric, confidently hopeful that both governments were "in the middle of an historic breakthrough." The problem (no need to ask which problem) facing the two governments had been "placed firmly on a new plane."[9] Everything was "on the table."[10] Since both Mr. Haughey and Mrs. Thatcher had agreed to keep the substance of their private conversation secret, only Mrs. Thatcher could dispute Mr. Haughey's interpretations of the summit, and she had her own very good reasons for not doing so. The secrecy, of course, added to the impression in the South that something important had really happened, and it added to the impression in the North that some monstrous betrayal was afoot. The joint communiqué issued at the close of the summit was significant

* See chapter 7, pp. 264–72, for a fuller discussion of the hunger strikes.

not for what it said but for the multiplicity of possible meanings the marvelously evasive wording allowed. Thus, there would be a further meeting to give "special consideration to the totality of relationships between these islands," and joint studies would cover a range of issues including "possible new institutional structures."[11]

Would these "new structures" cover only relationships between Britain and the Republic? Or Britain and Northern Ireland? Or all three political entities? Nothing, it seemed, was out of the question. "We set no limit," declared Mr. Haughey, "on what institutions might be brought forward, might be considered, might be designed, might be conceived."[12] The framework he had established "indicates bringing forward a solution through government-to-government cooperation."[13]

Historic. Breakthroughs. Solutions. The hint of history became history. The words spoke for themselves; and they did not speak of a framework that would ease the fears of Protestants and open the way to dialogue.

Mr. Haughey was quite explicit: the next meeting, which would give "special consideration to the totality of relationships within these islands," would "not exclude anything" that could contribute "to peace, reconciliation and stability, and to the improvement of relations between the people of [the] two countries."[14]

Were new constitutional structures in the offing? Mr. Haughey wouldn't say. Mrs. Thatcher would: they were not. The Union, she insisted, would not be prejudiced. There was no sellout, no united Ireland on the horizon; Protestants had "nothing to fear." Unionist opinion, however, was not mollified. Secret proceedings meant secret deals; secret deals meant unification. Nor was nationalist opinion convinced: it was understood that Mrs. Thatcher would have to deny the insinuation of constitutional change even if it were under consideration.

What appeared to escape attention in both parts of Ireland in the flood of confusing and often contradictory statements coming from both London and Dublin was the fact that despite Mr. Haughey's allusions to "new planes," "major steps forward," and "no limits" on what might happen next, the hunger strikes continued their inexorable course. Mr. Haughey might claim a "special relationship" with Mrs. Thatcher and insinuate the promise of great things to come, but he could not move her on the prison question.

Both, however, were in a position to use the summit as a buffer to deflect or at least to ameliorate the serious political repercussions that would almost certainly follow the death of a hunger striker. Mr. Haughey could argue that he was in fact making progress toward achieving unification, that an upsurge in support for the IRA would undermine the progress he had made. He could imply that the persistence of other hunger strikers in their protest jeopardized the prospects for an agreed settlement.

Mrs. Thatcher, on the other hand, could blunt international criticism of her handling of the situation by pointing to her accord with the Dublin government. Moreover, the more enthusiastic Mr. Haughey waxed over the fruits of their deliberations, the more reasonable her suggestion that his attitude amounted to less than an unequivocal rejection of her stand on the prison issue. The more extravagant his claims of their mutual agreements, the more trouble he would have in repudiating her intransigence should the prisoners die. Hence her tolerance, perhaps even covert encouragement, of statements by Mr. Haughey that would fail to withstand a closer scrutiny at a later date.

Mr. Haughey had at least two other reasons for needing the appearance of momentum on the Northern Ireland question. First, he had implemented stringent security measures along the Border, resulting in a dramatic reduction in the amount of explosives and ammunition moving into the North and in a sharp decline in Border-area IRA activity. To appease the extreme Republican elements in Fianna Fáil, especially in the Border constituencies, he had to show that his policies brought a quid pro quo from the British government. Second, the deterioration in the economic situation in the Republic was accelerating. The full measure of that deterioration, as Mr. Haughey well knew, was beyond the public's worst expectations. An early general election was imperative before the economy collapsed, bringing down Fianna Fáil in the shambles. It was only good politics for Mr. Haughey to try to make his Northern initiative the centerpiece of his campaign strategy, thereby turning the election into a referendum on his statesmanship and his formidable persuasive powers in bringing Mrs. Thatcher around to accepting a joint Anglo-Irish responsibility for resolving the Northern question, rather than on his record as chief steward of the nation's economic affairs.

Thus, the political and psychological dictates for a strong Anglo-Irish framework were subordinated to the immediate political needs of the protagonists. The Dublin summit became an end in itself, an expedient to redirect the impact of pressing political contingencies rather than a means to an end. If not stillborn, it was at the very least mongoloid.

Of course, a close reading of the 8 December communiqué reveals that it promised little. Perhaps it was the very lack of specificity that lent credibility to the speculation, since there was no yardstick to measure speculation against. Or perhaps the speculation was taken as verified when it was not denied. Or perhaps the media and the public were ready to believe that it was that easy — simply a cordial little tête-à-tête between two heads of government, the essence of summitry — to achieve a dramatic breakthrough. Thus, Mrs. Thatcher's insistence that the Union was as guaranteed as ever was, of course, necessary: what was the point in spelling out the unpalatable truth to the wild men of Loyalism who would, predictably, fly into one of their tiresome rages, threatening as always to fight Britain to remain part of Britain?

The communiqué started out with a statement of the obvious: "The Taoiseach and the Prime Minister agreed that the economic, social and political interests of the people of the United Kingdom of Great Britain and Northern Ireland and the Republic are inextricably linked."[15] This was followed by another statement of the obvious: "The full development of these links has been put under strain by division and dissent in Northern Ireland." The two governments' willingness, therefore, to accept "the need to bring forward policies and proposals to achieve peace, reconciliation and stability; and to improve relations between the peoples of the two countries" was no less than what any two reasonable and neighborly governments would seek to do under the circumstances and no more than what other British and Irish governments had sought to accomplish in the preceding decade. Accordingly, the context for the decision to have a further meeting to give "special consideration to the totality of relationships within these islands" and to commission "joint studies covering a range of issues including possible new institutional structures" was provided by the language of the communiqué itself: the "possible new institutional structures" were the upper bound; they set a limit to what might be achieved. The two countries were more closely tied to each other than to any other states. Besides the meetings between the two heads of government, there were ad hoc ministerial meetings, occasional meetings of the Joint Steering Group on Anglo-Irish Economic Cooperation, direct informal contacts between government departments, and meetings of the Anglo-Irish Parliamentary Group. Thus, a permanent institutional framework to coordinate and regulate Anglo-Irish consultations on a variety of relationships would, even in the absence of the Northern Ireland problem, make sense.

The British government's earlier reiteration of the constitutional guarantee to the Protestant majority in Ulster should have sufficed to banish thoughts of "constitutional breakthroughs," unless, of course, Mr. Haughey was preparing to take Ireland back into the Commonwealth, a move that would alter the relationship between Britain and the Republic but not between the Republic and Northern Ireland. The fact that the guarantee was not seen as precluding constitutional change indicates how close Southern thinking is to Unionist thinking. Neither puts much credence in Britain's affirmations of the guarantee; both believe she will end the guarantee when it is in her own best interest to do so.

But in the heady days following the summit there was no mention of the unity-by-consent declaration, only the encouragement of the perception that a process had been established that would eventually bring about unification.

Mr. Haughey claimed that he had persuaded the British government to the SDLP's position: namely, that since politicians in Northern Ireland had proved themselves incapable of finding a solution, the major initiatives had to be taken by London and Dublin acting together. Thus, the emphasis on finding an internal solution in Northern Ireland appeared to be subordinated to what was perceived as the framework of the whole problem — the framework of Britain and Ireland. The implicit, paradoxical, and certainly questionable assumption was that a settlement in Ireland as a whole could be achieved even if the two communities within Northern Ireland did not make peace with each other. The premise on which this assumption sought to support itself — that a more intimate relationship between London and Dublin would induce the North into a closer relationship with the South — was even more questionable, a matter of faith rather than of fact.

To summarize: the Anglo-Irish process was badly flawed at conception because both Mrs. Thatcher and Mr. Haughey used the summit that launched it to satisfy their own short-term political needs. Mrs. Thatcher allowed Mr. Haughey a certain leeway to exaggerate the outcome because it tied him all the more firmly to her in the event that the hunger strikers died and she faced an international political backlash. Mr. Haughey also secured some immediate protection from the national political backlash that would surely follow the death of the hunger strikers, but of far more importance was the excellent potential of the Anglo-Irish talks as an issue to deflect attention from the ailing economy during the forthcoming national elections. Thus, the manner in which the process came into being ensured the further alienation of the Unionist community, damaging, perhaps irreparably, an Anglo-Irish framework as a vehicle to address Protestant fears. The prospect of constitutional changes affecting the relationship between Ireland and Northern Ireland was moot, of course, as long as the British government conceded the guarantee to the Protestant majority in Ulster, and the prospect of a "solution" was also moot as long as the Irish government conceded unity only with the consent of a majority in Ulster.

• • •

The 8 December summit dramatized Mr. Haughey's ability to exploit to his full advantage a situation over which he had control. Control, however, slipped away in the months that followed. To the relief of all, the hunger strikes were called off unexpectedly on 18 December, but they were resumed the following March and pursued to the despairing end. The South's economy continued to decline, and Paisley continued to hold "Carson Trail"* demonstrations across Northern Ireland, whipping up Protestant sentiments against the Anglo-Irish talks. The death of Bobby Sands on 5 May 1981 resulted in demonstrations in support of the hunger strikers in both parts of Ireland.

H-Block committees and marches attracted thousands who theretofore had had no association with militant Republicanism. Sands's death and the deaths that followed made a mockery of Mr. Haughey's claim to a "special relationship with Mrs. Thatcher"; indeed, the "special relationship" became a liability as Mrs. Thatcher, insisting over and over again that "murder is murder is murder," adamantly refused to make any concession whatsoever to the striking prisoners. The general election Mr. Haughey could no longer postpone took place on 11 June. Once again, Fianna Fáil emerged with the largest number of seats but fell short of a majority. Eventually, a Fine Gael–Labour coalition government was formed with Dr. Garret FitzGerald as Taoiseach.

For the moment Charles J. Haughey was out in the cold.

• • •

Garret FitzGerald is the antithesis of Charles Haughey in almost every respect. Academic, pedant, journalist, moralizer, humorously known as "Garret the Good," he is open, unpretentious, almost compulsively without deceit, seemingly ingenuous, the epitome of the antipolitician. The two men do not like each other personally and appear to have little respect for each other professionally. In 1979 FitzGerald surprised many people, and

* Ian Paisley's Democratic Unionist Party organized a series of demonstrations across Northern Ireland, which Paisley referred to as the Carson Trail, after Sir Edward Carson (1854–1935), who led Unionist resistance to the Home Rule Bill of 1912. In place of Carson's Ulster Covenant, Paisley had Ulster's Declaration. See chapter 5, p. 188. For a Loyalist account of what the Carson Trails were all about, see Sam Wilson, *The Carson Trail.*

certainly embarrassed himself, with an unbecoming attack on Haughey when Haughey was nominated for Taoiseach. He has a fastidious appetite for facts, figures, and detail, and a mind that speaks in paragraphs, sentences leaping over each other in their haste to come to a conclusion. He is well liked, if perhaps a bit dull.

His father was Desmond FitzGerald, Minister for External Affairs in the first Free State government and later Minister for Defence.[16] His mother, a Protestant, came from an upper-class Belfast Unionist family. Both his parents took part in the 1916 Easter Rising and the War of Independence. They took different paths on the Anglo-Irish Treaty, his father supporting it, his mother opposing it, but his mother's opposition remained passive. FitzGerald was born in Dublin in 1926, educated at Belvedere College, University College, and the King's Inns. For some years he was a research analyst for Aer Lingus, the national airline, where he developed his formidable analytic skills in economics. Later he started his own economic consulting firm, wrote a weekly economic commentary for the *Irish Times,* was Irish correspondent for *The Economist* and the *Financial Times,* and lectured at University College, Dublin. He joined Fine Gael in 1964 and was elected to Dáil Éireann in 1969. Three years later, he led a major revolt to oust Liam Cosgrave as leader of the party. The attempt fizzled. Nevertheless, Cosgrave appointed FitzGerald Minister for Foreign Affairs when the Fine Gael–Labour coalition came to power early in 1973. FitzGerald excelled at the job, establishing an international reputation, especially during his tenure as President of the Council of Ministers in the European Economic Community (EEC). He was elected leader of Fine Gael in 1977.

After less than three months in office, FitzGerald moved to put his own imprimatur on the direction of Northern Ireland policy when he proposed a referendum to change the Constitution so that it would be acceptable to Northern Protestants. The Republic, he said, had become a state that was "not a nonsectarian state."[17] It was "inbred with the ethos of the majority." He ventured that if he were a Northern Protestant he would not be "attracted to getting involved with a state which is itself sectarian, though not in the acutely sectarian way that Northern Ireland was," but sectarian, nevertheless, to the extent that "our laws and our Constitution, our practices and our attitudes reflect those of a majority ethos and are not acceptable to Protestants in Northern Ireland." One of the specific changes in the Constitution he wanted was the deletion of Articles 2 and 3.

Article 2 of the Constitution lays claim to the whole of Ireland: "The national territory consists of the whole island of Ireland, its islands and the territorial seas." Article 3 bluntly asserts the right of the government of the Twenty-Six Counties to rule Northern Ireland: "Pending reintegration of the national territory, and without prejudice to the right of the Parliament and Government established by this Constitution to exercise jurisdiction over the whole of that territory, the laws enacted by that Parliament shall have the like area and extent of application as the laws of Saorstát Éireann [the Twenty-Six Counties] and the like extraterritorial effect."

FitzGerald argued that: "It is the implicit claim of a right of this twenty-six-county Parliament and Government to exercise jurisdictions over the whole of Ireland, including Northern Ireland, that represents such a stumbling block to progress towards Irish unity because it sticks in the throat of every Northern Unionist and gives power to their more extreme leaders to compete in demagoguery as they rant against this claim." Thus, repeal of Articles 2 and 3 would "reduce the pressures that give rise to their [Unionist] siege mentality and open up the possibility of easier dialogue between them and the nationalists in Northern Ireland."[18]

FitzGerald launched his Crusade: the case for changing the Constitution had several precedents. Had not "de Valera himself acknowledged that an overriding consideration in the drafting of the Constitution, which accounts for its confessional elements, was a desire to ensure that the Catholic Church of those times would support its provision"?[19] Had not de Valera's successor, Sean Lemass, called for changes in the Constitution every twenty-five years or so to reflect the country's evolution into a modern state?[20] Had not the informal all-party committee Lemass set up in 1966 to review the Constitution agreed that Article

3 should be amended, and had it not agreed with unanimity on the language to replace it? To wit: "The Irish Nation hereby proclaims its firm will that its national territory be reunited in harmony and brotherly affection between all Irishmen."[21] And had not Jack Lynch, Lemass's successor, gone on record with the statement that where there were "constitutional difficulties which are legitimately seen by people to be infringements of their civil liberties, then their views are worthy of extensive examination and we should try to accommodate them in our Constitution and in our laws"?[22]

Two weeks later, Mr. Haughey adamantly made Fianna Fáil's position clear at the unveiling of a memorial to de Valera at Ennis: "The Constitution," he declared, "enshrines in Articles 2 and 3 the clear assertion of the belief that this island should be one political unit — a belief stretching far back into history and asserted and reasserted time and again by the vast majority of our people North and South."[23] De Valera, he insisted, would have fought to defeat the efforts of the government "to give some legal validity to partition, and by doing so to abandon that aspiration to which generations of Irishmen and women have dedicated themselves." Partition was a British problem: de Valera, continued Haughey, "never failed to point out that as a British government had created the evil of partition, only the British government could take the initiative required to bring it to an end." Support for deleting Articles 2 and 3 came from "the remnants of that colonial mentality that still lingers on in Irish life, a mentality that cannot come to terms with the concept of a separate, independent Irish Ireland." The Irish-Irish were being put upon: "Once again we are being asked to accept a jaundiced view of ourselves. Once again we are asked to look only at our faults and to believe that somewhere else things are ordered much better than they are here, and there exists a superior form of society which we must imitate." There was no reason "to apologize to anyone for being what we are or for holding the beliefs we do; we angrily reject accusations of either inferiority or sectarianism." As far as Charles Haughey was concerned, the deletion of Articles 2 and 3 was a dead issue.

Less than a week later he was less rhetorical but more emphatic: "Irish unity remains our objective, and we are not going to alter our Constitution to weaken or diminish that. We also do not wish to give credence to the idea that unity can only be achieved if everybody sacrifices all that they hold dear."[24] Changes in the Constitution "should be undertaken on their merit, not with a view to impressing Northern Unionists, the British, or anyone else."[25] This was not the time, in his view, to make any such changes. Later he provided a scathing obituary describing the Constitutional Crusade as "unnecessary, divisive and unhelpful . . . the first time in history that a crusade was started by the infidels."[26]

Mr. Haughey was determined to make Dr. FitzGerald's imprimatur less than indelible.

• • •

The second Anglo-Irish summit took place at 10 Downing Street on 6 November 1981. Both Mrs. Thatcher and Dr. FitzGerald pronounced themselves well satisfied with the results: the exchange was "friendly and constructive and enjoyable"[27] according to Dr. FitzGerald; "warm, friendly, practical, constructive and workmanlike" according to Mrs. Thatcher.[28]

Their joint communiqué reflected their impressions. It reiterated the goal of successive Irish governments "to secure the unity of Ireland by agreement and in peace."[29] And it reiterated the British guarantee: "Any change in the constitutional status of Northern Ireland would require the consent of a majority of the people of Northern Ireland."[30] FitzGerald agreed to this stipulation, and Mrs. Thatcher, in turn, agreed to "support legislation in the British Parliament" to give effect to that consent if it "were expressed as a result of a poll conducted in accordance with the Northern Ireland Constitution Act of 1973." Both committed their governments to "promoting arrangements which might help to reduce tensions between them" and to reconciling "the people of the two parts of Ireland." They agreed, therefore, to establish an Anglo-Irish Intergovernmental Council, which would give institutional expression to the "unique character of the relationship between the two countries." The council would involve "regular meetings between the two governments at ministerial and official levels to discuss matters of common concern." They also agreed that it would be up to their respective governments "to consider at the appropriate time whether there should be an Anglo-Irish body at parliamentary level whose members would be drawn from the British and Irish Parliaments, the European Parliament, and any elected Assembly that might be established for Northern Ireland." The Anglo-Irish Intergovernmental Council would have the assistance of an advisory committee on cooperation; other arrangements called for cross-Border energy links and another look at the feasibility of an all-Ireland court. Finally, they agreed to publish the text of the Anglo-Irish *Joint Studies,* other than the security document, to reassure Northern Protestants that no dirty deeds were being done behind their backs, and to counter unrealistic expectations in the South.

At a press conference following the summit, Dr. FitzGerald provided more details — and more insight. Why the delay in announcing the parliamentary tier? Two reasons. First, "governments can't decide what Parliaments do"; second, "there was some merit in waiting to see if we get an Assembly in Northern Ireland."[31] The agreement to promote arrangements to reconcile the two major traditions in the two parts of Ireland was "an important step forward." Was this a tacit acknowledgment by Britain that the resolution of the Northern Ireland question was not solely the responsibility of the British government? FitzGerald wouldn't say that it wasn't — the communiqué "had to speak for itself." The agreement on the guarantee was a return to the Sunningdale position.* Britain's undertaking to accept

* The Sunningdale Conference was held at the Sunningdale (Berkshire) Civil Service College from 6 to 9 December 1973. Participating were the British and Irish governments, and the three parties — the Unionist Party, the Social Democratic and Labour Party, and the Alliance Party — that had formed a power-sharing Executive in Northern Ireland on 21 November 1973. The Sunningdale Agreement provided for a Council of Ireland; thus the Irish Dimension, consisting of two tiers. The first tier, the Council of Ministers, would have consisted of seven ministers from both the Dáil and the Northern Ireland Assembly. Decisions would require a unanimous vote. The second tier, a consultative Assembly, would have an advisory role. It would have sixty members — thirty from each side, elected by members of both Parliaments. The Sunningdale Agreement —and the power-sharing Executive — collapsed following the Ulster Workers' Council Strike in May 1974. See chapter 8, p. 317. See also W. D. Flackes, *Northern Ireland: A Political Directory,* pp. 147–48, and Robert Fisk, *Point of No Return.*

future majority consent for unity and to support legislation to bring it about was tantamount, in Dr. FitzGerald's view, to a declaration that she would not stand in the way of unity by consent. The possible refusal of a majority in a new Northern Assembly to take part in the parliamentary tier would "not preclude it operating."

Once again the emphasis of the government's remarks was on "progress," "steps forward," a greater role for the Irish government, and new structures with wide-ranging responsibilities. There was scant mention of bringing Protestants into the process. Indeed, Dr. FitzGerald found it easy to dismiss their possible abstention from the parliamentary tier as of no great consequence to the conduct of its business. Once again Unionists translated the language of reconciliation into the language of unification. And once again Mrs. Thatcher made her government's position clear: "A political settlement in Northern Ireland really has to be a matter for the Secretary of State and for the United Kingdom Government,"[32] she declared, but not many Unionists were listening. Even this declaration, though, was not as unequivocal as it sounded, because it referred only to the context of Northern Ireland and left unanswered the question of responsibility for a larger British-Irish context.

• • •

Mr. Haughey had set the stage for denouncing the outcome even before the summit took place by raising expectations of what should be achieved, indeed would be achieved, if he were still Taoiseach. After the summit he was quick to attack, accusing Dr. FitzGerald of a fundamental change in direction on the question of consent.[33] FitzGerald's agreement to the stipulation that "the consent of a majority would be required" for a change in the North's constitutional position was, he argued, a de jure recognition of partition. In contrast, his own commitment, expressed in the May 1980 communiqué of his meeting with Mrs. Thatcher, was limited to the stipulation that change "would only come about" with the consent of a majority. This was only a recognition of the "practical realities of the situation," at worst a de facto recognition of partition. The Fianna Fáil position, he declared, was that no part of the Irish nation had the right to opt out of the nation. Thus, FitzGerald's agreement to the change in the wording was a deliberate renunciation of this basic principle, consistent with his position on Articles 2 and 3 of the Constitution.[34]

Haughey's implication was clear: Garret FitzGerald conceded the legitimacy of the Unionist case.

In the Dáil, Mr. Haughey broadened his attack. Only one question had to be asked: had the Downing Street summit "brought us any closer to a settlement" or had it "taken us further away"?[35] Clearly it had "taken us further away." The outcome was a far cry from his own achievements at the Dublin summit when the British government agreed to his proposal that "the British and Irish governments had joint responsibility for the resolution of the Northern Ireland problem."

His objections were specific. First, the insertion of the word *intergovernmental* in the title of the Anglo-Irish Council deliberately excluded parliamentary participation and specifically excluded Northern Ireland. Thus, the British got a council no different from and of no more consequence than the Anglo-French Council. There was nothing in the council to express the dimension of the Northern Ireland question; it did not express "the totality" of relationships. Second, the agreement allowed the British government to separate the question of relations between the U.K. and the Republic from the question of relations between the U.K. and Northern Ireland. Thus, the British government could continue to assert that the solution to the Northern Ireland question was a matter for the U.K. Parliament only. Hence, the concept of joint responsibility had been rejected. Britain now could deal with Northern Ireland as an internal British problem with "the full agreement and acquiescence of the head of the Irish government." Third, the existence of a watered down Anglo-Irish Council was precisely what Britain had aimed for because it allowed her to give world opinion the impression that there were no problems between her and Ireland. Fourth, the council did not have "either the right or the duty" to take up the Northern question. Fifth, excluding a parliamentary tier excluded Northern Ireland's participation.

"Tiering," with a parliamentary tier in the distant future, destroyed the organic whole: the new arrangements merely institutionalized what was already going on. Sixth, FitzGerald either approved of or desired a new form of devolved government in the North — a sterile course, since it was "abundantly clear that no purely internal settlement could succeed." Seventh, Britain's undertaking to support legislative action to implement majority consent for a change in the North's constitutional status only acknowledged what had always been implicit: if a majority in the North opted for unification, Britain would support their position. The very least that FitzGerald should have settled for was a declaration by Britain of her support for Irish unity. And finally, the change in the wording on the consent stipulation was crucial: it made consent a prerequisite for a solution rather than a part of the solution itself.

And what would Mr. Haughey have settled for? Nothing less than an Anglo-Irish Council that had a ministerial arm charged with bringing forward "policies and proposals to achieve peace, reconciliation, and stability and to improve relations between the peoples of the two countries." This council would express the "acceptance in Dublin of joint responsibility for bringing forward a solution to the problem of Northern Ireland." The members of the council's parliamentary arm, including Northern members, would be appointed by the two governments. And then what?

The Haughey script for how things should proceed called for the British guarantee on the constitutional status of the North to be set aside, at which point proposals would be put to the people of Northern Ireland. In short, consent would come when Unionists realized that they had to make the best of an inevitable outcome. The responsibility for spelling out the inevitable outcome to Unionists, however, rested squarely with Britain.

In many respects Mr. Haughey's was an extraordinary performance. Nothing in the Dublin communiqué suggested that the settlement of the Northern question was an objective or that it would be an objective of a future meeting. Nor did the Dublin communiqué contain anything to remotely suggest that the British government agreed that the British and Irish governments had joint responsibility for the resolution of the Northern Ireland problem. The only mention of "solution" had come from Mr. Haughey's own lips in his numerous postconference assessments of his own achievements.

The publication of the joint studies exposed the unreality of some of his more grand assertions.[36] There had been no talk of solutions or settlements or even, for that matter, much mention of Northern Ireland, only a series of proposals to cooperate and to institutionalize the multiplicity of links that existed between the two countries. FitzGerald's contention that consideration of the parliamentary tier was delayed at his insistence because he felt Northern representatives should be members of an elective assembly rather than appointees of the Secretary of State was shown to be correct.

• • •

The public airing of differences following FitzGerald's constitutional initiative and the summit exposed not only the shortcomings of the Anglo-Irish framework as a mechanism for dealing with Northern Ireland but also the depth of the differences between Fianna Fáil and the Coalition parties on the issue. Moreover, the tone of the debate, especially the insinuations of some that others were less than Irish-Irish, confirmed to Northern Protestants that the process was designed not, as FitzGerald and Hume had so earnestly and hopefully envisioned, to alleviate Protestants' fears and to bring them into a dialogue but to achieve, as Mr. Haughey so bluntly put it, a settlement. The expectations raised by successive summits were expectations of progress toward something. That something, of course, was a united Ireland.

The media also saw the Anglo-Irish process from a "what's being achieved" perspective. This was inevitable, perhaps, in the case of the electronic media, which are singularly ill-equipped to deal with processes whose outcomes only slowly and imperceptibly work themselves out. Moreover, the constraints on the electronic media demand that something either happen or not happen. Television in particular devours complexity and spews out a simple equation and a simple philosophy: there are winners and there are losers and all the affairs of men can ultimately be made to fit into one or the other of these categories. Television's frame of reference focused only on Northern Ireland. The pendulum had to swing one way or the other: progress was either made or not made.

Exclusive emphasis on one aspect of the proceedings distorted the proportions of the whole. The important was not necessarily covered; what was covered, however, became the important. Questions at press conferences following the summits were invariably posed in the context of Northern Ireland, because the media had little interest in mundane "matters of common concern" such as electricity grids, interconnectors, and the nuts and bolts of economic cooperation. There was one overriding issue, and the importance of the others derived from their relationship to this one issue. Thus, the Taoiseach of the day was inadvertently put in a position of having to vindicate his performance. Even if he could not clearly show that "progress" had been made, he had to create the perception that it had, if only in the negative sense of not creating the perception that no progress had been made. Thus replies to questions were often evasive rather than straightforward, impressions were left to linger rather than dispelled, speculation was subtly encouraged rather than discounted, all of which left Northern Protestants to imagine the worst.

These problems, of course, are exacerbated when political parties in the South use the issue of Northern Ireland to make partisan political points. Accusations by one party that the "momentum" it created has not been sustained by the other party leads the other party to rebut the accusation, creating the impression that momentum has been not only sustained but quickened. When one party raises expectations of what should be negotiated in the future, it raises questions about what was really negotiated in the past. When the overriding consideration is to make it appear that progress is being made, large claims are made for small gestures. Hence the hysterical reactions of Unionists: "special relationships" suggest clandestine activities, goings-on behind closed doors, secret deals; "reconciliation" is a euphemism for "unification" and "new institutional arrangements" are code words for an all-Ireland state.

Unionists see the new institutions as mechanisms of coercion. They cannot participate because participation would legitimize the nature of the institutions, thus validating the purpose of their proceedings. Charles Haughey's insistence on the immediate implementation of the parliamentary arm of the Anglo-Irish Council in order to hasten progress toward a settlement (that is, unification) only guaranteed that Unionists would not voluntarily participate. His suggestion that they had better do so, if only to protect their own interests, betrayed an inherent incompatibility between the concept of unity by consent only and the concept of the Anglo-Irish process as a vehicle to allay Protestant fears. For Irish governments to talk in one breath of unity only with the consent of a majority and in the next of reaching agreement with the British government to advance "reconciliation of the two traditions" suggests to Unionists Machiavellian intrigue.

Is induced consent, consent freely given?

• • •

Garret FitzGerald may say, "As long as consent is not available — however long that may be — we are prepared to accept that decision. But we believe that we are entitled to work for that consent."[37] But for Robert McCartney, one of Northern Ireland's leading barristers, a prominent Unionist politician who has publicly rebuked Paisley for right-wing fascism, and an admirer of FitzGerald, there is a nagging contradiction, a dichotomy between the opportunity for the free exercise of choice implicit in the consent formula and the opportunity for the manipulation of choice implicit in the working-for-consent formula. Says McCartney:

In criminal law there's a crime called rape. Rape means having sexual intercourse with a woman without her consent. Consent in those circumstances or the absence of it is defined in three ways. It is not consent if you have her by force, and everyone agrees that in relation to Northern

Ireland force is out. It is not consent if you have her by fear, that is, by threatening her, which is what the Provisional IRA are doing. And it is not consent if you obtain her agreement by fraud. Everybody agrees that force is out, and the fear hasn't worked. Because people will not accept Northern Ireland's refusal, Unionists are now worried that her consent will be obtained by fraud through a series of careful structurings. First, there is the political structuring in the case of the Anglo-Irish talks, and then there will be an economic structuring so as to make the North and South mutually dependent, perhaps for energy sources. After a period of these closer working links she will be in a position where it will be impossible for her to refuse. She will be so committed, so bound and so attached that she will not be able to say no. And this, I think, breeds a lot of distrust.

What I think the parties should do, and the countries, England and the Republic, is say, "Right, we will accept Northern Ireland's refusal. She does not want to be our partner or to be absorbed by us. What we will do is we will show her that we can be her friend. We'll have a platonic relation with her. We'll not want into her bed but we'll share her ideas, to have cultural exchanges, to help each other — and who knows, ultimately when the barriers in her mind and in her heart are gone and there is a degree of confidence she may give her consent." It's like frightening a woman. Once she knows you are on a conscious course of structuring to get something from her that she doesn't want to give you, then every time you approach her, her heels go into the ground, and every move is interpreted as a deliberate move to gain by stealth what you cannot gain in the open. And that's not the way to win her. If Northern Ireland is to be wooed, it has got to be done honestly.[38]

Other Unionists echo these sentiments. James Molyneaux, leader of the Official Unionist Party:

What I find objectionable is to say on the one hand that the consent of a majority will be required for any change in Northern Ireland's constitutional status, and on the other hand then to say, "Let's see how we can pre-empt all that, and sabotage and erode all that by setting up structures that will through time erode and nibble away at the foundation of all that." The logical thing would be for people to say, for the Dublin government to say, for the SDLP to say, "In our political lifetime Northern Ireland is going to remain separate. It's going to remain part of the United Kingdom. Let's accept that fact of life, and settle down and behave like two neighboring nations should behave — the United Kingdom of Great Britain and Northern Ireland on the one hand, and the Republic of Ireland on the other." That's a perfectly respectable attitude. It's not for the EEC to say that while it accepts the fact that Spain and Portugal can't be united in the foreseeable future, never mind all that, we'll set up joint studies and councils in the hope that we can push them into it in advance of their deciding of their own free will to unite. That's what they're trying to do with all this summitry business. And that's why we're against it, and what we want to avoid is a situation where Northern Ireland would be dependent, energy-wise, on energy resources in the South.[39]

Harold McCusker, Official Unionist M.P. for Armagh, uses a broader context to voice his opposition to the talks:

You've got to put this Anglo-Irish Council in a context of an ongoing terrorist war being waged which doesn't lead people to a position of self-confidence. You've got to put it in the context of there being, up until recently anyway, a government in the Republic led by Charlie Haughey, who openly proclaims that it was a major step on the way to Irish unity. You've got to put it in the context of the Labour Party — the previous government, in the United Kingdom — now adopting as its official policy the goal of eventual unification. When you put developments such as the Anglo-Irish Council in these contexts, it's easy to understand why people in Northern Ireland are quite properly wary of it. It's called an Anglo-Irish Council. But it's not really designed to consider the full range of relations between Great Britain and the Republic. It's designed to allow the government of the Republic to have a say in the government of Northern Ireland . . . That's why we're so suspicious.[40]

John McMichael, chairman of the Ulster Loyalist Democratic Party, the political wing of the Ulster Defence Association:

The Anglo-Irish talks are seen by us as a great danger. We believe that the British parliamentary parties are moving positively towards a united Ireland solution. The Anglo-Irish talks are trying to bring about the resurrection of the Sunningdale Agreement with the emphasis on the economy rather than on political institutions. The idea is to make Northern Ireland economically dependent on Southern Ireland over a period of thirty or forty years. But we can't afford to spend the next thirty or forty years living in the conditions in which we are living now.[41]

For Ian Paisley, leader of the Democratic Unionist Party, it is simple duplicity: "The Anglo-Irish summit is saying, in effect, 'We're working for a united Ireland.' And then with a double tongue it's saying, 'Well, of course if a majority don't want it, it won't be.' Well, the majority don't want it."[42]

Thus, Unionists of every hue see the Anglo-Irish process as a stratagem on the part of the two governments to create an artificial consensus for unification. Their continued resistance to that process, and in particular their unwillingness to participate in the parliamentary arm, makes stable devolved government in Northern Ireland more difficult to achieve. Unionists are once again victims of their own intransigence. Their failure to consider any accommodation with the minority was responsible in large measure for making the British government receptive to an Anglo-Irish process in the first place. What they perceive as the direction of the process now reinforces the necessity to resist accommodation, but the more they resist the more they validate the need for the process. Things may be moving out of their control.

That, at least, is what Mr. Haughey and Fianna Fáil would have them believe. And moving things even further out of their control is the centerpiece of the Fianna Fáil strategy on Northern Ireland. It is very different from the Fine Gael strategy and carries with it a very different set of implications.

• • •

Dr. Martin Mansergh is Director of Research for Fianna Fáil, a prominent member of the party's think tank, and one of the architects of its position on Northern Ireland. Mr. Haughey, alone among the leaders of all political parties in both the North and the South, refuses to sit for a taped interview. He calls Mansergh. "Give him what he wants," he says.[43] Mansergh is happy to oblige.

The difference between the Fianna Fáil approach to Northern Ireland and Fine Gael's? Mansergh:*

It's very basic, and the so-called Constitutional Crusade has brought this out. It's fundamentally a difference of whether you accept that the Unionists have an entirely legitimate case, which is certainly the direction in which the Coalition has moved, and you work from that basis. Or you work from the basis that they are there and they have to be dealt with, but you don't necessarily accept the legitimacy of their case. Obviously we all accept the Union as a fact, but I think some of the things FitzGerald and O'Leary [Michael O'Leary, then leader of the Labour Party and deputy head of the Coalition government] have been saying suggest that they now think that the Unionists had a right to opt out of a united Ireland and that they still have that right. And that it is a question, if you want to change that, of trying to persuade them that it would be in their interests to change, whereas we believe that the Unionist position is based on the British guarantee, and that it isn't possible to talk much sense to them while that guarantee is there.[44]

While Fianna Fáil recognizes that any agreed arrangements in a new Ireland will come about only if Unionists give their consent, it has little faith in FitzGerald's belief that a certain proportion of Protestants can be won over. Indeed, it finds his approach somewhat devious:

Unionists would be right to be beware of Garret FitzGerald because his stated intention is to win over a sufficient number of Unionists — it need only be a maximum of 25 percent — and then to use the majority

* Dr. Mansergh's blunt comments on the differences between Fine Gael and Fianna Fáil on the Northern Ireland question are all the more interesting since approximately fourteen months after this interview was conducted (December 1981) both Fianna Fáil and Fine Gael agreed to participate with the SDLP in a forum that is charged with coming up with proposals for a new Ireland (see chapter 11, p. 382n, and chapter 14, p. 413n). Nothing happened in these fourteen months to lessen the differences between Fine Gael and Fianna Fáil on the issue. On the contrary, two general elections, the Falklands war, their very different responses to James Prior's initiatives (see chapter 11), and the emergence of more trenchant Republicanism in Fianna Fáil served to heighten, not lessen, the differences. One possible explanation as to why the two parties were prepared to participate in the forum is given in chapter 14, p. 413n.

so created — Catholics plus the 25 percent — to impose a solution on the rest. In other words, what he is seeking to do is to divide the Unionist camp, and isolate the hard-liners, though it's a bit ironic to talk about isolating people who form a vast majority of the Unionist camp.

Fianna Fáil, on the other hand, seeks to create no false impressions of where it stands. There is no reason why it should not be tolerable for Protestants to live as a minority in a state in which Catholics are a majority: "The Unionists have refused to come to terms with this. You could say their stated position is a conscientious objection to democracy. They are saying it would be intolerable for us to live in a state in which the majority were Catholics."

Fianna Fáil is in principle opposed to devolved government in the North because Northern Ireland is "a failed political entity," and to try once again for a devolved government would be "confining the problem within a framework which has proved itself incapable of providing a solution." The major initiatives, therefore, have to come from the Dublin and London governments acting in concert, with provision, of course, for Northern participation. This was what the Anglo-Irish process was all about, or at least had been about before FitzGerald's efforts sabotaged its objectives. The party agrees on the need for a new constitution but is "opposed to drawing one up or making substantial amendments without Northern participation." Constitutional changes solely to impress Unionists are a futile exercise. The party had traveled that particular route with no effect on Unionist opinion. It opposes removing Articles 2 and 3 because "if you remove them you are effectively recognizing the legitimacy of Northern Ireland." And if you recognize that legitimacy, "then you have very little basis for arguing that there ought to be a united Ireland if a majority in the North manifestly oppose it. And you've no basis whatsoever for asking the British to withdraw their guarantee." Northern Ireland "is going to impinge on us whether we like it or not." A solution has to be found, and "even if some form of a united Ireland would not at present arouse much enthusiasm among quite a large section of the population, that's also true of all sorts of political or economic solutions. You don't find much enthusiasm for extra taxation, but sometimes it's necessary."

The corollary of the Fianna Fáil position that the guarantee should go is that "the British should withdraw in an orderly manner at some time in the future." But there are different ways of getting to that objective. Since 1980 "the Anglo-Irish initiative was the path chosen. It was seen as something which in due course would unite the British and Irish governments and the parties in the North around a table." Does Fianna Fáil believe that Britain wants out? Yes:

> And that is a prospect which possibly alarms the coalition government a great deal more than it does us. At the level of general wishes, the British would like to get out but they don't see how they could get out at the moment. Obviously, if they could get out and the result wasn't catastrophic, they'd be very keen to get out. But that's not to say they have actually decided to get out . . .

Does Fianna Fáil have a concept of what a united Ireland should be? Indeed:

> We have a good conception, or at least a very clear conception, of what a united Ireland should be, although obviously it's something that has to be negotiated so it's not something that's going to depend solely on us. Back in the mid-seventies, in Jack Lynch's day, there was perhaps a strong preference for a federal solution — give Unionists Stormont back but under an all-Ireland umbrella. The Fine Gael policy of a confederal Ireland isn't so different from that except that the all-Ireland element is more attenuated than it would be in the federal system. Now there is no official party policy tying us to any particular form of a united Ireland. But preference has grown again for a unitary state with some legal administrative autonomy for Northern Ireland. This is the "Scottish model."

The Scottish model: Scotland has separate laws from England, separate law courts, separate police, and separate education systems. Within the British Parliament a Scottish Grand Committee deals with Scottish legislation. Mansergh:

Since it is not essential, nor in fact would it be practical, to immediately harmonize all laws, this is how you would get over any particular law having a conscientious dimension, be it divorce or censorship or whatever. You could have a separate divorce law for the Northern Ireland area, and have a separate divorce law, or nondivorce law, down here. There's no reason why that shouldn't operate. The thing that worked best in the old Stormont was the administration, not the government. And there is no reason why certain services, such as agriculture and so on — although not all aspects of agricultural policy, but particularly the implementation of policy — couldn't continue to be done from Belfast.

This would also provide a useful degree of decentralization and some recognition of Belfast's continuing status as a capital. As far as citizenship is concerned,

there's nothing to stop people in the North retaining British citizenship alongside Irish citizenship. In fact, those who didn't want to wouldn't even have to take up Irish citizenship. They could still enjoy the vast majority of civil rights — perhaps not become President or a few things like that. In other words, they could keep their personal connections with Britain to whatever extent they desired.

When a united Ireland is established, Fianna Fáil foresees a ten-year transitional period, perhaps during which the differences between social welfare benefits and civil service salaries would continue to be met by the British.

We would expect to get quite substantial EEC and perhaps American aid for reconstruction of the more battered parts of Northern Ireland. We might look to certain countries in the Commonwealth, such as Canada or Australia, to take the "irreducibles" who would find it absolutely intolerable to live in a united Ireland.

But would Protestants fight a united Ireland? That is problematical. The Protestant will to fight has never been tested.

They've never actually been pushed into a situation of having to carry out their threats. So let's put it this way: there is quite a big question mark over it. It all depends on the circumstances. No one is proposing that you try to impose this on them in the morning. It's more a question of gradually creating a situation in which this is the only way out or path forward — if necessary, going through certain transitional stages like the Anglo-Irish talks.

Fianna Fáil, therefore, puts great emphasis on creating situations. Kinsale gas is a good example. Belfast Gas wanted a supply of gas from the North Sea beds for both political and economic reasons. However, it would have involved such a heavy subsidy that the British refused to back the scheme. So Northerners were faced with a situation of having either Kinsale gas or no gas: "Faced with that choice they opted for gas from Kinsale, notwithstanding Paisley making comparisons between Kinsale gas and Belsen gas!"* Thus, the objective is to "set up that type of situation in other spheres where they either have the choice of doing something in cooperation with us or having nothing. Their choice will be to have something in cooperation with us."† Hence Fianna Fáil's greater emphasis on economic cooperation and new arrangements to "integrate and administer" sectors of the economy on an all-Ireland basis. As far as closer integration with the United Kingdom is concerned, Fianna Fáil is prepared to consider "any link which is based on the acceptance of the sovereignty or independence of the two countries." There is no question of going back into the Commonwealth:

* On 28 May 1982, approximately three months after Mr. Haughey had resumed office and five months after this interview with Dr. Mansergh was conducted, the British and Irish governments announced an agreement to pipe Kinsale gas to Belfast. The *Irish Times* reported that "consumers in Northern Ireland will obtain Kinsale gas at cheaper rates than their counterparts in Dublin and Cork . . . The result of the deal will be that Southern taxpayers will subsidize Northern gas-users." (29 May 1982.) Approximately eight months later, the *Irish Times* reported that the British government had agreed "to make a substantial contribution to the [Irish] government to help cover the costs of the new North-South gas pipeline from the Kinsale field." And it noted that the agreement was "certain to result in Loyalist opposition." See *Irish Times*, 19 January 1983.

† On 26 April 1982 a delegation headed by Mansergh visited engineering works in Belfast, including the Harland and Wolff shipyard, to see whether they might be able to supply the heavy engineering needs of some of the Republic's semistate bodies. (*Irish Times*, 26 April 1982.)

We're not going back to the situation of being an economic or perhaps even a political satellite of Britain. We left that behind us when we went into the EEC. We're not prepared to sell out in all directions in order to achieve unity. Nor would unity be achieved by that sort of method. That's where we differ a little bit from the present government, who seem to be much readier to appease.

• • •

There is, therefore, a consistency to Mr. Haughey's positions: make no changes, offer no suggestions, outline no alternatives, reveal nothing until Unionists either come or are brought to the conference table. You don't show the color of your cards until you have to, and don't deal away your bargaining chips before the play begins. And how would Unionists be "enticed" to the conference table? Easy. Create dependence. When you have them in an economic strangle hold, their hearts and minds will follow. End the guarantee and then have the two sovereign governments acting together put forward their proposals. This would force the Unionists, if only to protect their own interests, to participate. In Mr. Haughey's own words, "The inevitability of events would be such that no elected representative who would have a role in it could afford in the long run to stay out of it."[45] Out of the negotiations consent would emerge — and British withdrawal begin.

• • •

Some of the statements made by the present leadership of Fianna Fáil suggest that there is some idea of abandoning, without saying so, the concept of unification with consent, and of trying to seek some solution forced on the people of Northern Ireland over their heads . . . As long as that persists in Fianna Fáil it will be difficult to make progress.[46]

Dr. Garret FitzGerald speaks ever so rapidly, setting out the genesis of the Fine Gael–Labour coalition's — and his government's — policy on Northern Ireland in great detail: The Anglo-Irish initiative began with the Fine Gael policy paper of February 1979, which set out the idea of seeking a solution to the problems of North-South relations in the wider context of relationships between Ireland and Britain. The SDLP in November 1979 put forward its own proposal for an Anglo-Irish context that would enable the Unionists to participate without fear as part of a U.K. delegation that would also include the SDLP. This was "a very major concession indeed for a nationalist party in Northern Ireland to make in order to alleviate Unionist fears." However, "the presentation of the Anglo-Irish relationships from December 1980 onwards" was quite the opposite of what Fine Gael had envisaged:

> It was presented as the two ruling governments getting together as if to take decisions over the heads of the people of Northern Ireland. Instead of the Anglo-Irish context being seen as one that was helpful, it had the opposite effect. The damage done in December '80 was immense really. And it will take a long time to repair.

He got what he wanted from Mrs. Thatcher at the Downing Street summit: a declaration that "both governments should work together to reconcile the two traditions in the island," which is "the best definition of what we are about. No one seeks unity on any other basis than that."

Reconciliation is something Britain deeply desires:

> Reconciliation is a process which if it were complete would remove obstacles to unification, but it is a process and it may take time to reach that point. It will reach that point when a majority in Northern Ireland decide that it has reached that point.

You have to distinguish between the roles of the two governments in two different things. One concerns the internal devolution of power in Northern Ireland and the other the relationship between North and South. The devolution of power is constitutionally a function of the British government, hence a British responsibility: "We have an interest in it, obviously, because failure to devolve causes problems on devolution that lead in particular directions — like the restoration of Stormont could create problems for us."

It is up to the British government to take the initiative and not simply to wait for everybody to agree — a reluctant agreement is better than no agreement. However, North-South relations are a different matter:

There can be no resolution of that except on the basis of consent. It's quite different from finding a solution within Northern Ireland — consent is something to be given by the people of Northern Ireland to a relationship with us. Britain's role is in a sense secondary to creating conditions favorable to it — certainly not standing in the way — and doing whatever may be helpful to the evolution of good relations between North and South.

Thus the political strategy of the Coalition partners is designed "to create conditions in which a sufficient proportion of the Protestant population together with a large proportion, though probably not all, of the Catholic population would want a new political relationship with us." The South has to earn consent. Repealing Articles 2 and 3 would remove for some Unionists "one obstacle to the contemplation of a new relationship with us based on the common interests we share and in the context of an Anglo-Irish relationship so structured as to enable Unionists to retain their sense of a British-Irish identity, and citizenship of the U.K. if they wished to do that." When that consent emerges, then:

The moral strength of opposition to Irish unity would obviously be very limited if a majority in Northern Ireland wanted it. You'd then have a minority of a minority part of the island seeking to stand in the way of something which everyone else in the two parts of the island wants. At that stage the problem would be much nearer to resolution than today, although there could be some problems to overcome. You wouldn't necessarily wait for the first 51 percent vote and rush at it at that stage.

The Coalition strongly endorses devolved government in Northern Ireland. "Aside from being a preliminary to anything else, it's necessary in its own right if the people of Northern Ireland are to achieve a degree of internal cohesion that would make any real progress possible."

Those who are against devolution are following a sterile course:

By trying to prevent people in Northern Ireland from having their own representation and making their own decisions they are perpetuating the fear of people in Northern Ireland that decisions are being taken over their heads and behind their backs — something that is resented in both communities, though naturally more strongly in the Unionist community.

Should the guarantee be withdrawn? FitzGerald equivocates:

The process we are embarked on now is the most helpful one. No Irish government should contribute to a heightening of tensions. What we're trying to do is to reduce them, to eliminate the fears that certainly exist in Northern Ireland by publishing the joint studies, by making it clear in the communiqué how we're approaching these problems as one of reconciliation — not as a territorial claim — and by the constitutional initiative in which we set out to change the whole perspective within which these matters are being discussed.

At this point, even a declaration by Britain of its long-term interest in Irish unity would probably do more harm than good, provoking a backlash among Protestants and adding to fear and tension. How does FitzGerald feel about Haughey's curt dismissal of his efforts to remove Articles 2 and 3?

He has certain surprises coming. Far from being dead, the constitutional initiative is my chief motivation for being in politics. It will be pursued. It is clear that he is fearful of its consequences and his own very negative handling of it has caused considerable unrest in his own party.

Fine Gael favors an Irish confederation: two independent sovereign states "sharing those things in common which they can do better together." North and South would have equal representation in the confederation so that "there would be no fear of domination one by the other." As regards the kinds of things that would be done together: "They would be done in partnership on the basis of equality. They are things to be worked out — at some distance hence and by agreement — and no one is dogmatic."

Thus in a confederate Ireland Unionists would have power sharing at the confederate level: "They would hardly wish in an all-Ireland context, in the early stages in any event, to be in a position where they would be seen as a minority which could be dominated by a majority." The guarantee against that is power sharing on the basis of equality; and in those circumstances "it would also be logical to have it at the local level for a period if that were necessary." A confederate Ireland can only be seriously discussed when the situation within Northern Ireland has resolved itself and the two sides have come together in partnership:

> You would reach the point of talking about the North-South relationship in political terms when the two sides working together in government in Northern Ireland had created sufficient confidence in each other to be able to talk to us . . . So what you might have is a period of partnership in government in Northern Ireland normalizing the situation, after which it might be possible to revert to a normal political situation, since nobody saw either power sharing or partnership as other than a temporary phenomenon. You could end up, therefore, with a Northern Ireland which had been through a period of partnership and come back to a normal system of government moving into a confederation in which there would be power sharing at the confederate level.

• • •

Thus, the FitzGerald approach: there are two problems — the question of relations between the two communities within Northern Ireland and the question of relations between the two parts of Ireland. The onus for resolving the first lies with the British government and the onus for the second lies with the Irish government. Moreover, the first has to be settled before the second can be addressed in a substantive way. The solution to the first could, in fact, be imposed — a reluctant agreement that includes nobody's first choice. The solution to the second, however, could not be imposed. It has to take the form of a free and true acquiescence. The South, therefore, has to take steps to improve the climate for creating consent. Consent is something the North would give, something the South would earn. The Unionists have a case. It is up to the South to examine it, and to dismantle it, thus removing the obstacles to reconciliation.

Fianna Fáil is right: FitzGerald concedes a legitimacy to the Unionist case. And the Unionists are right: Fianna Fáil wants to create a situation of dependence and a set of economic and political structures that would make consent irrelevant in the face of an inevitable outcome.

• • •

For most of the period since 1968, when the troubles erupted again in Northern Ireland, the major political parties in the South managed a united front on the issue despite differences on particular questions that arose from time to time. All joined in condemnation of the Provisional IRA, all rejected force as a means of achieving unity, all aspired to the unification of Ireland by agreement and in peace. And all believed that, ultimately, Protestants would consent to unification. That united front is now shattered. The events of 1980 and 1981 revealed the deep-rooted differences between the two major parties, differences exacerbated by the acrimonious relationship between the party leaders themselves. The Anglo-Irish framework has not brought Northern Protestants into the process. It has, however, brought out the differences between Fianna Fáil's and Fine Gael's conceptions of the Northern problem. Nor has the Anglo-Irish framework provided a forum for the Northern Protestant parties to alleviate their fears. It has, however, provided a forum for the Southern Catholic parties to resurrect their distrust of each other. Old antagonisms lurk just beneath the surface of the national consciousness, the Civil War is not yet forgotten, and implicit suggestions that one party's delegates to a London summit were somehow insufficient plenipotentiaries have a disturbing ugliness about them. The more the two parties argue, the more they reveal the extent of their differences; the more fundamental their differences, the more suspicious are Unionists of what their real intentions are; the more suspicious are Protestants, the more difficult, if not impossible, is rapprochement.

Moreover, even if Loyalists were disposed to talking, their

incentive to do so lessens when one of the parties in the South starts making unilateral concessions. There is a huge difference between a confederate Ireland of two independent states sharing power equally at the confederate level and the Scottish model of administrative devolution in a unitary state. No Northern Protestant would think of accepting the latter if he thought there was even an outside chance of getting the former. A constitutional referendum to delete Articles 2 and 3 fought along party lines would almost certainly go down to defeat in an atmosphere of bitterness, accusations, and a reopening of old Civil War wounds, bringing back into the foreground of the body politic the ugliness of irredentist nationalism. It would risk losing more, on both sides of the Border, than it could possibly gain, since a reaffirmation of the territorial claim would convince Loyalists that consent meant conquest. The timing of FitzGerald's crusade was, therefore, unfortunate. The reaction it provoked in Fianna Fáil makes a referendum on the issue most unlikely in the immediate future. In that sense it has contributed to stalemate, and not, as had been intended, to opening the path to new considerations. What was perhaps the right impulse was stymied by the wrong politics. FitzGerald's inability, or unwillingness, to see things in their political context dims the luster of his aspirations. Politics, after all, is the art of changing aspirations into reality. Concessions made in a vacuum inspire silence in the hope that silence will inspire more concessions.

The Fianna Fáil position has hardened since the days of Jack Lynch, but it is, nonetheless, consistent with the long-standing Fianna Fáil perception of the problem. As befits the more Catholic and more Gaelic party, Fianna Fáil sees the question as a British problem. Hence, the withdrawal of the guarantee is the precursor of a general withdrawal. Thus, for Fianna Fáil the solution to the Northern Ireland problem rests primarily with the British. And although it condemns violence in unequivocal terms and believes that violence stands in the way of unification, it sees violence as a consequence of partition and not as the basic problem. The belief that an end to partition would mean an end to the violence is predicated on another belief: that when the hard-nosed Protestants accept unification as inevitable, in the sense of its being the only realistic or even feasible alternative in the face of a British withdrawal, they will not fight it. Thus, the case for withdrawal rests on the premise that if the British made clear their intentions to pull out, the parties in the North would be required by the new situation to work out their differences not only with each other but also with the South so as to produce a solution that would at the very least minimize the economic, social, and political dislocations that would result in the absence of an agreement.

Four other key assumptions underlie Fianna Fáil policy. First, that the British either can or will break the guarantee. Second, that the continued military presence of Britain during that process would or could preclude either civil war or a unilateral declaration of independence by the Unionists. Third, that Protestants would either behave rationally, in that they would be prepared to make the best of a bad situation, or failing that, that they would not behave *ir*rationally. It dismisses the Masada complex. Fourth, that the Loyalists would in fact come to the conference table rather than simply refuse to have any part in the proceedings.

The Coalition parties on the other hand, and especially Fine Gael, do not advocate a timed and phased withdrawal. They believe an internal agreement among the parties in the North is necessary before the subject of a Southern relationship can be raised. And even at that point they feel the onus is on the South to win the Unionists over. Moreover, Fine Gael, and especially FitzGerald, is far more likely to see IRA violence as *the* problem in Northern Ireland. His obsessive concern with the IRA as a threat to democracy leads FitzGerald to deny it any legitimacy whatsoever. When Owen Carron was elected M.P. for the Fermanagh–South Tyrone district after the death of Bobby Sands, FitzGerald refused to meet with him.* Carron, he maintained, did not represent the views of a majority of Northern Catholics or even of his constituents. Moreover, Carron's

* Sands's death was the result of his hunger strike. Carron was a prominent member of Provisional Sinn Féin. See chapter 3, pp. 122–26, for a fuller discussion of the Fermanagh–South Tyrone elections. And see chapter 7, pp. 264–72, for a fuller discussion of the hunger strikes.

unwillingness to repudiate the IRA was unacceptable to FitzGerald, who was not prepared to risk alienating "moderate" Unionist opinion by seeming to endorse a supporter of the IRA. Haughey, on the other hand, saw Carron.

The Fine Gael scenario for a united Ireland is also predicated on a number of assumptions, all of which are likely to be found wanting. First, it assumes that a majority consensus for some form of a united Ireland would, of itself, be sufficient to move things in the desired direction. However, that is unlikely to happen. At the moment there are not a sufficient number of "enlightened" Unionists to make even power sharing a reality. Second, the Fine Gael policy presupposes a power-sharing arrangement in the North. A consensus about power sharing would be far more palatable to Protestants in the context of a U.K. relationship than in the context of a Southern relationship. In the latter case, the prospect of the second step — confederation — would, in all likelihood, preclude the first — power sharing. Moreover, Protestant agreement to power sharing would pose a dilemma for Catholics: whether to accept it within the context of a U.K. relationship only or to reject it, thus inviting a Protestant backlash and setting the stage for civil war. Third, the policy assumes a monolithic Catholic preference in the North for any form of unification under all sets of circumstances. And, finally, it assumes that the ultra-Loyalists would accept a majority wish in Northern Ireland for some form of confederation. A sizable militant minority opposed to unification would, however, confront the Republic — and the security forces of the indigenous Northern Ireland state — with the task of enforcing the confederation. There is much reason to believe that such a Loyalist minority would prove to be as destabilizing in the North as the IRA now is; and there is no reason to believe that "the security forces" would be any more effective in dealing with the situation.

There is a crucial difference between a majority in Northern Ireland being for confederation and a majority of Protestants being for it. There is in fact an element of delusion in the attitude that condemns violence as a way of achieving unification while insisting that unification can be brought about with the consent of a majority. This attitude assumes that such a majority sentiment would easily, and peaceably, overcome resistance to the idea by a militant, well-armed, and well-financed minority. It is naive to believe that those Protestants who would at best be reluctant converts to the idea of confederation would continue to support it, even if it meant taking up arms against their fellow Protestants who were violently opposed to the idea.

• • •

The basic common assumption on the part of all political parties in the South is the belief that in the long run Northern Protestants will come to see their position as untenable, and a united Ireland as inevitable. Thus, notwithstanding FitzGerald's initiatives, the South awaits a change in attitude among Northern Protestants while doing little or nothing to bring about that change. It takes little note that a historical basis for such a change of attitude is nonexistent. In fact, just the contrary. Every time Ulster Protestants have felt that unification under a Catholic-dominated government was a possibility, even a remote possibility, they have flocked to a strident, militant Unionism. They reacted this way to Gladstone's Home Rule policy in 1886, to the Home Rule crisis of 1912, to the events leading to partition in 1921, and again to the proposed Council of Ireland in 1974.

FitzGerald poses the question: "Do you accept that reunification can only be with the consent of a majority, and if you do, how do you propose to create the conditions in which that consensus is most likely to be achieved?"

It raises a second question: Under what conditions would a majority in the South give their consent to unification? The aspiration to unity is real, but it must not be mistaken for consent.

For a consensus among the people of the South to emerge on this question, there must be a prior consensus among the Southern political parties. For the Anglo-Irish process to have any chance of working, there must be a prior consensus among the Southern political parties. And for Protestant fears to be assuaged, there must be a prior consensus among the Southern political parties. Before the question of the consent of a majority can be raised in a Northern context, it must first be resolved in a Southern context.

The failure of consensus to emerge is due to sixty years of silence, of blind allegiance to an aspiration that removed the necessity for debate.

2

The South: A Question of Commitment

We had fed the heart on fantasies . . .

— W. B. Yeats
"Meditations in Time of Civil War"

THE IRISH CIVIL WAR was not fought on the issue of partition. Indeed, the division of Ireland was scarcely mentioned during the Dáil debate on the Anglo-Irish Treaty of 1921. The pro- and anti-treaty factions split over something far more intangible — the formal international status of the new state. Northern Ireland's relationship to the new state was not an issue.[1] There appears to have been a willingness on all sides to accept Lloyd George's sly suggestion that the proposed Boundary Commission would redraw the Border in such a way as to make what was left of Northern Ireland an unviable economic unit. The question in 1921, therefore, was how to win "the freedom to achieve freedom," in Michael Collins's memorable phrase.

Besides, the Northern Ireland state was already a reality; no one contemplated the use of force to tear it down for the very good reason that no one believed it could be taken by force. However, when the Free State government accepted, albeit reuctantly, the Boundary Commission Report in 1925, it also accepted the Border as a permanent arrangement: the Ulster question had become an insoluble problem. Successive Irish governments, accepting that there was nothing they could do to change the situation, simply committed themselves to ending partition. The aspiration to unity took the place of a policy to achieve it.

Accordingly, during the first decades of its existence, the Free State gave its whole attention to terminating its dominion status within the Empire rather than to building bridges to the new state in Ulster, which might have eased the way to conciliation. The issue of sovereignty took precedence over the issue of unity. It was an extraordinarily shortsighted policy, responsible in large measure for the predicament the bickering parties in the South find themselves in today.

From the beginning, therefore, partition was treated only in the context of a continued British occupation of the Six Counties. There was no disagreement between political parties in the South on this issue; thus, their policies were nonpolicies simply calling for an end to the British occupation, and hence for an end to partition. By insisting that a foreign occupation was the only thing precluding unification, the Southern political parties were spared having to discuss the question of Northern Ireland, having to consider alternative possibilities, having to examine their assumptions about Irish nationalism, having to define the nature of political consent, having to develop the processes to achieve it, and most important, perhaps, having to understand the nature of Unionism and the identity of Northern Protestants.

The South took its own indigenous attributes as the attributes of the whole. Hence the gratuitous insensitivity to Northern Protestants that was a recurring feature of government action in the following decades. It looked as though the Catholic South was intent on proving to the Protestant North that Home Rule was indeed Rome Rule. Partition encouraged the confessional ethos of the state. The more the Free State asserted its independence, the more it asserted its Catholicity; and, with its Catholicity, its Gaelicism.[2]

First, there came a spate of legislation incorporating the Catholic moral code: a Censorship of Film Act in 1923, legislation prohibiting divorce in 1925, a Censorship of Publications Act in 1929, and in the 1930s laws requiring the licensing of dance halls and making the importation and sale of contraceptives a criminal offense. Second, with the election of Eamon de Valera in 1932 there came a concerted effort by the Dublin government to sever all remaining ties with Britain. Reality would be rearranged so as to conform with the myth of a Gaelic, Catholic state. The oath of allegiance was abolished in 1933; the governor-general was removed in 1936; and finally, the secular constitution of 1920 was abandoned in 1937 for a constitution acknowledging the "special position of the Catholic Church," incorporating Catholic social teaching, and forbidding divorce. The territorial claim to the whole of the island was reasserted: henceforth the government elected by some of the people was empowered to speak on behalf of all of the people. The fact that that government spoke with an unmistakably Catholic voice was accepted as an acknowledgment of what appeared indisputably obvious. Indeed, de Valera himself made the point with the quiet pride of smug assurance when he declared in the course of a broadcast to the United States that "we are a Catholic nation."[3]

• • •

No one disputed the claim, least of all the Protestants in the North and the Roman Catholic hierarchy in the South. The hierarchy's position in the new state was paramount: bishops had the right to interfere in public affairs where questions of faith and morals were involved, a right enhanced by the further acknowledgment that only the bishops had the authority to decide when questions of faith and morals were involved. Church interference in state matters was taken for granted, and proved conclusively to the satisfaction of all when the celebrated mother-and-child-health-scheme crisis erupted in 1951.

The facts are well known.[4] Dr. Noel Browne, the Minister for Health at the time, put forward a plan to provide free state medical care for children and their mothers. The hierarchy immediately condemned the proposal for being "in direct opposition to the rights of the family and of the individual"[5] and for constituting "a ready-made instrument for future totalitarian aggression."[6] The right to provide for the health of children, it insisted, belonged to parents, not the state. The arithmetic was awry, it not being "sound fiscal policy to impose a state-made medical service on the whole community on the pretext of relieving the necessitous 10 percent from the indignity of the means test."[7] What economics had to do with matters of faith and morals was left unsaid. The hierarchy was particularly insistent on one point: under no circumstances would it approve a scheme that did not include a means test.

There was no question of a debate on the merits of the issue. The government capitulated immediately. Browne resigned, the scheme was withdrawn, and members of Parliament fell over each other in their haste to acknowledge the rights of the Church to intervene whenever it felt that legislation was incompatible with Catholic teaching. At the time Seán O'Faoláin scathingly observed, "Here in the Republic, as this crisis has revealed to us, we have two parliaments: a Parliament at Maynooth and a Parliament at Dublin . . . the Dáil proposes; Maynooth disposes."[8]

And in case that message was lost, a leading Catholic theologian warned, shortly thereafter, that "it is a mistake to think as some of our politicians have been thinking that the moral law must be corralled into a partitioned area from which all social norms must be excluded. The distinction set up between the moral and the social teaching of the Church is an artificial and false teaching. Social teaching is no more than the application of moral principles to human social relations, all of which form part of God's plan."[9]

The Browne affair was revealing in other respects. The extreme deference of the state toward the hierarchy was matched by the extreme arrogance of the hierarchy toward the state. The Archbishop of Dublin "summoned" the head of the government, who responded on every occasion with breathtaking alacrity. Although the Archbishop was not the senior Church official in Ireland, he insisted on dealing only with the head of government. Ministers were very definitely lesser creatures and were seen only as a matter of courtesy. The hierarchy dictated: there was never a question of either negotiations or compromise. Its tone was cold, hostile, and aloof, underscoring the Church's arrogation of the right to take matters into its own hands whenever it alone saw fit to do so. Although spiritual matters, according to the most widely used religious textbook on apologetics, belonged exclusively to the Church and temporal matters to the state, there was to be no doubt as to who had the final say in matters of dispute: "the state inasmuch as it pursues the less important end must yield to the Church."[10]

The real and lasting power of the Church, however, comes from its involvement in every aspect of Irish life. It is not necessary to interfere in political matters because the entire apparatus of public affairs is conditioned to articulate and legislate what the Church wants without the Church having to lobby for it.* This conditioning goes back to the Church's total control over the entire educational process. It's a question of "give us the child and we'll answer for the man." The Church controls the educational system, the educational system begets the electorate, the electorate begets the political parties, and they in turn beget the government. The cycle is complete, rigid, and entirely self-contained. Catholic social and moral teaching is the basic influence at every level.

One noted scholar who could find only sixteen pieces of legislation in which Irish bishops had evinced an interest between 1926 and 1970 uses the figure to make the argument for a lack of Church interference, since some eighteen hundred pieces of legislation were enacted during the same period.[11] However, the fact that the clergy had to intervene openly on so few occasions is far more likely to reflect Parliament's sensitivity to the hierarchy's wishes: in general, legislators take good care not to bring down on themselves "the belt of a crozier."

The Church in the South stood aloof from and above the state. It was suspicious of the state, jealous of the state's prerogatives, obsessively concerned with threats to its own authority

* However, when the Church thinks that legislation close to its interests may be in jeopardy, it still does not hesitate to come out into the open in order to influence a political decision—as the proposed abortion amendment amply indicated. Instead, to many the Church's performance was reminiscent of its interference in the mother-and-child-health-scheme crisis, see p. 406n.

in a state that fully subscribed to all its teachings, quick to see opposition where none existed, a compulsive guardian of Catholic values in the face of all kinds of vague and imaginary dangers, and obstinately insistent on asserting itself on every occasion as though in constant fear of losing its power and position. It grew into an institution unsure of its grasp on a people who followed its every instruction unquestioningly; unwilling to entertain any idea that might erode its authority; almost intolerantly conservative, steadfastly insular, and rigidly uncompromising because it did not have to compete with opposing ideas. In the postwar era the Church in other countries had to do business with Communist regimes, and make accommodations with Communist or Socialist parties. The Church in Ireland, however, not only was not exposed to any opposing or even different ideologies, it became increasingly conservative, condemning "egalitarianism" at every opportunity: the siege mentality of the Protestant population in the North had its counterpart in the siege mentality of the Catholic Church in the South.

Some things are changing. Indeed, change was inevitable with the advent of television, the entry into Europe, and rapid urbanization. The cultural ethos has become increasingly secular. Between 1966 and 1974, religious vocations declined from 1409 to 547. The religious orders were hardest hit — vocations to communities of brothers declined 70 percent between 1966 and 1978, and to communities of sisters by 83 percent. By 1979 only 2300 out of 10,830 secondary teachers were from religious orders.[12] The younger generation, especially young single people, are less likely to attend mass and increasingly likely to believe that the use of birth control is morally acceptable.

The hierarchy, however, continues to fight a tenacious rearguard action. Although the Supreme Court found in 1973 that the Constitution's clause protecting privacy was violated by the law prohibiting the importation of contraceptives for the private use of married couples, the hierarchy was, nevertheless, grudging in its concessions. It took six years for the state to bring the law into line with the Court's ruling. And even when it did, the Church managed to plug the dykes against the rising flood of the loathed "contraception mentality."[13] Under the Family

Planning Act of 1979, contraceptives can be sold only in chemists' shops and only to married couples on doctors' prescriptions. Chemists, however, for reasons of conscience, can refuse to fill a prescription. Mr. Haughey, who was the Fianna Fáil minister responsible for the legislation, called it, without even a trace of facetiousness, "an Irish solution to an Irish problem."[14] Others were a good deal less charitable.

Some things are not changing. The hierarchy remains incorrigible on the question of mixed marriages, and the South's Protestant population continues to decline. Assimilation through intermarriage is the great fear of Northern Protestants. And the fear is not groundless. In 1911 Protestants accounted for 10 percent of the population of the South.[15] In the next fifteen years the number fell by almost one third; it fell again by a further 24 percent between 1926 and 1946 and by yet another 15 percent between 1946 and 1961.[16] Only 4.3 percent of the population called itself Protestant according to the census of 1971;[17] the birth rate for married women aged fifteen to forty-four was 1.7 times higher per thousand women among Catholics; and Catholic families were on the average 50 percent larger.[18] The Protestant birth rate remains the lowest in the world, with one minor exception, and the death rate significantly above average, the result of an abnormally aging population structure.[19] The low birth rate, however, cannot be solely attributed to Protestants choosing to have smaller families. By far the most important cause of the population hemorrhage is the fact that the children of many Protestants are brought up Catholic. In 1961, for example, about three out of every ten Protestant grooms and two out of every ten Protestant brides married Catholics.[20] The *Ne Temere* decree has taken a heavy toll: a mixed marriage in one generation almost invariably means a Catholic marriage in the next; ultimately assimilation means extinction.

The decree dates back to the Council of Trent in 1563, the modern version from 1918, when it was rewritten as part of the canon law code. It required parties to a "mixed" marriage to sign a four-point declaration: there would be no interference with the Catholic party's practice of his or her religion, the Catholic party would endeavor to convert the non-Catholic party to

Catholicism, there would be no non-Catholic marriage ceremony, and most important, the children of the marriage would be brought up as Catholics.

Although "mixed" marriages were forbidden by the hierarchy, the *Ne Temere* decree provided a fallback position: if a mixed marriage was unavoidable because failure to give permission might result in some even greater evil, it would take place only under circumstances and conditions that inflicted the maximum humiliation on the non-Catholic partner. No Protestant who read the *Ne Temere* decree could have any doubts as to what the Catholic Church thought of his religion. His religion was heresy—he could not pass it on to his children. He could not be married in a Protestant church or in a civil ceremony. He was not worthy enough to be married in a Catholic church; hence, the ceremony in mixed marriages took place on the church porch or in the sacristy. And even if he did convert to Catholicism, he had to be baptized a second time because his original baptism was somehow insufficient in the eyes of the Church to cleanse his soul of original sin. The Catholic partner had not only the right but was under a Church-mandated obligation to interfere at all times with the Protestant's practice of his or her religion, whereas the Protestant had to give a written pledge not to reciprocate such interference. The Catholic partner's "rights" were given legal weight by the Irish judiciary in 1948; the state abetted the Church's designs.*

The decree was modified in 1970. Only the Catholic partner is now required to make a declaration of the intent to bring up the children as Catholics. However, the modified decree gives a great deal of discretion to local bishops, and that discretion

* See Jack White, *Minority Report*, pp. 124–27. Article 44, section 2, of the Constitution stated that "the State recognizes the special position of the Holy Catholic Apostolic and Roman Church as the guardian of the Faith professed by the great majority of the citizens." In 1950 a court judgment held that the written pledge to bring up the children as Catholics required by the *Ne Temere* decree of the non-Catholic party to a mixed marriage was legally enforceable in view of the Church's officially recognized "special position." The Supreme Court upheld this judgment, the one vote of dissent coming from the one Protestant judge on the bench. Article 44, section 2, was repealed as the result of a constitutional referendum in December 1972.

has been exercised cautiously, to say the least, by the Irish hierarchy.

Moreover, for many Protestants the modification is not enough, since the object is the same: the Catholic Church's demands represent not only an intrusion into matters of individual privacy and a violation of the parents' right to bring up their children as they see fit but also proof of the Church's insidious and total influence.

Hence the intensity of Protestant fears: the Catholic Church's claim to be the One, True, Universal and Apostolic Church is no idle boast. Rather, its actions to back up its claim have decimated the ranks of Protestantism in the South. A united Ireland, Northern Protestants believe, would accelerate the process, opening the way to absorption.

The implications of unification are therefore ominous, for if the South was the willing instrument of the decline in the Protestant population in the South, even with the Protestant North looking silently on while the dastardly deed took place, how much more willing to hasten the process might she be if she had the Protestant North securely under her thumb?

Of course, the South vehemently denies a lack of religious toleration. She points to the fact that two of her first four Presidents were Protestant, that one of the most popular Lord Mayors of Dublin was a Jew. However, all the individuals involved not only accepted but sought to perpetuate the ethos of the state as Catholic and Gaelic.

Toleration is a function of diversity. The more heterogeneous the composition of a population, the greater the necessity for interaction. The greater the level of interaction, the better the environment for toleration. The absence of religious toleration in the South is benign; the pervasiveness of Catholicism preempts the development of a significant dissenting minority. There is no toleration because there is no tradition of toleration, because toleration has not had to be learned. Homogeneity has deprived the people of the tools to cope with diversity. Protestant fears are not taken seriously because Protestants are not taken seriously.

• • •

Paralleling the move to establish a Catholic nation was a second but less successful move to establish a Gaelic nation. Within weeks of assuming office in 1923, the new government made Irish a compulsory subject of primary and secondary education.[21] The revival of Gaelic as the language of the nation became a national aspiration. Failure to receive a passing mark in Gaelic in either of the two main official secondary school examinations meant failure in the whole examination. In 1937 the name of the state was changed to Éire. The major political parties insisted on Gaelic nomenclature — Fianna Fáil (Soldiers of Destiny), Fine Gael (Soldiers of Ireland) — and the head of government became Taoiseach (leader). All political parties were committed unequivocally to the ideal of a Gaelic-speaking nation. The attempts to impose the language failed, of course, but the accoutrements remain, dividing Irish men and women along cultural lines, adding to the exclusivity of "Irishness."

The South, under de Valera's direction, remained neutral in the Second World War. Neutrality became one more badge of sovereignty. Ireland would not fight alongside England as long as Ulster remained under English rule. During the war years it became increasingly insular, cut off from the great issues of the times, absorbed with its obsession to become more wholly Gaelic, more holy Catholic.

The severance of the last link between Éire and Britain occurred in 1948, when the coalition government dominated by Fine Gael declared Ireland a republic and took the country out of the Commonwealth. It was an extraordinary volte-face for Fine Gael, which had always advocated closer ties with Britain. Adding to the irony was Fianna Fáil's initial opposition to the move. *The* party of Republicanism argued, rightly, that cutting the Commonwealth link would make the abolition of partition more difficult. But when it came to the actual vote, Fianna Fáil could not, of course, publicly oppose an aspiration it was so strongly identified with. Indeed, one historian has astutely noted that "had the Irish government chosen to combine the status of a sovereign republic with membership of the Commonwealth, as India had done, the practical obstacles to unification would be less formidable than they presently are, given Ireland's complete separation from the Commonwealth."[22]

The British government responded to the Dublin government's unilateral declaration of a republic with the Ireland Act of 1949, which contained a provision introducing, for the first time, the concept of a British guarantee to the Northern majority:

> . . . Northern Ireland [shall] remain part of His Majesty's Dominions and of the United Kingdom and it is hereby affirmed that in no event will Northern Ireland or any part thereof cease to be part of His Majesty's Dominions and of the United Kingdom without the consent of the Parliament of Northern Ireland.[23]

Today, of course, a variation of that pledge continues to guarantee the constitutional position of Northern Ireland within the U.K.

• • •

The fact that successive actions on the part of Southern governments made unification more difficult is not all that surprising. The rationale was consistent: severing all links with the Commonwealth served to emphasize the separate identity of the Irish nation as a Catholic nation and a Gaelic nation: any relationship with Britain contaminated that image. The appearance of freedom was as important as freedom itself.

But these actions, coupled with ritualistic calls on Britain to end her occupation of the Six Counties, had a more far-reaching significance. They indicated that Southern political parties simply had no understanding of the differences that kept the two parts of Ireland apart. They encouraged the belief that Northern Ireland was something that Britain could in fact hand over to the South. They discounted the Irish Protestant and placed him in a political limbo outside the national consciousness.

The effects linger. Even today there are many who regard Protestants in the South at best as suspect Irish, at worst as the remnants of the old English Order. Many Southern Catholics do not feel Protestants are real Irish. Most do not feel that Northern Protestants have a sufficiently Irish "outlook" or "approach" to life. They pay Northern Protestants the ultimate insult of being indifferent to their concerns, yet they are always somewhat surprised when called to account, as though toleration were a question of honor rather than of attitude. Thus, they tend to see Northern Ireland in terms of "us" and "them" — "us" being the Catholic minority, "them" being the Protestant majority. When the British Army clashes with Protestant militants, Southern Catholics are apathetic. But when it clashes with Catholics, the reaction is far more visceral.

Unless the South acknowledges and accepts that the Northern Protestant with no knowledge of the Gaelic language or ties to Gaelic culture is as Irish as the Gaelic-speaking Catholic from Connemara, *consent* in either a Northern or Southern context will remain a word of divisiveness and not of reconciliation. Catholicism, not Irishness, is the distinctive characteristic of the South. Irishness she shares with the Six Counties of the North.

One dangerous manifestation of this "us" versus "them" mentality is the disposition on the part of some in the South to regard Northern Protestants as a colon class similar to the colons in Algeria in the 1960s. According to this view, a British withdrawal would not result in armed resistance by Protestants to a united Ireland. Rather, it holds that Protestants, like the colons in Algeria, would immigrate in droves to the "mother" country. It seems lost on Irish people who espouse this view that they are in fact talking about their fellow countrymen. And if they do not regard them as their fellow countrymen, are they prepared for an Irish state in which at least one quarter of the population might have to be classified as "aliens"?

• • •

In the 1960s the South shook herself free of chronic economic stagnation. A new Taoiseach, Sean Lemass, who had served as de Valera's chief lieutenant since 1932, was eager to put aside the mythology of the past, and more eager still to embark on an ambitious program of economic development. His 1965 meeting with the Northern Prime Minister, Terence O'Neill, which amounted to a de facto recognition of partition, raised little protest in the South, and the commemoration of the fiftieth anniversary of the Easter Rising the following year aroused little more than token interest.

The public was jaded with the past, demoralized by permanent economic debilitation and the massive hemorrhaging of emigration. The insularity had become suffocating, the suffocating insufferable. The IRA Border campaign of 1956–1961 had no popular support. And when Charles Haughey, the newly appointed Minister for Justice, introduced a Special Criminal Court in 1961 to crack down on IRA activity, he had the full support of both the people and their public representatives. From time to time the usual noises were made about partition, but repetition had robbed the ritual of meaning. The South knew little of her Catholic co-religionists in the North, and less of the Protestants, only that they were British, and in that sense also part of the "foreign" occupation. The national consensus on Northern Ireland, if in fact there was one, extended to a general agreement that partition was Britain's fault and that only she, and she alone, could abolish it. And since there was no way of putting pressure on her to do so, there was no point in pursuing the matter.

There was, of course, no diminution in the enthusiasm for a united Ireland, the aspiration remaining a much-honored element of the national grail. Indeed, since there was no prospect of it, the enthusiasm for it was all the greater. Enthusiasm cost nothing, involved no risk, entailed no sacrifice, and required no thought. There was no need for a national consensus on what to do about Northern Ireland because it was accepted that nothing could be done. For the public the ideal of unification, something unsubstantive, intangible yet preordained, did not impinge upon the very tangible reality of a Northern Ireland state about which they knew little and seemed not to want to know much more.

Thus the ritualistic adherence to the aspiration of unity left the South in almost total ignorance of every aspect of the Northern Ireland state. Few of her citizens went there, few evinced interest in how the state was run, few thought of the Catholics there as a disadvantaged minority, if indeed they thought of them at all. Because the South did not recognize the North, the North did not exist. Because she did not exist, there was no need to discuss her, or for a government to have a policy that took into account the reality of her existence. That the South knew little of the discrimination against Catholics there is perhaps not surprising, since the Nationalist Party in Northern Ireland rarely raised such "mundane" matters in the Stormont Parliament.[24] To call on the state to redress an injustice is to recognize the legitimacy of the state. When the abolition of the state is your only political imperative, you cannot compromise the imperative by appearing to recognize the state's legitimacy.

The South entered the late 1960s enjoying the benefits of its first economic boom. A second program for economic expansion replaced the first, and a third the second. Growth in GNP, raising capital-labor ratios, increasing productivity, industrialization, keeping unit costs down, developing export markets — these were the passwords to a future of abundance. The advent of television was a watershed. The first tentative liberalizing influences of the Vatican Council chipped away at the fissures in conservative Catholicism. The country was looking to Europe for its future, changing rapidly from a backward, insular, agricultural society to a more secular, outward-looking, modern, mass-consumer society. The economic boom altered the South's perception of herself, creating a sense of national confidence and spawning a native entrepreneurial elite. Mammon had come to stay.

Occasionally, the North came to her attention, but only in a way that invited comparison to her own growing sophistication. Hence, the shooting dead of a Catholic barman on Malvern Street and the subsequent arrest of some members of the Ulster Volunteer Force* only served to remind the South of how she

* On Saturday, 25 June 1966, Peter Ward, a barman at the International Hotel, Belfast, who was from the South, was shot dead when he emerged from the Malvern Arms with three companions. Three persons, all members of the Ulster Volunteer Force, including Gusty Spence (the paramilitary organization's founder), were arrested, tried, and convicted of murder and sentenced to life imprisonment. See David Boulton, *The UVF, 1966–73*, pp. 48–61.

The Ulster Volunteer Force is an illegal Protestant paramilitary organization named after the Ulster Volunteer Force, which was established in 1912 by the Unionist Sir Edward Carson to fight Home Rule. After the shooting of Peter had put all that nonsense behind her; and the antics of Ian Paisley, whether in Belfast, London, or Rome, only served to reflect the North's comparative insularity, her hermetic preoccupation with the theology of the seventeenth century in contrast to the South's confident acceptance of the technological promise of the twentieth century. Accordingly, when television brought the ugly scenes of sectarian violence in Belfast and Derry into Southern homes in 1969, people there found they were looking at a foreign country.

And a foreign country she remains.

People in the South continue to know little of their Northern neighbors. Most feel that Catholics and Protestants in the North have more in common with each other, despite the endemic and seemingly intractable divisions between them, than they have with the people of the South. Travel to Northern Ireland has dwindled to a trickle. In 1978 only 10 percent of Southerners had gone there in the previous year, and only 10 percent more had gone there at any time in the preceding ten years. A majority had never set foot in the place.[25]

Indeed, the most remarkable feature of the last fifteen years has been the lack of popular support in the South for the nationalist cause in the North. With two notable exceptions — the torrent of emotion unleashed following Bloody Sunday, which culminated in the burning of the British Embassy in Dublin, and the massive H-Block demonstrations during the hunger strikes — Southern reaction to events in the North has bordered on a sullen passiveness. Northern Catholics are often seen as their own worst enemies: petulant to the point of inviting retaliation, demanding to the point of inviting denial, insistent to the point

---

Ward, Prime Minister Terence O'Neill declared the organization to be illegal. The UVF may have reached its peak strength in 1972, when it probably had about fifteen hundred members. The organization was heavily involved in the random assassination of Catholics. In March 1977, after the most costly trial in the history of Northern Ireland, twenty-six UVF members were sentenced between them to seven hundred years in prison after facing fifty-five charges, including four murders (two were murders of Ulster Defence Association men). According to W. D. Flackes, *Northern Ireland: A Political Directory*, "The UVF probably maintains a small but ruthless organization in Belfast" (p. 147). See David Boulton, *The UVF, 1966–73*, for a detailed account of its origins and early days.

of inviting recalcitrance. Even the H-Block demonstrations petered out, certainly to the surprise of the government, which pleaded with Mrs. Thatcher to make some concessions on the question of special status if only to obviate what it perceived as a threat to the stability of the South posed by the hunger strikers. Moreover, there has been a consistent unwillingness to consider change, apart from the token gesture of deleting the reference in the Constitution to the special position of the Catholic Church. Each time a government party has tried to make Northern Ireland an election issue the electorate has rejected the attempt, making it clear that the state of the economy in the South concerns it far more than the state of the state in the North.

• • •

When the situation did erupt, the South, caught, of course, by surprise, fell back on the predictable shibboleths of the past. One day after the Battle of the Bogside had engulfed Derry, Jack Lynch, leader of Fianna Fáil and Taoiseach, commanded the airwaves to assert the Irish Catholic perspective:

> . . . the reunification of the national territory can provide the only permanent solution for the problem, [and] it is our intention to request the British government to enter into early negotiations with the Irish government to review the present constitutional position of the six counties of Northern Ireland.[26]

Dr. Patrick Hillery, Minister for External Affairs, was dispatched to the United Nations to plead Catholic Ireland's claim:

> The claim of Ireland, the claim of the Irish nation to control the totality of Ireland, has been asserted over the centuries by successive generations of Irish men and women and it is one that no spokesman for the Irish nation could ever renounce.[27]

Reflexive action was a substitute for government policy in the years that followed. Lip service to the aspiration demanded a show of concern. Hence Lynch's "the Irish government can no-longer stand by" remarks and the setting up of field hospitals along the Border to give at least the appearance of action. The object was to appease militant elements within Fianna Fáil, but Northern Protestants did not see it that way: invasion was imminent; 1641 had come again. The invasion, of course, did not take place, nor was one ever seriously contemplated. But when the extent of the plans under consideration by the Dublin government to arm Northern Catholics so that they would be in a position to defend themselves against the attacks of Northern Protestants was made clear during the Arms Trial of 1970, the Protestant sense of vindication was complete: the civil rights movement of the late 1960s was just another subversive attempt by Catholics to bring about union with the South. The circle of collusion between the Dublin government and Republican activists in the North was complete.

The Protestant paranoia was perhaps understandable. For fifty years the South had laid claim to Ulster, insisting she spoke on behalf of all the Irish people, proclaiming Ireland an exclusively Gaelic culture and an even more exclusively Catholic nation. Even though the reality of modern Ireland is quite different, it does not dispel the paranoia of Northern Protestants that the South will stoop to any devious stratagem to dupe them. Thus, the South's recognition of the separate existence of Northern Ireland shortly after the Sunningdale talks in December 1973 did nothing to still Loyalist fears. Rather, it was seen as a cynical ploy to sell Ulster on the idea of a Council of Ireland.

During most of the 1970s, successive Irish governments continued their reactive responses, the only certainty the consistency of their inconsistencies. They objected strenuously to internment without trial, conveniently forgetting that Irish governments in the past had used internment without trial on numerous occasions to deal with suspected IRA members. They objected to provisions of the Northern Ireland (Emergency Provisions) Act yet introduced amendments to the South's Offenses Against the State Act, which incorporated many of the features they had theretofore found so objectionable. They cracked down hard on IRA suspects in the South, yet refused to consider extradition of IRA suspects to the North. They had problems with the Diplock Courts, yet the Special Courts in the Republic often presented similar problems. They urged — *begged* might be a better word — the British government to make concessions to the hunger strikers in the Maze in 1981, yet were fully prepared to make no concessions whatsoever to striking prisoners in Port Laoise in 1977. Historically — in the 1920s, 1930s, and 1940s — Irish governments allowed IRA prisoners on hunger strike to die rather than accede to any of their demands. The principle, it seems, is not so inviolate when the political repercussions are more immediate. Or perhaps there is a subtle distinction between "our" government letting "our" IRA "boys" die and "their" government making them die.

The ill-advised insistence by the Irish government on there being an Irish Dimension to the Sunningdale Agreement doomed the prospects for power sharing. Ignorance of the nature of Unionism, of the fragile alliances that held it together, of the power and intensity of militant Protestantism, and of the conflicting Protestant traditions led the Irish government to assume that a monolithic Unionism could deliver both power sharing and a Council of Ireland. Had it settled for power sharing only, and allowed the new alliance of Unionists and the SDLP a wide berth in which to develop a mutual trust under the least demanding of circumstances, some fundamental change in the direction of Northern Ireland might have been put in motion. But once again a precipitate demand, the insistence on the gesture in the direction of unity, the preoccupation with symbol and the appearance of things, had their predictable effects on the Protestant mentality. Indeed, the Sunningdale Agreement, hailed as the "solution" to the Irish question by the parties to the agreement, shows just how little the South was prepared to settle for. The proposed Council of Ireland was a token institution, devoid of real purpose, a skeletal institutional framework with few responsibilities and fewer decision-making powers. It was both a genuflection to the aspiration of unity and the expression of a marginal commitment to its realization. It epitomized the Irish ideal: unification with no economic cost, no political cost, and no social cost.

• • •

The unwillingness or inability of Southern political parties to formulate comprehensive policies on Northern Ireland or even to recognize the need for a common policy both reflects and ensures the public's unwillingness or inability to face the problem. There is perhaps a benign hope that it will somehow solve itself, that an internal solution will emerge that will ensure some form of devolved government acceptable to the minority, and that the IRA will fade away, as it has in the past. The aspiration to unity could, of course, continue to be enunciated vigorously from time to time. Unity by consent is safe when majority consent seems impossible.

But when unification is demystified, robbed of its heroic pretensions, examined harshly in the context of real alternatives, the public is put in the uncomfortable position of having to face up to the unpleasant possibility that they may not want that which they have aspired to so unthinkingly for so long.

Unification will have costs, something the South is becoming painfully aware of; the benefits, however, are not so apparent. The costs will be incurred on behalf of the two communities in the North, neither of which the South has much in common with and both of which have more in common with each other than with the South. Unification will involve sacrifice, but the sacrifice the South will be called on to make is on behalf of a people who are remote from her everyday life and concerns. The bitter consequence of past silence, of virtuous aspiration in lieu of honest debate, is a lack of real identification in the South with Catholics in the North. They were strangers, and they remain strangers, but their actions and demands are increasingly seen by the South as a threat to her way of life.

The past silence smothered the raising of questions that might have revealed a chasm between the level of the aspiration to unity and the depth of the commitment to it. The South continues to evade the hard questions because the answers may prove to be profoundly disconcerting, posing unpalatable — even impossible — choices, triggering, perhaps, a crisis of national self-identity. What if the South is unwilling to bear the costs of unification, unwilling to drop the aspiration to unity, and unwilling to make a tradeoff between the two? The real consensus may be that the consequences of a united Ireland are not worth the cost. Not wanting to face the implications of that possible dilemma, the South has chosen to avoid it.

The hard questions: Under what circumstances is there majority consent in the South for a united Ireland? How does the level of consent vary with the form of the arrangement? How does the level of consent vary with the probable costs of alternative arrangements? How does the level of consent vary with the likelihood of violent opposition to unification spilling over into the South? How does consent vary with considerations of the enormous economic, social, and political strains the South would be subjected to; of increased opportunities for the possible destabilization that might result; of the more stringent infringements on civil liberties that might be necessary to curtail terrorism; of the militarization of society in the name of security? How does consent vary with considerations of the economic costs, the social costs, the security costs? How does consent vary with considerations of having to bear these costs immediately? And if consent is not there for the immediate assumption of these costs, then when is it likely to be forthcoming? How would consent vary if Catholics and Protestants in the North found an acceptable internal solution? Would the South give her consent to a solution that did not involve unification in the foreseeable future but did not require her to give up the aspiration to eventual unity? How does the level of consent vary with the level of IRA activity? Is consent conditional on there being benefits to unification? How would the level of consent vary with a form of unification that involved significant economic and social costs, yet was not a sufficient expression of the national aspiration to appease the IRA? How does consent vary with considerations of ability to bear the costs as distinct from the willingness to do so? Can the South in fact afford unification? And if she can't, is she now in the unenviable position of not being able *not* to afford it?

• • •

The aspiration to unity remains strong, though it is by no means universal. Survey data taken since 1970 show that between 60 percent and 70 percent of the public in the South consistently endorse the idea of unification. Ten years after the conflict erupted, however, only 57 percent felt that the Border would in fact ever disappear: people do make a distinction between what they wish for and what they expect to happen.[28]

Expectations, of course, are related to intensity of commitment. On the one hand, the more intense the level of commitment to a particular goal, the stronger the expectation that the desired outcome will eventually happen. On the other hand, a lesser level of commitment is likely to be associated with lower expectations, and conversely, lower expectations with a lesser level of commitment. Expectations also temper the public's attitudes toward "best," "workable," or "acceptable" solutions. For example, in a 1978 Gallup poll for the BBC, only 54 percent were prepared to say that a "united Ireland" would be the "best answer" to the problem, while another 6 percent supported the idea of joint control by Dublin and London.[29] The rest either chose a solution that had no Irish Dimension or they were unable to make any choice. A major attitudinal survey by Dublin's prestigious Economic and Social Research Institute (ESRI) later the same year provided a more comprehensive compilation of attitudes.[30] It found that 41 percent were in favor of an Ireland unified under one central government as "the most workable and acceptable solution" and another 27 percent were in favor of a federal solution—regional parliaments in both parts of the country and a strong central government.[31]

More important, however, was the finding that those who chose a federal Ireland had a lower commitment to ending partition: the Border was not something that absolutely had to go. Since this segment of the public tended to have higher levels of education and to come from urban backgrounds, the likelihood increasingly is, as levels of urbanization and education continue to rise, that the level of commitment to ending partition will continue to decline.[32] There appears to be a growing tendency, therefore, for people to see the question of unification apart from the question of partition.

However, although there was a majority choice for some form of a united Ireland, the choice was not made with any great degree of optimism. Seventeen percent of those who favored some form of a united Ireland felt that the Border would never disappear.[33] When these respondents were factored out, only 56 percent were left who saw a united Ireland as a "best" solution that would actually happen. Even allowing for the coexistence of the Border and a federal Ireland — the two being by no means incompatible — the factoring out of the 12 percent of respondents opting for a unitary state who maintained, nevertheless, that the Border would never go reduced the number who saw a united Ireland as a "best" solution to a not overwhelming 60 percent.

Furthermore, those who opted for a unitary state as the "best" solution were among the least optimistic. Twenty-one percent of respondents in this group felt that the Border would never disappear, thus reducing the "hard-core" support for that particular solution to just 33 percent.[34] Other signs of the public's proclivity to distinguish between what they aspire to and what they expect: overall, 26 percent felt that the Border would never disappear, and another 8 percent that it would not disappear for at least fifty years.[35]

The intensity of the public's feelings is, of course, a measure of their commitment to a desired outcome. The ESRI survey found that there was widespread opposition to partition (72 percent opposed it), but only 46 percent would say they felt either strongly or even moderately about it.[36] And again, although 69 percent agreed that unification was essential for any solution to the problem, only 52 percent felt strongly about it.[37]

Thus, while the aspiration to unity in the South remains strong, though not overwhelming, the commitment to it is far less strong, either because the public's expectations are low — they believe it will not happen — or other considerations dampen their enthusiasm for it.

The apparent willingness of a growing number of people to settle for a federal Ireland raises other questions. For although it is reasonable to assume at this point that those who now opt for a federal solution would accept a unitary state, it is by no means certain that those who opt for a unitary state would accept a federal state. If, somehow, a consensus for a federal solution did emerge, would a sufficient minority still hold out, encouraging and incubating support for a continued military campaign for "real unification"?

This in fact may already be the situation in the North of Ireland. Surveys consistently show that under 50 percent of Catholics there regard unification in either the federal or unitary form as the most "acceptable and workable" solution.[38] On the other hand, almost 50 percent of Northern Catholics continue to see some form of association with the United Kingdom as the most "acceptable and workable" outcome.[39]

In a late 1981 survey, two thirds of the Northern Catholic respondents indicated that they would regard a Northern Ireland state with a power-sharing assembly within a U.K. framework as *an* acceptable resolution of the conflict.[40]* In contrast, most people in the South unabashedly reject the suggestion of a continued U.K. link without an Irish Dimension as an acceptable outcome, which suggests, at first glance, that Southern Catholics are more nationalistic than their Northern co-religionists. But most people in the South, of course, are far removed from the problem, and being far removed, they find it easy to reject an option when they do not understand either the costs or implications of the alternatives. Moreover, the more distant some people are from Northern Ireland, the greater their proclivity for more extreme solutions, since distance seduces them into believing that they will escape the repercussions of what they espouse. Not that the aspiration to unity is less strong among Northern Catholics than it is among their Southern co-religionists. However, their very closeness to the realities of the situation and the toll of fifteen years of violence and division have forced them to make a clear-cut distinction between what they aspire to and what they will ultimately settle for. The South must now embark on the painful process of reconciling the dichotomy im-

* The same survey found that 71 percent of Catholics (and 20 percent of Protestants) were in favor of Northern Ireland becoming part of a Federal Irish State with its own assemblies and guarantees for Protestants. There is, therefore, at least on the part of Northern Catholics, a propensity to make a distinction between a *preferred* outcome, which they may see as being either impossible or not workable, and an *acceptable* outcome in the sense of its being both possible and workable.

plicit in the distinction she must make between what she aspires to and what her ultimate commitment to achieving that aspiration is, before she can address the question of her own consent. Consent is a matter not of aspiration but of commitment, and commitment in turn is a matter of concern. To judge from the last fifteen years, the South's concern is selfish, not altruistic, focused less on what might happen in Northern Ireland if unification becomes a reality and more on what could happen in the South if unification provokes a violent Loyalist reaction. Her concern at this point appears to be superficial: Northern Ireland consistently ranks as one of the South's lesser concerns, ranking only fourth in a list of problems facing the country in 1973, listed by only 5 percent as an important issue in the 1977 elections, by less than 3 percent in the 1981 elections, and by an insignificant 1 percent in the February 1982 elections.[41]

The fact, however, that the IRA can still so successfully convey the impression that Northern Ireland's Catholics are fighting for their "freedom" from British "oppression" reinforces the myth perpetuated by the South: that Northern Ireland is primarily a British problem. If a majority of Northern Ireland's Catholics are not actively seeking a united Ireland, and if a large number will settle for an outcome that does not necessarily involve a link with the South, and if there is no real depth of commitment to unification in the South herself, then the question must be raised: who does want a united Ireland?

And a corollary must be answered: if a majority in the South would settle for a solution that was unacceptable to a more irredentist, nationalist-minded minority in the South — but acceptable nonetheless to a majority of Northern Protestants — would the whole of Ireland become as destabilized as the North of Ireland is today? Is a minority of the minority in the North and a minority of the majority in the South trying to force the majority of the minority in the North and the majority of the majority in the South into new constitutional arrangements that they do not really want, that are an anathema to a majority of the majority in the North, and that may not even satisfy the pristine aspirations of these elitist minorities? Is the real problem, perhaps, not one of competing national aspirations or differences of identity or religious divides but rather the existence for more than three hundred years of two concurrent traditions in Irish history, the constitutional and the unconstitutional? As long as there is even an implicit toleration of the unconstitutional as a legitimate political tool — and there is, because "history" accords that validation — then the tail will always wag the dog.

• • •

For a while the heady performance of the Southern economy had some people thinking that the Republic might actually *produce* its way into unification. Traditionally, the South lagged far behind the North in matters of per capita income and overall economic performance. But the last twenty years changed all that. Between 1959 and 1969, the decade preceding the outbreak of violence, manufacturing output in the South grew 60 percent faster than in the North; between 1969 and 1973 it spurted ahead of the North's by another 20 percent; and between 1973 and 1977 manufacturing output actually declined by 10 percent in the North but increased by 12 percent in the South. The net result was that over a period of eighteen years, from 1959 to 1977, manufacturing output increased two and a half times more rapidly in the Republic than in Northern Ireland — by 177 percent compared to 72 percent.[42]

The impact of this upon employment was striking. In 1960 the South, with twice the North's population, had only the same number of workers employed in manufacturing. In 1977, however, the South's industrial labor force was over half as large again as the North's — 220,000 versus 143,000, a net increase of 30,000 manufacturing jobs in the South in contrast to a decline of 47,000 such jobs in the North.[43]

In terms of per capita income, the South also made considerable progress in catching up. In 1958 per capita personal income in the South was just 67 percent of the Northern figure; in 1976 it had climbed to 86 percent, and personal disposable income had actually inched its way up to 93 percent of the Northern level. In fact, for the first time there was reason to believe that without the scale of British subsidies to Northern Ireland output and living standards there would actually be lower than they were in the Republic.[44]

The boom, of course, didn't last. By 1980 the steam had begun to run out of the economy. Because of the very rapid growth in the country's population — an expansion of 1½ percent per year[45] — the growth in output between 1973 and 1980 had been sufficient only to provide a minuscule annual increase in per capita income. The adverse turn in the terms of trade after 1973 because of the rise in imported oil prices and the relative decline in agricultural export prices as the decade closed resulted in a sharp dilution in living standards and purchasing power. The advance in living standards that was achieved between 1973 and 1980 was in effect illusory, purchased with borrowed money.[46]

In 1981 the alarming deterioration in the country's economic situation had become catastrophic. Per capita income was falling, as the growth in population outstripped the growth in output; real farm incomes had fallen by 50 percent in two years.[47] The government's total indebtedness came to 10 billion Irish pounds,* almost half of which had been borrowed abroad.[48] In other words, foreign borrowings were equal to almost 50 percent of GNP. In just two years the government's external debt had increased by 145 percent.[49] Public-sector borrowing in 1981 accounted for 17 percent of GNP,[50] foreign borrowing for 15 percent of GNP,[51] and government interest on foreign borrowing for 3 percent of GNP.[52] The budget deficit came to 8 percent of GNP.[53] Each member of the work force would have had to shoulder a 24 percent increase in taxation to eliminate the budget deficit.[54] The trade gap — the excess of imports over exports — came to 17 percent of GNP, and the balance-of-payments deficit to 15 percent of GNP.[55] Inflation jumped to 20 percent,[56] and unemployment to 10 percent.[57] And the number of unemployed was expected to climb to 15 percent by 1985.[58]

* The Irish pound freely fluctuates against both the dollar and sterling. Between 1981 and the beginning of 1983, the rate of exchange fluctuated between $1.55 and $1.35 for one Irish pound, and 0.90 to 0.80 pounds sterling for one Irish pound.

The Organization for Economic Cooperation and Development forecast that among its twenty-four member countries, Ireland would have the lowest rate of growth in 1982, the fourth highest level of unemployment, the second highest rate of inflation, the worst balance-of-payments deficit, the highest level of foreign debt, and the highest level of debt repayment.[59] Ireland is the poor man of the EEC, with the highest rate of population growth, the highest birth rate, the highest number of dependents per member of the work force, the lowest share of industrial employment, and the lowest standards of living, not only in terms of per capita income but also in terms of everyday amenities such as automobiles and telephones.[60]

The continuing net inflow of migration, rapid population growth, and an increasingly younger population — almost one third of the population is under fourteen and almost one half is under twenty-five — will put even further strains on the economy in the future.[61] Despite the much ballyhooed movement of labor from agriculture into industry and services, the number of full-time jobs has remained remarkably constant in the last twenty years.[62] Continuing high levels of unemployment; the need for investment in social infrastructure, particularly schools, health, and housing; a high dependency ratio (number of dependents per member of the work force) that will go still higher, adding to the overall burden on individual taxpayers; and the need to reduce the extraordinary excess of public spending make it highly improbable that the South can bear any additional financial burden associated with the North.

The economic costs are also likely to weigh more heavily in the future because of the changing demographic pattern in the South. The South's population increased 20 percent between 1961 and 1979.[63] And although the traditionally high fertility rate has been falling, the marriage rate, particularly among younger people, has been steadily rising, resulting in a birth rate that is now the highest in Europe and is likely to remain so for some time to come. Whereas the South has only 1.9 times as many people over forty-five as Northern Ireland, it has 2.65 times the number of people under five years of age.[64] The higher burden of family support coupled with rising unemployment (between 1976 and 1986 the labor force may increase by 15 percent with no comparable increase in job opportunities in sight)[65] and higher taxes to eliminate the excesses of the past will put severe strains on the South's fragile economic structure, and especially on the taxpayer. Thus, quite apart from the question of whether the South is willing to assume the costs of unification is the question of whether she can in fact afford to.

• • •

Both the willingness and the capacity of the South to assume the economic costs of unification are, of course, related to the relative position of the North's economy. Other things being equal, a vigorous economy in the North would make political integration more attractive, whereas a weak economy there would only add to the burden of transfers from the South to the North.

Northern Ireland, unfortunately, also qualifies as one of the most distressed areas of Europe. The population is declining; industrial output is falling; the unemployment rate hovers at 20 percent and rises to 50 percent in the inner-city areas of Belfast and Derry. The system is supported almost entirely by public expenditure. In fact, the growth of real public expenditure accounts for the greater part of the growth in real income since the mid-1970s. The level of public expenditure, both direct in the form of transfer payments and indirect in the form of employment support schemes, is now more than 50 percent higher on a per capita basis in Northern Ireland than in the U.K. as a whole.[66]

Northern Ireland, of course, cannot generate the resources necessary to sustain this level of public expenditure. Hence the Northern Ireland subvention — the difference between total public expenditures in Northern Ireland and the tax revenue attributable to her, which represents the net transfer from the U.K. government. These subventions grew from approximately one quarter of total public expenditure in Northern Ireland in 1972–73 to approximately 50 percent in 1979–80.[67] And though the proportion has been dropping in recent years — in part due to Mrs. Thatcher's monetarist economic policies, and in part due to the distribution of North Sea oil revenues — the 1982–83 subvention of £1.2 billion accounted for approximately 34 percent of the £3.5 billion in public expenditure earmarked for Northern Ireland.*

At present, given the chronically depressed state of Northern Ireland and its extreme reliance on public expenditure to generate economic growth (in just four years, 1974 to 1978, real public expenditure increased 15 percent in Northern Ireland in contrast to a drop of almost 3 percent in the rest of the U.K.),[68] even a relatively healthy and prosperous Southern economy of some 3.4 million people would be unable to take over the cost of supporting Northern Ireland at its present income level, a cost that is now shared by some 55 million people. The fact that the future in Northern Ireland holds little promise of improvement — indeed, the promise is of just the opposite as cutbacks in the level of public expenditure take effect — makes consideration of an economic support program financed entirely by the South even more implausible. And the fact that the South will be hard put to deal with its own internal strains will make it impossible.

The cost of bringing social benefits alone in the South into line with benefits in the North would require at least a 12 percent increase in per capita taxes.[69] According to a study conducted back in 1975, the cost of absorbing the subvention in a federal Ireland would require residents of the Republic to give up 15 percent of their income.[70] In 1979–80 the cost of absorbing the subvention would have required an increase of 50 percent in the South's total tax receipts.[71] The figures today, given the enormous increase in public expenditure in the North, would certainly be no less. Moreover, the transfer of substantial sums

* Although there is disagreement as to what the precise amount of the subvention is, in 1980 most commentators were prepared to accept the figure of one billion pounds sterling. See *The Guardian*, 19 February 1980. The figure of £1.2 billion for 1982–83 was supplied by the Northern Ireland Office on 21 February 1983. The public expenditure figure is taken from Secretary of State for Northern Ireland James Prior's statement on the matter, 6 January 1982. For details see *The Economist*, 9 January 1982, p. 52.

Note: The British pound freely fluctuates against the dollar. In 1980, for example, one pound was worth approximately $2.30. Early in 1983, however, the rate of exchange was at one point as low as $1.45 for one pound.

from the South to the North would further weaken the already seriously weakened potential for economic growth in the Republic.

The ability to pay for unity seems woefully inadequate.

When the question of the economic costs of unification is brought to the forefront, the South undergoes a metamorphosis of sorts. Repeatedly, public opinion polls indicate that less than a majority are prepared to pay higher taxes to support a united Ireland. In one survey, respondents went even further: 50 percent opted for unity only if either the social, economic and political costs were not too great (32 percent) or there were no costs involved at all (18 percent).[72] More surprising, perhaps, was the ESRI finding that only 51 percent of those opting for a unitary state were willing to assume a higher tax burden in order to see their aspirations fulfilled, and only 54 percent of those opting for a federal arrangement were similarly disposed.[73] Clearly, at the very least it is questionable whether the South is willing to assume a significant — or perhaps even any — part of the financial cost that might make a united Ireland a reality.

The willingness to pay for unity seems woefully absent.

However, this disagreeable, even selfish, propensity to put the economic well-being of self before the mythical well-being of the aspiration is taken care of by the blithe assumption that the U.K. would continue to underwrite Northern Ireland's financial situation in the event of unification. The rationale for this line of thinking is as follows: first, there is the assumption that Britain is so anxious to have Northern Ireland off her hands that she would be more than willing to foot the bill for a while if only to get rid of the mess. Thus, the South might be persuaded to accept the burden of the politics if Britain continues to assume the burden of the economics. Second, there is the assumption of reparation for historical wrongdoing: Northern Ireland is the creation of Britain, the direct result of centuries of attempted conquest; partition, a solution imposed by Britain despite the wishes of the majority; the subsequent discrimination against Catholics, the result of Britain's benign neglect — hence the moral obligation on her to acknowledge her guilt and pay the price for it. And even if the U.K. balked at bearing the full cost, there is the further assumption that the EEC would step in to pick up a share, or the United States or some yet-to-be-defined consortium of nation-states who for their own obscure reasons would be all too happy to defray the costs of a united Ireland rather than make the Irish themselves undertake the disagreeable task.

At the moment, therefore, there appears to be neither the capacity nor the willingness in the Republic to underwrite the economic costs of unification. One, of course, is a function of the other, and if the capacity to assume the burden somehow improves in the decades to come, a willingness to assume it may follow, but not necessarily. Indeed, the reverse may be true: a willingness to assume the burden may be more forthcoming when the capacity to translate the willingness into reality is nonexistent.

Questions of economics also affect the way Southerners perceive the motivation of Northern Protestants. According to one Gallup survey, a majority in the South believe that the economic subsidies Northern Ireland receives are the main reason the "Loyalists" are loyal.[74] Presumably, therefore, one way to bring the Loyalists around to a more compromising position on a united Ireland would be to have Britain turn off the economic spigot — but only, of course, until the Loyalists changed their minds. In a new Ireland, a benevolent Britain would turn the spigot back up to its former level.

Questions of economics may also be a reason why more "non-Loyalists" are not more disloyal as Northern Catholics look to a South struggling to eliminate deficits in the budget and her balance of payments, to curtail her foreign borrowing, and to cope with dramatic increases in her labor force and climbing unemployment. Many may find the security of the U.K. subvention more appealing than the hollow calls of nationalism.

Thus the South: having lived beyond her means for a number of years, the country at present is painfully incapable of assuming any additional economic burden. She faces immense social and economic problems as the population soars and job opportunities fail to keep pace. Stiff tax increases and austerity measures are an absolute necessity to bring some semblance of order to her chaotic economic condition.

There is, therefore, more than substantial reason to question whether consent exists on the issue of assuming additional financial costs to pay for an all-Ireland state. On the one hand, the more lasting the economic crisis in the South, and the more severe the measures to remedy the situation, the more resistant the South is likely to remain to the suggestion of having to absorb part of the costs of unification. And again, the more intractable the economic situation in the North, the more rapid the erosion in industrial employment, the more incapable she appears of attracting new investment and the greater her dependence on public expenditure, the more likely the South is to withhold enthusiastic approval of unification. On the other hand, both sets of circumstances — a chronic economic recession in the North and severe economic problems in the South — are also more likely to make Catholics in the North less than fully enthusiastic about the prospects of unification.

• • •

Considerations of violence also temper the South's commitment to unification. Every survey of opinion has found that a large majority would oppose an attempt to impose unification by force, indicating that there is, at least, a clear understanding that unification cannot be imposed.[75] The ESRI survey found widespread support for the view that a united Ireland would be opposed by the Loyalist paramilitaries: 60 percent believed that Loyalist paramilitaries would pose more of a problem in a united Ireland than the IRA does today.[76]

Unfortunately, the wording of the question — "If Ireland were ever united, [do you think] the Loyalist paramilitaries would be more of a problem than the IRA is today[?]" — begged the further question: would be more of a problem to whom? It did not make clear to respondents whether they should consider future Protestant paramilitary opposition only in the context of Northern Ireland, that being the IRA's present theater of war, or whether they should also consider it in the context of the South. In other words, it was left up to respondents to decide for themselves whether Protestant paramilitary opposition to a united Ireland would confine itself mainly to the North or whether it might somehow establish as menacing and entrenched a presence in the South as the IRA's today in the North.

However, notwithstanding the ambiguities, some conclusions can be drawn from the data, suggesting a relationship, tenuous but nevertheless implicit, between the choice of a most workable and acceptable solution and the expectation of Loyalist paramilitary violence. Those who expected opposition from Loyalist paramilitaries to pose more of a problem than the IRA violence of today gave slightly below average support to an all-Ireland solution and above average support to a non–united Ireland solution. On the other hand, those who tended to discount the threat of Loyalist paramilitary opposition were more supportive of an all-Ireland solution and correspondingly less supportive of a non–united Ireland solution.[77]

The relationships — and again they are tenuous — also appear to work in the opposite directions. Thus, those who chose an all-Ireland solution in one form or the other were a little less likely to agree that Loyalist paramilitary violence would be more of a problem than the IRA's now is, while those who chose a non–all-Ireland solution were more likely to believe the opposite.[78]

Thus, the public's perceptions of Loyalist paramilitary opposition to a united Ireland have a bearing on their commitment to an all-Ireland solution, even though they may not define that opposition in terms of its having a direct bearing on their own position. The less their expectations that a united Ireland would trigger violent resistance, the greater their commitment to it. The converse also holds, but to a lesser extent, perhaps because the public in the South do not see themselves as being among the victims of the violence that would ensue. If they start to do so, however, the trend already apparent in embryonic form may assume a full-life form, ensuring that the public's commitment to unification will lessen when their expectations that unification will in fact trigger a violent and contiguous resistance to it increase.

• • •

There is a striking concurrence between the people of Britain and the Republic on the question of a political settlement for Northern Ireland. An absolute majority in the Republic and either a majority or a large plurality in Britain consistently endorse some form of a united Ireland.[79] Moreover, majorities in both countries are in favor of Britain making a declaration of intent to withdraw her troops from the North at some time in the future. Indeed, the people of both countries are more disposed to a military withdrawal than the Catholics of Ulster are.[80] Not that this should be surprising. After all, it is the Catholics of Ulster who would bear the brunt of the violence that might — many would say would — follow the withdrawal. For the moment at least, what they perceive as their vulnerability to Protestant attack outweighs their animosity toward the security forces.

The British public's predilection for a united Ireland is not, of course, the expression of a commitment to bring it about. Rather it is the expression of a wish to make Britain's Irish problem Ireland's Irish problem.

In the South support for a British military withdrawal is also, in many respects, the expression of a wish rather than a demand for action. The wish represents the obverse of the aspiration to unity. Hence, it suppresses the conscious examination of the implications of the possible consequences of the action. Thus, the following: the ESRI survey found that 71 percent in the Republic were in favor of a declaration by Britain of her intent to withdraw, whether or not a majority in Northern Ireland agreed to it.[81] At the same time 59 percent believed that British withdrawal without the consent of the two communities in the North would lead to a significant increase in violence there.[82] Nor did respondents believe that withdrawal would lead to a resolution of the conflict. On the contrary, only 43 percent felt that a unilateral withdrawal would lead to a negotiated settlement.[83] Even the most pessimistic — the 37 percent who felt that withdrawal would result only in a great increase in violence — hewed to the withdrawal line, 55 percent agreeing that the British government should declare its intention to withdraw whether a majority in Northern Ireland agreed to it or not.[84]

Other data add to the contradictions. The Gallup poll conducted in 1978 for the BBC indicated that 76 percent of the people in the Republic felt that the people of Northern Ireland should be able to decide for themselves whether they are in favor of unification.[85] But 76 percent of these *same* people also wanted a declaration by Britain of her intent to withdraw, whether or not a majority in Northern Ireland gave their consent![86]

People in the South and their public representatives tend to be far more audacious in their demands when the perceived consequences are seen as falling on others and not on themselves, or when the demands are not associated with consequences. Thus, in 1975 the Fianna Fáil platform called on the British government to "declare Britain's commitment to implement an ordered withdrawal from her involvement in the six counties of Northern Ireland."[87] Some years later, when Fianna Fáil had again assumed power, Jack Lynch, the Taoiseach, was called upon to clarify what this meant. Mr. Lynch was more attuned to consequences: The Irish government, he said, regarded "the ultimate unification of Ireland as the only long-term solution."[88] But it did not want the British government to make "a proposal to withdraw at a given time," since "if a date were given — five, ten or fifteen years hence — there would be a possible build-up of preparedness by militants for that date."[89] And that, of course, could prove to be disastrous. Hence, the phrase "declaration of intent" for withdrawal came to be replaced by the demand for a declaration of intent for Irish unity. Presumably this would have represented some sort of moral victory, a kind of delayed mea culpa by Britain for the past, a tacit admission that it was, after all, her fault. Meanwhile, the Republic could remain as aloof as ever from the consideration of the changes she would have to make to bring about the "reconciliation" she so earnestly desired. Not only were a majority unwilling to pay higher taxes to bring about a united Ireland, but a majority, at least in 1979, also felt that the Irish government should continue to articulate the goal of unification, a majority opposed removing the territorial claim of Northern Ireland from the Constitution even as a gesture of goodwill to Northern Protestants, and a majority, albeit a slender one, opposed changes in the nation's divorce laws.[90]*

These attitudes beg the questions: If the South is unprepared to make even the gestures of reconciliation, which cost nothing, is she really prepared to absorb the real costs? Are her beliefs that someone else — the EEC, the British, the United States, or whoever — will open their financial coffers real or fantasy? And if they are fantasy, is she prepared to deal with the reality? Or does she want to induce Unionists to the point of accepting some form of unity only to find that she is unprepared, or unable, to pay the price of that arrangement?

• • •

In short, there is the consent of a majority in the South for unification if unification comes easily, costs little, and leaves the status quo virtually unchanged. This is the legacy of sixty years of silence: ignorance begets simplicity. Hence, the problem in the North is the fault of Northern Protestants — 78 percent of respondents in the ESRI survey agreed that the basic problem in Ulster is the determination of Protestants to defend their privileges at all costs,[91] while 68 percent continued to insist that Northern Ireland is a British problem.[92] Thus the belief that withdrawal is the key to a settlement; that withdrawal will set in motion a series of actions ultimately leading to unification; that unification will come about when the "un-Irish" Northern Protestants are persuaded of the futility of their resistance, especially with the loss, or the threatened loss, of the British subsidy; and that Britain will continue to subsidize the Ulster part of a united Ireland. To repeat, then, unification is welcome but only if it comes easily and at little cost. However, the prospect of violence, particularly of the violence spilling over into the South,

* More recent survey data indicate that attitudes toward divorce are undergoing further change. It now appears that a majority (about 53 percent) favor the introduction of divorce. See summary of survey data since 1971 on the subject in the *Sunday Independent*, 17 April 1983.

has a powerfully tempering influence on these expectations.

The "wishful-thinking"—some might say the "hard-nosed"—character of Southern attitudes toward unification is exemplified by the fact that one quarter of those choosing a united Ireland as the most workable solution believe it will take more than fifty years to happen or that it will never happen. It is entirely possible that they either subconsciously or consciously want to put off implementation of their own preferred solution in order to avoid the inescapable costs it will involve. It may well be a question of not wanting something to happen rather than of not believing it will happen. The desire is no expression of commitment to or even of interest in achieving the outcome.

Unification is no longer an article of faith in the South. The ability to pay for it is absent, the willingness questionable. Increasingly there is a fear that a united Ireland would be an unstable Ireland. The South has seen the economic paralysis that protracted violence has wrought in the North. She knows too well there is no effective defense against paramilitary assault. Having gained a little, she is loath to lose all on behalf of Northern Catholics with whom she shares little other than a common religious denomination.

The aspiration to unity may still be strong, but the commitment to it is far less so. And to assume that that commitment somehow extends into the "consent of a majority" for national unification is a prescription for national self-delusion which might even be cause for mild merriment were it not that the possible consequences could be so awfully tragic.

3

The Social Democratic and Labour Party: A Question of Guarantees

But we have hidden in our hearts the flame out of the eyes
Of Cathleen, the daughter of Houlihan

— W. B. Yeats
"Red Hanrahan's Song About Ireland"

REPORTING ON THE 1975 ANNUAL CONFERENCE of the SDLP,[1] a seasoned observer of the Northern Ireland political situation captured the mood of the convention at the Europa Hotel in Belfast:

> There were a few waverers [on the Irish Dimension] before the conference started: some who felt that the insistence on a Council of Ireland was the major factor in wrecking Sunningdale, that the very term Irish Dimension was the Green Flag to the Orange Bull. But when John Hume, in a speech of passionate conviction, reaffirmed that the Party would continue on the road to partnership within the North and between North and South, rather than the path of conflict with one side dominating in the North, and North and South living in mutual hostility and suspicion, he was thunderously applauded and their commitment was stronger than ever.
>
> . . . Familiarity with their leaders has brought respect rather than contempt. And Gerry Fitt, with that unique blend of humanity, wit

and native intelligence which is the secret of his political flair, has no serious rivals for the leadership. There is, of course, a residual faction of the more academic or formal whose instincts are for a more controllable leader, but he can usually make them laugh too. Shortly after acknowledging an outstanding ovation for an address in which he had them laughing and cheering, he was jokingly asked, "So it looks as if you're going to stay in the Party for another while, Gerry?" "Aye, as long as it's going my way," he replied. There is more than a grain of truth in the observation that if the time ever comes when he is totally happy with the Party, either he will be finished or the Party will.[2]

Four years later, the SDLP was no longer going his way, and Gerry Fitt, clearly unhappy, resigned from the party he had co-founded and led from its inception. His priorities were no longer the party's: "What we must do," he said shortly afterwards, "is to go out and find a solution within Northern Ireland on the power-sharing issue. After you have done that and allowed time to build up trust between the communities, then you can begin to think about Irish Dimensions. To try to institutionalize them both at the same time is self-defeating."[3]

• • •

Nonsense, says John Hume, who succeeded Fitt as the party's leader. His passionate conviction is as strong as ever.

He is the brain, proof that for all their pretension to ascendency, Unionists are unable to produce one of their own who can match his intellectual skills, the acuity of his thinking, his masterful propensity for conceptualization, his formidable on-camera presence. His rumpled insouciance is more disarming because it appears uncontrived, more touching because it belies his intensity. Politicians admire him because he is adept at not appearing self-servingly political; the media, both in Ireland and abroad, because he is articulate, tireless, and talented; his opponents, if only grudgingly, because of his visceral ability to survive.

And John Hume has a plan, a clear vision of how the future can be made to work: establish a viable Anglo-Irish framework, abrogate the guarantee, and the combination of the two will alchemize a solution.

First, the guarantee:

> The whole thrust of our argument on the guarantee is that it is a sectarian guarantee, a unilateral guarantee, and an unconditional guarantee. It is a guarantee of perpetual sectarianism. When the state came into being it was set up on the basis of a sectarian head-count.
>
> That having been done, the British government then said, "We guarantee you can stay with us as long as the majority want to." By doing that they trapped the Unionist population into perpetual sectarianism, because in effect what they were saying is "In order to maintain your power and your privilege you must behave as a sectarian bloc." And that's exactly how Unionism has behaved. No other group of people in the same circumstances would behave any differently.
>
> If one is to break down the sectarianism, one has to remove that guarantee, leave people standing on their own two feet, allow them to define their relationships with other people. At the moment there is no relationship, there is only separation, which leads to conflict.[4]

Accordingly, Hume argues that a solution can come about only when the underwriters of the guarantee withdraw it:

> British policy should be: "There are no guarantees for any section of this community anymore. Our policy, the reason we are here, is to promote the coming together of the people of this island in a manner and form they can both agree to." The British should join the ranks of the persuaders.[5]

But the ending of the guarantee must be put into a strategic context. It is the means to an end, not an end in itself. Hume:

> If the British made the kind of declaration I am suggesting about the guarantee, the immediate response from the Protestants would not be to go to war, because the British would still be there. That's why we're not saying the British should withdraw their presence or even make a declaration of intent to withdraw. Under these circumstances, therefore, the Protestants would opt for independence. However, you can't have an independent state without a recognition of that state by Dublin. Thus, Dublin would have to be brought into the process at the negotiating table. When we get to the table we would come away with what in my view would be an autonomous Northern Ireland within an Irish state. The structure I am talking about is not very far from an independent Northern Ireland.[6]

But for Dublin to be brought into the process, there must be the machinery already in place that both facilitates the negotiating process and is in itself an implicit recognition of the dimensions of the problem. Therefore, the problem must be taken out of its Northern Ireland context:

Over the last ten years successive attempts have been made to get agreement internally on the North. They have all failed because every attempt at an internal solution will founder on the rock of the guarantee.[7]

Which leaves you with two choices:

You either keep on trying something you know is going to fail or you move on to a wider stage — the Anglo-Irish approach. I was the one who advocated that we move on to that approach because in the end we're not simply dealing with the question of the relations between Catholics and Protestants in the North; it's a question of relations within Ireland between North and South and of relations between Britain and Ireland.

Thus the rationale for the Anglo-Irish process:

Since the framework of the problem is all the interlocking relationships between the two islands, the framework for a solution must be exactly the same. The thesis was for the two governments to start a process, and that at some stage in the process the Northern political parties would be drawn into it.

The Protestants, Hume maintains, keep stressing that any solution must be acceptable to them, but they fail to put that right into a political perspective:

Their right to an acceptable solution is not an absolute right. It's a right that's qualified by the right of the minority to an acceptable solution and by the rights of the British and Irish governments who will be called upon to enforce or pay for any settlement. This means that in practice all these parties must be involved in negotiations. That again is why the Anglo-Irish process is so important.

How will this process unfold?

First, the governments start the process of negotiations. They invite the parties from the North in. The Unionists come in and ask for their independence. And then the real negotiations begin, because the first thing you ask when they ask for independence is, "How do they get the consent of the minority for that?" Because you can't have an independent state if one third of the population is against it. How do you get the recognition of the South? How do you get the agreement of Britain, particularly for the financial agreements that would be involved? So, immediately you're locked in to real negotiations for the first time. Then, in my view, we respond at that point by saying, "We're not agreeable to independence but we are agreeable to autonomy."

And how will this tradeoff between independence and autonomy occur?

At the end of the day I see the Unionist or Protestant position as saying two things. One, we're British, and two, we're Protestant. I'm not sure which they place the most emphasis on, and I'm not sure they're too sure themselves. The crisis of identity in that community is at the heart of the problem.

Protestantism, in my opinion, can be protected by the powers which the autonomous state will have. The autonomous state would give Protestants absolute control over the thing they fear most — which is being subsumed into a Catholic state which is hostile to them. The Britishness would be protected by the Anglo-Irish Council, an institutional link with Britain which would provide for British citizenship. The Irishness of the minority would be protected by the federal link.

No arrangement can work, however, that does not contain, at the very least, a federal link:

The only victim of the 1920 settlement was the minority in Northern Ireland. Indeed, without a minority in Northern Ireland the 1920 settlement would have been perfect. The minority were the victims then and they've been the victims of it since, not only in terms of economics, but also in terms which are essential to the cohesion of any state.

Most democratic states survive because they have an identity to which the whole population subscribes. Identity is the focus of order and authority. But the identity of the minority in Northern Ireland is not recognized. The minority have no source of authority.

That's why ambivalence on violence is not ambivalence on violence per se but an ambivalence on how to deal with it. And the ambivalence on how to deal with it comes from the absence of a central authority to which they can give their allegiance. Therefore, an essential element to any solution has to be a recognition of the identity of the minority.*

Unionism, says Hume, must come to terms with the concept of accommodation. Its seemingly intractable reluctance to do so means that the debate going on within Unionism may be not only misdirected but possibly destructive:

The situation in Unionism in the last few years has basically been a competition to see who can out-Paisley Paisley. To date the struggle in Unionism has not been about policy and direction. It's been about virility. About who can be more virulently pro-Unionist in the traditional sense than about the means whereby Unionism can reach an accommodation with the rest of society in the North and in these islands.

Unless voices start emerging on the Protestant side that see a means of accommodating Protestantism within Ireland which is acceptable to Protestantism, we're not going to get very far. Unionism has represented itself as the only possible savior of Protestantism, and after sixty years I think it's fair to ask the question: has it done so? Because it is now being represented by Paisleyism, and Official Unionism is simply competing with Paisleyism in an attempt to out-Paisley Paisley.

And my question to Protestants is: where in Paisleyism are the traditional Protestant values and principles of individual freedom, of civil and religious liberty, of freedom of speech? Is it not time to ask the question whether the traditional values of Protestantism and the tradition of dissent in Ireland are in fact being destroyed by the siege mentality and its by-product, Paisleyism? Is it not time to look at other ways of protecting Protestantism within Ireland and of having also relationships with the rest of Ireland which would produce a genuinely pluralistic Ireland?[8]

The differences between the Official Unionists and Paisley's Democratic Unionists? None, according to Hume:

* The question was, "Is there a way of making this whole thing work without a federal link?" Hume's reply began, "I can't see it. Because if you look at the minority situation the only victim . . ."

The Official Unionists simply say politely what Paisley says in a loud voice. The Official Unionists say "not an inch," Paisley says "not a millimeter." But that's the only difference.[9]

Thus, while the Official Unionists vie with the Democratic Unionists for leadership of the Protestant people, the question of how to accommodate Protestantism within Ireland is not being addressed, a problem that has much to do with the nature of Unionism itself:

because Unionism is by its very nature defensive. It's born from the siege mentality. It exists purely on the basis of sectarian solidarity reinforced by the British guarantee. Therefore, it never had to accommodate anybody else. It simply had to maintain the laager. As such it wasn't political. It didn't have to reach out to anyone.

Now it's clear that for survival — not only of the Protestant community but of the rest of us — that they must accommodate. And it's that debate — how do you accommodate while at the same time protecting your own identity? — that they must address. As long as the guarantee exists, there is no necessity to accommodate.[10]

Despite its pretensions to moderation, Hume maintains, the Official Unionist Party does not believe in parliamentary democracy. If it did, he argues, it would accept the democratic will of the U.K. Parliament with respect to how government in Northern Ireland should work:

Overwhelmingly the U.K. Parliament has decided that within Northern Ireland majority rule is not democracy. Majority rule is not democracy anywhere where the majority and the minority are fixed. So, the United Kingdom Parliament in its wisdom decided that a new form of government was necessary to reflect democracy, but Mr. Molyneaux won't accept that. So he doesn't accept parliamentary democracy. He accepts it when it suits him, which has been the Unionist position throughout — independence within the United Kingdom. The sooner they're faced with what that means, the sooner we'll get a movement.[11]

Thus, the more pressure that can be put on Unionists to think in terms of independence, the better. Above all, the British government should confront Paisley with the logic of his own position:

His antics in the British Parliament were tantamount to saying "I will only accept the will of the Parliament as long as I agree with it"—and that's independence. When he wants the guarantee reiterated but doesn't want anything said about how Northern Ireland should be governed within the U.K., that's a declaration of independence. When he launched the Third Force, that was a unilateral declaration of independence because it was a declaration that the existing legitimate security forces were unacceptable.*

The British government should confront him with that logic, and say, "Well, you can't have independence unless you get the agreement of the minority, unless you get agreement of the British and Irish governments."[12]

And at that point the trap is sprung, because the British government must then confront Paisley with the inevitable corollary:

"If that is what you want," [the British must say], "you must come into the process already under way.† Because the very process you are objecting to is necessary even for getting what you want yourself."[13]

* On 14 November 1981, Rev. Robert Bradford, Official Unionist M.P. for South Belfast, was shot dead by IRA gunmen at Finaghty Community Center, where he was meeting constituents. On Monday, 16 November, Paisley and his party colleagues Peter Robinson and John McQuade—all M.P.s—were suspended from the House of Commons after they disrupted speeches about Bradford. Paisley said he despaired of getting change through Westminster and called for a "Day of Action" on 23 November. "If we do not have a democracy, then the person with the strongest force is going to win," he said. Six hundred members of Paisley's "Third Force" marched in Enniskillen. At Bradford's funeral on 17 November, James Prior, the Secretary of State for Northern Ireland, was verbally abused. Paisley threatened to make the province ungovernable. On 23 November, the Day of Action was strongly supported in Protestant areas. On 27 November, Paisley challenged the Chief Constable to arrest him if the Third Force was illegal. See *Fortnight*, no. 184 (December 1981/January 1982), pp. 17–18. See chapter 5, p. 192n, for a description of what the Third Force stands for.

† This statement was a continuation of Hume's previous one. The initial question was "Some Protestant politicians seem to be talking more about independence. Do you see this as a hopeful sign?" Hume's response began, "Yes, I do see it as a hopeful sign. In fact, last week I was saying in response to Paisley's carry-on that the British government should sieze the opportunity and confront him with his own logic."

Hume:

Paisley has said to me that Unionists cannot break the link themselves but that if the British break it that's a different matter. I feel Paisley isn't all that sure what he wants because his role is really anti. If you look at his whole history it's always against something. It's "O'Neill must go," "Chichester-Clark must go," "Faulkner must go," "Wilson's a liar, Callaghan's a liar, Thatcher's a liar."* It's very difficult to find out what he is really for. But I think that underlying all that confusion, where the only clear-cut message is that he's against everything, is a message of independence.[14]

And if that is the case, Loyalists must be made to face the logic of what they want: "They must seek the recognition of the minority within Northern Ireland, the recognition of the Republic, and the approval of the British. Once again we're back to the Anglo-Irish process."[15]

• • •

Robert McCartney, the Belfast barrister and member of the Official Unionist Party who likes to describe himself as a unionist spelled with a small "u," is also a rational man:

This term *guarantee* is nonsense. When the British government or the Southern political parties say they are not interested in unity other than with consent, they are not giving anything or guaranteeing anything. They're merely acknowledging a reality — because it is well known that the British government and the British Army would be totally incapable of dealing with a Protestant majority in the North fully united and freely committed to resisting a particular course of government action.

Military experts and experts on Northern Ireland have said that the British Army could only stay here three or four weeks if the entire Protestant population rose up in insurrection. So it's just a load of

* Terence O'Neill was Prime Minister of Northern Ireland from 1963 to 1969; James Chichester-Clark was Prime Minister from 1969 to 1971; Brian Faulkner was Prime Minister from 1971 to 1972 and Chief Executive in the 1974 power-sharing administration; Harold Wilson was Labour Prime Minister of Britain from 1964 to 1970 and from 1974 to 1976; and James Callaghan was Labour Prime Minister of Britain from 1976 to 1979.

rubbish to talk of anyone guaranteeing the Northern Ireland constitutional position or, alternatively, of an external force taking Northern Ireland by force, when all of them instinctively—and, I think, rationally—recognize that there is no other way than by consent. But whether the British government or the Southern government guarantee it is neither here nor there.[16]

Indeed, with the exception of the IRA, there is unanimity on every side and among all parties that unification can come about only with the consent of a majority of the people of Northern Ireland. The SDLP has committed itself unequivocally to unity only with the consent of a majority, the Southern political parties and successive Irish governments have made solemn declarations to that effect, and the British government reiterates its unswerving commitment to the condition of consent prior to every initiative it attempts.

Accordingly, as long as the consent of *a* majority is required there is no greater onus on *the* majority to be more receptive to "entering a dialogue" or to "modifying" their behavior than there is under the existing guarantee. It is hard to argue that Northern Protestants would be less intransigent on such matters as the structure of a devolved government if their position were not "guaranteed," since it is just as plausible to argue that their intransigence is due to the fact that the SDLP in the North and successive governments in the South willingly, in fact almost insistently, argue that unity will require the consent of a majority in the North.

Moreover, ending the guarantee would not affect the North's position within the United Kingdom. It would, in fact, put her on an equal footing with Scotland and Wales, neither of which has a "guarantee" of her position in the U.K. And although it could be construed as a necessary move for breaking the U.K. link, it is not a sufficient one.

Nor is it sufficient to bring about either unity or the consent for unity. For, as Hume points out: "You [the British government] should realize that in withdrawing your consent to the guarantee you would not be destroying the right of a majority in Northern Ireland to decide their future."[17] Accordingly, even in the absence of a guarantee there is no prima-facie reason why Protestants should change their behavior as long as they are mindful of the solidarity of their numbers. Therefore, if the rationale for ending the guarantee is that it will somehow induce either a more "responsible" or less sectarian Protestant attitude to other initiatives or that it will make Protestants less assiduously conscious of the paramount necessity for solidarity in the face of every threat, it may be seriously, perhaps even irreparably, flawed by the parallel guarantee implicit in the "unity only with the consent of a majority" formula. And, if that tiny minority of Protestants do exist who contemplate a new relationship with the Republic, they have developed despite the guarantee — in which case the guarantee is not an absolute barrier to change. It is somewhat presumptuous to believe that ending the guarantee would encourage the growth of that minority by "liberating" "moderate" Protestants from having to live up to the sectarian "obligations" of the guarantee.

Indeed, insofar as the conditional guarantee provides a measure of security if it is accepted at face value, Protestants are under less pressure to react and therefore in a better position to contemplate with more assurance where they are going and the implications of possible relationships with the Republic, especially as new considerations assume more importance with time.

In fact, since the necessity for solidarity would undoubtedly become more pressing in the absence of the guarantee, it is as feasible to argue that its termination would hasten a closing of the ranks, fueling the siege mentality and making consent less likely rather than more likely, since consent even on matters on which there is consent (such as the wretched state of the economy) would become highly symbolic, and therefore far more likely to be misconstrued. The appearance of things would assume a far greater significance than the reality. When agreement on anything could be perceived as a harbinger of possible agreement on everything, there will be agreement on nothing.

To summarize: If Ulster Protestants act *rationally,* accept the logic of their numbers, embrace the concomitant guarantee implicit in the unity-only-with-consent formula, then the ending of the constitutional guarantee would have no impact on the reality of their situation. Indeed, if they were to demand a quid pro quo for agreeing to the guarantee's termination — such as a joint guarantee by the SDLP, Dublin, and Westminster that gave legal expression to the declaration that unity shall require the consent of a majority — or if they were to indicate a willingness to trade off the guarantee for the removal of Articles 2 and 3 of the Republic's Constitution, they could end up in many respects more secure in their position rather than less secure.

However, even in the absence of such "horse trading," the new situation would create no incentive for Protestants either to alter their behavior or to modify their positions, provided, of course, that they acted *rationally,* since the guarantee appears to give no more than a legal expression to a consent formula that all parties publicly adhere to.

But there *is* one subtle distinction between the two: To assert that the constitutional position of Northern Ireland within the U.K. will not be changed without the consent of a majority is a guarantee of the state's continuing status within the U.K. On the other hand, to assert that unification will take place only when a majority in Northern Ireland agree to it is, in effect, a guarantee of the state's continuing status outside an all-Ireland structure. Thus, vitiating the former and reiterating the latter opens up the way to just one other possibility: independence. This is the first purpose of the exercise.

The second purpose is implicit in the first: once the window of independence is opened, Protestants must be encouraged to step out onto the ledge. And when they do, the window is closed. But for this to happen Protestants must act *irrationally.* After all, if the proceedings of the second Anglo-Irish summit, which reiterated the guarantee more strongly than ever, led to hundreds of Loyalists protesting the actions of the British government in the predawn hours in the hills of County Antrim, would not the withdrawal of the guarantee be likely to trigger a large-scale irrational reaction? And if, as Hume insists, what the British government is saying to Unionists is tantamount to a man saying to his wife, "I will stay with you as long as you like, because I am obliged to do so under the guarantee clause of the 1973 Marriage Act, but the very instant you agree to a divorce you shall have it, and what is more I wish you to know that I have my lawyer on permanent retainer, so there will be no delay in arranging the separation,"[18] then would not the ending of the guarantee be tantamount to a man bringing his mistress home, in the hope that by adding insult to injury the wife would finally walk out, thereby precipitating divorce?

Thus the second purpose of the exercise: ending the guarantee would induce an *irrational* reaction on the part of Protestants, a call for independence by Paisley that would move things in an irreversible political direction. Hence, Hume's confident assertion that "if the British make the kind of declaration I am suggesting about the guarantee, the immediate response from Protestants would not be to go to war because the British would still be there. Under the circumstances, therefore, the Protestants would opt for independence."[19]

Ending the guarantee, therefore, is a mechanism to trigger an end to the conditional loyalty of Unionists to the United Kingdom.* When Britain appears to be breaking the Union, then Loyalists are in a political position to do so. Under these circumstances, the question of consent takes on a new meaning because the frame of reference has changed.

James Molyneaux, leader of the Official Unionists:

> Something like FitzGerald's solution with two more or less independent states linked by a confederal tier might be something that might be attractive to Paisley, because in a private remark to some Fine Gael representative to the EEC he said something to the effect that "I can do nothing until you persuade the British government to get rid of the guarantee. My hands are tied until you get rid of the guarantee."[20]

Hume, of course, also sees Paisley moving in the direction of independence. Hence the Hume logic and the Hume assumptions: the Anglo-Irish process acknowledges the framework of a problem, and therefore the dimensions of the solution. Protes-

* For the reference for the concept of conditional loyalty, see note 41, chapter 4.

tant participation must be induced. You achieve this by ending the guarantee, thereby triggering a massive *irrational* reaction in the Loyalist community. Civil war is averted by the presence of the British Army — in fact, Britain is called on not only to break the guarantee but then to place herself between the two communities in the North to ensure that the two tribes don't attempt to implement their own final solution. The irrational Loyalists call for their independence. However, now that their irrational behavior has moved them in a direction that is irreversible, they become rational. Moreover, the hard-nosed business Loyalists would understand that a Northern Ireland bereft of the British subsidy, shut out of Europe, and beset by massive political, economic, and security problems would simply not be viable. Therefore, they accept an invitation to participate in the Anglo-Irish process to negotiate their independence. They accept the rational arguments of the other parties — that independence requires the consent of the minority in the North, of the government to the South, and of mainland Britain. They agree to bargain, and out of that bargaining there would emerge some form of an autonomous Northern Ireland, a restored Stormont Parliament, perhaps, but with one important difference — Westminster would transfer its reserve powers over Northern Ireland to Dublin. Hence there would exist a federal Ireland. But the Anglo-Irish Council would continue to guarantee a special link with Britain, and of course a new constitution would guarantee the political and religious rights of Protestants. For good measure those who wanted to maintain their U.K. citizenship would be more than welcome to do so. In fact, every effort would be made to acknowledge and accommodate the "British Dimension."

Consent, therefore, would become the by-product of a process, not a precondition for the process itself.

Hume is explicit on the question of consent: "If you had a 51 percent–49 percent situation [for unity] there still would be strong resistance. Therefore, you have to get the broad consent of the Protestant community as to where you are going."[21]

But the concept itself, he says, is not negotiable:

It's a mistake to get caught up in the casuistry of words. We all know what we mean. There's been a great deal of political argument over the word *consent.* Conor Cruise O'Brien* says consent means the right to say no. That's clever but it doesn't get us any further ahead. What I'm saying — and mean by consent — is that if we are going to get the Irish problem solved, then there are two traditions in Ireland, broadly speaking, and you've got to get both sides of them to sit down. And to hammer out an agreement that broadly speaking both traditions will accept.[22]

Robert McCartney, on the other hand, counterpoints what he perceives as the contradictions of the guarantee with the prerequisites for consent:

This talk about guarantees is nonsense. What is the guarantee at the moment to the majority? It's no guarantee at all, because they're giving up nothing. They're not guaranteeing us anything. They're only saying "This will have to be, because even if we wished otherwise we couldn't do anything about it." That's the first basic premise.

The second premise is that at the moment they are not guaranteeing anything to the present generation of Unionists. Because they are not protecting their most fundamental rights by their security policies — the right to live, the right to farm your fields in Fermanagh, the right to have a normal life.

What they are saying by their guarantee is "We will guarantee the rights of tomorrow's Republicans." That when they get 51 percent we will, I think Margaret Thatcher said, "institute legislation for making the necessary arrangements to take account of the will of the majority." But that is such ludicrous nonsense because if at that time the minds are not converted, if the differences are not abolished, if the partition in hearts is not removed, we'd be back exactly where we started.

There'd still be a three quarters of a million people saying "No! —

* Conor Cruise O'Brien is the author of *States of Ireland* and other books, former editor in chief of *The Observer* of London, former Minister for Posts and Telegraphs in the coalition government of Liam Cosgrave, and former representative of the UN Secretary General in Katanga. He is a frequent and controversial commentator on Northern Ireland. While Minister for Posts and Telegraphs, he banned broadcasts by illegal paramilitary organizations and Sinn Féin. Among other things, he has called for repartition of Northern Ireland as the least worst outcome.

no matter what institutions you announce from Westminster, no matter what acts of Parliament you pass, you're still going to have a civil war situation in Ireland."[23]

Paddy Harte, former Fine Gael spokesman on Northern Ireland, agrees:

If tomorrow morning there was a plebiscite on what the future of Northern Ireland should be and 51 percent voted for a united Ireland, the stage would be set for a civil war. Percentages in the North are not relevant. You could have 75 percent in favor of a united Ireland; the other 25 percent would resist it. You might have a twenty-seven- or thirty-county Ireland, but you would not have a thirty-two-county Ireland.[24]

Thus, again, the logic of the Hume position and the network of interlocking assumptions: if consent is chameleonlike and elusive in a framework that makes the outcome it mandates perhaps more remote even as consent for that outcome grows, the status quo will remain permanently frozen. To unfreeze the status quo you need to dismantle its framework. Therefore, you alter the context of what is to be resolved: make the issue one of Northern Ireland either having or demanding to change her relationship with the U.K. rather than having to resolve her relationship with the Republic. By putting the primary emphasis on the former, you alter the context in which consent for the latter is a consideration. By altering the context in which consent is sought, you alter the meaning of consent, especially as a question of ratiocination.

The Hume scenario is, of course, the basis of the Fianna Fáil "policy" on Northern Ireland. And since Fianna Fáil opposes devolved government in Ulster, it is perhaps not surprising that the SDLP is increasingly reluctant to commit itself to that route once more. Hume:

It depends on the context in which a devolved structure is created. If you're talking about a devolved structure along the lines that have been attempted since 1972, then it will fail. If it's part of a broader Anglo-Irish process, I don't see a problem with it.[25]*

There are, of course, other considerations. First, with an Anglo-Irish structure in place, the absence of an internal Northern Ireland structure would diminish the Belfast-London axis and substantially increase the role of the Dublin-London axis. Recalcitrant Protestant parties in the North, therefore, would be increasingly isolated. If the guarantee was withdrawn and the Loyalists, as conventional nationalist opinion expects, did opt for independence, there would be only one avenue through which to pursue it. The absence of an internal governmental structure would make a Unilateral Declaration of Independence more difficult, perhaps even impossible, since the entire machinery and administration of government would remain in British hands. The outcome, therefore, would be immediately subordinated to the context of the deliberations of two sovereign governments. It would not be so much a matter of "inviting" Loyalists into the Anglo-Irish process so that they could demand their "independence" as a situation in which the "irrational" demand for independence would precede, indeed precipitate, their participation in the Anglo-Irish forum. Moreover, stalemate on the issue of devolution will make Britain more disposed toward an initiative that does not involve devolution, especially if it appears that obdurate Loyalists once again will not yield on the issue of power sharing — a guarantee of power to the minority — which Britain has always insisted upon as a nonnegotiable precondition for devolution.† In fact, the failure to achieve devolution in the past opened the way to the Anglo-Irish process, and

* In April 1982 — approximately three months after this interview with John Hume was conducted — the British government unveiled its new proposals for a devolved government in Northern Ireland. The SDLP did not regard Secretary of State James Prior's proposals as being part of "a broader Anglo-Irish process." Hence its rejection of Prior's plan and its subsequent boycott of the Assembly. See chapter 11.

† Although the Prior initiative unveiled in the April 1982 White Paper did not insist on power sharing as the "right" of the minority, the concept of broad cross-community support and the 70 percent formula would give an effective veto to the minority over proposals for devolved government. See chapter 11.

continued failure could lead Britain to consider a withdrawal of the guarantee or at least to use the threat of its withdrawal to make Loyalists more accommodating on devolution. At which point, of course, it is still in the interests of the SDLP to resist accommodation while somehow making it appear that the Loyalists are, as always, at fault.

• • •

It's a chess game. Ending the guarantee is an opening gambit that will ensure the consent of one player to resign on the thirty-fifth move when he realizes the inevitability of certain checkmate on the fifty-third. Or at least that's the reasoning behind it. Ultimately, ending the guarantee has little to do with breaking down sectarian solidarity and everything to do with inducing sectarian irrationality.

But only at first, and therein lies the worm at the core, the internal inconsistency, for success is predicated on rational action following irrational reaction. First, there is the assumption that ending the guarantee will precipitate a call for independence. This, given the pathology of Protestant behavior, is a rational assumption. Nonetheless, such a response would in fact be irrational given the obverse guarantees implicit in the numerous multilateral declarations that unity will require the consent of a majority. The second assumption is that this irrational response would be followed by a series of rational actions, bringing Protestants to the judicious conclusion that an independent Northern Ireland would be untenable. And this second assumption is, of course, itself irrational.

Says Hume:

It's always been the Unionist case that the reason why they opted out of Ireland was because Ireland did not accommodate them. That's been their case against unity. They should not be surprised when those who believe in unity come back and try to propose a form of unity which does accommodate them as an alternative option.

When the options are all on the table of a unity which does accommodate them as opposed to a union with Britain which does not accommodate the minority in any manner, shape, or fashion, or as opposed to what we have at the moment, which is Direct Rule with the clear failure of it, then what I want is for all these options to be put to people, and I would have faith enough that if they're put to people properly, that people would study them objectively, and that there would be a shift in opinion as a result.[26]

Thus, "rational" Protestants would come to accept the "guarantees" that would protect their positions and interests in a new Ireland. Articles 2 and 3 are a case in point. Rather than a constitutional referendum in the South on Articles 2 and 3, which might prove to be extraordinarily divisive, even destabilizing, Hume advocates that:

. . . the parties in the Dáil [should] make a solemn declaration that in any new Ireland there will be absolute guarantees for the Protestant position, and they should make that declaration now . . .[27] even going so far as to lodge it with the United Nations.[28]

The irony of the proposal is inescapable. The SDLP demands that Britain should end a long-standing guarantee to the Protestant community that secures its position within the U.K. Yet the SDLP also solemnly offers the Protestant community a guarantee to secure its position within an all-Ireland state. Similarly, Mr. Haughey can consistently call on Britain to break her guarantee to the Northern majority, all the while asking Protestants to take at face value his own solemn guarantee that "in any discussion or negotiations which may be proposed, the safety and welfare of our countrymen of the Protestant faith in Northern Ireland would be for me personally a special priority."[29] And that "it would be my concern to ensure that their place in the Ireland of the future was secure, and their talents and industry were given every opportunity to develop and flourish, that their traditions were honored and respected."[30]

The contradictions appear inexplicable; the implicit inconsistencies inhibit dialogue. The result: a deepening distrust among Protestants of every Catholic initiative. How can those who decry one set of guarantees be taken seriously when they do an about-face and offer their own set of guarantees? How are Protestants to reconcile the promises of guarantees to protect them in a new Ireland made by those who insistently demand the revocation of the guarantees they presently have? Indeed, if the SDLP and Fianna Fáil were to acknowledge that guarantees were in fact made to be kept, might not Protestants be more open to suggestions that their position in an all-Ireland arrangement could in fact be guaranteed?

One thing is certain: if Britain did withdraw the guarantee, it would be seen by the Protestant community as capitulation to the SDLP and Fianna Fáil. A future accommodation between North and South on the basis of "guarantees" would be impossible, since the Catholic parties would have shown by their prior actions what Protestants believe in their hearts: Catholics do not regard guarantees as binding; guarantees are a ruse to get either into or out of something; thus, Catholics will offer all kinds of guarantees to lure Protestants into a united Ireland, only to renege on the promises so solemnly given when Protestants are securely — and permanently — entrapped.

• • •

The very rationality of Hume's proposals works against them because the obverse is implicit in many of his conclusions. For example, if an autonomous Northern Ireland with a federal link to the Republic and an institutional link to the U.K. should provide a framework to accommodate what is important to Protestants — their "Britishness" and their "Protestantism" — should not Protestants inquire of Hume whether he would accept a framework that accommodates what is important to Northern Catholics — their "Irishness" and their "Catholicism"? Such a framework, for example, might amount to a variation of the Sunningdale model: an autonomous Northern Ireland with a power-sharing government, a federal link with the U.K., and an institutional link with the Republic that would recognize, among other things, the "Irishness" of Northern Catholics. And again, if the ambivalence of the minority on how to deal with violence "comes from the absence of a central authority to which they can give their allegiance,"[31] might not a Protestant minority in an all-Ireland state find themselves ineluctably drawn into a similar situation if, despite their "autonomy," they cannot give a sufficient allegiance to a central authority in Dublin? The assertion that "an essential element to any solution has to be a recognition of the identity of the minority"[32] is probably beyond dispute, but it does not necessarily follow that this can be accomplished only through a federal link with the rest of Ireland. For if it did, one would have to accept the converse: a federal link with the rest of the U.K. as the only way to accomplish a second essential element to any solution, which is, of course, the recognition of the identity of the majority in Northern Ireland.

The question of accommodation also cuts both ways. Though it is indisputably correct to say that Unionists have no history of accommodation, it is also a fact that for most of the history of Northern Ireland the minority were no more accommodating than the majority. After the settlement of 1921, the pervasive belief among nationalists "that the border was a temporary expedient led to intermittent abstentionism from the Stormont Parliament and to an unconstructive attitude to the institutions of the State."[33] Along the way, Catholics were instructed to get as much out of the welfare state as possible and then "to act stupid, demand explanations, object, anything at all that will clog the departmental machinery."[34] The nationalists had "no policy except to wait for the unification of Ireland. No matter what the social and economic orientation of the Nationalist member at Stormont, he was first and foremost a Nationalist."[35] Hence, for a very long period the unwillingness of Protestants to accommodate had little to do with the "guarantee" of their position. Even if they had had sufficient foresight to wean Catholics into the process, Catholics would have rejected the attempt.

The sectarianism of the majority was reinforced by the nationalism of the minority. The will of the majority to maintain the state was counterpointed by the aspiration of the minority to destroy it. The undisguised belligerency of the minority coupled with their absolute resolve neither to acknowledge the existence of the state, nor even to appear to acknowledge its existence by participating in its government, probably had as much to do with encouraging the solidarity of Protestants, which ensured their "special position of privilege and power," as the provisions in the Act of 1920 that brought the state into being. Nationalists, in fact, would almost certainly have felt repudiated, perhaps even insulted, had they not been treated as the "enemies" of the state. Moreover, the extraordinarily close identification of nationalism with Catholicism ensured that the sectarian solidarity of the majority was matched by the sectarian solidarity of the minority.* In the few towns where Catholics were able to muster a majority in local elections, they were as adept at discriminating against the Protestant "minority" as were Protestants at discriminating against Catholics in the towns where they enjoyed majority power.[36] Unfortunately for Catholics, the latter situations vastly outnumbered the former.

But these, perhaps, are debating points, peripheral to some disturbing corollaries that follow from an SDLP policy designed to maneuver Unionists into demanding their independence.

• • •

After Robert Bradford, Official Unionist member of the Westminster Parliament for South Belfast, was murdered by the IRA, the IRA followed up the action with a concentrated campaign against the indigenous Ulster segment of the security forces. Harold McCusker, Official Unionist M.P. for Armagh, was incensed:

The last time we talked [August 1981], I was making the point that independence seemed a tidy solution for people who couldn't come

* See Ian McAllister, "Political Opposition in Northern Ireland." "Having no consistent organization the [Nationalist] Party had therefore no formal membership which presented problems in selecting candidates for elections. This gave rise to the 'convention' system by which prominent Catholics in the constituency, often invited by the local priest, came together to select a candidate. A contemporary critic observed that 'charges of "fixing" and selective invitations by the sponsors to such conventions have been the rule rather than the exception.' Clerical influence in Nationalist politics was in fact a consistent theme. Direct involvement by the Roman Catholic clergy was usually limited to election periods, especially when disputes arose between contenders for the nationalist role . . ." (p.356). According to J. L. McCracken, this identification of nationalism and Catholicism "detracted from the effectiveness of opposition criticism" and it "encouraged a narrow sectarian approach on the part of some nationalist members." See J. L. McCracken, "Political Scene in Northern Ireland 1926–37," p. 154.

up with any other solution or who weren't prepared to face the unpleasant consequences of other solutions. But I've got to say to you that the tide of murders in the last six months has very substantially changed people's attitudes up here. There is almost a feeling — and it's a feeling I share as well — as the hopelessness grips you, you can't help it, you say, "Hell, let's get it in our own hands. If we're going to be slaughtered, let's at least feel that we've done something to stop ourselves being slaughtered."[37]

Thus, the IRA's actions and the perceived inadequacy of the government's response lead increasing numbers of Protestants in the direction of "independence." When John Hume wants the British government to confront Ian Paisley with the "logic" of his actions, Paisley's actions more often than not have been a reaction to the actions of the IRA. If the Third Force should be construed as an instrument of a Unilateral Declaration of Independence, then the IRA is responsible for moving Paisley in that direction.

The point is this: when the IRA murders Ulster-born members or former members of the security forces, which is happening with increasing frequency in the Border areas, Protestants see the murders as a calculated attempt by the IRA to systematically kill off the Protestant people — a matter of the most serious concern to them. And when the British authorities fail to respond to these murders with large-scale assaults on suspected IRA strongholds — in fact, with a scale of response that would not be possible without alienating the Catholic community to the point of political resistance — then at a general level Protestants feel that the British authorities are not serious about taking on the IRA, and at the personal level they feel that the murder of Protestants is not a matter of serious concern to the authorities. Thus, the chain of conditional loyalty is further weakened, the temptation to go it alone more enticing: ultimately, the Provisional IRA's campaign of violence and the SDLP's call for an end to the guarantee complement each other.

The unconstitutional and the constitutional become symbiotic. Not that there is any question about John Hume's — or the SDLP's — attitude toward the IRA. It has been one of consistent and unequivocal condemnation. At the SDLP's annual conference at Newcastle, County Down, in the aftermath of Robert Bradford's murder, Hume was scathing in his denunciation of the Provisional IRA campaign:

The SDLP [he declared] will always recognize this evil for what it is and call it by its name: murder. We say to the Provisionals, you are not Irish Republicans, you are extremists who have dishonored and are dishonoring the deepest ideals of the Irish people. Can we remind you yet again that those whose inheritance you so falsely claim laid down their arms in 1916 lest they cause undue suffering to the Irish people.[38]

Yet there is a convergence of interests, if not of methods. The unconstitutional could ultimately facilitate the constitutional. More tragically, perhaps, the converse could also be true if the ending of the guarantee precipitated a Masada-like Unilateral Declaration of Independence by diehard Loyalists — a response made to fit for the Provisionals — rather than a demand for independence within the Anglo-Irish framework.

• • •

And there are other convergences, or at least the perceptions of convergences, among Protestants that make it difficult for them to accept what the SDLP says as a measure of its true intentions. McCusker:

I can understand how the Provisional IRA feel when they are condemned by Hume. Because in many respects they see the SDLP, deliberately or otherwise, using the threat of IRA violence to achieve their political objectives insofar as they say, "If you don't guarantee us places in the government, this violence is going to continue." The IRA provides them with a very substantial lever in their negotiations. And, therefore, I think the IRA would feel quite sore that they're always on the receiving end . . . The threat posed by the IRA, the threat of violence, enables the SDLP to negotiate from a position of some power. Now they mightn't be very honest when they say it, but the suggestion is, you see, that they can end this violence. [They say,] "If you'll only give us a chance we'll end this violence, and if you don't give us a chance this violence won't end." [And] they say, "Now, we don't like this violence but it's going to continue until you give us guaranteed jobs in government." I think the Provisionals see through that particular argument and don't take too kindly to it.[39]

The pressure on the SDLP to become more "Green" increases as other indigenous political parties threaten to erode their political constituency. At crucial political moments they cannot appear to be outflanked by the IRA, hence the appearance of complicity. The Irish Independence Party, launched in 1977 on a platform calling for British withdrawal, also looms as a threat to the more irredentist nationalist elements within the SDLP's constituency. Indeed, in the 1981 local elections, the IIP secured 22 percent of the vote in some Border constituencies — admittedly, constituencies where the SDLP has always been weak.* The decision by Provisional Sinn Féin to contest elections, which grew directly out of its success in the Fermanagh–South Tyrone by-elections where the SDLP failed to field a candidate, adds to the difficulties the SDLP now has in not appearing to be less nationalist-minded than the next party.† This, in turn, increases its propensity to put less emphasis on an internal settlement as a first step toward some ultimate new arrangement. There is an inexorable pressure not to accommodate.

Fermanagh–South Tyrone: Northern Ireland's "valley of hate" according to one observer.[40] In Fermanagh alone, with its meager population of fifty-one thousand and beautiful landscape of gentle, undulating hills, lakes, wetlands, forests, and small scattered rural communities, more than sixty people have been gunned down in the last ten years — almost all of them Protestant. Suspi-

* In the May 1981 local elections the IIP took 4 percent of the first-preference poll. *Fortnight* noted that "in the country areas there was the traditionally high poll, and the SDLP lost ground to the IIP and other Republican independents . . . It is significant that IIP easily outpolled the SDLP in Fermanagh." *Fortnight*, no. 182 (July/August 1981), p. 8. For a brief history of the IIP see W. D. Flackes, *Northern Ireland: A Political Directory*, p. 71.

† Provisional Sinn Féin contested the Northern Ireland Assembly elections in October 1982. It won three seats and 10 percent of the first-preference vote, to the dismay of the SDLP, the British government, and the Irish government. See chapter 11 and chapter 13. For Provisonal Sinn Féin's strategy to displace the SDLP as the spokesparty for the nationalist community, see chapter 7.

cion between Catholic and Protestant runs deep: to this day, nothing interferes with the integrity of their quarrel. Murder is often in the eye of the beholder.

Catholic voters in the district outnumber Protestants by about five thousand, so a Unionist candidate can in fact win only against a divided opposition. The mathematics are simple: elections are merely a matter of tribal head-counts.

When Owen Carron, who had been Bobby Sands's election agent when the hunger-striking Sands was elected to the Westminster seat for the district, decided to put himself forward as a candidate for the seat following Sands's death, the SDLP decided not to contest the election, even though Carron made it clear he was the candidate of the Provisional IRA.*

Their decision drew widespread criticism, but Hume argues the SDLP position with a cold tenacity.[41] First, the party's Executive voted to contest the election and sent its recommendation to the local constituency. But the local constituency voted not to field a candidate. Second, the SDLP's constitution does not allow the Executive to override the local constituency on such issues. Third, the SDLP always had problems in that area. If they had contested the election, they would have finished third — which would have meant that in their first head-to-head confrontation with the Provisional IRA, the Provisionals would have beaten the SDLP, a result that would have provided the IRA with great propaganda fodder. "If you're going to take them on," said Hume "take them in a place of your own choosing. In fact, everywhere else we took on H-Block candidates in the

* On 5 March 1981, Frank Maguire, Independent M.P. for Fermanagh–South Tyrone, died suddenly of a heart attack. On 26 March, representatives of Bobby Sands, who had been on hunger strike for "political status" at the Maze Prison since 1 March, announced his candidacy for the by-election. On 30 March, nominations closed with only two candidates — the Republican, Sands, and the Official Unionist, Harry West. Noel Maguire, the late M.P.'s brother, had at first announced his candidacy and then withdrawn it at a very late stage. Many believe he had been put under severe pressure to do so, so as not to split the Catholic vote. Earlier, the SDLP Executive had decided to withdraw Austin Currie's nomination for the by-election. See *Fortnight,* no. 181 (May/June 1981), pp. 12–14. Owen Carron was a member of Provisional Sinn Féin, the political wing of the Provisional IRA. Among his statements: "There is nothing wrong with people fighting for their country." Quoted in *Fortnight,* no.183 (October/November 1981), p. 16.

local elections and we hammered them."[42] And finally, with ten hunger strikers dead, and seven more on the conveyor belt of death, the Unionist candidate would have won the seat:

The SDLP would have been accused of lifting the siege of pressure on the British. That would have reverberated through other elections. It was a no-win situation. We would have drowned in the deluge. Politics are not only about principles but about the ability to put principles into practice. The second is as important as the first. There are times when it is necessary to speak more quietly in order to speak more often. The SDLP was being put in a situation that was not of its own choosing. It could have become one more victim of British policy.[43]

The logic is indisputable, but the Fermanagh–South Tyrone election once again illustrated the insidious collusion between the constitutional and the unconstitutional, and the contamination of the morality of the political process that results when the one is made to bend to the other.

It confirmed to Protestants — not that much confirming was needed — their suspicions that the SDLP's condemnations of IRA violence were a charade, a cynical ploy to manipulate ingenuous Protestants into the belief that there were in fact differences between the various "brands" of Republicanism. It undermined the SDLP's claim to be the moral and political bulwark against the IRA. And it allowed Unionists to rationalize their own self-serving actions in the light of the SDLP's lack of action. The tail was very definitely wagging the dog.

Harold McCusker, for example:

The SDLP ran away from the fight. The choice was whether they wanted a Protestant democrat in Parliament who disagreed with them politically or a Republican gunman who wouldn't go to Parliament. And by abstaining they gave their mandate to the Republican gunman, and in doing so they have abdicated their responsibility in Fermanagh–South Tyrone. Now the SDLP will never be able to fight that seat. They have encouraged the Provos to the point where they are now saying "We'll fight West Belfast."

The only argument they had for backing down was that they were not prepared to split the Catholic vote. And if you're not prepared to split the Catholic vote in Fermanagh–South Tyrone, why should you be prepared to split it in West Belfast or South Armagh or Mid-Ulster or Londonderry? I think the SDLP abdicated seriously from their responsibilities.

For me — and as you know I stand foursquare against the attitude of the DUP — the ideal situation in Fermanagh–South Tyrone was for the DUP to put its hat in the ring, the OUP to put its hat in, the SDLP to put its hat in, and Carron would have been the candidate of the Provisional movement.

The electorate would then have had a choice between the various brands of Republicanism and the various brands of Unionism. It might well be that the same result would have emerged, but at least all the democratic parties would have participated in the process.[44]

And Robert McCartney:

John Hume is a very astute politician. But I think the decision of the SDLP not to run a candidate in Fermanagh–South Tyrone showed a tremendous lack of political courage. I've heard his logic. It makes political sense. When John Hume condemns the IRA as murderers I believe he is sincere. But I also believe there is an element of expediency.

There is a time when all political caution must be thrown to the winds. You must mount your white charger. You must believe in your principles. Likewise I believe the Official Unionist Party must declare itself in relation to Paisley. And it has to run the risk that in the short run it will lose a lot of support.

Similarly, if the SDLP took a comparable stand it would undoubtedly have lost support in Fermanagh–South Tyrone. But I think both these central parties could secure an influx of those people who would be attracted to their courageous stands.[45]

Jim Allister, spokesman for the Democratic Unionists, not surprisingly sees his party's failure to contest Fermanagh–South Tyrone in an entirely different light than the SDLP's failure to do so:

We did it openly. For the purpose of securing the maximum Unionist vote. Because it was a straight fight. And it has always been the policy between the two Unionist parties that wherever there was a straight fight that some kind of agreement should be reached on a Unionist candidate. We opted out but gave our backing to the OUP candidate openly.

The SDLP opted out but they were not even honest enough to give their backing to Carron openly. I think it has put the SDLP in a peculiar predicament because their voters have gone and voted for Owen Carron and the SDLP is faced with the problem of getting them back.

A vote for Carron was a vote for the IRA. The Catholic community has held up its hands in horror and said, "We disown the IRA. We are as appalled as you are at the atrocities they commit." Yet that same Catholic community went to the polls and voted for the IRA virtually to a man. That is something which speaks volumes to the Protestant community.

Whereas the DUP did not fight, it gave its support to someone who was not a gunman. But the SDLP by not fighting gave its support to the IRA. So much for the SDLP saying it hates the IRA as much as anybody.[46]

Ian Paisley makes no distinctions whatsoever: the SDLP and the IRA are synonymous:

John Hume's politics and the politics of the IRA are one and the same. They both want a united Ireland. In Stormont he opposed legislation that would deal with the IRA and he has consistently opposed every piece of legislation that would put down the IRA. He opposed everything that would be effective in dealing with the IRA.

And of course, he does not support — his party does not support — the security forces. Nor will he invite his people to join the security forces, and yet he tells us people should fight the IRA. So the people of Northern Ireland have no faith in the integrity of John Hume. Why should they?

Here's a man who condemns everybody who does anything to give safety to the Protestant people, and then he says, "You must support the forces of the Crown," and then when he's asked by his party, "Do you support them?" he says, "Definitely not." [And when he's asked,] "Will you ask the Roman Catholic people to join them?" he says, "Definitely not." And yet he hounds them from pillar to post. So when you're a Protestant and you join the security forces you get no support from John Hume.[47]

The OUP's James Molyneaux is hardly less sparing:

When John Hume comes out and calls the IRA murderers and an abomination against every form of democratic government, I believe that he means it. Because the IRA have to a very large extent sabotaged what John Hume was up to. They've spoiled his nice political position and all that sort of thing. He's saying that out of exasperation and not necessarily condemnation.

I suppose we've all fairly long memories in Northern Ireland, but we don't have to go back that far—just ten or twelve years, when John Hume's activities, not just his statements, were synonymous with those of the IRA. So we're inclined to be a wee bit skeptical about what Hume says for these reasons.

I don't think the SDLP have attempted to take on the IRA. They've been more inclined to join them. It's very difficult for them to take on the IRA because their political objectives are the same.[48]

This ultimately is what defines the Unionists' perspective, even in the party that purports to put forward the "acceptable" face of Unionism: the SDLP is not a Northern Ireland political party. Hence the SDLP's condemnations of the IRA are self-serving. Since both aspire to the same political end, they are, when all is said and done, fellow travelers. Reconciliation is a Catholic word for unification. Unification means conquest. Nothing has changed—a nationalist is a nationalist is a nationalist. Molyneaux:

If the SDLP were a party which said, "Right, we represent a lot of Catholics in Northern Ireland and we'd like to do business with you to make Northern Ireland a better place for Protestants and Catholics to live and work in," that would be a very different matter. But they say nothing of the kind.

They say, "Well, right, we're going to do everything we can to achieve unification. So be on your guard and well aware that everything we do is designed to achieve unification, and to get you prised out of the positions which you occupy as citizens of the United Kingdom." And furthermore, they not only say that but gave evidence of it, when they were in the Faulkner power-sharing Executive. They showed that their allegiance was to a nation other than the one to which they belonged by going down to Dublin as a body, as an SDLP nationalist element, as a Republican element within the power-sharing Executive, taking their secret confidential Cabinet papers to Dublin and spreading them out in front of the then Taoiseach and saying, "Look, we'd like your advice on how we should vote when we go back and meet with Faulkner and his colleagues next Tuesday."

I can tell you in confidence that that exasperated even their most ardent sympathizers in high places in the London government at that time — and I'm not excluding even the top person of that time, who was completely aghast when he discovered what they were up to.

Because if there was anything that was calculated to show distrust, it was that; by simply saying, "Well, here we are sitting at the polished table in Stormont but don't be under any misapprehension, we are the Fifth Column and as soon as we can get the Enterprise Express down to Dublin we'll be down to tell them what we're about around this table, and furthermore take their advice as to how we should vote on this particular piece of legislation."

Now, that proves that you simply can't work with a body whose object is not to make Northern Ireland a happy or more prosperous place but to get Northern Ireland prised out of the United Kingdom. That's the big divide. And it's important for people to realize. It's not a question of whether you're a Catholic or a Protestant, it's a question of which nation you want to belong to. And on that rock all these experiments of reconciliation founder.[49]

If the DUP equates the SDLP with the IRA, Seamus Lynch, Regional Chairman of the Workers' Party's Republican Clubs (still allegedly the political wing of the Official IRA), equates the DUP with the SDLP:

The only difference between the SDLP and the DUP is their religion. The DUP is to the Protestant population what the SDLP is to the nationalist population. To us the agreement between the DUP and OUP to field one Protestant candidate and the agreement between Provos, the IIP, and the SDLP to field one Catholic candidate meant that once again we had an election being fought on very sectarian grounds. It was very much dividing and polarizing the communities in Northern Ireland.

The SDLP, who we have condemned over the years for being a sectarian party, at last showed their true colors and showed themselves to be a Catholic, nationalist party. They refused to participate in that election because they didn't want to split the Catholic vote. The DUP didn't want to participate because it didn't want to split the Protestant vote. We were in there to fly the flag of the worker on a nonsectarian basis.

We think the SDLP are nothing more than a political wing of the Provos. They have lost all credibility as a serious, moderate political party in Northern Ireland. Even the Alliance, with whom we are in disagreement on most things, had the gumption to contest the election.[50]

And Oliver Napier, leader of the Alliance Party, which also contested the election, accuses the SDLP of having given in to Provisional IRA pressure: "The SDLP caved in to the Provos. They had given a guarantee following their withdrawal from the Sands election that they would contest all future elections. The SDLP has moved from being a progressive party to being a nationalist one."[51]

Even Paddy Harte, former Fine Gael spokesman on Northern Ireland, is critical:

I can freely go along with the difficulties the SDLP found themselves in, that if the Unionists won the election because of a split Catholic vote, then the SDLP would be blamed for losing that election. That's the negative way of looking at it. Because the Sinn Féin Republican Party could also have been blamed.

No party in Northern Ireland had a mandate to contest the election more than the SDLP. I think the SDLP were afraid to lose. Being in politics isn't that you should always win. You argue your case and you seek to have it endorsed. I have sympathy with the SDLP for the particular circumstances they found themselves in. But I do not excuse them for not contesting the election. They should have been there, even if they finished fifth.

In the local government elections, they had a strong mandate as the spokesparty for the nationalist community in Northern Ireland. For them to then say that in the Fermanagh–South Tyrone by-election they didn't have a mandate and that the people who had the mandate were the Republicans, well, I don't understand that logic. It's an abdication of their responsibility.[52]

Only the Ulster Defence Association exhibits some sympathy for the SDLP's position. John McMichael:

The Protestants look at Fermanagh–South Tyrone and see thirty thousand Provos. They blame the SDLP—that they didn't step into the arena and show the voters that they were not supporters of the IRA. But the SDLP say they couldn't, and I accept that because they would have been blamed for losing the seat. And that was unpalatable to them.

If it had been a split election on both sides, it would have given everybody an opportunity. Everybody should have thrown their hat in the ring. We considered it. But we were caught in the same bind.[53]

On the question of whether Hume's denunciations of the IRA are to be taken at face value, McMichael also offers some insights that illuminate the depth of the problem:

You do not believe those you do not trust. John Hume has come out very anti-IRA. But there are different ways of looking at it. The average Ulster Protestant wouldn't believe that. I've heard the SDLP called the political wing of Sinn Féin, and that's from people in the Catholic community.

John Hume is distrusted. The Ulster Protestant wouldn't be convinced by him at all. At the same time, I do believe the SDLP is anti-IRA, that they're antiviolence. They have to deal with their own communities and adapt as the temperature changes. I don't think it's a matter of being anti-IRA or politically expedient. It's a mixture of everything.

The Provisional IRA can't be defeated militarily. They can only be defeated when the Catholic population withdraws its support totally, but the SDLP's attitude seems to be "Why should we take them on?" because it will be a very bitter battle and it would leave deep scars within the minority community unless there's something tangible for them to get as a reward.

I can understand that. Why should they engage in something that's going to divide their own community? Unfortunately, John Hume is regarded by the Protestant community as being extremely Republican. It doesn't matter what he actually says. As long as the Provos continue a violent war against the Ulster people, the SDLP will always be suspect, because some of the fallout rubs off on everybody.[54]

• • •

"Those who claim the right to kill and the right to die in the name of what they conceive to be Irish unity," says John Hume, "subvert not only the hope and meaning of unity but the integrity of their own tradition. When the most fundamental right, the right to live, is made subsidiary to a political principle, all other civic and religious values are diminished. The challenge now to my tradition is to reject violence unambiguously and to redefine and communicate a true vision of reconciliation between the two traditions on this island."[55]

These are fine and noble sentiments. But when reconciliation means unification, albeit an agreed unification, when consent can only acknowledge the form of an outcome and not the outcome itself, when it appears that consent is to be induced and not freely given, then Protestants find it difficult to take the condemnation of violence seriously because the violence aims to bring about broadly similar outcomes. The SDLP may dispute the means, but it does not dispute the end: unity is unity is unity.

Whenever principle is sacrificed to expediency, no matter how justifiable the circumstances, the principle is corrupted. The SDLP's call to reject violence loses its moral authority to lift the party's condemnation of violence out of the realm of political rhetoric whenever there is even the appearance that the men of violence can in fact force the SDLP to a political decision that accommodates, even if unwittingly, the IRA's purposes. And the SDLP is compromised yet again whenever the actions of the IRA, no matter how loudly condemned they are by the SDLP, give tactical support to the SDLP's strategic designs.

"The nationalists of the North," Hume passionately asserts, "see in the Provisionals' activity the destruction of the integrity of their own political values, a direct attack on the real meaning of Irish unity. We also see in those parts of the community where the Provisional IRA are most active the spread of a foul social cancer . . . What has followed is a gross distortion of moral values in society, the promotion of the pornography of death and nihilism on our gable walls, and the deep corruption of the young."[56] Again he reiterates that "the SDLP will always recognize this evil for what it is and call it by its name. Murder."[57]

But the corollary poses a brutal dilemma for the SDLP. Its insistence on an all-Ireland solution as the only way forward reinforces the perception that it is, like the Provisionals, the party of "Green." Only the shade of the color, not the color itself, is in question. Ultimately, the collusion of interests between the two undermines the SDLP's moral identity.

Moreover, the SDLP's strategy, with its emphasis on ending the guarantee in the hope of driving Protestants to demand their independence, is not only based on a set of questionable, even contradictory, assumptions, it has at its core an inconsistency that would appear to be irresoluble: rational behavior must follow irrational behavior. Given the history of the conflict, it seems more likely that once the irrational has taken hold the prescription for murder will be filled.

Perhaps the only way for the SDLP to make the rejection of violence unambiguously clear is to take a step back, to redefine its direction in a manner that ends the collusion of interests.

4

Official Unionism: A Question of Consistency

O land of password, handgrip, wink and nod,
Of open minds, as open as a trap.

— Seamus Heaney
"Whatever You Say, Say Nothing"

THEY CAME TO DUBLIN in October 1981 — "professional and business people of the Unionist tradition"[1] — to make their case in the aftermath of Dr. FitzGerald's call for a Constitutional Crusade.

"The case for the Union of Northern Ireland with the rest of the United Kingdom," their manifesto, written by the liberal Official Unionist Robert McCartney, began, "is an honourable one."[2] "For too long," it went on, "the only acceptable source of information available to the government and people of the Republic about what Northern Unionists think or what they may do in certain circumstances has been the representatives of the Northern minority. The colouring and imbalance of such information requires correcting, for it has led successive Southern governments erroneously to believe that the application of external pressure from Dublin, London and Washington will bring about Unionist acceptance of a packaged political settlement."[3] It warned that "any initiative based on this premise has no prospect of success and any consent obtained by fear or fraud would lead to open conflict."[4]

Dr. FitzGerald described the OUP manifesto, titled "The Case for the Unionists," as "the authentic voice of Unionism,"[5] while Dublin's *Irish Independent* editorialized that the document should become "required reading on this side of the Border."[6]

• • •

The Unionist case,[7] or at least the Unionist case that is espoused by a "large section of moderate unionist opinion,"[8] rests on the reiteration of a simple reality: "Over one million Northern Unionists are totally opposed to the concept of a United Ireland and the activities of the Provisional IRA have done nothing but entrench them in such opposition."

That opposition springs from two primary sources. First, there is the question of the nature of the Southern state: "The Northern Unionist believes it is inevitable in a country where 95% of the population subscribes to the Roman Catholic faith, that the teaching of that church as reflecting the views of the overwhelming majority will be mirrored in the laws of the state." And second, there is the question of the claims of the Southern state: "The national aspiration of the Republic, its people and its parties is claimed to be the absorption of the North into a United Ireland. This objective is given legal validity by articles 2 and 3 of the constitution." This claim is a fundamental source of offense to the Northern Unionist, since "it belies his most basic political belief and heritage." Such claims also give "a spurious legitimacy to the worst excesses of the Provisional IRA." And since the objective of a united Ireland is also favored by the Catholic hierarchy, "it is hardly surprising," the manifesto continues, "with both the state and the church supporting the same objective of unity as the Provisional IRA, that the great mass of Roman Catholics in Ireland find that the legitimacy of the Provisional IRA campaign can be couched in terms which they find difficult to reject."

Moreover, the territorial claim is also fundamental to the Provisional IRA campaign for the withdrawal of the British Army from Northern Ireland, since "the whole concept of the British Army as one of occupation is founded on the premise that Northern Ireland is not legitimately part of the United Kingdom despite the Northern Unionist's total identification with the British Army being as much his as that of a Yorkshire man." Hence, "the most significant blow that can be struck by the Republic against the pseudo legitimacy of the Provisional IRA is the abandonment of the territorial claim in the constitution of the Republic."

Furthermore, the manifesto asserts that "the fact that Republicanism and Roman Catholicism are virtually co-extensive in Ireland inevitably means that Catholics and Republicans are for all practical purposes synonymous — Roman Catholicism equals Republicanism" and "few Southern politicians or members of the Irish hierarchy have done much to dispel this view."

The core of the problem: "Northern Unionists hold the view that the Roman Catholic Church is in such a position of entrenched power because of the control it exercises indirectly through the minds and attitudes of the faithful, as to be able to dictate policy to the state on matters which the church considers essential to the maintenance of its position." Such is the extent of this power that "conflict between state and church barely arises, and the power is so effective in real things that the badges of it such as the special position of the church in the constitution are no longer necessary and can be dispensed with." Accordingly, "the Northern Unionist considered that the amendment of the constitution to remove the special significance clause was of no significance."

And since the source of the Church's power is "the sum of the individual Catholic's commitment to the church's teaching," control of education is "essential for its maintenance." Northern Unionists believe that the Roman Catholic Church has "a grip on education of unique strength," and that while there are other countries in the world "having educational systems which are denominationally controlled, only in the Republic of Ireland is it clerically controlled." In addition, they are also convinced that the Catholic Church's insistence on "separateness of education for its members" in the North has been "a significant factor in the polarization of the communities," which leads to the continuing instability.

The Catholic moral code is enshrined in the law of the Republic. Article 41 "would require not merely the passing of a statute but the amendment of the constitution to legalize divorce." Article 42 stresses the limited nature of the state's rights in the area of education, thereby placing "the education of 95% of the population effectively in the hands of the Roman Catholic church." Hence the machinery "for perpetrating a Roman Catholic theocracy is built into the constitution."

A statement of Eamon de Valera's during the Dáil debates on the Constitution in 1937, quoted in the manifesto, provides the raison d'être for resistance:

> "There are 93% of the people in this part of Ireland who belong to the Catholic Church and 75% of the people of Ireland as a whole who belong to the Catholic Church, who believe in its teachings and whose whole philosophy of life is the philosophy which comes from its teachings. If we are going to have a democratic state, if we are going to be ruled by the representatives of the people, it is clear their whole philosophy of life is going to reflect that and that has to be borne in mind and the recognition of it is important."

This is grist for the mills of Unionist opposition. "One million Protestants," the manifesto declares, "would find the above expression of opinion close to anathema. It expresses exactly what they fear, that in a United Ireland the will of the majority would be a Roman Catholic will in circumstances where the constitution not only did not recognize their rights to divorce, contraception, state schools, uncensored reading and other matters involving the exercise of individual conscience, but might require constitutional amendments to secure them." Hence, "the aspect of the Republic's present arrangements which reinforces Northern Unionist opposition to any form of unification is the absence of any real prospect or possibility of change."

Radical influences are weak: "the circumstances in which even the Health (Family Planning) Act was put on the statute book and the difficulties evident in its implementation because of the Catholic conscience of doctors and chemists [are] but an example." If there is to be any hope that the two traditions in Ireland might ultimately meet upon the same road, then "the process of transforming the Republic from something bordering on a theocracy to a pluralistic society" has to be undertaken.

Accordingly, the challenges before the people of the Republic are: first, "to decide whether they are willing to abandon a claim to the territory of Northern Ireland which is used by the Provisional IRA as a licence to murder," and second, "to decide whether the current relationship between church and state and the power which the church exercises in the areas of education and health are to be drastically modified so that the state becomes a pluralistic and non-sectarian state." The alternative is "to underwrite partition on a permanent basis and make any normal relationship between North and South impossible." Thus the cornerstone of the Unionist case: "Those parties or groups who allege that there is no requirement for constitutional change must face the challenge head-on and accept that this means their endorsement of either partition or the unification of Ireland by force."

But even if these changes are made, it would be wrong to assume that Northern Unionists would "consent to any unification of Ireland" because "the position of the Northern Unionist is dependent neither on the guarantee of the British government (which is also a guarantee of the minority's safety) nor on the posturing of loyalist extremists but on his identification of interest with Britain in peace and in war." The Unionist is "psychologically bound to her with bonds of blood, history and common adversity which cannot be bartered away in some political package no matter how attractive that might seem." Even more important, he embodies "theological, philosophical, cultural and political principles and ideas that materially affect his attitude on government, clerical authority and morality so that his views on these matters are profoundly different from his Roman Catholic neighbour." As a result, "the real partition is not a line drawn upon the map of Ireland but in the hearts and minds of men."

Moreover, "the ambivalent attitude of successive governments of the Republic to the issue of extradition and the more recent decision not to implement the European Convention on Terrorism" are seen by "the ordinary Northern Unionist as evidence of a real unwillingness to do what is morally right unless it is also expedient in terms of the South's domestic politics." Which leads the manifesto to conclude that "the defensive attitude of the Northern Unionist to the Roman Catholic minority is exacerbated by the activities of the Provisional IRA and the external threat of what he sees as a sectarian Republic which not only claims his territory but to which the minority looks for support." This external pressure so polarizes the communities as to make meaningful discussion and rational concession impossible. Accordingly, "failure to remove the territorial claim and the consequences which we have sought to show flow inevitably from it, almost totally precludes the necessary preconditions for any settlement of the minority's claim within Northern Ireland and the United Kingdom."[9]

• • •

The fact that the "minority" in Northern Ireland is mentioned but once in "The Case for the Unionists" is perhaps sufficient indication of its psychological prejudice: McCartney was not making a case for the majority in Northern Ireland but for what he perceives as the minority in all of Ireland. Indeed, one of the anomalies of the conflict is the fact that the Northern Ireland question is to a large extent a tale of two minorities. Catholics see themselves as a minority in Northern Ireland, while Protestants see themselves as a minority in the whole of Ireland. They both look at things the same way; it is the things they look at that are different.

Ultimately, the Unionist case as presented in the manifesto is an argument on behalf of Northern Protestants for not joining a united Ireland rather than an argument for their remaining in the U.K. On the one hand it says, "We cannot join you because you are a Catholic state." On the other hand, however, it also says, "We would not join you even if you were not a Catholic state because we see ourselves as British." But these attitudes beg the question: what if the British do not see you as British?

What, in fact, if the British wish to expel you from the United Kingdom? The Reverend Martin Smyth, Imperial Grand Master of the Orange Order, puts the Unionist response most forcefully:

Even if we are put out of the United Kingdom we will not move into a united Ireland. And while there are some of us who would yearn for proper neighborly relations with the South and try to work together as, for example, Canada and the United States, the bulk of our people would look upon it as an abomination to be linked in an Irish federal relation with the nation who more than any other has been an instrument of our destruction during the last decade. Both the Official IRA and the Provisional IRA have been allowed to work openly out of their headquarters in Dublin, and while the South protests that it has no participation in either, it allows attacks on the North from the South. As a result, I know of very few Unionists who would ever consider a confederation with the South.[10]

Hence the political and psychological contradictions of the Unionist case, because Unionists to a man believe that Britain wishes to rid herself of her unruly Northern Ireland appendage. The logic of the Unionist case, therefore, rests on one premise: they cannot be forced to do what they don't want to do. Their refuge is the solidarity of their numbers; their most awful fear is that they themselves will undermine their own solidarity. McCartney:

I have always preached the doctrine that what the Northern Ireland people need to be told is that no power on God's earth can direct a million-plus people to go where they don't want to go, or to accept a constitutional arrangement which they don't wish to accept. And that's why I'm so critical of Paisley, and of Unionist politicians who tend to follow on his coattails, for not telling the people that cries of sellout are absolutely meaningless, because the only people who can sell out the people of Northern Ireland are the people of Northern Ireland themselves.

It is meaningless to say — for the British government to say — that we will guarantee that so long as the majority withholds its consent there will be no united Ireland. Because the corollary of that is that when there are 51 percent in the North who say they want to go into a united Ireland that someone can deliver the 49 percent who would still amount to half a million–plus. At that point all you will have done will be to have converted the present Northern Ireland majority into a minority in Ireland. And if 33 percent of the population — say five hundred thousand people in total, of whom perhaps only five thousand are real activists — can make the North ungovernable, then, by God, a million Prods on the rampage can make the whole of Ireland totally and utterly ungovernable.[11]

The sentiments have not changed for sixty years. They are still the sentiments of negative nationalism. McCartney will not even concede the context of consent:

Even if 51 percent of the people in Northern Ireland opted for unification, you can't take that 51 percent in isolation from the rest of the United Kingdom. We are, whether they like it or not, part of the United Kingdom, part of a constitutional fifty-five million people.[12]

But what if 51 percent of the people of the United Kingdom, including 51 percent of the people of Northern Ireland, opted in a free and open referendum to become part of a united Ireland, could he. McCartney, go along with that? He equivocates:

I'd have to raise a number of questions. What sort of South? I cannot live in a society where one cannot be divorced, where one cannot purchase contraceptives without a very convoluted procedure depending on the whim or the conscience of the local Catholic doctor or priest. That is just not on. I'd also have to see how many of my brothers — brother Unionists — are prepared to take up arms. After all, in terms of historical perspectives Robert E. Lee, when offered the Commander in Chief's position in the Union Army, said with the greatest of sadness, "No, I've got to go with Virginia." These are all considerations that must be taken into account.[13]

James Molyneaux, too, equates consent with the threat of violence:

If 51 percent of the people of Northern Ireland in a free and open election opted for some form of unification, my party would have to accept it democratically. When you say "accept," presumably you're asking whether we would take up arms to resist it. As a political party

I don't think that we would. But then you'd be leaving out of account the people who wouldn't be under the influence of any politicians — and there would be a growing number of them in those circumstances who would, if they felt that they were being pushed into a united Ireland against their will, without adequate safeguards and all the rest of it; then I think you'll find the strength of the paramilitaries vastly increased. You'd have a terrorist situation, the reverse of what it is now. It would be a question for the South of Ireland to decide, if it would be either prudent or desirable to go for unification if they were going to have that kind of problem on their hands. You wouldn't simply make people acquiesce by signing a document. That would be the problem. Accordingly, under these circumstances it would be up to the South to decide what it wanted to do.[14]

• • •

The problem, of course, goes deeper. Although both McCartney and Molyneaux pay lip service to the concept of consent "freely given" — indeed, they go out of their way to condemn structures that would "induce" consent — they are, nevertheless, reluctant to accept openly the implications of freely given consent. On the one hand, they insist that majority rule in the North is democratic rule, dismissing the fact that Britain's refusal to restore majority rule to Northern Ireland is a clear indication that she does not recognize majority rule in Northern Ireland as democratic rule in the British sense. As British subjects they refuse to accept the obligations of British citizenship and adopt the rules of the British Parliament. Yet, on the other hand, they will only give the most grudging and qualified support even to the freely given consent of a majority for some form of unity. The inference is that they would stand aside, or would have to stand aside, or would even, unwillingly perhaps, have to stand shoulder to shoulder with the minority in their own community who would feel compelled to take up arms to fight the good fight.

Nor is there a genuine consistency to their position. McCartney can point out what he considers to be the obnoxious features of a Catholic state, and insist that these features of Southern society are unacceptable to Northern Unionists. And although he is careful to point out that even their removal would not make Protestants any more disposed toward unity, he implies nevertheless that changes in the South are a prerequisite for any kind of progress.

Molyneaux, on the other hand, is dismissive of constitutional reforms and the like:

> I don't doubt that a few Unionist politicians for their own ends do, as one of them put it to me, send signals down South that this kind of operation, the Constitutional Crusade on which FitzGerald has embarked, will transform the situation and all the rest of it. Well, within the limits of my communication with Dublin I've sought to transmit the opposite, and I hope more realistic, message: that the so-called reforms in the Constitution are good news for the citizens of the Irish Republic, but they won't transform the thinking of people in Northern Ireland. They'll simply say, "That's jolly good news, isn't it?" They're bringing them up to the same level of civil rights in the South of Ireland as we've got in the U.K. It doesn't make us — and when I say "us" (I don't want to use the word *majority* because that's simply equated with the Loyalist majority), I mean the greater number of people in Northern Ireland [who] simply won't say, "Now that they're on par with U.K. civil rights we'll jump out of the U.K. into the Irish Republic." That's not real. It's wrong-headed for any of them to imagine that they are going to make an impression on Northern Ireland.[15]

In fact, Molyneaux flatly contradicts McCartney's rationale:

> I've always taken the view [he says] that it's not for us as Orangemen to suggest that things be done differently in the South, because we're haunted by the specter that if you do break the influence of the Church in the South what will replace it? Will you get the awful pattern you get in other countries which were formerly dominated by the Roman Catholic Church and which have now gone completely Marxist? They don't necessarily become more democratic in the terms you and I understand it. This, I think, is a very real fear.[16]

More distressing still, however, is the fact that while the "authentic" voices of Unionism rant about the Provisional IRA, the complicity between Catholicism and Republicanism, and what they consider to be the covert approval given to the IRA by successive Dublin governments, they themselves raise the threat of Protestant paramilitary force to subvert the concept of a freely given consent in the North to some form of unity. In short, they want the South to give up its territorial claims, they want majority rule within the province, but they are unprepared to say that they would stand by the majority if the majority were to go against their wishes. They cannot — or will not — dissociate the position of *the* majority from the position of *a* majority.

Nor is there agreement among them as to who should be consulted on the question of consent. If McCartney believes that the larger unit — the United Kingdom — should become the unit of reference, then he must face up to the corollaries: a majority in the U.K. would rather that Northern Ireland not remain part of the United Kingdom;[17] and a plurality in the U.K. believe that unification may be the best solution to the problem.[18] Molyneaux, at least, is sensitive to what consequences would follow a U.K. referendum. In fact, he uses Paisley's call for a U.K. referendum* as one more indication that Paisley is after independence. Says Molyneaux:

> That's the only meaning of the proposal to have a referendum in Great Britain, knowing as he does that it would go against us — and I'm not being pessimistic, because in a referendum unless you've got the electorate very well educated beforehand on the issue, you're going to get a very confused result. And if you have a referendum you can depend on it that the three, four, or five million people in England of Irish descent are going to come out and vote while the ordinary Englishman is not going to bother to go out and vote on the future of what he sees as an obscure province of the U.K. which is a bit of a nuisance anyway. So it's bound to go against us. Paisley will then say, "We're being thrust out. I've done my best but they don't want us, so now we must go and do our thing, and I'm the only strong man to whom you can turn."[19]

Moreover, for all the apparent reasonableness of the presentation, McCartney takes occasional liberty with the facts. For exam-

* On 14 December, 1981, Paisley called for a referendum in England, Scotland, and Wales to decide the future of Northern Ireland. If Britain no longer wished to maintain the Union, he said, there should be an Independent Ulster. See *Fortnight*, no. 150 (March/April 1981), p. 10.

ple, the Protestant churches must share the blame for the denominational structure of Northern Ireland education. Even an eminent historian of Unionism has pointed out that while "the first minister for Education, Londonderry, had a happy vision of all denominations being educated . . . the 1923 Act completely underestimated the determination of the Churches to maintain their control over education. The Protestants set the pace. The combined organization of the Orange Order and the United Education Committee of the Protestant Churches virtually turned elementary schools into Protestant establishments."[20]

Furthermore, when the Unionist manifesto is put in the context of Molyneaux's, Smyth's, and McCartney's remarks — and these are the voices of "moderate" Unionism — something profoundly disturbing emerges. For what they are saying is that as a group of people, Unionists, who presumably consider themselves part of the civilized world, are opposed almost to the point of physical revulsion to the thought of any association, under *all* sets of circumstances, with the rest of Ireland.

"We have to ask," says John Austin Baker, former subdean of Westminister and chaplain to the Speaker of the House of Commons, now Bishop of Salisbury, "what it is that makes differences which in other societies can be tolerated intolerable here, even in contemplation. For what we have in Northern Ireland is the sight of one section of the people, the majority, saying to the rest, 'We could never live in a country where you were in the majority.' Now that is deeply hurtful, it is an insult . . . We have to be quite clear that this rejection of the minority, this sense of alienation from them as not sharing certain basic values essential to a tolerable society is the reason for devotion to the United Kingdom, not the other way around. The majority in Northern Ireland do not have such a wonderful opinion of the English or of Westminster government. They are simply evils that have to be borne lest a worse thing befall, which means, I would guess, that the rope which keeps Protestant Ulster from UDI [a Unilateral Declaration of Independence] is pretty thin, and might well in certain circumstances snap."[21]

And there is a second corollary. If Unionists find even the contemplation of an association with the rest of Ireland intolerable, how can they expect the minority in Northern Ireland to take even their limited offers of accommodation within a U.K. framework seriously? For Catholics to be in a position to accept Unionist "guarantees" that might make an internal solution work, the future possibility of an external association with the rest of Ireland must be conceded by Unionists, because if Unionists can only relate to Catholics when they form a permanent minority, then they do not regard them as equals. And if they do not regard Catholics as equals, no internal solution can work.

It is this inability or unwillingness on the Unionist side to see Catholics as equals that precludes them from acknowledging any dimension of the problem other than their own. McCartney can say:

> If anyone was the loser in successive Unionist administrations since 1921 it was the Protestant working classes. I don't see them as having benefited any more than their Catholic neighbors from Unionism. However, it would be quite wrong to take the view, as is commonly held, that the fifty years of Unionist rule were fifty years of misrule. There was a lot of misguided rule, but I don't think it would be doing justice to many decent but limited Unionist politicians to describe those fifty years as such.[22]

However, the Protestant working classes were marginally better off, if only in the sense that they "belonged" to the ruling class. Even for those Protestants who were close to the bottom of the economic heap, it was comforting to know that Catholics, as a class, were worse off. It fed the myth of superiority, of ascendency, of exclusivity. Hence Protestants — even the poorest — were in some sense "better." Again, any concession to Catholics threatened the marginal advantage of the Protestant poor. Making Catholics equal made Protestants inferior. Moreover, to argue the Unionist case on the basis of the Unionists' "identification of interest with Britain in peace and war"[23] and not to acknowledge even in passing that the minority has a similar identification of interest with the Republic in peace and war is an astonishing feat of ingenuous argument. If the people of the South are being asked to accept the Northern Unionist's identification with Britain as a historical reality and to accommodate that reality, should not Northern Unionists have to reciprocate, thereby acknowledging that they too must accept the minority's identification with the South as a historical reality, which in turn must be accommodated in some manner?

Contemporary Unionists may decry the Catholic state to the South, but they remain strangely reluctant to acknowledge the fact that Northern Ireland rapidly transformed itself into a Protestant state. James Craig, later Lord Craigavon, Northern Ireland's first Prime Minister, pointedly asserted in 1932 that "we are a Protestant Parliament for a Protestant people."[24] And Basil Brooke, later Lord Brookeborough, who became Northern Ireland's third Prime Minister in 1943, put the matter in as uncertain terms as possible when he remarked on one occasion in 1933 that "many in the audience employ Catholics but I have not one about the place . . . In Northern Ireland the Catholic population is increasing to a great extent. Ninety-seven percent of Roman Catholics in Ireland are disloyal and disruptive . . . If we in Northern Ireland allow Roman Catholics to work on our farms we are traitors to Ulster."[25]

And shortly after he resigned as Prime Minister, in 1969, Terence O'Neill, the "liberal" Unionist whose overtures to Catholics opened the schisms in Unionism, still saw the situation as one in which "the basic fear of the Protestants in Northern Ireland is that they will be outbred by the Roman Catholics. It's as simple as that. It is frightfully hard to explain to a Protestant that if you give Roman Catholics a good job and a good home they will live like Protestants because they will see neighbors with cars and television sets. They will refuse to have eighteen children, but if the Roman Catholic is jobless and lives in a most ghastly hovel, he will rear eighteen children on national assistance. It is impossible to explain this to a militant Protestant. He cannot understand in fact that if you treat Roman Catholics with due consideration and kindness they will live like Protestants in spite of the authoritative nature of their Church."[26]

Even leaving aside the gratuitous condescension of O'Neill's statement, the corollary posed a terrible dilemma. For if Northern Ireland did turn itself into a modern state in the Western sense of the word, and if the economic progress provided Catholics with jobs and resulted in a fall in Catholic emigration, might not the higher Catholic birth rate no longer offset by a higher emigration rate turn the minority into a majority? And if so, what then?

• • •

Underlying the Unionists' dilemma is the fact that they refuse to examine the basis, and more important the validity, of their own negative attitudes toward Catholicism. McCartney might say that "the Northern Unionist's or Northern Protestant's ideas are not religious in any theological sense,"[27] and define the Northern Protestant as the Northern non-Catholic:

> The Protestant's attitude on issues such as contraceptives, divorce, and abortion is on much more logical grounds, humanist grounds if you like. All of it is entirely irreligious rather than religious. They're not afraid of Catholicism or absorption by a Catholic state. What they are intent on is maintaining the social liberties which they have at present, which are in keeping with the social liberties which would be afforded them in the United Kingdom, in the United States, in France, or even in Italy.[28]

But the matter is not quite that simple. On the one hand, church attendance among Northern Protestants is higher than anywhere else in the world.[29] On the other hand, since less than half of the Protestants attend church at least once a week, the Protestant churches serve only as a *membership* group for many Protestants rather than as a *reference* group providing them with standards of religious behavior.[30] These standards are provided by the individual denominations within the Protestant umbrella (there were fifty-five denominations according to the 1961 census), and they vary considerably from one denomination to the next. In religious matters, however, sociologists have found that Protestants of almost all denominations do share common negative attitudes toward Catholicism, "especially in doctrinal matters or on the question of the authority of the priests."[31] The reason this generalized anti-Catholicism is an important part of the

Unionist's political identity has to do with the way in which the Northern state came into being and with the problems of national identity that followed.

Northern Ireland exists because no one wanted it.[32] Protestants did not want it (they sought only to maintain the Union with Britain),* and Catholics certainly did not want it. The South, of course, never accepted its existence; and although she was obliged to acknowledge its constitutional position in the Treaty of 1921 and was party to an agreement in 1925 following the demise of the Boundary Commission, which ratified the North's existing boundaries,† the Constitution of 1937 set the record straight.[33]

* James Craig, head of the Northern government, wrote to the British Prime Minister, Lloyd George, that "as a final settlement and supreme sacrifice in the interests of peace, the Government of Ireland Act, 1920, was accepted by Northern Ireland although not asked for by her representatives." Quoted by D. H. Akenson in *United States and Ireland,* p. 90. After the partition of Ireland, Sir Edward Carson himself lost interest in the cause of Ulster. See G. Bell, *Protestants of Ulster,* p. 38: "For him [Carson], the greater battle, preventing Home Rule for the whole of Ireland, had been lost. So he left Northern Ireland to be lorded over by others, in particular James Craig, its first Prime Minister." Carson himself remarked to Arthur Balfour, "It is only for Ireland that I am in politics." (J. C. Beckett, "Northern Ireland," p. 124.)

† The Anglo-Irish Treaty of 1921 contained a provision for a Boundary Commission that would consist of three persons — one chosen by the Irish government, one chosen by the Northern Ireland government, and a chairman, who would be chosen by the British government. The commission would determine "in accordance with the wishes of the inhabitants, so far as may be compatible with economic and geographic conditions, the boundaries between Northern Ireland and the rest of Ireland." Thus, the treaty, in Michael Collins's view, provided the "freedom to win the freedoms," since he felt that no commission could overlook the nationalist majorities in Fermanagh and Tyrone, and nationalist enclaves in Derry and Armagh. On the other hand, it seemed that the South stood to lose only a small area of Donegal that had Unionist leanings. The net result, he believed, would produce a Northern Ireland greatly reduced in size and essentially economically nonviable. The Boundary Commission met throughout 1924 under the chairmanship of Judge Feetham of South Africa. The Northern Ireland government refused to name a member. The British government, however, named one to represent the North's interests. When the London *Morning Post* on 25 November leaked the commission's purported findings, which would have resulted in only minor changes in the existing boundaries but actually would have enlarged the North's territory by adding an area in East Donegal to it, the South's representative, Professor Eoin MacNeill, Minister for Education, resigned, the commission dissolved, and its findings were put on the shelf. See D. H. Akenson, *United States and Ireland,* pp. 211–12.

The Ulster state came into being solely because of the opposition of Northern Protestants to Irish nationalism: negative nationalism had its way. According to the historian J. C. Beckett, Northern Ireland's creation "was an expedient created by a hard-pressed British cabinet which sought to keep two groups of Irishmen from each other's throats, and to give them an opportunity to live peaceably apart since they could not live peaceably together."[34]

But despite the agreement of 1925, the new state was accepted neither by the Catholic minority in the North nor by successive Dublin governments.[35] Accordingly, the words and actions of successive Dublin governments buttressing their claims to sovereignty over the whole of Ireland confirmed Northern Protestants in their view of the external threat of attack and the internal threat of subversion. The Unionist state became a state of siege. Unionists might perhaps be forgiven for feeling threatened when the "enemy within" willingly admitted to being the enemy within. The Nationalists did not want to be regarded as a constitutional political party: they had no central organization or local branches,[36] and the sight of Nationalist members of Stormont marching to Dublin a few days before the 1959 general election there to pledge their loyalty to the President of Ireland "in the name of hundreds of thousands of Nationalists"[37] must have convinced Unionists of the righteousness of their course. That righteousness demanded that all Catholics be viewed as subversives and all Catholic actions interpretated in that context; any compromise with Catholics in a political sense was seen as potentially undermining Protestant hegemony. The result: widespread discrimination against Catholics, especially for jobs and housing;[38] keeping their numbers down by keeping their emigration up;[39] stereotyping; and a society that put the utmost premium on spatial divisions, that developed along close communal lines, and in which religion became the badge of political allegiance.[40]

Not that the Loyalists are particularly pro-English. In fact, many have a strong anti-English streak; they regard themselves as British only in the most generalized cultural definition of the term: what Loyalism continues to represent is opposition to any move to absorb Ulster into a united Ireland. Allegiance to Britain is therefore conditional,[41] and to this extent the term *Loyalism* is a misnomer.

The conditional element of the link to Britain accounts in part for the ambiguity Northern Protestants have about their identity. Before 1921 there was, of course, no such ambiguity. All inhabitants of Ireland were Irish — and they were British. After 1921, however, the term *Irish* was more or less appropriated by the Free State, leaving Northern Protestants in particular in a quandary as to who they were and what they should call themselves. Whereas the people of Scotland, Wales, and England all readily identify themselves with their individual nations, Northern Protestants are far less prone to do so. In Ulster national identity "is a variable, not a constant."[42] The Rose Loyalty Survey* found that only 20 percent of Protestants regarded themselves as Irish, while 76 percent of Catholics identified themselves in this way; a plurality of Protestants (39 percent) called themselves British, compared to 15 percent of Catholics who described themselves as such. A significant number of Protestants (32 percent) described themselves as Ulstermen, but only 5 percent of Catholics made that association.[43] Protestants' predilection for regarding themselves as British actually compounds their identity problem because being British is not, of course, a nationality. It supplements a national identification, but it cannot take the place of one. It would involve being part English, part Scottish, and part Welsh. Moreover, there is a case for maintaining that British is the one thing the Northern Irish are not. By definition the United Kingdom refers to both Great Britain and Northern Ireland: while Northern Ireland is a part of the United Kingdom, it is not a part of Great Britain. Thus, Northern Ireland is not in the same category as England, Scotland, and Wales.

The upshot is that Ulster Protestants are a lot more clear about what they are not than about what they are. And because

* The Loyalty Survey was carried out by Richard Rose between March 1968 and August 1968. Thus, it was completed before the conflict erupted. Rose interviewed 757 Protestants and 534 Catholics. The results of the survey appear in Rose's book, *Governing Without Consensus.*

they are more unsure than Ulster Catholics of what their political identity is, they are more insecure about it and tend to compensate by feeling more strongly about it. The Rose Loyalty Survey found that Protestants felt more strongly than Catholics about their identification — no matter what identification they chose — and those who identified most strongly with a particular national label had the most extreme political views.[44]

One drawback of the Loyalty Survey is that it did not allow respondents to specify a secondary national identity. Group loyalties are not necessarily mutually exclusive; people may simultaneously have strong identifications with different social groups and with different nationalities.[45] For example, Irish Americans have no problem in thinking of themselves as both American and Irish; indeed, in many cases they are both more Irish than the native Irish, and more American than the average American.

Another study points out that "there is among Ulster Protestants a reasonably general, clandestine affection for the Irish label and a willingness to acknowledge under certain circumstances that the label is appropriate to them."[46] In some sense their reluctance to call themselves Irish may have more to do with their feeling that to do so would acknowledge in some way the Republic's claim to the whole of the island than it has with any clear-cut identification with Britain. In fact, the identification with Britain is often nebulous and ill-defined despite McCartney's claim that the Unionist is "psychologically bound to her with bonds of blood, history and common adversity."[47] The Rose Loyalty Survey, for example found that more than 66 percent of Northern Protestants felt that their co-religionists in England were a lot different from themselves.[48]

In Ulster, therefore, the question of identity, particularly among Protestants, is extraordinarily complex. Because they do not have a strong sense of political identity, they fall back on their religion for symbols of identity. And because they take their cohesion in religious matters from an anti-Catholic bias that is common to all their denominations, anti-Catholicism becomes an expression of a shared identity.

Partition, in fact, created two confessional states. To condemn the one — as Protestants are wont to do — without acknowledging the existence of the other, is a form of moral obfuscation.

• • •

There is no doubt in Harold McCusker's mind that the British would like to get out of Northern Ireland:

By and large the British people and politicians are moderate and reasonable, [and they] can't understand why all people aren't moderate and reasonable. And that's why they don't understand the Unionists, because Unionists very seldom are moderate or reasonable. And now they've discovered that most of the Catholic community aren't very moderate or reasonable either. Because if you hold strong views on Ireland one way or the other you're unlikely to want to compromise.[49]

That, of course, runs counter to the British approach to politics and life, which is: "Let's get by as easy as we can to our mutual advantage. And if that means that I don't get what I want and you don't get what you want, well, by and large we can come to a reasonable settlement."

However, since McCusker recognizes that the fundamental grievance of the Roman Catholic community "is that they are being denied their national aspirations," he feels that the British are confronted with a situation where they see that the only way they can remove that grievance is to "grant something which would create an even bigger grievance in the larger section of the community in Northern Ireland." In short, "to satisfy the minority they have to betray the majority."

Hence the British dilemma: since there is no reasonable settlement to the Northern Ireland question, they must come down on either one side or the other. Which means that either way they are in a no-win situation. McCusker:

You can't make a minority into a majority and give it majority rights, and you can't turn a majority into a minority and give it minority rights. Confronted with that conundrum, the average Englishman says, "How can we get rid of these totally unreasonable, totally irrational people?" And having tried for ten years to find an honorable settlement, the British now see disengagement as the only sensible thing.

But the wish is one thing, the reality of the situation another:

It's one thing to want that or even to want it and embark on a course to achieve it, and another thing to think out the implications of it and the probability of what's going to happen. In the long run they may be faced with problems greater and even more intractable than the ones we face today.

McCusker recalls going to see James Prior, Secretary of State for Northern Ireland, following the spate of killings in November 1981 and saying to him, "One of these days, Mr. Prior, we'll be coming up to see you to tell you to pack your bags and go home, because if you can't govern this province properly we'll govern it ourselves."[50] Prior's reaction?

He stamped one fist into the palm of his hand and he said, "I want to tell you now that I'll bring all the troops I need into Northern Ireland to make sure Northern Ireland stays within the United Kingdom."

This reaction of Prior's confirmed, says McCusker, what he already knew: the British want to get out of Northern Ireland.

But they want to get out over a period of time with minimum trouble to themselves and they want to hand us over to the Irish Republic with minimum trouble to the Irish Republic. And the thing that can prevent that happening would be for us to get effective control of our own affairs back into our hands again.

Although McCusker accepts that Northern Ireland doesn't have the same strategic importance it had twenty or thirty years ago, he believes nevertheless that "the sort of problems that could come out of the turmoil, especially if it spilled over into the South of Ireland, could turn all of Ireland into another 'trouble spot,' something neither the British nor the Americans nor the European community would want."

What the British will attempt to do, therefore, "is to carefully maneuver the situation over a period of ten or twenty years, which would enable the whole transition to take place very gently."

Hence, the essence of the Official Unionist Party's strategy, according to McCusker, must be based on the premise that "if Mr. Prior is so concerned that he talks openly about bringing as many troops into Northern Ireland as it would take to hold Northern Ireland within the U.K., then there's a fair distance we can push them."

Like every Unionist politician, McCusker unquestioningly accepts that even in the face of Britain's predilection to disengage, the "guarantee of Northern Ireland's position within the U.K." comes from "the confidence and solidarity of the majority in Northern Ireland to maintain the Union. Because as long as that majority wants to maintain that Union, it goes without saying that the Union will continue to exist. And that doesn't require Charlie Haughey or Garret FitzGerald or Mrs. Thatcher or anyone else to reiterate the guarantee to the majority."

Moreover, should Unionists become entirely disenchanted with Britain and decide to take their affairs into their own hands, the result would not necessarily mean independence. McCusker:

> The reason why it wouldn't necessarily mean independence is that I think the British government are so intent on holding on to us, and in this respect they would be strongly supported by the Republic, who would be afraid of the consequences, that it might be possible for us to negotiate a reasonable structure of government in Northern Ireland under the United Kingdom — not going back to the old Stormont regime.

McCusker accepts that there is no going back to the old Stormont, and he believes Prior understands that there is no going back to the 1974 power-sharing arrangements: "There has to be perhaps something between these two."

Above all, McCusker sees the need for some form of Assembly in Northern Ireland, because it would change the whole basis of negotiations between Unionists and the British government:

> At the moment [he says], we're invited up to Stormont like serfs to talk with their master, and if you had an election we'll be sitting there as the elected representatives of the people, elected to get something

done for them, talking with the British government. We're not doing that at the moment. We're knocking at the door, going in as beggars.*

Thus, one of the reasons he became such an ardent convert to devolution "was to get out of the position of always going cap in hand looking for something."†

But why should an attempt at devolution now prove any more successful than in the past? Were there not the same seemingly insurmountable problems? Yes, there were problems, but they were the result of misguided British policy. The British government had made demands on the majority that were unreasonable and that would never be met by the majority. McCusker:

If you talk to a lot of minority politicians other than John Hume, you'll find there is a far greater realization among them that there is no going back to 1974. They know that if they are to have a political future there must be some form of devolved government. If the most unreasonable demand — the power-sharing demand — were dropped, some agreement could be reached.

But on power sharing he is adamant. Not that he disputes that "you must give the Catholic community as big a share as you possibly can in whatever structure you establish." But that does not mean that "you can guarantee before an election that you're going to give anyone as a right a place in government, because the very people who are themselves offering a place in government to others may not be elected." What you must

* At the time McCusker made these remarks (29 December 1981), James Prior had not yet announced his plans for a Northern Ireland Assembly. The Unionists got their Assembly in October 1982. See chapters 11, 13, and 14.

† In fact, up until 1980, McCusker was a full-fledged "integrationist," espousing the position that only the full integration of Northern Ireland with the U.K. would solve the problem. The rationale for the integrationist position came from Enoch Powell, the former Conservative Minister for Health (1960–63) and M.P. for Wolverhampton S.W. (1950–74), who left the Conservative Party for the OUP in 1974 and was subsequently elected Westminster M.P. for South Down. The Powell logic: violence in Northern Ireland, especially IRA violence, is due to the uncertainty regarding her future constitutional position. As long as that uncertainty exists, the IRA will persist. End the uncertainty and the raison d'être for the violence disappears. Integration, he maintains, would end that uncertainty once and for all.

develop, therefore, is a structure that will ensure minority parties "a major role short of Cabinet positions." Accordingly, one of the things the Unionists had suggested was a small cabinet that "maintains its integrity in that it represents the majority viewpoint as expressed at the ballot box." Below it you would have "a mirror image in the form of committees modeled along the lines of congressional committees in the U.S. [but] weighted in favor of the minority and with chairmanships weighted in favor of the minority." These committees "could initiate legislation, and call the Executive to account." In fact, the committees would have "all sorts of almost Executive-like functions."

One reason for past failures to achieve a devolved government, McCusker argues, is that the SDLP negotiated only from the position of "the British government want the minority to be given power in Northern Ireland; how are you going to give it to us?" But Jim Prior was not saying that now. The British governments were now saying to the SDLP, "We are going to do our best to make sure that you get a fair deal." And that, according to McCusker, "puts the SDLP for the first time into a negotiating position. Now they'll have to negotiate a fair deal for themselves."

McCusker acknowledges an Irish Dimension, but for the moment he will not spell out what he means by it.

> There'll be an Irish Dimension [he says], but I'm not prepared to describe what I mean by that in detail. Once you had a parliament established in Northern Ireland, and once the Constitution of the Irish Republic had been amended to change Articles 2 and 3, the two countries couldn't exist on a small island without doing a thousand and one things to their mutual advantage.

Nor would he object to Articles 2 and 3 being replaced by a clause in a new constitution that expressed the aspiration to unity. What Unionists most object to, he maintains, is the way it's presently expressed. And if things were allowed to follow their natural course, then:

> If in the fullness of time those matters of mutual interest become more than that, it's not for me to judge generations to come. I doubt if

they could change me. But I'm not so pigheaded to believe that my children might not think differently. But that's the sort of time scale you have to talk about. And any discussion must proceed from both sides talking from a position of security. I don't lay any claim to the Republic. And I don't believe they have any right to lay claim to me.

Talk of unification leads McCusker to raise what he considers one of the key issues: the presumption that Britain would finance whatever new arrangement might be arrived at.

There is this cozy belief that Britain will go on bailing us all out in any new arrangement. Now if Britain does want to cut her links with Northern Ireland, she's not going to go on pouring one billion pounds a year into this island. And she's certainly not going to pour them into Charlie Haughey's grubby little hands in the hope that he will dispense some of it equitably into Northern Ireland.

You know this idea that for the first fifteen years Britain would go on maintaining — well, how would they do that? Would they write out a check for a billion pounds and send it to the Exchequer in Dublin in the hope that it would find its way back to Northern Ireland? They might believe that. But I don't. And I certainly have no intention of putting myself into hock to the gentlemen into whose hands it would come.

• • •

Thus the Unionist scenario according to McCusker: the British want out but the possible consequences — spillover effects on the mainland, and the prospect of the whole of Ireland erupting and becoming a major trouble spot on Britain's doorstep — mean that she will proceed judiciously, carefully trying to maneuver the situation to her own advantage. But here she may be caught in a double bind. On the one hand, the solidarity of the Unionists for the Union, even in the face of Britain's desire to withdraw, leaves Britain with no way of extricating herself without severely jeopardizing her other interests. And on the other hand, Britain would resist any hasty attempt by Unionists to go the independence route if she felt that that would damage her own strategic interests. Prior's threat to bring in whatever number of British troops it would take to keep Northern Ireland within the U.K. leaves McCusker in no doubt that for the time being Northern Ireland's continued presence in the U.K. serves Britain's interests. Furthermore, despite her posturing and rhetoric, the Republic would not be overly enthusiastic about having to deal with a Northern Ireland suddenly bereft of a British presence. Therefore, the threat of going it alone is a weapon the Unionists can use to hammer out an agreement that would keep Northern Ireland in the U.K. because — for the moment at least — the threat they would pose to Britain's national and strategic interests if they attempted to break the connection outweighs whatever advantages might accrue to Britain if she were to withdraw, leaving the irrational and unreasonable natives to their own irrational and unreasonable devices. And unless she could hand over Northern Ireland to the Republic on a magic platter, those perceived advantages might turn out to be a terrible — and costly — miscalculation. Furthermore, even if she did find that magic platter, which would, of course, take time, it was extremely unlikely that she would go on bailing out the island to the tune of £1 billion–plus per year.

Two potential developments endanger McCusker's scenario. First, an Anglo-Irish process that continues to evolve could facilitate Britain's maneuvering to withdraw, especially if the parties within Northern Ireland cannot agree on a structure of devolved government. Indeed, McCusker's remark that "they [the SDLP] know that if they are to have a political future there must be some form of devolved government" is in many respects a form of Freudian projection. Certainly it is far more pertinent in reference to his own party than to the SDLP. Continued deadlock on devolution will only attenuate the London-Belfast axis, and this in turn will automatically strengthen the London-Dublin axis. A solution within an all-Ireland framework doesn't necessarily require that the SDLP have a political future, but an internal solution within the U.K. framework requires that the Official Unionist Party have one, unless, of course, it is willing to concede its turf to Paisley.

The second potential danger is the time element. The more time Britain has to manipulate the variables to fit her own purposes, the less leeway open to Unionists; for the successful implementation of the McCusker scenario depends not on seeking independence but on being able to use the threat of doing so as bargaining leverage in circumstances that are less than propitious to Britain's strategic interests. Thus, the McCusker strategy is predicated above all else on Unionists being able to perform an exquisite balancing act. "We've got to have sufficient confidence in ourselves," he says, "that we can take a risk and turn it to our advantage." The risk with McCusker's scenario is the assumption that making out doesn't mean you have to go the whole way. Maybe not, but it certainly encourages it, and if they do go the whole way the McCusker scenario and the Hume scenario become one and the same.

Meanwhile, no power sharing with Catholics. The SDLP's unreasonable insistence on power sharing, abetted by the misguided policies of successive British governments, accounts for the failure to reach agreement on devolved government. Majority rule with committee chairmanships weighted in favor of the minority is as far as Unionists are prepared to go. And an Irish Dimension, tentative at best, could be considered only after the Republic repeals Articles 2 and 3. The "fullness of time" would take care of the future. Hardly the politics of compromise. And hardly surprising that McCusker would say, "The norm in Ireland has always been internal strife, and I don't see any end to it."[51]

• • •

James Molyneaux, leader of the Official Unionist Party, also has a strategy for maintaining Northern Ireland's position within the U.K.* His focus: the British Parliament.

When you ask whether Britain wants out [he says], it depends on what you mean by Britain. If you mean the man in the street who, in an unthinking way, if you were to confront him with a microphone, would say, "Yes, let's get rid of the lot of them," he would say the same

* Molyneaux is an integrationist despite the party's official position, which, of course, favors devolved government. He favors "administrative" devolution, an arrangement under which Northern Ireland would have an administrative body with participation by all parties rather than an elected parliament. In short, the Union would be preserved by promoting fuller integration with the U.K.

with equal enthusiasm if you had some kind of trouble in Glasgow. However, the people who really count are the people in Parliament who make the decisions.[52]

And when that is remembered, the questions of guarantees and the like become irrelevant:

Supposing that the British were to drop the guarantee and supposing that after a general election the British government of the day were to bring forward a bill which said, "We're going to detach that part of the United Kingdom which lies across the Irish Sea, and we're going to hopefully transfer it to the jurisdiction of Dublin," well, Parliament would simply say to the government, "You want your head examined. The majority of the people there [in Northern Ireland] have said quite the opposite — they've no intention of going, so we're not going to do it."

Hence the Molyneaux logic: since the guarantee only states the obvious — that the greater number of people in Northern Ireland don't want any change for the moment — the British Parliament will always respect the wishes of that majority, and that majority is not likely to change its position for a very long time to come, if ever.

But what if it does become clear that Britain is going to embark on a course of withdrawal? Would the Official Unionist Party consider a negotiated independence? It wouldn't be a matter of considering, says Molyneaux:

We'd be faced with a situation which would be created by the British Parliament being asked to do a most unlikely job, that is, enacting legislation to expel part of the Kingdom from the Queen's realm. That, mind you, would take some doing, because I can't see any Parliament being sympathetic to that kind of suggestion. It would have to be followed by other enabling legislation. It wouldn't be a question of negotiated independence. They don't have to make provision for Northern Ireland being able to run its own affairs or powers being transferred in an orderly fashion from Westminster to some body in Belfast. It wouldn't — and couldn't — remove us at one swipe, and it's very important for people to realize that, from the authority and jurisdiction of the London Parliament to the authority and jurisdiction of the Dublin Parliament. That's not on.

Since it would be a question of independence being thrust on Northern Ireland, there would be no question of considering options. Only one course would remain open. Molyneaux:

> We would then set out — and I emphasize we're only talking about a hypothetical situation — to see how the Unionist Party with all its experience in running the affairs of Northern Ireland would continue to do that.

But what about the new Anglo-Irish institutional structures? Might they not ultimately make the North less viable economically and more interdependent with the Republic? Might they not become instruments of persuasion, altering the will of the majority rather than allowing it to evolve naturally over time? And if so, what can the Official Unionist Party do about it? "You can fight it a lot of ways," says Molyneaux, "by exposing what's going on and especially by exposing to British ministers what's going on." He doesn't believe there has been any basic shift in the Conservative Party's attitude since the day in 1978 when Margaret Thatcher, on her third visit to Northern Ireland as Leader of the Opposition, reiterated in the strongest terms her support of the U.K. link, even going so far as to say that although it was the fashion to talk of a federal Ireland, it was a fashion her party did not intend to follow.[53] In fact, since the Anglo-Irish summit between Mrs. Thatcher and Dr. FitzGerald, "people in Conservative associations across Britain have been taking the trouble to write and the proportion is running about nine to one against what's going on." Which leads Molyneaux to conclude that "the Prime Minister herself hasn't basically changed her position."

What, then, has happened? According to Molyneaux, the villain of the piece is the Foreign Office:

> What has happened is that the civil servants, the Foreign Office, and the Northern Ireland Office, which contains a fair chunk of former Foreign Office establishment people, were determined even before Airey Neave was murdered that they would move the incoming Secretary of State away from what they knew was going to be in the Conservative Manifesto. Airey Neave himself knew that before he was murdered.

So it was easy for them when they got someone like Humphrey Atkins who was like a blank piece of paper — you could write on him what you liked — to turn him completely away from it.*

But could all this take place without Mrs. Thatcher's knowing about it? Molyneaux:

I think the answer lies in the fact that she has many complicated problems on her plate. For example, in the day or two before the summit, and at the summit itself, she could do no more than glance at the very complicated communiqué which was in preparation for eleven months before the summit took place. So, I think if you look at her words since the summit, once she realized what she had been let in for, you'll find then that she's retreating back to the genuine Thatcher.

But has not the present Secretary of State, James Prior, said that there is an Irish Dimension, and that this Irish Dimension has to be accommodated? Yes, but that is just one more example of Foreign Office jingoism. Irish Dimensions do not impress Mr. Molyneaux:

Humphrey Atkins said the same thing before him. But all that is Foreign Office language. This is the natural sort of thing they get up to. I mean, a Foreign Office official one night, when he was perhaps lubricated a little, said to me — not privately — he just simply said, "Mr. Molyneaux, you and I are intelligent enough to know that the only real solution is a united Ireland." Now, he was a fairly senior official in the Foreign Office. So it's not surprising that they put into the mouth of an incoming Secretary of State sentiments like "an Irish Dimension." I mean, it's Foreign Office jargon, isn't it?

* Airey Neave, the confidant of Margaret Thatcher, masterminded her election as Conservative leader and headed her private office from 1975 to 1979. He was also Conservative spokesman on Northern Ireland during the same period. He opposed power sharing, calling it "no longer practical politics," and urged the setting up of regional councils — a measure favored by the integrationist wing of the Official Unionist Party. He was killed by a car bomb as he drove out of the House of Commons garage. The Irish National Liberation Army took responsibility for the killing. Humphrey Atkins was James Prior's predecessor as Secretary of State for Northern Ireland. He served from May 1979 to September 1981. He owed his appointment to the post to the assassination of Airey Neave.

Look at Nick Ridley,* standing up one day in the House of Commons, making a statement on his return from the Falkland Islands and relating what he had said to the Islanders. If you shut your eyes and just inserted Northern Ireland for the Falkland Islands it would be exactly the same claptrap.

"I did beg them to acknowledge that there was an Argentinian Dimension," said he. "I asked them to recognize that Argentina was their nearest trading neighbor and it made sense for them to have economic structures which would have improved their economic conditions and so forth. I said to them there was no question of their ceasing to be British citizens. It might be that we would transfer the territory to the Argentines but then we would lease it back on a twenty-five-year basis, but they could be assured that they would remain British citizens for as long as they wanted to. But they'd have to remember there was an Argentinian Dimension."

They say the same about Gibraltar, don't they? "Now, for heaven's sake, don't go having referenda showing that 98 percent want to stay British, because that irritates the Spaniards, and don't paint Union Jacks on the rocks because Spaniards can see them from across the frontier, and do recognize that there is a Spanish Dimension. Don't invite the royal couple on their honeymoon to stop off because that too would annoy Madrid. You've really got to be reasonable, all you people."

All these three places have that in common. You've only got to change the name — the jargon is exactly the same.

The instability in Northern Ireland, Molyneaux maintains, has not been created by the IRA. Rather, instability feeds the IRA, and this instability is due to the policies of successive British governments:

The instability which we've had is a result of the shilly-shallying of the British government, particularly over the last twelve years, which has encouraged the IRA to keep going in the hope that one more push and we have them. And if you remember the IRA's one great demand, and the SDLP were with them on it, was in demanding an end to Stormont — well then, you can hardly blame the IRA for saying on the morning after the abolition of Stormont: "All right now, maybe

* At the time of this interview, December 1981, Nicholas Ridley was Conservative M.P. for Cirencester and Tewkesbury and Minister of State at the Foreign and Commonwealth Office.

if we turn the screws a little bit harder we'll get them out of the United Kingdom into independence. And from independence we'll get them into a united Ireland. Then when we have a united Ireland — goodbye to FitzGerald, Haughey, and all that lot; they're all Tories anyway — what we're going to have is a Marxist united Ireland."

In short, Molyneaux argues that British governments are the best recruiting agent for the IRA, because their inconsistent policies in the last fifteen years have appeared to leave the constitutional position of Northern Ireland in the balance. They have talked with the IRA. They have set up institutional structures with the Republic. And by appearing to be uncertain about what the future of Northern Ireland might be they have encouraged the IRA to persist, because from the IRA's point of view it's logical to believe that where there is uncertainty today, there will be capitulation tomorrow.

To deal with the IRA, Molyneaux insists, everybody must face political reality:

Everybody, including the Dublin government, must say, "Well look, this is the fact of the situation, the political reality is that that part of Northern Ireland which lies to the North is going to remain part of the United Kingdom, full stop for the foreseeable future. So let's all settle down and accept that." That would be the biggest blow to the IRA imaginable. There'd be nothing left for them to fight for.

Thus the Molyneaux solution: "The ideal way to solve the whole Irish question is for the South of Ireland to come back into the unity of the British Isles."

As regards that tiny minority of Protestants Hume and FitzGerald talk of, who see some form of a united Ireland as inevitable and whose numbers might be expected to grow given a "nurturing" environment, Molyneaux is dismissive:

They're fooling themselves and they're not facing the fact that a very large proportion of the Catholic population also wouldn't want a united Ireland. So they're not talking about just having to convert Protestants — they'd have to convert Catholics as well. Had it not been for the troubles, the hunger strikes and so forth, you would have found that year by year a growing proportion of the Catholic population, while not wildly in favor of the United Kingdom in the sense that the Shankill Road people would look at it, were saying to themselves, "On balance we're better off within that bigger unit of the U.K. than tied up with that lot down South," because you have to remember, there's very little common ground between Catholics in Northern Ireland and their counterparts in the South. I think that's a very significant factor.

But what of those Catholics who don't accept the Union, who want some form of association with the rest of Ireland? Molyneaux puts one question to them:

I've said to those Catholics who say their true interests can only be safeguarded in a united Ireland, I say to them, "Well, what privileges are you being denied in Northern Ireland which are enjoyed by your fellow Catholics in Great Britain?" Of course, they can never answer that. And how could they answer it when we've been under Westminster rule for the last nine years? I can't point to anything that a Catholic in Birmingham is enjoying which a Catholic in Belfast is denied under the same U.K. Parliament.

• • •

Thus, in the Molyneaux scheme of things there is, on the one hand, a harried Prime Minister who is on occasion the unwitting victim of the machinations of the Foreign Office and, on the other hand, empty-headed secretaries of state who are easily manipulated by the same Foreign Office establishment. There are no Irish Dimensions — only the language Foreign Office bureaucrats create to paper over irresoluble differences. Anglo-Irish frameworks encourage Foreign Office intrigues; they are an attempt to induce consent. Hence, Anglo-Irish frameworks should be abandoned. The future of Northern Ireland rests in the hands of the Parliament of the United Kingdom. That Parliament will never expel Northern Ireland from the U.K. as long as it is clear that a majority of the people of Northern Ireland wish to remain within the U.K. And if for some utterly unfathomable reason Britain did set out to expel Northern Ireland from the U.K., then the Official Unionist Party would take the necessary steps to make self-government in Northern Ireland a reality.

There would be no question of submitting to a link with Dublin.

The Molyneaux strategy: forget opinion polls and referenda and what the man in the street thinks. Pay attention to the workings of Parliament. Win friends and influence people in that arena. Expose the Machiavellian intrigues of the Foreign Office for what they are and how they complement the equally Machiavellian designs of governments in the South. And always remember: a majority is a majority is a majority. Which is why the Labour Party's endorsement of the unification of Ireland in the long term with the consent of a majority does not bother him because "they're simply saying — and saying a contradictory thing — 'Yes, we'd like a united Ireland but it's not going to come about in the foreseeable future, and we in the Labour Party have no intention of forcing the majority to change their minds.' So they're saying what we're saying: that you won't have a united Ireland in the foreseeable future because a majority of people — and by majority I mean the greater number of people — don't want it."

And what of the minority? They have nothing to complain of: they enjoy the same rights as Catholics in any other part of the U.K. In fact, Dublin governments should face the problems they would have converting many Northern Catholics to the idea of a united Ireland before they talk of converting Protestants to the idea. IRA violence would cease if both the Dublin government and the British government openly acknowledged what was obvious: there will be no united Ireland in the foreseeable future. "We stand for the maintenance of the Union above and beyond all else," says Molyneaux, "and consistent with that, we want a devolved government in a form that will not threaten the Union." Which means no power sharing. And no arrangements that attempt to impose an Irish Dimension.

Molyneaux's strategy is not so much a strategy as a set of assumptions ranging from the calculating (his belief that a British Parliament would find it traumatic, perhaps even impossible, to expel part of the U.K. against the wishes of a majority in the area) to the ingenuous (his belief that the Foreign Office establishment is somehow hoodwinking successive secretaries of state and, more especially, the British Prime Minister) to the inscrutable (his belief that there is no Irish Dimension) to the naive (his belief that the IRA would wither away if both Dublin and London agreed that a united Ireland was out of the question in the foreseeable future).

But the assumptions, whether valid or invalid, dubious or foolish, are only a smoke screen, for the heart of the Unionist case beats to a seemingly immutable tune: not an inch, not now, not ever.

• • •

There are ironic parallels: Fianna Fáil — moderate Republicans, at least by the IRA's standards — is unwilling to concede that the minority in all of Ireland may have even the semblance of a legitimate case, while the Official Unionist Party — moderate Unionists, at least by Paisley's standards — likewise is unwilling to concede that the minority in Northern Ireland may have even the semblance of a legitimate case.* The moderate Unionists praise — qualifiedly, of course — Dr. FitzGerald for the direction of his policies and are harsh in their condemnation of Mr. Haughey's. Yet there is no reaching out on their part to reciprocate FitzGerald's gestures. They appear unable to understand that their ability to persuade the South to acknowledge a British Dimension to the problem depends on their willingness to acknowledge an Irish Dimension. Their steadfast refusal to face up to the Irish Dimension no matter how persuasive the argument made on its behalf may, perhaps, be explained by their own insecurities: to concede an Irish Dimension is somehow to concede that unification is inevitable. Or it may be explained by the more deeply imbedded inconsistencies in their own position, for it is these inconsistencies that ultimately make their "case" untenable.

Consistency demands that they accept without equivocation the principle of unity with "freely given" consent, for not to do so undermines the rationale of their own most deeply cherished and often promulgated, albeit mistaken, belief: that major-

* Also ironic: integrationists also consider Northern Ireland to be a "failed political entity."

ity rule is democratic rule. Consistency also demands they acknowledge, without equivocation, that an internal solution in a U.K. framework can work only if they are willing to concede the *possibility* of a solution in an all-Ireland context, for not to do so reduces the minority to being less than their equal.

Robert McCartney says that the Official Unionist Party must

> get ourselves properly led and direct ourselves in two ways. First, in regard to our relations with the U.K., by putting our case properly, acting rationally, winning friends and influencing people, and convincing sections of the British political scene and the British public as to why we should remain linked with them. And second, by saying directly and simply to the South: "Look, our house is not for sale, it's not for exchange, and it's not for absorption. But we are content to peaceably coexist with you, and to enter into any such economic arrangements about roads, terrorism, in fact about anything which benefits us both, but without any institutional or structural ties."[54]

But if Unionists cannot envisage "institutional" or "structural" ties between the two parts of Ireland even after the repeal of Articles 2 and 3, then McCartney's further statement that "the Constitutional Crusade being launched by Garret FitzGerald is to try and create an atmosphere whereby the Northern Unionists will feel less besieged, will feel that the Dublin government is less antagonistic, and therefore Unionists can perhaps take a more conciliatory atmosphere where rational concessions can be made"[55] rings hollow. It puts the onus on the South to accommodate the North to the Unionists' view of history, while relieving Unionists of any obligation to accommodate the minority in the North to their view of history. It suggests that if the accommodations on the part of the South are forthcoming, well and good, but if not, well, so it goes. On the other hand, concessions on the part of Unionists may be made out of charity, or even to appease, but not, it appears, out of a genuine recognition that an internal solution can work only if it provides a context that accommodates in some manner the minority's legitimate sense of its own identity.

5

Paisleyism: A Question of Intent

Here in the narrow passage and the pitiless north, perpetual
Betrayals, relentless resultless fighting.
A random fury of dirks in the dark: a struggle for survival
Of hungry blind cells of life in the womb.

— Robinson Jeffers
"Antrim"

NO ONE, OF COURSE, took him seriously. He was a throwback, a raving, outrageous, somewhat uncouth religious zealot out of the backwoods of Ulster. He was the lunatic preacher, the simple-minded bigot, the often belligerent buffoon whose hell-fire fulminations were cause for amusement, good for pub conversation. His bizarre antics were sometimes repulsive, like his staging of a mock mass in Ulster Hall in 1959, or comical, like his journey in 1963 to the Vatican ("Harlot City" in his words) to protest the ecumenical council, or even embarrassing, like his illegal march on Belfast City Hall later the same year to protest the City's decision to fly the Union Jack at half-mast when Pope John XXIII died.

But today few are laughing, and none take the Reverend Dr. Ian Paisley lightly.[1] Of the major Protestant leaders who came to prominence in Northern Ireland in the late 1960s and the early 1970s, he alone remains at center stage. He brought down three Prime Ministers—Terence O'Neill, James Chichester-Clark, and Brian Faulkner. He destroyed the hegemony of the Unionist Party, which had stood as the sole voice of Protestant opposition to a united Ireland since 1892. And he claims, with some justification, to be *the* leader of the Protestant people of Northern Ireland since 1979, when he topped the polls for a seat in the European Parliament.

His success does not surprise him. Says Paisley:

> We are traditional Unionists, walking completely in the Carson mold, and in the Carson stand. The Official Unionist Party has changed its coat too many times. It has gone in for the denial of democracy in the power-sharing Executive; it has gone in for the Sunningdale Agreement and the united Ireland concept; it changes as often as its leaders change.[2]

"Traditional Unionists," on the other hand, do not change. They are loyal above all else only to

> the Williamite Revolution Settlement Constitution and the Queen, being Protestant. It's as simple as that. My loyalty is to the Williamite Revolution Settlement Act, which guarantees civil and religious liberties for all men, and to the Protestant monarchy because it has been seen, as the Act says, it has been seen that it is not good for a nation to be controlled by a Roman prince, whose first loyalty is to a foreign monarch, that is, the King of the Vatican, that is, the Pope.[3]

Hindsight, of course, lends insight, and on reflection it is not at all surprising that he should have come so far, for if Paisley had not found the Protestant people of Ulster, they surely would have found him. Ultimately, Paisleyism is a far more enduring phenomenon than Paisley. He is only an instrument, albeit a charismatic one, giving powerful, perhaps even exaggerated, expression to what is already there; he is the personification of the "fearful Protestant," the embodiment of the Scots-Presbyterian tradition of uncompromising Calvinism that has always been the bedrock of militant Protestant opposition to a unified Ireland. It is a tradition shaped by a siege mentality, and the almost obsessive compulsion to confirm the need for unyielding vigilance.

Fear breeds the need to justify it.

• • •

At its nearest point Scotland lies just thirteen miles off the coast of Antrim. For centuries Scots had poured into Ulster, intermingling with the natives, assimilating, and often becoming, as had been said of the Normans elsewhere in Ireland, "more Irish than the Irish themselves." But the Scottish settlements that took place in Antrim and Down following the granting of extensive estates there to the Scottish entrepreneurs James Hamilton and Hugh Montgomery in 1605, and the subsequent plantation of Ulster with Scottish and English settlers in 1607, were different. The Scots were Presbyterians of the strictest and most doctrinaire kind; the English, Episcopal Protestants. Thus, from the beginning, land and religion were inextricably mixed, and religion remained the barrier to assimilation because the colonizations took place in the wider context of the Counter Reformation.

Moreover, the colonizations were partial. At all times the new settlers lived in conditions of maximum insecurity. Surrounded on every side by a dispossessed and hostile native population, they were always vulnerable to attack. And since the settlements themselves were often scattered, the threat to survival was far greater. Insecurity and the fear it bred became a permanent part of the Protestant mentality.

First, there was the fear of being overrun and massacred by the Catholic majority. Then came the fear of what would happen if the Act of Union were repealed. Later it was fear of Home Rule. And finally, there has always been the fear of being abandoned by the British or sold out by their own.

Protestant fears are endemic. They encapsulate the entire Protestant experience in Ulster. They are so deeply rooted, so pervasive, so impervious to the passage of time that it is almost possible to think of them as being genetically encoded — a mechanism, like anxiety, necessary for the survival of the species.

No understanding of the Northern Ireland question is possible without an understanding of the basis for, and perhaps more important, the intensity of Protestant fears. No solution is possible that does not address them. Southern politicians, who all too readily dismiss Protestant fears as either irrational or something that can be taken care of in a new constitution, simply do not understand the nature of the problem. Nor do they understand that the continued insistence of successive Irish governments that unification is the only feasible long-term solution confirms Protestants in their belief that their worst fears are indeed justified. The constant references to unification as "inevitable" make its realization more unlikely. And they ignore history.

History, of course, is a question of starting points. For Gaelic Catholic Ireland it begins in 1170, for Protestant Northern Ireland in 1641, when the long-feared uprising by the native Irish to reclaim their lands finally took place. The reality did justice to the awful anticipation. Actual events overwhelmed the worst expectations, and when a number of Protestants were in fact slaughtered by vengeful Catholics, the myth of siege was reinforced by the myth of massacre. The massacres, of course, were exaggerated in the telling, but their extraordinary symbolic significance transcended exaggeration.[4] They became a vindication for fearfulness, vigilance, and distrust; they made paranoia necessary for survival.

The events of 1688, when the native Catholics again rose up to support James II, the deposed Catholic monarch, affirmed the lessons of 1641. They were reaffirmed yet again in 1798 with the slaughter of Protestants at Scullavogue and Wexford Bridge.[5] And in the nineteenth century, when the mass movements first for repeal of the Union and then for Home Rule took hold, the specter of "1641 come again" became permanently imminent because the granting of Catholic emancipation in 1829 ensured that either repeal of the Union or Home Rule would have a most deleterious effect on the status of Irish Protestants: they would go from being part of a Protestant majority in a U.K. parliament to being a permanent minority in an Irish parliament.

Presbyterians had added cause for a sense of vulnerability.

The Episcopal ascendancy did not reward their standing firm for the Protestant King, their beloved William of Orange. Rather, after his death, they too as nonconformists came under the constrictions of the penal laws, though to a lesser extent than Catholics. They had to pay tithes to the Episcopalian Church, they could not participate in politics, their marriages were not recognized, and their civil liberties were severely curtailed. Hence the steady stream of Presbyterian immigration to the United States in the eighteenth century.* And hence the special Presbyterian dilemma: in fear of Catholics and suppressed by the Episcopalian ascendancy, deeply distrustful of the one and deeply resentful of the other, the Presbyterians hewed to their own exacting counsel, the bitter divisions between themselves and Episcopalians reinforcing the bitter divisions between themselves and Catholics, and giving Presbyterianism in Ulster its unique characteristics and special exaggerations.

• • •

The exegesis of Protestant fears, however, goes deeper than the historical belief that the Catholic majority were always poised to rise up and drive Protestants from the lands they had settled. At a more fundamental level, Protestants felt the threat to their values of an omnipresent Catholicism that contemptuously rejected their religious beliefs as heresy, wicked in the eyes of God. Their fear was the fear of being submerged by and absorbed into a church that put man's relationship to his church before his relationship to his God.[6]

* The best estimates of Presbyterian immigration to the United States put the figure at two hundred thousand during the eighteenth century. According to D. H. Akenson, "In 1790 about one quarter of a million living Americans had Ulster Scots ancestry . . . During the early years of American independence, men of Ulster Scots descent were politically prominent. Andrew Jackson, James Buchanan, and Chester Alan Arthur were all first generation and all presidents of the United States. In addition, the following presidents were also of Ulster descent: James Polk, Ulysses S. Grant, Woodrow Wilson, Andrew Johnson, Grover Cleveland, Benjamin Harrison and William McKinley . . . In the atmosphere of prejudice which greeted the Catholic Irish immigrants (during the post-Famine years), the Americans of Ulster Scots descent who had previously not objected to being called 'Irish' took to calling themselves 'Scotch-Irish' in order to dissociate themselves from the newcomers." See *United States and Ireland,* p. 90.

These fears have not abated. Northern Protestants continue to fear what they perceive as the power of the Roman Catholic Church to control individual judgment, and the political power of the Catholic Church to manipulate events, peoples, and nations.[7] Paisleyism is the extreme manifestation of these fears: the Roman Catholic Church is pervasive, indivisible, clandestine, sinister, ruthless, perverse, and insidious. No intrigue is beyond her cunning, no duplicity beyond her design, no mendacity beyond her machinations, no corruption beyond her capacity. And though she could "paint her face and attire her face like Jezebel of Old,"[8] true Protestants "could still recognize the murderous wrinkles on the brow of the old scarlet-robed hag."[9] They are not deceived by her stratagems to entrap: she could "clothe herself in the finest attire" but they know that "underneath the gorgeous robes [are] the leperous garments of all whoredom."[10] At the outer edges, religious pornography masquerades as puritanical denunciation.*

The Papacy has a political constitution:

> Romanism is more properly a government than a worship — a vast and complicated secular organization including, under the style and externals of a devotional system, all the elements of a civil polity — a political crowned head, a statute book of political institutes called Canon Law, a magistracy of various ranks, decked in canonicals but drilled in diplomacy, and an indivisible police bearing the title of Jesuits or the followers of Jesus but in reality the followers of a set of maxims so well calculated to bring both subjects and civil rulers under the sway of the Pope, that at one period or another almost every state in Europe has been obliged to banish from its territories this army of conspirators against the independence of sovereigns and the civil and religious liberty of subjects.[11]

The Pope is the anti-Christ; transubstantiation, "a blasphemous fable."[12] Rome seeks nothing more than the "full recovery of the political and social status which she lost by the exercise of her intolerant and treasonable principles."[13] But the forces

* These vividly worded extracts are taken from the *Protestant Telegraph*, a paper Paisley helped launch in 1966. Over the years it has continued to be his mouthpiece.

of Truth and Right will prevail. "In luminous fulfillment of prophecy, 'the horns' [the civil powers] had turned to 'hate the whore' and 'to eat her flesh' . . . The spoils of a thousand years, the domains of priestcraft, the mansions of monkery, as well as her political dominancy, are fast disappearing before the retributive vial which is now being poured on 'the seat of the beast.' "[14]

Northern Protestants also oppose religious unity between Catholics and Protestants, whereas Northern Catholics do not.[15] Catholic support of ecumenism, however, is not surprising: Catholics don't feel threatened by it. Ecumenism is simply a way of bringing erring Christian brethren back into the True Fold. Catholics see it as requiring no compromises on their part, no theological concessions, no substantial doctrinal changes. In short, ecumenism is palatable to Northern Catholics because they do not take Protestantism seriously. There is One, True, Holy and Apostolic Church, and the others are the fallout of heresy. On the other hand, the attitude of Northern Protestants toward ecumenism reflects, yet again, Protestant fears. Ecumenism is one more stratagem to absorb Protestants and extend the control of the Catholic Church. It is something that would compel them to surrender part of their identity. It would pose unconscionable acts of compromise.

But when Paisley is asked about Protestant fears, he resists the insinuation. *Fear* is a smear word, implying *coward.* Protestants, he says, are not cowards:

I don't know what they mean by Protestant fears. I think this is an expression used by Roman Catholics and Republican politicians. I don't fear anything. I believe in liberty, and I'm prepared to fight for my liberties and I don't think Protestants are walking about in fear. I think the only thing Protestants are legitimately afraid of is a dirty, underhanded deal done behind their backs, because while we have the majority we have absolutely no political power whatsoever. We're in the hands of our English masters. And we understand they are not our friends. They would like to destroy us. So that's our only fear, but we're not wandering about in fear of anybody.[16]

• • •

He was born in 1926 in Armagh and christened Ian Richard Kyle Paisley.[17] His father, a Baptist minister, was a strict Puritan, noted for his vehement anti-Catholicism. But his anti-Catholicism did not extend to individual Catholics. His spleen, it seems, was eschatological, not personal. The father is remembered as a generous and warm-hearted man, despite his dour exterior and the fact that he was a harsh disciplinarian. The young Paisley appears to have been genuinely close to his father in what was, by all accounts, a close, happy, and often hungry family. Paisley followed in his father's footsteps, becoming a Baptist minister in 1946 and founding his own church in 1951. The Free Presbyterian Church now has branches in Northern Ireland, the Republic, Canada, and the United States. He also inherited his father's virulent anti-Catholicism, yet he too distinguishes between Catholicism as an institution and Catholics as people. From the beginning of his career he linked politics to a militant evangelicalism in the tradition of the great militant evangelists of the nineteenth century, Henry Cooke, Thomas Drew, and "Roaring" Hugh Hanna. Paisley's doctorate is an honorary award from Bob Jones University in Greenville, South Carolina, a strict Bible Belt college that forbids, among other things, interracial dating and marriage.

No one doubts his oratorical gifts or his charismatic presence. No one disputes his scriptural knowledge, or the excellence of his pastoral performance, or his impressive record of service as an M.P. on behalf of both Catholic and Protestant constituents. Bernadette Devlin found herself nonplused by the warmth, closeness, and normalcy of his family when she visited him in 1968.[18] The leading politicians in the South who have met him speak warmly of him as a person. The voice that is easily raised in demagogic denunciation of Pope or Prime Minister or peer is as easily raised in laughter. In the midst of conflict and in the shadow of cataclysmic civil war, one thing is clear: Ian Paisley is enjoying himself hugely. And why not? He is a member of the Westminster Parliament, a member of the European Parliament, moderator of the Free Presbyterian Church, and undisputed leader of the Democratic Unionist Party (DUP), which may yet become the largest and most powerful political organ of the Protestant people.* The back-street preacher has very definitely arrived.

• • •

Historically, two traditions emerged among the Northern Presbyterians. The "New Light" emphasized personal and civil liberties, religious tolerance, and equality for Catholics, while the "Old Light" emphasized fundamentalism, rigid, uncompromising Calvinism, the Pope as anti-Christ, the Catholic Church as abomination. New Light Presbyterians were drawn to the radical thinking of the French Revolution and to the United Irishmen, and for a time it appeared that an alliance between Catholics and Presbyterians might prove to be insurmountable. However, the Old Light was to triumph.

The issue that brought Presbyterian divisions to a head was the question of subscribing to the *Westminster Confession of Faith.*† The liberal Henry Montgomery, the personification of the New Light, opposed subscription, finding the document's description of the Pope as anti-Christ highly repugnant. The conservative Henry Cooke, the personification of the Old Light, demanded that all Presbyterian ministers subscribe to the confession. In 1829 Cooke prevailed, and from that point on Presbyterianism in Ulster moved toward an evangelicalism that is, in some ways, no less pronounced today than it was a hundred and fifty years ago.[19]

Moreover, along with the evangelicalism, which preached that salvation came through grace alone, there also came a renewed

* In October 1982 he became a member of yet another elected body, the Northern Ireland Assembly. See chapter 11.

† The *Westminster Confession* was a confession of faith of English-speaking Presbyterians. It was formulated by the Westminster Assembly, which was called into session by the British Parliament in 1643 during the English Civil War and met until 1649. The confession was completed in 1646 and presented to Parliament, which approved a revised form of it in 1648. When the English monarchy was restored in 1660, the Presbyterian confession lost its official status in England. Among other things, the confession stated that the sole doctrinal authority was Scripture, and it subscribed to the doctrine of predestination: "Some men and angels are predestined unto everlasting life and others foreordained to everlasting death." The confession was adopted by the Church of Scotland in 1647 and by various American and English Presbyterian bodies.

emphasis on fundamentalism, which looked on the Bible not just as the Book of God but as His literal word. And since the Roman Catholic Church claimed a special authority to interpret and preach the written word of God, Catholicism became an even more perverted and evil institution in the eyes of the evangelical fundamentalists. The difference between Catholics and Protestants was the difference between those who were saved and had access to the Truth and those who were damned and in Darkness.[20] There could never be a question of compromise.

This concept of "Protestant Liberty," dating back to the seventeenth century, has been pivotal to the aspirations of conservative Protestantism in Ulster for the last one and a half centuries. It is a religious metaphor for political action. There is a clearly identifiable enemy: a Roman Catholicism whose primary politico-religious aim is to crush Protestant Liberty. The defense of that liberty becomes the rallying point for opposition to a united Ireland because the Republic of Ireland is seen as the vassal of Rome — "Home Rule is Rome Rule." Says Paisley:

> Protestants love their liberty too much to put themselves into a state where there is censorship, a state where you can't have divorce, a state where even the elementary liberties of husband and wife are severely curtailed by the law. When one looks at the South of Ireland one can see the genocide that has taken place. When the country was divided it was something like 10 percent Protestants in the South of Ireland and now it's something like 3 percent. So you have a complete annihilation, almost, of the Protestant population in the South of Ireland."[21]

The Protestant perspective is, therefore, essentially religious.[22] Protestants are motivated in large measure by the fear of being overwhelmed by Roman Catholicism. Their fear of unification is symptomatic of a far more deeply rooted fear — the fear of religious and spiritual absorption, the fear of Catholic power. Paisley:

> The struggle to destroy Ulster Protestantism cannot be viewed in isolation. Ulster is the last bastion of Bible Protestantism in Europe, and as such Ulster stands as the sole obstacle at this time against the great

objective of the Roman Catholic See: a United Roman Catholic Europe.[23]

For many Protestants, any concession to Catholics in order to gain their support is a mistake, since concessions will not change the basic Catholic objective of unification. Concessions only weaken the foundation of the state. They set the stage for surrender. Paisley:

So, behind all the rhetoric and window dressing, we know exactly what our enemies want to do. They want to put us out of our own country. And we're not prepared to accept that. As far as Catholicism is concerned in Northern Ireland, Catholics don't want a share in the government of Northern Ireland. They want Northern Ireland to be destroyed, and to have a united Ireland. Their only agitation for a share in government is until such time as they can destroy it. Mr. Hume has said that it's a united Ireland or nothing. And even if they were to join a government it's only until such time as they can destroy the government and the state.[24]

Accordingly, the overtures Terence O'Neill made in the 1960s to Catholics opened up yet again deep schisms between liberal Protestants, who thought it possible to gain Catholic support for the regime, and conservative Protestants, who believed that any conciliatory gesture to Catholics undermined the very Protestant solidarity that was the backbone of the state.

Indeed, over the years whenever a movement developed that threatened to divide Protestant ranks, the hard-line conservatives were quick to point to the ever-present danger: Protestant divisions provided an opportunity that might work to the advantage of Catholics. As a result it was almost impossible to effect a division among Protestants no matter what the inner conflicts at work.

And there were many. The poorer Protestant who was invariably more opposed to a united Ireland than his better-off coreligionists was deeply suspicious of his social superiors. He neither liked nor trusted them, yet he had no option but to vote for them in order to preserve his independence from the hated Republic.[25] The dependence made him both resentful and fearful. In fact, there is a curious paradox at work. For though Catholics have had more to complain about than Protestants — having borne the brunt of the discrimination in housing and employment, having suffered the major dislocations following the disturbances of 1969, having endured a systematic exclusion from political power, and being in every sense of the term the oppressed minority — Protestants appear to be more embittered, more prejudiced, and far more fearful.[26] Their fears of Catholicism are augmented by yet another set of fears: the fear some Protestants have that others of their co-religionists will compromise their position.

The Ulster Workers' Council strike in 1974 brought the schism into the open.* The collapse of the ruling Unionist establishment became inevitable when one segment of the Protestant community felt that the ruling classes themselves were betraying Protestant interests. Paisley was both the architect of that collapse and the chief beneficiary, creating division on the one hand and taking advantage of it on the other.

The division and suspicions remain. And they have helped to give the conflict its insoluble quality. The Protestants of Ulster are probably more deeply divided today than at any time since the 1880s. No Protestant leader is able to deliver the support of his community. None dares to take his support for granted. Stepping ahead can mean falling behind. The collapse of the Unionist establishment has had a crippling impact on Britain's capacity to influence events. In 1969, she was, for the first time since 1921, directly determining the course of policy in Northern Ireland, and the Unionist establishment was powerless to stop her. However, with the collapse of the Unionist ruling classes and the emergence of a more intransigent and militant Protestant leadership, Britain has lost the power to enforce policy short of threatening either to cut off the flow of subsidies or to withdraw. The collapse of the Executive and the Assembly in 1974 made clear, for the first time, that the dominant feature of Protes-

* See Robert Fisk, *Point of No Return,* for a comprehensive account of the strike. Also see chapter 8, p. 317, for a brief account.

tant Ulster was the widespread support for the hard-line perspective.

• • •

Protestant fears are directed at Catholicism as an institution and a power in its own right rather than at Catholics as people. And though the fears are pervasive, they are to a large extent amorphous — 49 percent of Protestants, according to the Rose Loyalty Survey, could not name a single characteristic about the Catholic Church they disliked.[27] Thus, the fear of Catholic power rests much more on what is perceived to be true than on any specific knowledge of Catholicism itself. It is the cornerstone of Protestants' insecurities, supporting a host of lesser fears arising out of the artificial nature of their society, the teachings of their own religion, the perceived hostility of the world in which they live, the demands of the siege mentality, and the inherent instability of a society that has no social center of gravity.

The fear of Catholics as Catholics and Catholicism as an organization spills over into the socioeconomic area: Catholics are "disloyal," hence Catholics do not want to work; Catholic unemployment is part of a sinister ruse to overload the welfare system, thereby draining the country economically; Catholics consciously opt for high unemployment and high birth rates to subvert the state by depleting its resources. Catholics are "loyal to the half-crown but not the Crown."[28]

Protestant response to every Catholic action is reflexive: behind every Catholic demand is the intent to destroy the state. It entirely escaped them, therefore, that the civil rights campaign of 1968 was a middle-class movement demanding equal rights (in other words, full British rights) for Catholics. The tacit acceptance of the constitutional position was coupled with the demand for the rights and privileges it was supposed to confer.[29] Protestants, however, were conditioned to respond according to their own prior notions and interpretations of Catholic behavior.

And since for many any organized Catholic action had to be an act of subversion to bring about a united Ireland and the subjugation of Protestants by the Catholic Church, all previous

Catholic action having been for that purpose, their response was predictable: they behaved as they had been conditioned to behave when they felt threatened; hence their violence. This violence, of course, was seen by Catholics as a threat to their own communities; hence their counterviolence. But this, of course, was taken by Protestants as a confirmation that the Civil Rights Association was just what they had thought — a front organization for an armed rebellion planned in Dublin.

Protestant fears therefore tend to be self-fulfilling: the more Protestants behave as though they are threatened by Catholics, the more Catholics behave in a way that reaffirms Protestants in their view that they are in fact threatened. At which point Protestant perspectives polarize, the hard line becomes the only line, and Paisleyism comes to the fore. The source of its allure is its power to convince many that their particular positions depend on the maintenance of Protestant power, whether they do or not.

• • •

The ideology is sectarian. Its roots go back to the savage competition for land in the latter part of the eighteenth century. The growth in the population had gone from rapid to explosive, putting tremendous pressure on resources but especially on land, where rents were determined by the inexorable laws of supply and demand.

The awful economic conditions bred agrarian violence. Secret societies proliferated. In Munster the Catholic White Boys prowled the countryside, burning the homes and killing the livestock of Protestant landlords. In Ulster the Presbyterians used a network of secret societies, the most notorious being the Oakboys and the Steelboys, to keep Protestant landlords from raising rents.

The competition for land between Catholics and Protestants in Ulster became particularly excruciating because of a system of land tenure unique to the area. Under the "Ulster Custom," tenants had fairly comprehensive rights, including freedom from eviction so long as they paid their rents, and compensation for improvements to leaseholds. Accordingly, Protestant tenants in Ulster were better off than tenants in the rest of the country. However, when the Catholic Relief Acts of 1778 and 1782 permitted Catholics to purchase and hold leases on an equal footing with Protestants, that situation began to change. Catholics were eager to move into Ulster to compete for the land vacated by Presbyterians who had immigrated to America. Since they were more accustomed to a lower standard of living, they were prepared to bid up the price of land and accept a bare subsistence standard of living.

But Presbyterian tenants were not. Their secret societies turned their attention from Protestant landlords to Catholic tenants. The "have-littles" fought the "have-nots" along strict sectarian lines. Once more it was a question of land and religion in Ulster.

The Peep O'Day Boys, made up primarily of former Steelboys and Oakboys, emerged in the mid-1780s to terrorize Catholics, especially in Armagh, into moving to other parts of the country as they raided Catholic homes on the pretext of looking for arms, which Catholics were forbidden to carry. In response, Catholics formed their own protection society — the Defenders. The distinctive feature of both societies was their strict sectarian orientation. The Protestant society was aimed exclusively at Catholic tenants, while the Catholic organization retaliated exclusively against Protestant tenants in Ulster and, later, Protestant landowners in the rest of Ireland.

The paradigm was set. In the nineteenth century when the rapid influx of new residents, especially Catholics from the hinterlands, transformed Belfast from a Presbyterian town of some nineteen thousand residents at the start of the century into a teeming polyglot of some four hundred thousand residents at its close, competition for jobs took the place of competition for land. The sectarian rioting that ravaged the city sporadically — fourteen major riots occurred in one hundred years — had its roots in the brutal agrarian violence of the previous century.[30] The cleavages of the nineteenth century were reinforced by the events of the twentieth. Even today the main locations for sectarian clashes remain remarkably unchanged since the riots of the nineteenth century: the tradition of violence had bred an ideology of violence to justify it.[31]

The prerogatives of supremacy were guarded all the more jealously because they were so marginal. Hence the predicament of poor Protestants: while poor Catholics had an explanation for their situation (an oppressive and "foreign" regime holding them in bondage), poor Protestants did not. It was, after all, *their* state, and *their* government supposedly protecting *their* way of life. Since they could not take their rage out on the system, they took it out on the system's state-appointed scapegoats—the Catholics. And when the Sunningdale Agreement made it appear that the Unionist establishment was prepared to betray Protestant interests, "Official" Unionists also became the target of their hostility.

No one could be trusted.

• • •

The politics of fear is, of course, the politics of protest, and Paisley understands what good politicians everywhere instinctively grasp: it is easier to arouse people against something than for something. Only the enemies are real, and they are many: the Orange Order, the Unionist establishment, the Vatican Council, the Pope, the Irish government, the British government, the Roman Catholic Church, the other Protestant churches, and, of course, Republicans. To protest violence he has created occasions of violence. Time and again he has held up the awful specter of violence that would engulf Ulster if Britain were to leave. The fundamental tenets of undiluted Unionism are followed in all things: not an inch; no surrender.

He has opposed internment without trial, the Sunningdale Agreement, power sharing, the Common Market, and the Anglo-Irish talks. Why does he regard the Anglo-Irish talks as such a sellout?

Because the Anglo-Irish talks are saying, in effect, "We're working for a united Ireland." And then with a double tongue [they're] saying, "Well, of course, if a majority don't want it, it won't be." The majority don't want it. Mrs. Thatcher has now come to the conclusion that the solution to the problem is a united Ireland. She has done a complete U-turn. She has said over and over again that the problem of Northern Ireland is a matter solely for the people of Northern Ireland, her Parliament, and the people of the United Kingdom. Now she has made it a matter for her government and the government of Dublin. And everybody admits that. Of course, they denied what I said at the time: that it was all done in secret. But now it's out in the open and even all my enemies say, "Paisley was right; this is exactly what's taking place," and so it is.[32]

He has denounced British Prime Ministers Edward Heath, Harold Wilson, and James Callaghan and has branded Margaret Thatcher "a liar and a traitor." His tantrums in the House of Commons have shocked his parliamentary colleagues and the British public to the point where many believe he is more anti-English than the IRA. But Paisley is quick to make a distinction:

I'm not anti-English in the sense that I'm opposed to the English people. But I am certainly anti-English politicians — and no doubt about that. I utterly detest them. Because all we've had in Northern Ireland since Direct Rule is a bunch of liars. They won't tell the truth and they've been proved lying over and over again. I've said this to Mrs. Thatcher straight and plain: "Let's have the truth, Mrs. Thatcher. Let's have no more nonsense. Let's stand and talk the truth." And because I say these things I'm not liked. I am not a beggar with a begging bowl going to an English politician and asking for a mess of pottage. If anything, the British government owes to Northern Ireland more than we ever owed to them.[33]

He turned down an invitation to the royal wedding because the presence of the Catholic Archbishop of Canterbury, Cardinal Hume, would "undermine the Protestant foundation of our nation."[34] More recently, he condemned the new diplomatic relationship between the Vatican and the U.K. as "a direct violation of the Williamite Revolutionary Settlement."[35] And he objected vociferously to the visit of Pope John Paul II, the "anti-Christ," to the U.K.[36] He insists on closing public sports and leisure facilities on Sundays in towns where his party has a majority on the town council. Even here the fundamentalist perspective is at work: the belief that if Protestant sabbatarian values are not upheld, some implicit advantage somehow accrues to Catholics.

He is consumed with the rout of his "enemies"; they will be driven to concede that he, after all, is right. It is the role of the Prophet reviled in his own time, the Bearer of Truth who is mocked yet vindicated, a quasi-religious extension of the public persona. Paisley:

> They [the representatives of the minority community] hate my guts. Of all people, they would like to see my demise, so they have planned it in many ways. But they have found that while they have been able to destroy other Protestant leaders, they haven't been able to destroy me because I'm a man of integrity. I don't go by the wind. Nothing will move me from my integrity. Other Loyalists were prepared to negotiate deals behind backs in secret for their own political ends, and they all fell by the wayside. Of course the opposition has tried that with me, but they've found, just as the British government have found, that Ian Paisley cannot be licked or bought.[37]

The Big Man stands alone.

• • •

His success is due in no small measure to the fact that the politico-religious line he articulates feeds the siege mentality with massive doses of evangelical fundamentalism. The combination of the two exaggerates the worst features of both.

The positive commitment to the evangelical standard expresses itself through its negative counterpoint. Roman Catholicism is the enemy: it is inimical to the political and religious liberties of Protestants; hence Protestants must act politically to counter these threats.

> Victory for our enemies [says Paisley] would put us under the jackboot of priestly tyranny. To submit to Rome and Dublin would be worse than death. Better, therefore, to die fighting our enemies and battling for freedom than to live under a system which is in itself a living death.[38]

The failure of the British Army and the RUC to protect the Protestant community gives Loyalists a right to take matters into their own hands. Paisley:

If we cannot arrest the IRA and disarm them and they are going to kill us, we have not only the right but the duty to kill them before they kill me, my family, or others. That is my duty before God and under the law.[39]

He will not tolerate the forces of the Crown, misdirected by Sir Jack Hermon, the Prime Minister, or anyone else, to rob Protestants of the right to defend themselves:

The Chief Constable had better know and Mrs. Thatcher had better know and James Prior had better know that the Protestants of Ulster have no intention no matter what Mr. Girvan says — or eleven Presbyterians or umpteen ex-moderators or umpteen ex-Methodist presidents, and the whole galaxy of gartered bishops and archbishops of the Church of Ireland — he better know this, that the ordinary Ulster man is not going to surrender to the IRA or be betrayed into a united Ireland or put his neck under the jackboot of popery. He better learn that, and this is war, and so be it.[40]

Furthermore, "If the Crown in Parliament decreed to put Ulster into a united Ireland, we would be disloyal to Her Majesty if we did not resist such a surrender to our enemies."[41]

Loyalty to Britain is seen as the only way to preclude incorporation into the Catholic-dominated Republic. But it is a conditional loyalty and does not necessarily indicate support for maintaining the U.K. link.

The attitude is almost prenationalistic — a contractarian conception of obligation going back to feudal times. Subjects owe a conditional allegiance to their ruler. But when the ruler fails to live up to his obligations, the subjects are entitled to look after their own interests, even to the extent of taking up arms against the ruler to bring him back to his senses.[42] It is the message of 1912. Jim Allister, Press Officer for the DUP:

If Britain decided tomorrow to expel us, she should remember what happened in 1912 when Britain sought to expel the whole of Ireland.

The people of Northern Ireland not only said, "We don't wish to go," they said, "We won't go." And it paid off. So there's a message there: that the people of Northern Ireland have it within their power to say "We won't go." And they took action in 1912–13 that reversed the British government's attitude.[43]

1912. Nothing, it appeared, could stop the Third Home Rule Bill from becoming law. But Ulster Protestants would not have it; the Ulster Covenant was the signal of their resolve to resist. Nearly half a million men and women signed a declaration to use "all means which may be found necessary to defeat the present conspiracy to set up a Home Rule Parliament in Ireland."[44] The Ulster Volunteer Force was formed to give efficacy to the oath. Almost a hundred thousand volunteers enrolled. The army was disciplined, professional, and well-armed. The unwillingness of the British Army to move against the Volunteers precipitated the "Curragh mutiny" in 1914. The Home Rule crisis, it seemed, was veering out of control. Ulster could not, would not, be coerced into a united Ireland. Only the outbreak of World War I forestalled what appeared to be inevitable — either a constitutional crisis or a clash between the British Army and the Ulster militia. Home Rule was put on the shelf for the duration of hostilities. And there it stayed.

Thus, Paisley's reaction to the Thatcher/Haughey talks: a reenactment of "that glorious moment in Ulster's history," a walk in the trail of Carson, a call to Loyalists to pledge once again to use "all means which may be found necessary to defeat the present conspiracy hatched at the Thatcher/Haughey Dublin Summit to edge Northern Ireland out of the United Kingdom and to establish an on-going process of all-Ireland integration."[45] It may have been inspired improvisation, one more example of his inimitable capacity to seize the moment. Or it may have been an unconscious predisposition on his part to turn instinctively to what one noted historian calls "the only source of wisdom applicable to such circumstances — the inherited folk memory of what had been done in the past, both good and bad."[46] Or perhaps elements of both were involved. Whatever the case, the guiding principle was the same: when the future threatens, turn to the past.

As political theater, however, the campaign against the Anglo-Irish talks was vintage Paisley. He claimed with the modesty befitting the accomplishment that "the commission [to cover constitutional matters] was dropped following the opposition demonstrated by the Unionists of Northern Ireland through the Carson Trail campaign."[47] The fact that such a commission was never contemplated was of little consequence. The sweetest victories are victories over nonexistent foes; the larger the claim, the more beguiling its adumbrations.

The guiding principle of Paisleyism is total suspicion of any Catholic movement toward cooperation. Nothing is accepted at face value. Every Catholic action is part of a conspiracy to achieve unification, and where the reality does not bear out preconceptions, reality is simply rearranged so as to confirm a larger scheme of deception.

It is the politics of paranoia. Is there complicity between Catholicism and Republicanism? Of course, says Paisley:

> Everyone knows that. There's no doubt about it. It would be interesting to note how many arms, how many caches of arms, have been found in Roman Catholic Church property—both in schools and churches. A very large cache of arms was found in the Lurgan church some time ago.[48]

And is the Republic a Catholic state taking its orders from Rome?

> Very much so. Very much so. And the bishops are the strongest possible political lobby. And that has been illustrated in their history down through the years. I believe that even Garret FitzGerald called it in many ways a sectarian constitution. He himself said that. So, quote themselves. When your enemies say, "Yes, we've got a sectarian constitution," there's no need for an Ian Paisley to make any comment.[49]

Catholicism and Republicanism: the hunger strikes provided final corroboration of the collusion between the two, and of the church's prevarication on the issue. Jim Allister elaborates:

The Roman Catholic Church teaches that suicide is a sin. Yet not only did the various prison chaplains encourage the hunger strikers and give them full burial, but we also find that the Pope himself sent an envoy who, it has been revealed, brought with him a specially blessed crucifix for each of the hunger strikers.[50] *

And the crucifixes, malignant instruments that they were, assuaged the suffering of the hunger strikers, strengthening their resolve to endure, and worse still, they gave solace in the hour of death:

Now here was a man, Bobby Sands, who according to Catholic teaching is committing a mortal sin, and yet to comfort him in his death he was brought from the Pope a specially blessed crucifix.

The potency of these specially blessed crucifixes was brought home to Allister when he heard Raymond McCreesh's mother being interviewed after his death:

She was asked the question: "Well, how did your son face death? Surely it must have been a terrible ordeal." And she said, "He faced it in great peace, holding on his heart a crucifix that the Pope had sent him." Now, if that is not the Roman Catholic Church involving itself in the continuation of the hunger strikes instead of doing what it would surely do if it believed its own teaching and getting them off the hunger strike.

All the Church had to do to end the hunger strikes was to demand it, to say, " 'You're to come off the hunger strike, you're committing mortal sin, there'll be no last rites, no church rites at your funeral.' " Instead of that demand, however, "they got everything that is held dear by Catholics and they were treated

* On 28 April 1981, Pope John Paul II sent Father John Magee, his private secretary and a native of Northern Ireland, to Belfast in an attempt to dissuade the hunger strikers from continuing their fasts. Magee met with Sands, McCreesh, and O'Hara, but his efforts came to naught. Perhaps the real significance of his visit was the fact that the IRA and the INLA hunger strikers said "no" to the Pope.

like saints." The Catholic Church, therefore, was as guilty as the IRA in perpetuating the hunger strikes.

• • •

The politics of paranoia: when he lectures in the Bible Belt states where he has a reputation as a virulent anti-Communist, Paisley effortlessly switches from attacks on Catholicism to attacks on Communism, which is to many Bible Belt Americans what Catholicism is to many Ulster Protestants. But for Paisley there is no difference between the two:

> Both Romanism and Communism have absorbed the basic elements of pagan philosophy to bolster up their false and anti-God systems. Rome deployed and developed pagan ritual within the framework of counterfeit Christianity. Communism prior to the French Revolution adopted the pagan and pantheistic doctrine of creation. The resulting formula came to be known as dialectical materialism.[51]

Nor is there a difference between Rome and Dublin or even for that matter between Mrs. Thatcher, "the perfidious woman of 10 Downing Street,"[52] and the IRA. "Her goal," he charges, "and that of the IRA murderers is now one and the same. Both are in league with the ecumenical clergy and the evangelical compromisers."[53]

Thus the conspiracy: Rome and Dublin; Catholicism and Communism; Mrs. Thatcher and the IRA; each posing a threat to Biblical Protestantism, isolated in its last bastion of survival in a far outpost of Europe, and each, therefore, interchangeable.

• • •

He demands unquestioning obedience from his followers. Only he has served as moderator of the Free Presbyterian Church, and only he has served as leader of the Democratic Unionist Party. He exercises a degree of authority over church matters that even the Pope might envy.

In political matters he is both cautious and daring, but when the daring overreaches the caution he is quick to retreat. In

1971 he appeared to imply, to the amazement of many, that some accommodation with the South might be possible: "If the 1937 Constitution of the Republic was scrapped," he said in the course of a radio interview, "and if it came to be even that the Catholic hierarchy no longer exercised the power, influence, and control over the government of Dublin, then Protestants in Northern Ireland would look upon the Republic in a different light and there would be good neighbourliness in the highest possible sense."[54] The confusion among Loyalists that the remark evinced led Paisley to make a quick retraction. Less than a week later he was unequivocal on his position in the *Protestant Telegraph.* It was "no" to a united Ireland, then, now, and forever. In 1977 he called a general strike to protest security measures, vowing to retire from public life if the strike was not a success. It was not. He, however, simply walked away from the debacle, declaring himself well satisfied with the results. He has a gift for stunts and an adman's felicity for catch phrases: Carson Trail, Days of Action, Third Force.*

He attracts others to violence yet is careful to separate himself from it. While he attacks institutions, or persons as the figureheads of institutions, his less discriminating followers often retaliate against persons as individuals. In one celebrated case when members of the present-day Ulster Volunteer Force (UVF) were charged with the murder of a Catholic, one allegedly told police, "I am sorry I ever heard of that man Paisley or decided to follow him."[55] His Third Force — with its emphasis on mass parades, the display of arms, and the intimidating paraphernalia of neofascism — took Northern Ireland one step closer to the brink. His

* The Carson Trail was the name Paisley gave to the demonstrations he called for after the first Anglo-Irish summit. His itinerary followed that of Sir Edward Carson's in 1912. The Day of Action was the name he gave to the demonstration he called for on 23 November 1981 to protest the second Anglo-Irish summit. Following Robert Bradford's death, it became an expression of Unionist opposition to what Unionists considered to be the government's inadequate security policies. The Third Force was the name he gave to the paramilitary group that materialized following the second Anglo-Irish summit. According to Richard Clutterbuck (in *Protest and the Urban Guerilla*), "In almost all countries except Britain there is a 'Third Force' — that is, a paramilitary force as a bridge between the police and the Army — especially designed, trained, and equipped for riot control and sometimes for additional duties such as disaster relief." (p. 35.)

actions often suggest that he may not yet know where he is going. And even if he does, it is clear that he has no plan, no carefully formulated political strategy. But he will always be seen to be doing something, his sense of the opportunity dictating the intensity of his response. And though his actions may often seem contradictory and even confusing, there is, nevertheless, an underlying consistency, the consistency that comes from the knowledge that he, too, is a hostage to Paisleyism. If he were to forget that, he would in all likelihood find himself in the company of the political opponents he has so thoroughly discredited.

• • •

What does Paisley want? Only to save the Union, he maintains. Nonsense, maintain his "enemies," it's power he's after. For Daithi O'Conaill, leading IRA strategist and currently a vice president of Provisional Sinn Féin, the movement's political wing, there is no uncertainty:

> Power. Power is the name of the game for Paisley. He's a power-hungry person. He's consistently advanced from one policy to another, and if you look at the state of play at the moment, he's at the point of eliminating Molyneaux, just as he eliminated Faulkner, Chichester-Clark, and Terence O'Neill. They all fell before his blunt, rash approach. He's been expert at exploiting the beliefs of Protestant people, at engendering fears among them. Basically, the way I see Paisley is as a fascist out and out, an arch manipulator who has no qualms about offending the British on his road towards absolute power.[56]

However, O'Conaill insists in very measured tones that Paisley is unlikely at this point to become a target of the IRA:

> There has been a belief for a long time that Ian Paisley has helped expose the whole rotten mess of the Six-County state. He brought home to the people of Ireland that the thing was artificial and corrupt, and internationally he has done the same. The recognition has been there that Paisley in his own idiotic way has helped the Republican cause by exposing the fascist nature of Loyalist ideology — that recognition has been there for a long time.[57]

On occasion Paisley's objectives appear to coincide with the IRA's. When he launched the Third Force with a vow to make Northern Ireland ungovernable, he was echoing the IRA's often-repeated sentiments. O'Conaill: "The thing is, whether Paisley knew it or not he was playing into the hands of the IRA in that he was helping to destabilize the Six-County state."[58] John McMichael, spokesman for the Protestant paramilitary Ulster Defence Association, agrees: "Ian Paisley makes himself out to be a target of the Provisional IRA or INLA [Irish National Liberation Army]. But they wouldn't shoot him for two million pounds. Because he's worth millions in propaganda."[59]

Paisley, of course, scoffs at the charge, and insists that the IRA would like to see him dead:

Well, David O'Connell [Daithi O'Conaill] is an IRA spokesman who has planned the killing of Protestant people, and who now is, of course, identified with the murder of Robert Bradford because of his IRA connections. I would say that as far as I'm concerned this is just smear propaganda that is put out by the liars of the IRA. The Republicans have tried to murder me. I was shot at by the INLA just recently in an ambush. So to say they are loath to kill me is, of course, an absolute lie. As far as "ungovernable" is concerned, I made it perfectly clear that what I meant by that was not anarchy but was to make it impossible for the Queen's ministers to properly govern Northern Ireland — and we have done that. We have brought to a standstill every District Council in Northern Ireland. And the Ministers have been told, "You're not welcome in these towns." And what the Ministers are doing [is] jumping about secretly from place to place. Well, if that's the way you govern a country when those who should be in control of the country are jumping here and jumping there, not prepared to tell where they're going because of protests, when they've been thrown out of Council meetings as they have been, thrown out of board meetings and their lives made absolutely unbearable, well, that's what I mean by making this country ungovernable.

I don't believe in anarchy. I believe in keeping the law. I believe in respecting the forces of the law. The IRA knows perfectly well, and they made it perfectly clear when the Third Force came into existence that they saw it as the greatest threat to its existence. And it ill-becomes a spokesman for the IRA, like David O'Connell, to say that I and the

Third Force are doing their work. I mean, that's an absolute and blatant lie — and everybody knows that. It's the joke of the century.[60]

Perhaps. But it's clear nevertheless that the Provisional IRA and Paisley feed off each other. Republican terrorism begets Loyalist fascism; fascism in turn begets terrorism. Paisley's rantings, his hooded and well-armed Third Force paramilitaries, his threats to answer murder with murder arouse the fears of Catholics and legitimize the IRA as the protector of the minority. Each spate of IRA killings, on the other hand, legitimizes Paisley's calls for retribution, for meeting fire with fire, and this in turn fuels the fears of Catholics. Thus, the more successful the IRA is in getting Protestants to retaliate for the murder of Protestant members of the security forces by killing Catholics, the more inexorable the slide toward sectarian civil war, and the more ungovernable Northern Ireland becomes.

James Molyneaux, leader of the Official Unionist Party, doesn't see Paisley as "idiotic." On the contrary:

I think it's part of a plan on Paisley's part, no matter what he says about the Union, to weaken the Union by presenting the British people with the unacceptable face of Unionism, the unacceptable face of Protestantism. So it's not as much of an accident as O'Conaill might imagine.[61]

And the objective? "Well, he's after independence, quite clearly." [62]

• • •

He is a huge man: the physical proportions displace; he expands to fill the space available. He is affable and businesslike; his replies are unhesitating.

Is Britain trying to get out of Northern Ireland? Of course they are: "I accept that. I've been saying that for years, but the pundits wouldn't believe me. But they're believing me now."[63] Northern Ireland has no option but for one, to remain within the United Kingdom. But what if Britain were saying, "We're trying to kick you out"? Paisley: "Well, we just say to

Britain, 'Try it.' That's all we're saying: 'Try it.' " What about Mr. Molyneaux's opinion that he, Paisley, wanted an independent Northern Ireland?

Well, I didn't know Mr. Molyneaux had made that statement, and if he has I would severely rebuke him. Because I have never toyed with the idea of an independent Ulster. His party has been riddled with people who have toyed with that idea. It's Mr. Molyneaux's party which has gone for independence, not the Democratic Unionists. The Democratic Unionists have always been rock-solid on the Union. We're going to remain completely within the United Kingdom. We have no options but one: and that is to remain within the United Kingdom. We're not in any way flirting with an independent Ulster. We don't discuss it. We're not considering it. And that's it. And that has always been our position.

Why, then, would Mr. Molyneaux made such an allegation? "Because we licked them so effectively at the ballot box. In the last Council elections we beat the Official Unionists two to one in their own territory."

Since he is adamantly opposed to power sharing, insisting on the rule of majority, how would he react if 51 percent of the people of Northern Ireland in a free and open election opted for some form of unification with the South? Could he go along with that decision?

Well, I happen to be a democrat. And I believe in the rule of the majority. And I would say that if the majority of the people in Northern Ireland want to become part of the Republic, well, as far as I'm concerned, that's it. I would, of course, in those circumstances, do my best to protect the interests of the people that I represent. But I mean I'm a democrat, and if that's what happens in Northern Ireland at any time I've got to accept that.

What faith has he in the British government's guarantee not to change the constitutional position of Northern Ireland without the consent of a majority? Paisley:

There is no use people talking about a guarantee. The only guarantee in this country is the strength and will and might of the majority. You can have a majority in a country but if you don't have the will, the courage, and the might, it's finished. The message now to the British government is that the Protestant majority have had enough. We're not having any more. The fact is coming more and more clear that the IRA will only listen, and will only take heat from the Protestants when Protestants show their determination to resist them. Since the Third Force came into existence there has been a complete lull in the whole terrorist activity of Northern Ireland. Why is that? Because the IRA realize that while they can take on the British, and can take on the security forces with their hands handcuffed behind their backs, they can't take on the whole Protestant population.

Would he talk with political leaders in the Republic? "Well, I wouldn't be talking to them as long as they claim jurisdiction over Northern Ireland, which I don't think I need worry about." And if they weren't claiming jurisdiction?

I would only talk to them in the way the leaders of the Stormont government in the past talked to leaders of the South — and that was to do with matters that would help us in Northern Ireland — we talked about the Northern railway. We talked about the Northern drainage scheme, electricity, and so on and so forth. But that's departmental. I've no ambitions as an elected leader of Northern Ireland to talk to the leaders of the South. We're poles apart. There's no such thing as reconciliation. When you marry Christ to Beelzebub, then we'll be ready for talks with them. We're poles apart.

Garret FitzGerald has launched a crusade to repeal Articles 2 and 3 of the Republic's Constitution. Is this a move in the right direction?

I think he destroyed his credibility when he said it was done to get a united Ireland. I don't care what constitution they've got in the South — there's not going to be a united Ireland. What people don't realize is that when this island was divided in 1920, the constitution of the South was the same as the constitution of Stormont. Our forefathers wouldn't accept a united Ireland under a constitution similar to Stormont. So it's hardly likely that we're going to accept a united Ireland under a constitution which would really only be a revamping of the 1937 Constitution.

What does he think of Cardinal O'Fiaich? "He comes from Crossmaglen. You can take him out of Crossmaglen, but you can't take Crossmaglen out of him."*

Many would say that Paisley's concepts of morality as they relate to pornography, homosexuality, divorce, and so forth are really close to Catholic concepts:

I don't accept that. I accept that the concepts I have are Biblical concepts and I don't accept that the Roman Catholic Church takes a strong stand on some of them. There wasn't a squeak of protest from the Roman Catholic Church in regard to the sodomy bill, which the government tried to put through the House of Commons to legalize homosexuality in Northern Ireland. The SDLP backed that sodomy bill. My morality stems from the Bible. If the Church of Rome agrees with the concept of Biblical morality, well and good, although I would very much doubt it.

How about Paisley versus Paisleyism? In his absence would the Democratic Unionist Party continue to thrive?

If I was removed? Yes, if I was removed the people wouldn't change their minds. The DUP will continue to battle even if I were removed tomorrow. I think the IRA probably knows that. They might, of course, let me say, get a rougher leader. I mean, I'm a very tolerant man, and have been prepared to negotiate and I've told the British government, "You should be very happy that I happen to be the leader of the Ulster people because you could get a worse figure who wouldn't tolerate." And I happen to be a pledged democrat. That's the only thing that the British government better get, that message, that they've a democrat at the moment. But maybe if they get rid of the democrat they might find a far different type of leadership.

• • •

* Cardinal Tomas O'Fiaich, Archbishop of Armagh and Primate of All Ireland, became spiritual leader of Ireland's 3.5 million Catholics in 1977. He has spoken out strongly on Northern Ireland, condemning the violence on every side. He made several forceful statements during the hunger strikes. (See chapter 7, p. 270.) Paisley makes the reference to Crossmaglen because O'Fiaich was born in Northern Ireland near the South Armagh village of one thousand that is just four miles from the Border. The area has a long history of militant support for the IRA.

"We just say to Britain: 'Try it.' That's all we're saying: 'Try it' ": the statement speaks for the man, the blend of challenge and defiance suggesting a redoubtable presence, insinuating the expectation of excess. His shrewd assessment that Britain's unwillingness to confront the Northern Ireland issue head-on undermines her willingness to take risks impels him to take more risks to reinforce her unwillingness. His intuitive understanding that Britain's knowledge of her own actual weakness outweighs her estimate of his potential strength gives him a scintilla of advantage he adroitly exploits.

The illusion of power is as important as power itself. The appearance of irrational action — the midnight maneuvers on the mountainsides of County Antrim; the shrill, almost hysterical reaction to the Anglo-Irish summits; the torrents of abuse heaped on Westminster; the Carson Trail, with its threat of treason; the ring of plangent invective on his Day of Action — gives his opponents pause. If small changes, or the appearance of change, or even the absence of change, can provoke such frenzied responses, might not a real change or the appearance of a major change provoke an uncontrollable backlash? Thus, by overreacting to small things, Paisley is ensuring that he will not have to react to bigger things because his opponents dare not take the risk of incurring his wrath. And to this extent his power is an illusion resting on the assumption that he could bring about the nightmare he so vividly paints. It is, of course, an untested assumption — bluff, perhaps, but as yet no one has been willing to call his hand. The possible price remains greater than the anticipated benefits.

He has no options. His tactics are necessarily negative and uncompromising. Absolute positions cannot appear to be less than absolute, otherwise they are not positions at all. "No surrender" cannot accommodate "not too much surrender." "Not an inch" cannot subsume "no more than an inch." "No" to a united Ireland means no under all circumstances, notwithstanding his agreement to some form of unification if that were the wish of a majority. That agreement is easily given because he does not believe it will ever happen, or at least "not until Christ shall marry Beelzebub." But it makes him look good, consistent in his adherence to the primacy of the ballot box: he is, after all, a democrat, and 51 percent should have their say no matter what the circumstances; majority rule is democratic rule, and so on. But though the agreement is easily given, there are implied caveats: he would, of course, have to protect the interests of the people he represents; and even if a majority might want to opt out of the Union, he would, nevertheless, reserve his democratic right to fight for the Union. And therein lies the contradiction. For if that is his position, the criticisms he now levels at the minority, which reserves its democratic right to fight for a united Ireland, are criticisms he might yet have to level at himself. He is not disconcerted: circumstances are always paramount — when in the majority, demand the rights of the majority; when in the minority, insist on the rights of the minority.

The Paisley strategy, therefore, is not a strategy at all. It is pure improvisation backed up by one of the best political organizations in Ulster. In the short run Paisley wants to establish himself as the undisputed head of Protestantism in Ulster. Hence his predilection for elections, since every percentage point his party gains on the Official Unionist Party, the more valid his claim to speak for all and the less valid his opponents' claim that he does not represent the authentic voice of political Protestantism.

The authentic voice of political Protestantism is not, of course, the authentic voice of Unionism. Although the two coexist, they are antithetical; the one can only flourish at the expense of the other. But the fact that they do coexist, if only uneasily and not without a degree of mutual dependence, may account for the volatile interplay of conflicting tensions that is the hallmark of Loyalism today. The psychology of political Protestantism, which is intent on keeping Northern Ireland out of a united Ireland at all costs, is quite different, antagonistic even, to the psychology of Unionism, which is intent on keeping Northern Ireland within the United Kingdom at all costs.

Were a complete union of Northern Ireland and Britain to take place, leading to the full integration of Ulster with the rest of the United Kingdom, political Protestantism would lose its raison d'être and disintegrate. For Protestantism to exist as a political force, Northern Ireland must exist as a state.[64] Integration, of course, would settle the question of unification once and for all, thereby vitiating the rationale behind the campaign to keep Northern Ireland out of the Republic. Without that rationale there would be neither the need of nor a place for political Protestantism. Accordingly, to the extent that only Britain is in a position to bring about an end to the state of Northern Ireland, she is responsible for political Protestantism — Paisleyism in its present manifestation — and, therefore, the acts it commits in the name of the Union. And to the extent that only the Republic's insistence on the inevitability of a united Ireland perpetuates the raison d'être of Paisleyism, she too, paradoxically, is also responsible for political Protestantism, and, therefore, the acts it commits in the name of non-Union.

But if Paisley were intent beyond any other consideration on maintaining the Union, he would press for full integration, despite the fact that integration would erode the source of his own power. The loss of power would be a small price to pay for achieving so cherished a goal. Furthermore, the fairly obvious fact that integration will never happen would appear to make calling for it more attractive politically, since the position would command the advantages that come from being on the "right" side without having to incur the disadvantages success would bring, unless, of course, the act of championing the position put obstacles in the way of a more cherished goal — the consolidation of Protestant power. Which may explain why Paisley put the integration platform behind him a long time ago, well before his own vertiginous climb to the pinnacle.

The consolidation of Protestant political power, however, is just a first step; the second calls for a forum in which that power might express itself. Hence his railing against Direct Rule and his insistence on a simple majority-rule Stormont government. Direct Rule is inimical to Protestant interests; therefore Direct Rule must go, despite the fact that Direct Rule fosters closer links between Northern Ireland and the U.K. than any other form of government aside from integration.

Direct Rule is one more bogeyman: all kinds of malaises are laid at its doorstep. It is responsible for the woeful economic conditions, the inadequate security measures, and the devious concoctions of Dublin and Westminster. Putting the reins of government back into the hands of the people of Northern Ireland will miraculously cure the assorted woes. The nomenclature "the people of Northern Ireland" is, of course, an exclusive term, strictly Protestant in connotation: when Catholics behave like good Protestants, good government will prevail. However, the preservation of the link with Britain is not sufficient to appease political Protestantism. The organism must have its own government, else it will perish: it must have independence within the protective framework of the United Kingdom.

But there is a more pressing need for a devolved government. Should Westminster decide at some point to legislate Northern Ireland out of the U.K. or should Loyalists themselves opt for a Unilateral Declaration of Independence (UDI), establishing an independent Northern Ireland would be a far more viable proposition if much of the apparatus of government was already in the hands of Loyalists. A declaration of independence coming from a lawfully elected Assembly would have an a priori legitimacy that a declaration from an ad hoc nonelected committee claiming to speak for a majority would conspicuously lack. In fact, in the case of UDI, the latter would be an act of treason: the call to Loyalists to seize the reins of government would be, in fact, a call to overthrow the government.

Independence, of course, is a step of last resort, possible only if Britain breaks the link and is clearly seen to do so, feasible, therefore, only under certain circumstances. Paisley could not admit to the intention even if it were foremost in his mind, yet he can nevertheless insist on it having to happen if Britain betrays political Protestantism. Independence, of course, would represent the apotheosis of political Protestantism; it is hard, indeed impossible, to imagine circumstances in which it would not lead to civil war. On the one hand, an agreed independence seems unworkable, since it would perpetuate political Protestantism with all its ugly sectarian ramifications; on the other, UDI is a prescription to disaster.

• • •

There is no long run. Indeed, the idea of one is incompatible with improvisation. Events are always reacted to, every reaction an immediate response to what is perceived as an exigency, the political landscape strewn with the debris of past responses.

"I'm a very tolerant man," Paisley says. There are many government officials in Dublin who want desperately to believe that he is. According to their script, Paisley, being above all else a man attuned to the nuances of power, will ultimately strike an accommodation with the South when it becomes clear to Northern Protestants that some form of unification is inevitable given Britain's predilection to disengage. What they overlook, however, is that while Paisley may well succeed in breaking the connection with England, he cannot deliver his followers into a united Ireland.

The failure to recognize this could be tragic.

6

Britain: A Question of Inconsistency

If you madden the people it is impossible to calculate the strength of insanity.

— from Locker-Lampson's *Consideration of the State of Ireland,* quoted by Thomas Jones in *Whitehall Diary,* Volume 3

THE BRITISH HAVE NO PLAN; their attitude today toward Northern Ireland is the same as it was sixty years ago. Their own interests are of paramount importance, and their interests, today as in the 1920s, make them unwilling to coerce the Loyalists.* In the twenties the overriding necessity was to main-

* In October 1921, when Lloyd George was accused by Arthur Griffith of abandoning the principle of unity to which Liberal governments theretofore had pledged themselves, he replied: "Attempts have been made to settle the Irish problem since 1886 on the basis of autonomy. Gladstone . . . tried to do it but he came up against Ulster . . . We tried from 1911 to 1913. Ulster defeated Gladstone. Ulster would have defeated us. Ulster was arming and would fight. We were powerless. It is no use ignoring facts, however unpleasant they may be. The politician who thinks he can deal out abstract justice without reference to forces around him cannot govern. You had to ask the British to use force to put Ulster out of one combination in which she had been for generations into another which she professed to abhor and did abhor whether for political or religious reasons. We could not do it. If we tried the instrument would have broken in our hands." (Lloyd George quoted in Thomas Jones, *Whitehall Diary,* Volume 3, pp. 129–30.) The British, of course, still believe the instrument would break in their hands.

tain Cabinet unity.[1] A large number of English Unionists had served in the War Cabinet and in the coalition governments that followed. If Ulster fought, the government would fall: coercion therefore was simply not on. There was also, of course, the fear of setting a precedent for other dominions: an Ireland without a tie to Britain could set the stage for a Canada, an Australia, or an India to follow in her footsteps. A solution, therefore, could not be seen as a first step toward a possible dismantling of the Empire. And today a solution cannot be seen as a first step toward a possible dismantling of the U.K. The frame of reference may have shrunk, but for many the thinking is the same: what comes to pass in Northern Ireland today may come to pass in Scotland tomorrow.

But if partition was seen as a necessity it was also seen as a temporary expedient. Hence the provision for a Council of Ireland in the Government of Ireland Act (1920). Lloyd George, master of prestidigitation that he was, argued to Collins and Griffith that "in order to persuade Ulster to come in there is an advantage in her having a Catholic population. I think you will get Ulster into an Irish unit on agreed terms. We promise to stand aside and you will not only have our neutrality but our benevolent neutrality."[2]

• • •

Benevolent neutrality: many would argue that that is precisely Britain's position today. Hence the distrust she arouses on both sides of the divide, as she seeks to appease two communities that have diametrically opposing aspirations. On the one hand, she seeks to convey the impression that Northern Ireland is an integral part of the U.K.; on the other, that she would not stand in the way of some form of association with the rest of Ireland. She cannot, of course, formulate a policy to accommodate both ends, and her attempts to do so only highlight the underlying incongruities and magnify the distrust. Having no long-term policy, she is unable to achieve short-term objectives or to develop a set of complementary strategies to deal with complementary aspects of the conflict. The result is one of confusion and contradiction suggesting opportunism, ambivalence and equivocation inviting cynicism.

In 1920 Britain would not declare herself in favor of Irish unity; nor would she do so in 1973. Yet in 1920 she attempted to provide some sort of mechanism that might bring it about, and she did so again in 1973. She is neither for unification nor against it: if unification is the wish of a majority in Northern Ireland, she will take steps to disengage; if it is not, she will remain.

Thus the anomalies: the Republic has no part whatsoever to play in what is purely an internal U.K. matter; the Republic has a role to play. The prisoners warrant special-category status; the prisoners do not. Negotiate with the IRA; do not negotiate. Insist on power sharing; avoid the action necessary to make it succeed. Accept the existence of an "Irish Dimension," yet do not impose the view on Loyalists. One Opposition leader announces a plan for unification within fifteen years in 1971, yet, when Prime Minister, takes no action to save the power-sharing Executive in 1974. Another Opposition leader boasts she is "rock-solid" for the Union in 1978, yet embraces an Anglo-Irish Intergovernmental Council when Prime Minister in 1981. A former Prime Minister calls for independence, and a former Secretary of State for Northern Ireland calls for an end to the guarantee. The British Army sent in to protect a besieged Catholic community in August 1969 is given virtually unlimited power to search, seize, detain, and intern—powers the Army used almost exclusively against the Catholics it was supposed to protect. Always Britain balances the cost of a given action against the cost of inaction, and often she concludes that a policy of maximum inaction pays higher dividends than a policy of minimum action. Ultimately she faces a dichotomy: to solve the problem of political Protestantism she must destroy its fears of unification, and that may require closer links between Ulster and the rest of the U.K.; to solve the problem of the IRA she must destroy its raison d'être, and that may require looser links between Ulster and the rest of the U.K.

She, too, of course, sees herself as the victim of history, albeit history largely of her own making. Though abused by both sides, she continues to pour money, men, and arms into the province, ostensibly for the sole purpose of stopping the natives from executing their murderous designs on one another. Meanwhile, her initiatives are rejected, her soldiers shot, her efforts to mediate scorned, and her international image sullied. The war against the IRA is a war she knows she cannot win; the war against political Protestantism is one she is unprepared to wage.

• • •

By early 1970 the Northern Ireland Civil Rights Association had achieved its major objectives. There was a permanent ombudsman and a commission to investigate citizen complaints against government bodies; the gerrymandered, Unionist-dominated City Council in Derry had been abolished, the hated "B-Specials" disbanded, the RUC disarmed; and one man–one vote in local elections was the law. In 1971 the allocation of public housing was taken out of the hands of local authorities and placed under the jurisdiction of a new Central Housing Executive.

But these reforms were not enough. The dynamics of the political situation had changed with the arrival of the British Army. It was a new variable. The relationship of the two communities to the Army defined and exacerbated the nature of their relationship to each other, and this in turn altered their relationships to the Army. The Army's pervasive presence became a symbol of old hatreds, a symbol that at last provided a renascent IRA with an opportunity it couldn't ignore: there were old enemies to be vanquished, new enemies to be made.

By mid-1970 the Provisional IRA had fifteen hundred members, six hundred of whom were believed to be in Belfast. Secure in their sanctuaries in the "no-go" areas, they waged a campaign of harassment against the Army. The strategy was meant to invite retaliation, and it succeeded. The Army-imposed curfew in the Lower Falls in June 1970 lasted thirty-four hours, during which a house-to-house search of the area was made. When the curfew was lifted, five civilians were dead and fifteen soldiers and sixty civilians were injured: the alienation was complete. During the winter and spring of 1971, the Army, still believing that it could defeat the IRA, continued to counter IRA harassment with retaliation against Catholics in general but especially in the ghetto enclaves in West Belfast and Derry, thus consolidating support for the IRA, whose actions were perceived as defensive measures on behalf of the community. Each civilian killed or maimed by the security forces resulted in a rush of recruits to the IRA to avenge the victim.

A bad situation was made intolerably worse when internment without trial was introduced. The botched circumstances of the initial operation ensured its failure. At 4:00 A.M. on 9 August, 350 arrests were made. But intelligence was poor, many of those arrested had nothing to do with the IRA, and some were simply too old, so that 104 had to be released within forty-eight hours. But the horrifying circumstances of that morning were never to be forgotten. Whole areas were sealed off, paratroopers smashing down doors and literally dragging men from their homes in front of hysterical wives and terrified children, the brutal knock in the middle of the night reeking of totalitarianism about its dirty work. The random brutality, the abuse of rights, the uncertainty, the spread of rumors and counter-rumors, the callous indifference of the Army to inquiries as to the whereabouts or the fate of internees, and the holding of a small number at secret locations for interrogation in depth transformed the psychology of the conflict. The Army, "the Brits," had become the enemy. Once more it was a question of Irish nationalism versus British imperialism. Alienation turned to hostility; the violence hardened and worsened.

Internment united the Catholic community. The IRA became victim, the persecuted rather than the persecutor. Recruitment soared, and Irish-Americans took to the cause and their pocketbooks. The SDLP called for a rent and rates strike, which at one point involved close to thirty thousand tenants,[3] while the Republic's Taoiseach, Jack Lynch, called for the abolition of the Stormont regime.*

* On 12 August 1971, Mr. Lynch said in a statement that "as an immediate objective of political action the Stormont government should be replaced by an administration in which power and decision-making will be equally shared between Unionist and non-Unionist. The Stormont regime which has consistently repressed the non-Unionist population and bears responsibility for recurring violence in the Northern community must be brought to an end." For a chronological account of the events preceding and following internment, see Richard Deutsch and Vivien Magowan, *Northern Ireland 1968–1973*, pp. 114–31.

Those released brought back stories of hooding, of deprivation of sleep, of having to stand for long periods spread-eagled against walls, of insolent soldiers and sadistic guards.[4] The European Court of Human Rights later found that those who were "interrogated in depth" had been subjected to "inhuman and degrading" treatment but not torture. In the atmosphere of 1971, however, the distinction was moot. The propaganda mills poured out details of atrocity, feeding the public's imagination, heightening their sense of insecurity, strengthening their sense of collective consciousness to stand firm against the enemy. Brutality would be met by brutality, the abuse on one side indistinguishable from abuse on the other. No matter how grotesque the action, it could be justified, because one side could always point an accusing finger at a comparable action on the other. Murder justified murder.

Bloody Sunday completed the cycle: the thirteen civilians shot dead by the Army became a cause that reverberated around the world.* The Army had become the hard men of violence, and when the Catholic clergy called on its flock to reject the men of violence they responded: they rejected the Army.

• • •

The Army's strategy — break the IRA and bring a halt to its operations by arresting as many IRA officers as possible and putting them behind bars — not only was fallacious in conception, it actually spawned a new generation of IRA leaders who revitalized the movement in the late 1970s.[5] Implementation called for the screening of almost the entire Catholic population in militant areas. But the large-scale identification of Catholics

* A fourteenth civilian died later. The civil rights march took place on 30 January 1972 in Londonderry's Bogside. The official inquiry into the shootings, conducted by Lord Widgery (*Report of the Tribunal Appointed to Inquire into the Events of Sunday, 30 January 1972, Which Led to Loss of Life in Connection with the Procession in Londonderry on That Day*), concluded that there would have been no deaths if there had not been an illegal march. He also found that the soldiers had been fired on first, although none of the dead were shown to have been shot while handling a gun. The report was vehemently attacked by, among others, Samuel Dash, who later gained fame in the United States during the Watergate hearings. (See Dash's "Justice Denied.")

was possible only if large numbers were arrested; hence the sporadic sweeps of entire streets and housing estates. The Emergency Provisions Act* gave the Army the power to arrest and question any person for up to four hours, which was, of course, more than sufficient time to compile a dossier. Thus the Army pursued a policy under which every Catholic was treated as a potential IRA member or supporter; hence the arbitrary arrests and screening, hence the residue of smoldering resentment incubating support for the IRA. Screening was self-defeating: by treating every Catholic as a potential subversive, the Army made actual subversives of many.

The unevenhandedness of the Army's policy also rankled. Since the Army was not out to "defeat" the Loyalist paramilitary organizations, inclining to view Loyalist violence as a misguided, defensive reaction to IRA provocation, no such large-scale screenings were taken against the Protestant community.[6] Hence the Catholic sense of injustice and anger spilling out into a swelling sea and finally cresting in support of the IRA. They were heady days for the movement.

The failure of the Army campaign was due to a failure to define the objective, whether it was to restore law and order or to "win" a guerrilla war. In the short run, the latter is not necessarily compatible with the former: restoring law and order may be perceived as a consequence of, rather than a condition

* The Northern Ireland (Emergency Provisons) Act of 1973 (amended slightly in 1978) arose directly from recommendations made by the Diplock Commission, appointed in 1972 to consider how the administration of justice in Northern Ireland might be rearranged to "deal more effectively" with terrorist organizations. The Act defined terrorism as the use of violence for political ends, and for all terrorist-type offenses it altered normal common-law practices relating to arrest, period of detention before charging, bail application procedures, and the right to trial by jury. Although the Act was amended in 1978, and its most notorious provision (permitting internment without trial) has been allowed to lapse, the main 1973 provisions are still in force; any person suspected of being a terrorist may be arrested without warrant and detained for up to seventy-two hours by the police, while the Army has a similar power of detention but only for a maximum of four hours. Further, trials of all "scheduled" (terrorist-type) offenses are held by a senior judge, sitting alone without a jury. In June 1982, the Northern Ireland Secretary, James Prior, announced a judicial review of the Emergency Provisions Act, which will follow the 1983 review of the U.K. Prevention of Terrorism Act.

for, winning the war. Moreover, if restoring law and order is subordinated to winning the war but the latter cannot be achieved, then neither can the former. And the sense of injustice that the absence of law and order contributes to also adds to the instability, and to the impossibility of winning the war.

Although the clause of the Northern Ireland (Emergency Provisions) Act authorizing internment was kept on the books until 1980, internment was abandoned in 1976 for a new policy.* More authority was given to the police, the role of the Army was reduced, and the emphasis was put on "normal" policing and "normal" police procedures. Henceforth, suspected terrorists would be dealt with through the court system. There would be no more special-category status for persons convicted of so-called political offenses. They would be treated as ordinary criminals.[7]

The circumstances of their trials, however, continued to be anything but ordinary. The one judge–no jury "Diplock Courts," introduced in 1973, were an attempt to resolve the dilemma posed in the Diplock Report:[8]

> The minimum requirements [for a proper criminal trial] are based upon the assumption that witnesses to a crime will be able to give evidence in a court of law without risk to their lives, their families or their property. Unless the state can secure their safety, then it would be unreasonable to expect them to testify voluntarily and morally wrong to compel them to do so. This assumption, basic to the very functioning of courts of law, cannot be made today in Northern Ireland.[9]

Witnesses were informers. In Ireland the word has a special pejorative: informers are ostracized at best, dead men at worst. The knowledge of almost certain reprisal is a marvelous incentive to keep the mouth shut, the eyes closed, the mind a blank.

* Open-ended internment of suspected terrorists without trial was introduced by Northern Ireland's last Prime Minister, Brian Faulkner. On assuming Direct Rule in 1972, the British government announced that this practice would be gradually phased out. Although the last internees were released in December 1975, it was not until July 1980 that the internment clause in the Emergency Provisions Act was allowed by Parliament to lapse at the Secretary of State's request.

The Diplock solution: special powers to the police and the courts. Suspects could be held for up to three days under the Northern Ireland (Emergency Provisions) Act, and later for up to seven days under the Prevention of Terrorism Act, a U.K. statute introduced in the aftermath of the Birmingham bombings in November 1974.* As a result, police had a high degree of success in securing confessions. The rules of admissibility were also altered so that statements made by a defendant could be used as evidence provided they were not obtained by "torture or by degrading treatment." And because juries could be subjected to intimidation, jury trials were suspended, the evidence presented before a single judge.

The safeguards were loose, the results predictable: overreaction on the part of the police, and abuse of the powers they had under the security legislation.[10] For example, in one twelve-month period during 1977–78, more than twenty-eight hundred people were arrested under the three-day power, yet only 35 percent were charged with a crime.[11] The police were still using their powers to screen the population; their actions, therefore, were at variance with both the procedures and principles of normal policing.

The routine was simple enough: the suspect was arrested, usually in the early morning by a joint Army/police squad, and taken to an interrogation center. Interrogation began in mid-morning and continued under relays of detectives with short breaks for lunch and supper until late evening, usually 10:00 or 11:00 P.M. Often suspects spent six to eight hours per day under interrogation.[12] Almost three quarters of the cases brought to trial were based solely on confessions obtained through this process.

The abuse in the scale of arrests, however, was paralleled by abuses in obtaining confessions. In 1978 Amnesty International reported: "On the basis of the information available to

* Nineteen people died when bombs went off in two Birmingham pubs on 21 November 1974. The Provisional IRA denied responsibility. However, it never carried out a promised investigation into the bombings. Six men were jailed for life for the bombings. Fr. Dennis Faul and Fr. Raymond Murray argue in *The Birmingham Framework* that the six are innocent.

it, Amnesty International believes that maltreatment of suspected terrorists by the RUC has taken place with sufficient frequency to warrant the establishment of a public inquiry to investigate it."[13]

In response to the Amnesty International report, the government established a committee, chaired by Judge Bennett, to inquire into police interrogation procedures in Northern Ireland. It concluded that there was sufficient evidence of maltreatment to warrant major reforms.[14] Among the reforms introduced as a result of Bennett's report: suspects are entitled to closed-circuit television cameras in interview rooms, attention of a medical officer every twenty-four hours, access to a solicitor after forty-eight hours, and a limit on the number of police officers questioning them.

The reports of physical mistreatment have practically disappeared. However, the evidence suggests that the emergency legislation is still being used for "screening, building up dossiers of information on people in the area, harassment and inducing suspects to pass on information."* The biggest abuse remains the abuse of the emergency powers of arrest. While that abuse remains, an effective policy of law enforcement is impossible and the Catholic community will remain estranged, the sea

* The Administration of Justice in Northern Ireland: Conference; Belfast, 13 June 1981. See also Dermot Walsh, *Arrest, Interrogation, and Diplock Courts.* Among Walsh's conclusions: (1) Ninety percent of all those arrested under emergency legislation were released without charge after being held for up to four hours, three days, or seven days, depending on which power was used. These people were mostly arrested for intelligence gathering or harassment as opposed to being suspected of a crime. This, he concludes, was an abuse of the particular power of arrest. (2) Emergency powers of arrest and interrogation were used as a primary means of policing in Republican areas. They had largely supplanted all the normal policing techniques. The police approach to investigation was to arrest any relevant persons and interrogate them in police custody for three to seven days. This was so whether the information sought related to a serious crime or was simply concerned with local information gathering. (3) Of those who were charged before Diplock Courts, 40 percent were ordinary suspected criminals — that is, they had no terrorist involvement. (4) For almost 75 percent of those charged, the evidence against them consisted wholly or substantially of a confession. These confessions had been obtained by interrogation techniques that often breached Bennett's recommendations, and many of them would have been inadmissible at common law. (Summary of findings was provided to author by Dermot Walsh prior to the study's publication.)

choppy, husbanding its unpredictable energies for the first signs of storm.

• • •

The response of the authorities to criticism compounds their problems, especially with regard to how they are perceived in the minority community. The Widgery Report[15] on Bloody Sunday, the political decision not to take action against military personnel involved in the incident, the grudging response to Amnesty International and the unwillingness to let its reporters into the Maze Prison, the highhanded treatment of the Irish Commission for Justice and Peace* during the hunger strikes, the reluctance to forego the use of plastic bullets despite the documented evidence of their potential lethality, and the propensity not to prosecute any member of the security forces against whom complaints are made are problems of arrogance. Because the British see themselves as the ones put upon, as the "good guys" keeping the contumacious natives from tearing each other apart, as the bearers of standards of democracy and "fair play" not adhered to by their ruthless and cowardly opponents, they have an arrogance that persists in their trying to justify their every action. If there are aberrations, it's only because there are a few rotten apples in every barrel. Aberrations are not policy, and certainly their aberrations are neither on the scale of nor of the same magnitude as the French Army's actions in Algeria or the U.S. Army's actions in Vietnam. Allegations are investigated, committees sit, recommendations are put forward, and reforms are made. They would agree wholeheartedly with the observer who wrote: "Seldom, perhaps never before in history, has a military force been subjected to such close scrutiny of its conduct, over so long a period, and by such a variety of umpires and emerged with such credit."[16]

The use of plastic bullets exemplifies best, perhaps, the extent of the authorities' hubris. They are either unwilling or unable to understand that the methods the security forces employ must have political acceptability if the security forces are ever to win

* A peace and human rights lobby group working within the Catholic Church.

political legitimacy in the Catholic community. The plastic bullet does not. It has become one more symbol of repression. The Army will not concur in the view that plastic bullets are more lethal than their rubber predecessors, despite a substantial body of evidence that they are.

A plastic bullet is a solid PVC cylinder four inches in length and one and a half inches in diameter, weighing five ounces and with an operational range of thirty-six to seventy-two yards.[17] Unlike the rubber bullet, the plastic counterpart is designed to be fired directly at targets, not ricocheted off the ground. Research in the United States has amply demonstrated that any crowd-control weapon based on direct impact can cause severe damage — skull fractures, rupture of the kidney and heart, fragmentation of the liver, and hemorrhages — if its energy impact exceeds 90 foot-pounds. However, at a five-yard range the plastic bullet has an energy impact of 210 foot-pounds, and at fifty yards an impact of 110 foot-pounds.

During the riots that followed the deaths of the hunger strikers in May and June of 1981, the shortcomings of the plastic bullet as a crowd-containment instrument became manifestly obvious. Four people were killed and three partially blinded; another three suffered permanent brain damage; and a hundred more needed hospital treatment for injuries ranging from flesh wounds to broken bones and damaged internal organs. Many of the casualties were children — a fourteen-year-old girl died on 13 May from injuries she had received when she was struck on the head by a plastic bullet the previous evening, and nine days later a twelve-year-old girl died from similar injuries.* Since plastic bullets were first used in February 1973, more than forty-two thousand of them have been fired;† eleven people have

* Later the inquest on the twelve-year-old girl, Carol Ann Kelly, determined that she had not been in a riot when she was hit by the plastic bullet that killed her.

† Of the total number of plastic bullets fired in Northern Ireland since 1973, 29,665 were fired in 1981; 16,656 of them in the month of May 1981 alone. See written reply given by Northern Ireland Secretary of State James Prior to Mr. Kilroy-Silk in House of Commons. *Hansard: Written Answers,* 19 November 1981, col. 200.

died and at least another sixty have been seriously injured.* Yet not a single member of the security forces involved has been called to account by the Director of Public Prosecutions despite the extraordinarily dubious circumstances surrounding many of the deaths and injuries. But on each occasion the ghettos closed in on themselves, rage and grief authenticating the IRA in its role as defender of the community against the callous and contemptible security forces who made innocent children the victims of their arbitrary actions.

They will remember.

• • •

Britain's unwillingness to confront the problem works against her own best interests. The absence of a long-run policy, and thus the absence of a clear-cut distinction between the short run and the long run, especially in regard to security policy, where decisions are often made to maximize short-run considerations, has probably narrowed the range of long-run political options available to her.

At the height of the IRA offensive in 1972, when 468 people died, there were over twenty-one thousand troops from the "mainland" and nine thousand members of the Ulster Defence Regiment (UDR) in Northern Ireland.† At the beginning of 1983, there were about ten thousand troops and seventy-two hundred members of the UDR on active service.[18] However, though there has been a significant, in fact drastic, reduction in the number of troops from the mainland, the relatively small drop in the number of UDR members has altered the composition of the

* Statistics supplied by Professor Kevin Boyle, University College, Galway, 22 February 1983. On 13 May 1982 the European Parliament voted to ban the use of plastic bullets in the EEC, though the decision was not binding on member countries. The British security forces, however, indicated that they would continue to use plastic bullets in Northern Ireland.

† The Ulster Defence Regiment (UDR), which became operational in April 1970, is a locally based and mainly part-time force that provides back-up services for Northern Ireland's police force, the Royal Ulster Constabulary (RUC). The UDR was intended to replace the B-Specials but not to be open to the same objection of being exclusively Protestant. The 1972 data are quoted in the Labour Party's *Northern Ireland: Statement by the National Executive Committee*, p. 14.

security forces. The UDR constituted 30 percent of the military force in 1972; at the beginning of 1983 it accounted for 42 percent, and the proportion is growing. British military withdrawal in the face of this development assumes a new connotation. For although the UDR is an integral part of the British Army, it cannot be "withdrawn"; its members are drawn only from Ulster, and the regiment was formed to serve only in Ulster. One third of its members are full-time soldiers and two thirds serve in a part-time capacity. It is almost exclusively Protestant, the number of Catholics having fallen from 18 percent in 1972 to an insignificant 2 percent in 1980, thanks to the IRA's success at persuading Catholics that it was not in their best interests to join the security forces.[19] Altogether about twenty-one thousand men have served in the force since 1970. Their loyalties are unmistakable. Ulster is their country. And they know the enemy.

When the manpower of the Royal Ulster Constabulary (about seventy-eight hundred) and the RUC Reserve (about forty-eight hundred) is added,[20] the problems attendant on withdrawal would appear to be insurmountable. Local full-time security forces equal in number the level of mainland Army manpower, while local reserves are almost as much again. Thus, withdrawal of the mainland troops would leave Northern Ireland policed by a segment of the British Army whose primary loyalty is almost certainly not to Westminster but to Protestant Ulster. The antipathy of Catholics toward the mainland Army is exceeded only by their antipathy toward the UDR and their fear of and vulnerability to Protestant attack in the event of the mainland Army's withdrawal.

A declaration of intent by Britain to withdraw would pose a further set of difficulties. It could pit one segment of the Army against another if the UDR was called on to turn in its weapons. And if the UDR was not called on to turn in its weapons, it would be under enormous — indeed, almost irresistible — pressure to stockpile, leading to a situation where Britain ultimately would be abandoning Northern Ireland to an army resolutely hostile to the Catholic minority, which she herself had trained and armed. It is inconceivable that Britain would take this course of action, but the alternative — disarming the UDR and the RUC — may be equally inconceivable in her eyes. In short, she may have no way out of the dilemma.

It is hardly surprising, therefore, that support for the Army's withdrawal varies in inverse proportion to distance from the epicenter. The Northern Ireland Attitude Survey found that 49 percent of Catholics in the North agreed that "the British government should declare their intention to withdraw whether the majority in Northern Ireland agrees or not":[21] 71 percent of Southern respondents in the ESRI survey were in favor of this course of action and 56 percent of British respondents concurred.[22] Thus, Catholics in North Ireland are less than clamorous for British withdrawal: they know too well that they would be the first to feel the consequences. The available firepower is awesome: aside from the weapons used by the police force and the UDR, more than eighty-five thousand firearm licenses for some one hundred ten thousand guns have been issued in Northern Ireland, most of them held by Protestants, and most of them, no doubt, in excellent working order, the meticulous care nursing presentiments of "1641 come again."[23]

• • •

Successive British governments have concurred on one issue. Northern Ireland will remain a part of the United Kingdom so long as that is the wish of a majority in Northern Ireland. Even the Labour Party, which at its 1981 Annual Conference came out in favor of the long-term unification of Ireland — "by peaceful means and on the basis of consent" — upholds the right of a majority to self-determination. Accordingly, its position on the guarantee straddles the equivocal and the evasive:

> Labour's position [according to the party's 1981 manifesto on Northern Ireland] as set out in Labour's Program of 1976, is that the party "respects and supports the right of the Northern Ireland people to remain within the U.K." Nevertheless, we do not intend to allow this to halt progress towards a political settlement in Northern Ireland. The guarantee, as understood by the party, is that the people of Northern Ireland will not be expelled from the United Kingdom against their wishes.

It must not mean a veto on political development in the hands of Unionist leaders.[24]

But having made what appears to be, at the least, the assertion of a willingness to confront Loyalist intransigence, the Labour Party resurrects the familiar caveats:

At the end of the day it would be no part of the political program of the Labour Party to force Northern Ireland out of the United Kingdom or into the Republic of Ireland. Before any constitutional change is made, therefore, we would seek to obtain the consent of the people of Northern Ireland.[25]

Don Concannon, M.P., is the Labour Party spokesman on Northern Ireland and a former Minister of State for Northern Ireland. Would he elaborate on Labour's position on the guarantee? Of course:

The guarantee on paper is absolutely worthless. Taking it away on paper is not the big objective. The objective is taking away the guarantee from the hearts and minds of a million Protestants. The guarantee is for the million Protestants who don't want to go into the South. So the guarantee's not on the piece of paper but what's in the hearts and minds of a million Protestants.[26]

How does he square that distinction with John Hume's insistence that the guarantee on paper has to be withdrawn if progress is to be made? Concannon:

I don't see it as important, to be quite honest. I don't think John Hume sees it as important. Ian Paisley certainly doesn't see it as important. Everyone knows that the guarantee is not the piece of paper but a million souls who are prepared to get off their backsides and do something about it.

In short, Labour's position on the guarantee does not call for repeal of the 1973 legislation. It simply dismisses it as unimportant, since the reality is so irrefutable. Repealing the guarantee could have undesirable side effects without achieving anything positive. The direction of change should be the reverse: change the hearts and minds of the recalcitrant one million and then change the legislation. Concannon:

I think there's too much emphasis put on the guarantee — on the paper guarantee, that is. That's why our policy tends to ignore the paper guarantee. It says we will just work towards a peaceful political solution to the problem, because at the end of the day it's not the piece of paper that matters. I just wonder why people still talk about withdrawing the piece of paper when it's the five hundred people that Paisley can get on a mountainside in the evening which is the guarantee.

Thus Labour's predilection: replace Direct Rule with a power-sharing Assembly, and then with the Assembly working in tandem with Westminster, Labour would hope that "the people would work in their own time and in their own way and with the British government giving them good government, so that they would see their way into unification." There will, however, be no question of coercing people into any arrangement. What the Labour Party has to do is "to work steadily and hard to win the hearts and minds of a million Protestants."

The assumption — dubious, at best — is that when the people of Northern Ireland are the beneficiaries of good government, they will be more disposed toward obeying the edicts of that government:

If you're bringing good government to the people of Northern Ireland — and by that I mean bringing them jobs, bringing them good housing, giving them welfare and giving them virtual parity with the rest of the United Kingdom — then, of course, they will look upon and respect, I think, the people that are governing them.

Would a Labour government take steps to induce consent? No, it wouldn't:

Consent will have to be freely given consent. There's no way in which we can coerce people, in which you can coerce a million Protestants into doing something that they freely don't want to do. That is recognized by everyone.

Does Britain want to get out of Northern Ireland?

The two governments [Labour and Conservative] would be perfectly happy to see a political solution to the problem. We [Labour] see that political solution as one of unification. But with a caveat — by free consent. I would suspect that the Tory government would like, of course, to see some form of accommodation under which they could withdraw, if you like, from the scene in Northern Ireland . . . and they, I'm sure, would not go amiss if the plebiscite which comes next time on a free vote showed that the vast majority of the people of Northern Ireland wanted unification with the South. I don't suppose a Tory government, same as our government, would stand in the way. So if you're saying would they want to get out, yes. I think that both Labour and Tory governments would like to see a political solution to the problem. But what we couldn't do, neither of us, would be to force the issue over the heads of the people of Northern Ireland.

Thus, the question of legislating Northern Ireland out of the U.K. would only arise if the action had the consent of the people of Northern Ireland. Without that consent, "the Labour Party couldn't do it."

What, then, are the differences between the Labour Party's approach to the problem and the Conservative Party's? Labour puts more emphasis on the Irish Dimension: While the Conservatives "will go for an Assembly," says Concannon, "what they won't do is give the same kind of emphasis which we would be giving to power sharing and the Irish Dimension, which is there, whether you talk about it or not." Thus the Labour Party would press for implementation of the parliamentary tier of the Anglo-Irish Intergovernmental Council:

We're behind this process and we're trying to get it moving as quickly as we possibly can. The more talk that goes on between the three sides — Belfast, London, and Dublin — the better. There is an Irish Dimension and it's no good trying to ignore it.

As for the Republic, Concannon says:

They would certainly like to see unification, but they would certainly only wish to see it in the same way as we would. They know full well there's not much use taking on Northern Ireland. Another million disgruntled people who are willing to, if you like, do what the IRA is doing at the moment. So they know that there's a lot of hard work, a lot of things that have to be done to win, as I say, the hearts and minds of those one million people. They certainly don't want it forced onto the people of Ireland.

• • •

Thus the Labour policy — for there is no strategy. Just a set of aims, all of which have been expressed before, all of which are seen in a mutually inclusive framework, the contradictions in some precluding the achievement of others. Labour is for unification, when a majority give their consent to it. Consent, of course, must be freely given. And Protestants, of course, must be given a set of guarantees to protect their rights and liberties in the new Ireland. The present guarantee must not be interpreted as the right of the majority either to obstruct every initiative or to veto any new arrangement, especially when internal changes are in question. Thus, the majority do not have the right, under the guarantee, to veto either power sharing or an Anglo-Irish Intergovernmental Council. They do, however, have the right to veto any change in their constitutional position. But the fact is, the two positions are not necessarily mutually independent. However unassailable Labour's sentiments, its logic is wanting — because once the right of veto with respect to the constitutional position is explicitly conceded, Protestants acquire an implicit veto over internal arrangements, since their refusal to participate carries with it no threat to their external status — and only the external status matters.

The elusive consent will emerge when Protestants realize that Britain is not trying to unload them without their consent, and when her actions — her "good" government — put Northern Ireland on a par in every way with the rest of the United Kingdom. The implication is that once Protestants accept that Britain is acting in their best interests, they will accept her judgment willingly as to where their constitutional future should lie. Once they see themselves treated as equals within the U.K., they will somehow consent to leave it. But there is no question of a withdrawal, even a troop withdrawal, prior to a political solution — "there is no dishonorable way out," says Concannon.

The Labour Party wants out. A Labour government would want out. And the Labour Party believes that the Tory government wants out. Labour makes good government virtually synonymous with improving economic conditions, which in turn depends on increasing levels of public expenditure. However, Northern Ireland could hardly be more dependent on the public sector and public expenditure. In 1979–80 public expenditure per head of population was £1648 sterling, almost £400 more than in Great Britain. Expenditure per head on health and social services, social security, education, and law and order was higher than in England, Scotland, or Wales. Only Scotland had a higher per capita expenditure on housing.[27] Yet the economic situation continues to deteriorate, and unemployment continues its pitiless advance. Labour's program for "direct employment creation through increased public expenditure"[28] seems timeworn, tested, and wanting. This, of course, is not to dismiss the need for an even higher level of public expenditure in Ulster. But it's not a prescription for improvement. It's a palliative: without it an intolerable situation would become simply impossible.

The North's dependence on public expenditure has had secondary effects. By binding the North's economy so completely to the British public sector it has created a situation that may be impossible to reverse. The North's economy, more than ever, is integrated with and dependent on the U.K.'s, especially on the largess of the British Exchequer. There may be no way the South could ever assume the burden without substantial assistance. Therefore, to the extent that IRA violence has contributed to the economic decline in the North — and the conventional wisdom is that it has, though it is by no means the sole agent of that decline[29] — Britain's attempts to limit the repercussions through higher public expenditure have made the North more dependent on an external subvention. The greater that dependence, the greater the economic burden that would have to be assumed by the South; and the greater that burden, the more unlikely unification.

• • •

James Dunn, M.P., is a former Labour Minister of State for Northern Ireland and currently the Social Democratic Party's spokesman on Northern Ireland.

Does the SDP endorse the long-term unification of Ireland "by peaceful means and on the basis of consent"? Dunn:

> It has to come by common acceptance and consent, and the only way you're going to achieve that sort of acceptability is first by answering the fears of those in Northern Ireland who have grave reservations about it. It should be put to the people of Northern Ireland that it is in their interest in the long term to have a closer association with the Republic. But if the people of Northern Ireland don't want that, then it shouldn't be imposed on them. Any imposition would bring about disaster. The only solution to the problem is by encouraging and providing the means for the people of Northern Ireland to determine their own future.[30]

Dissimulation has virtues to commend it:

> Any government at this moment who, for whatever reason, were to tell the Northern Ireland people where they believe their real future lies would probably inherit some of the legends and aspirations of opposition immediately, and what they're seeking to achieve could be demolished overnight.

Which brings up the matter of the guarantee. Dunn:

> It can't be withdrawn at this moment in time because there would be overwhelming opposition to any attempt to modify or withdraw it . . . What we have to do is demonstrate quite clearly that nothing will be imposed on the people of Northern Ireland against their wishes.

Does this mean that the SDP is opposed to the withdrawal of the guarantee? No, it doesn't:

It's impossible for us to do so because as yet there has been no consideration given to a comprehensive policy on Northern Ireland. We're only just twelve months old. We've really had so much to do on demand that this matter has not been prominent.

An SDP government would, however, put more emphasis on partnership than on power sharing as the way forward:

Power sharing as such was not a success. The way forward is in partnership, and if in legislation there are protections given to minorities without vesting a power of veto in their hands — because while minorities have rights, they also have responsibilities, and they must recognize that majorities cannot easily be dismissed, and provisional upon that majority being unable to impose any form of discrimination or political constraint — then every option is open. And that's the thing that the SDP is trying to encourage.

And how about the assumption of Irish governments that Britain would opt out if she could find some way of extricating herself? It is incorrect:

Britain has a responsibility, and until such time as that responsibility is changed by the consent, or indeed at the request, of the people of Northern Ireland, the responsibility that [she has] will be discharged properly. For those who want other things, they claim that the British government wants out.

• • •

Ultimately, James Dunn concedes that "I couldn't honestly tell you what the policy of the Social Democratic Party will be on Northern Ireland." The absence of a policy is perhaps understandable. Founded in 1981, the party is a relative newcomer to the British political stage. The necessity to organize, the contesting of elections, the sudden metamorphosis from splinter party of malcontents to national party, and the prospect of forming a future government put tremendous strains on the party's resources. But Dunn's remark that "we've really had so much to do on demand that this matter has not been prominent" should not be taken as peculiar to the SDP. Rather, it is germane to the question, part of the problem being that neither the public nor Parliament cares to think of the problem too often or too deeply.

Northern Ireland, in fact, occupies a very low position on the British national agenda. Between 1922 and 1969 it occupied no position at all. The Speaker of the House of Commons ruled that a British government could not be asked about matters that were properly deemed to be the responsibility of the Northern Ireland government. Little deeming was necessary, since few evinced a proclivity to inquire into what might properly be Westminster's concern.* In the 1970 general election, one year after British troops had been dispatched to Northern Ireland, it was a nonissue.[31] In fact, only when internment made Northern Ireland headlines news in Britain, television dramatizing for the first time the scope of the conflict between the Army and the IRA, did it gain a brief ascendancy as Britain's number-one problem, that being the view held by 20 percent of the public.[32] But even that was short-lived. According to Rose et al., the last time more than 10 percent of the British public thought of Ulster as being the nation's either first or second most important issue was in December 1975. In general, they report, "its position in the Gallup poll has fluctuated between nil mention and coming at the bottom of a list of ten or a dozen issues."[33]

Nor is public opinion swayed by either the level of violence in Northern Ireland or by the fate of political initiatives. Observe Rose et al.: "It appears that political killings in Northern Ireland, whether they involve British soldiers or Ulster men, have become 'boring.' "[34] Only violence in England appears to stimulate concern. Thus, in December 1974, "23% of respondents said they considered Ulster the first or second most important problem, a figure that has not been approached since."[35] The question, however, was asked shortly after the pub bombings in Birming-

* In 1935, for example, nine Catholics were killed in what appeared to be an attempted pogrom, but when the matter was raised in Westminster, the Prime Minister, Stanley Baldwin, said that riots were solely a matter for the Northern Ireland government and could not be raised at Westminster. See G. Bell, *Protestants of Ulster*, p. 241.

ham that resulted in nineteen deaths and dozens of injuries.

Moreover, since June 1974 British opinion has been consistently coming down on the side of a military withdrawal. One series of surveys conducted over a two-and-a-half-year period indicated that on average 57 percent of respondents favored withdrawal, 19 percent favored maintaining current levels of deployment, and 13 percent wanted to increase the number of troops.[36] There has also been a consistent consensus for ending the Union. Between June 1974 and December 1980, only 28 percent, on average, favored the maintenance of the Union. Nor did the figure fluctuate during the period, despite the fact that 131 British soldiers were killed.[37] Ulster Protestants may see themselves as British; the feeling, however, clearly isn't reciprocated by the mainland British.

The lack of British concern with Northern Ireland is not surprising. It constitutes less than 3 percent of the U.K.'s population and accounts for just 12 of the 635 Members of Parliament;* and since Northern Ireland Members of Parliament are not directly affiliated with the Labour or Conservative parties, they never become part of the governmental structure. The conflict in Ireland is seen as being the result of "Paddy" intransigence and bullheadedness. "Paddy," much to the chagrin of Northern Protestants, includes them too. The lack of public concern with concerns Irish — the "boredom" threshold Rose et al. refer to — reflects itself in policy initiatives. The pace is desultory, the will lacking.

The first White Paper on Northern Ireland's constitutional future appeared in March 1973.[38] It proposed a new, seventy-eight-member Assembly for Northern Ireland elected by proportional representation. The Assembly would take over the day-to-day government of Northern Ireland, though Westminster would retain control over security. The White Paper also advanced the idea of power sharing to guarantee minority participation in the government. Elections for the new Assembly were held in June, and after five months of wrangling, the SDLP,

* With the 1983 British general election the number of Northern Ireland parliamentary seats increased to seventeen.

the Unionist Party, and the Alliance Party agreed to form a power-sharing Executive. Within a month the three parties met with the British and Irish governments at Sunningdale to work out the political framework in which the new government would operate. The Irish government, for the first time, recognized the de jure existence of Northern Ireland when it agreed to the stipulation that a change in the constitutional status of Northern Ireland would require the consent of a majority of the people there. For its part, the British government gave a positive expression of its willingness not to stand in the way of a united Ireland if consent did emerge, and the Northern Ireland Executive, under pressure from Westminster, agreed to a Council of Ireland (shades of the Government of Ireland Act of 1920) to give institutional expression to the Irish Dimension.

The arrangements were short-lived. Rather than face down the militant Ulster Workers' Council strike called in May 1974 to protest the proposed Council of Ireland, the newly elected Labour government — dependent for its survival on a slender majority — stood aside, thus ensuring the collapse of the Sunningdale Agreement and the experiment in power sharing.* Thereafter, the "initiatives" were, for the most part, exercises in form. The Constitutional Convention of 1975–76 produced a majority report predictably unacceptable.† A "framework" for an interim form of devolution was the brain child of the fourth Secretary of State, Roy Mason, in 1977–78. His call for negotia-

* See Robert Fisk, *Point of No Return.* He writes, "It was the Army's influence, the military expression of military impotence that caused Wilson to place a new 'interpretation' upon his promise to the executive of action against the UWC; but it was the Prime Minister's own fear of the executive's imminent disintegration — and his belief that this collapse would contaminate the stability of his own Government if he continued to support it — that made the coalition's abandonment inevitable." (p. 198.)

† The Constitutional Convention was an elected conference of Northern Ireland parties established by the British government in 1975 to consider what type of government was most likely to command widespread acceptance throughout Northern Ireland. A majority of seats in the Convention were held by Unionists; and the report submitted to Westminster at the end of 1975 recommended a return to majority rule. This proposal was rejected by the British Parliament, and although the Convention was recalled at the start of 1976 to reconsider its findings, it ended its sittings in March of that year without reaching any agreement acceptable to Westminster.

tions was rejected by both the SDLP and the OUP. In 1980, the fifth Secretary of State, Humphrey Atkins, produced yet another White Paper setting out two options for safeguarding the interests of the minority, but his negotiations with the political parties simply petered out.[39]

The impasse is simple and complete. On the Protestant side, no power sharing and no Irish Dimension. On the Catholic side, power sharing and an Irish Dimension. On the British side, no propensity to wield "the stick."

• • •

The sixth Secretary of State for Northern Ireland, James Prior, was appointed on 12 September 1981; by all accounts he was a reluctant appointee. Many said it was the Thatcher form of revenge, a borrowed Irishness, not to get mad but to get even. As her Employment Secretary he had been less than enthusiastic about her monetarist policies, but when she reshuffled her Cabinet, she showed her displeasure not by dropping him from the government but by consigning him to a fate, worse in the eyes of many, of having to assume the portfolio for Northern Ireland. That, or oblivion — a distinction lost on some.

Prior set to the task with great verve. He would, he said, "stake his political reputation on returning political life to Northern Ireland."[40] In the aftermath of the hunger strikes his gestures were conciliatory: he visited the Maze, talked to protesting prisoners, made reforms.

One month after his appointment, he informed the Conservative Party Conference of his intention to promote yet another political initiative: he wanted closer economic ties between Northern Ireland and the Republic, a new Assembly with safeguards for the minority, and interparliamentary institutions. Ulster politicians, he said, had to make "a serious effort"; Britain's "patience" was running out.[41] And he spoke openly of the Republic having to have a say in Northern Ireland's affairs.[42] Dublin was plainly pleased; Loyalists were obviously dismayed.

Speaking to a group of Conservatives at the House of Commons the following February, he set out the considerations that would guide his policy initiatives.[43] Security, the economy, and political development were inseparable; there could be no lasting improvement in either security or the economy unless there was political progress.

Direct Rule was a failure: "We have to face the fact," he said, "that we cannot make Direct Rule work indefinitely. It is a remarkable achievement that we have made it work as well as it has. Direct Rule has brought to the province a fair and impartial system of administration. But it is only a second best. It cannot offer anything more than a temporary answer."[44]

Moreover, to continue with Direct Rule "would be to resign ourselves to a very unsatisfactory security situation. At best there would be continuing loss of life, a continuing heavy cost in resources, and always the risk of a sudden flare-up. At worst security would deteriorate because of the prolonged uncertainty."[45] And there would be "little hope of establishing a sound economic base in the Province while the political uncertainty which accompanies Direct Rule continues."[46]

Integration was not a realistic option. The four major political parties were opposed to it. The province could not be governed as though it were Yorkshire, Norfolk, or Dorset. In the upper-tier local government authorities there would be the problem of permanent Unionist majorities. Control of the authorities would not alternate between parties as it did throughout most of Great Britain. In addition, the history, geography, and society of the province were different. And the fact that it was part of the island of Ireland "made it quite distinct from any other part of the United Kingdom."[47]

Thus, there was only one way forward: devolved government was necessary to bring about improvements in both the security situation and the economic situation. Improvements in these two areas would reinforce each other, strengthening the political framework and making people more confident in its ability to deliver just and equitable government.

Prior's task was not to achieve full agreement from the parties but "to try and narrow the differences, to try and bring the disagreement within proportions which are at least manageable."[48] Any new initiative had to be of the kind that would enable "the Northern Ireland politicians and parties to operate it and to work it for themselves."[49]

• • •

James Prior is relaxed, urbane, his responses interspersed with sudden shafts of self-deprecating humor and turns of slight irony. He conveys an aura of convincing purpose: a man sure of himself and of what he is doing, principled but also pragmatic, determined rather than insistent, familiar, perhaps too familiar, with the course of outrageous fortune, but nevertheless undeterred.

Would he address himself to the assumption prevalent among government and opposition officials in Dublin that Britain wanted out of Northern Ireland? Certainly:

They make the problem more difficult. I don't think Britain is in any way trying to force Ulster out of the United Kingdom. Why should we go on pouring money and blood and finance into Northern Ireland if we merely wanted to see the end of Northern Ireland as part of the United Kingdom? We are absolutely determined that as long as the majority of the citizens in the North wish to belong to the United Kingdom they should have a perfect right to do so. But we also feel that there is a relationship and an identity of many people among the minority in the North with the South and that it would be ridiculous if you denied that relationship, and if you didn't recognize it and allow it to be identified in some manner.[50]

Would a British government ever consider withdrawing the guarantee?

The will of the people alone guarantees [that there will not be a united Ireland]. Therefore, I regard section one of the 1973 Act as being, if you like, no more than a belt-and-braces approach in giving a legislative guarantee. I think it isn't so much the value of the guarantee as such, as the problems that would be created and the suspicions that would be created if you withdrew it, and therefore it is there, and there it remains. But if there had never been a guarantee, I don't think it would have made the slightest difference to the actual perception of the people of the North, and the fact that there is no way in which I can see that they would be prepared to join with the South.

Does the insistence of Southern politicians that unification is ultimately inevitable make its prospects less likely?

There are two elements here. Or perhaps even more than two. Let's take three elements. One, the more the demands come from the South for unification of the island, the less likely it is to come. That is something which is not properly understood in the South, although Garret FitzGerald did understand it and was seeking to meet it. He was quite exceptional in his point of view. The second thing is the very deep suspicion that there is by Unionists that some deal will be done behind their backs between London and Dublin, and that too is totally counterproductive. But the third and most fruitful approach would be for the North itself to have a degree of self-government in which the nationalist element was involved, unlike the old Stormont government, and for this self-government in the North to build a degree of self-confidence in itself which will enable it to have a totally different relationship with the South than is possible if they think the first two things are likely to come about.

But successive Irish Prime Ministers, notably Mr. Haughey and Dr. FitzGerald, equate the statements in the communiqués issued at the conclusions of the two summits that both governments wished to bring about the reconciliation of the two traditions in Ireland, with consent and in peace, as tantamount to British agreement to the eventual unification of Ireland. Is this an erroneous assumption on their part? Yes, it is:

Because it might suggest that the unification of the island could come about other than by the consent of the people of the North. It is perfectly clear that that consent is not forthcoming now, either in a numerical term or in an emotional term, and to that extent if reconciliation of the two traditions means unification, then the wording used has been unfortunate, because I don't believe that's what it's about.

In other words, reconciliation between the traditions does not necessarily imply consent to unity:

The idea that in the near future there would be a form of reconciliation, to use that word, which would result in the unification of Ireland has never seemed to me, at least in the time that I've been looking at the Northern Ireland problem, as being a likely outcome. I would have thought the Border Poll* is one reason, but also far more important than that the will of the people and the self-determination of the people themselves too.

Is he saying that reconciliation carried with it the right to say "no" to unity? Would the South have to become "reconciled" to the fact that unification is not in the cards for a very long time, if ever? Prior:

Yes, I think that's probably right, and I think that applies to those in the North who would take the nationalist point of view. However, there is an obvious need for nationalists in the North to be able to identify much more with the South and with Dublin. I don't think there's anything inconsistent between that wish to identify, to feel that they are, as it were, part of Ireland much more than just part of the U.K. I don't think there's any difficulty with them taking that point of view and still remaining part of Northern Ireland, governed, as it will be for a very long time to come, within the confines and within the concepts of the U.K.

In these circumstances how does the government propose to solve the problem of IRA violence?

What is necessary to defeat terrorism, apart from all that we're doing, is for the minority community to believe that they're going to be treated fairly and reasonably, particularly by the forces of law and order, and so the day will come when they can support freely the forces of law and order, and by support I mean joining in the police force and joining the UDR, and taking a free part in those activities and in the normal

* The purpose of the Border Poll introduced in the Northern Ireland Constitution Act (1973) is to establish the extent to which there is support for a continued link with Great Britain. The poll, intended to be held every ten years, was first held on 8 March 1973. Five hundred ninety-one thousand people voted to remain part of the U.K. and 6463 voted to join the Republic. The SDLP and most nationalists boycotted the poll.

activities associated with government. Then I believe we can isolate the IRA, and under those circumstances there will be no comfort or aid given to the IRA, and that will be the best way of defeating them.

And just how does he propose to get the minority to take part in "the normal activities associated with government"?

By having an Assembly in the North and by giving very strong guarantees about no transfer of power unless and until there is proper cross-community support, we are ensuring that the minority point of view is adequately represented.

But should not Britain spell out more clearly how she sees the future of Ireland and the relationship between the two islands? Yes and no:

The time will come when we ought to spell it out more clearly. But I'm not certain that today is the right time to do it.* I myself see a degree of self-government in the North, with the politicians here being far more responsible for their own destiny, with the situation in which those who are in politics have a responsibility for their actions, whereas they don't at the moment. And for them to be making much more of the relationship that they can develop with the South, away from the suspicions that someone else is seeking to push them against their will to do something.

An Assembly with devolved powers would quickly gain confidence in itself, and since it would face the severe economic difficulties small countries are jointly up against, it would want "to make sensible economic arrangements with the South as well as retaining the economic links with Great Britain." It would be "along these lines that at last some means of learning to live together would eventually come."

* Prior's statement, "But I'm not certain that today is the right time to do it" in regard to Britain spelling out more clearly how she sees the future of Ireland and the relationship between the two islands refers to the deterioration of Anglo-Irish relations in the wake of the Falklands war and Haughey's reiteration of Ireland's neutrality. The interview with Prior took place on 25 May 1982, at the height of the Falklands crisis. See chapter 12.

Would not a straightforward declaration that some form of Irish unity was in the best interests of both Britain and Ireland be helpful? Prior:

No, I mean it would be meaningless. It would lead to an enormous degree of suspicion which would be totally counterproductive. It would be in the interests neither of the Republic nor of the people of Northern Ireland. It would merely have a counterproductive result. You would merely find the antagonism of the Unionist element in the North towards the South would be much greater.

Would the removal of Articles 2 and 3 have a beneficial impact?

In the long run these gestures are important. Garret FitzGerald is moving along the right lines in all this, but I don't believe it would make a fundamental difference in the space of a few years. I think a number of things that we were beginning to move towards last winter were helpful and would have borne fruit in a period of time. But I don't think you can expect the prejudices, the deep prejudices which have been added to by the events in the last ten years or so, and the feeling in the North that terrorists have been able to take refuge in the South — you're not going to solve that in a short space of time. On the other hand, I think there is among Unionists a view that they just can't go on as they were going on before, and I fancy that there are many Unionists who, in the interests of Northern Ireland, are prepared to come out of their fixed positions and to recognize that there has to be a government with cross-community support.

Should the parliamentary tier of the Anglo-Irish Council be implemented? Correction:

It's not a parliamentary tier. It's a parliamentary body. I know from my personal experience with Parliament at Westminster that Members of Parliament are not going to give any share of their sovereignty to this particular body, and so I don't believe that this body is going to be of great significance for some time. Which is why I think the Unionists make a lot of unnecessary noise and fuss about this body. On the other hand, the SDLP holds out too many hopes and expectations for this body. Personally I hope a body will be set up. I think it would be a good thing for it to be set up, and in due course I expect it will.

On the differences between Charles Haughey and Garret Fitz-Gerald:

Garret FitzGerald was certainly taking the view that until one had some form of parliamentary body in the North one couldn't have any representatives for it in the Anglo-Irish parliamentary body. So in the communiqué last November [1981] it was written very clearly the words that the membership should consist of members of the House of Commons, the Dáil, members of the European Parliament, and any Assembly that was set up for the North, and so FitzGerald in fact was hinting that he would welcome a form of devolved government so much that the Unionists have accused me of wishing to set up a devolved government in the North in order that it might move towards some all-Ireland parliamentary body — so whatever way one wants to go one gets caught! That's why it's very important that there shouldn't be this view that Charles Haughey sometimes gives, and London sometimes gives, that Dublin and London are going to sort it out, and that Belfast is not going to have a say in it. It simply will not work that way.

If Britain were to contemplate withdrawal at some point, would the possibility of all of Ireland erupting into a trouble spot at Britain's back door preclude withdrawal as a viable option? Prior:

Yes. I think I would put it in two different ways. Obviously that is one consideration which would be very important. The other consideration is that Britain has brought about enough suffering in Ireland throughout the last two hundred and fifty years or more. And it really would be intolerable if we added to that suffering by a unilateral withdrawal now.

According to Nicholas Scott, Parliamentary Under-Secretary for Northern Ireland, the strategic implications are clear-cut:

The biggest challenge that the governments of the United Kingdom, the Republic of Ireland, and, I believe, the governments of Europe face is that the IRA campaign should succeed in the North, because if it [did] it would certainly mean that they would turn their sights on a government of the Republic and pursue their aim of a thirty-two-county socialist workers' republic, and Europe would then be faced with an offshore island and center for subversion that would not be very dissimilar from what the United States and the central and northern parts of Latin America have endured from Cuba for the last twenty years. I think that's the first danger and the first real problem of instability that we face, and that's one of the reasons why we're determined to make sure that the IRA campaign does not succeed in the North.[51]

Little, it seems, has changed in the four hundred years since Henry VIII set out to consolidate his control over Ireland primarily for strategic purposes. Back then the advance in technology that vastly increased the range and capability of long-distance sailing ships had made England more and more vulnerable to attack through Ireland. In fact, the Spaniards, her arch-foes, landed a force in 1601; the French did so in 1689 and again in 1798; and German submarines landed off the coast of Kerry in 1916. Even in 1951 the Commonwealth Relations Office continued to make the case for Northern Ireland remaining in the Commonwealth on the basis of defense considerations:

Historically [it argued], Ireland, which has never been able to protect herself against invasion, has been, as she is today, a potential base of attack on the United Kingdom. It is the more important that a part of the island, and that one strategically well-placed, should, and of its own free will, wish to remain part of the United Kingdom and of the United Kingdom defense scheme.[52]

The same considerations hardly apply today. But in a world where "trouble spots" have become the arenas in which the superpowers play out their elaborate games of force and counterforce, seeking marginal yet potentially crucial advantage to nudge the balance of power in their own favor, a socialist, hostile, unstable Ireland at Europe's back door would not be tolerable. A small, peripheral country cannot be allowed to exercise a degree of threat to the order of things disproportionate to her size, power, and resources. She is a pawn in the larger scheme.

Prior sums up his government's position:

It is incorrect to think that Britain wants to leave Northern Ireland. Britain wants Northern Ireland to do more for herself and to have self-government, but it doesn't want to leave Northern Ireland. It has a responsibility to the people of Northern Ireland and will fulfill that responsibility. As far as reconciliation between the two traditions is concerned, we want to see reconciliation between the two traditions, but we don't in any way regard that as synonymous with the unification of the island. It is synonymous with the recognition that there are people in the North who have an aspiration towards the unification of the island. It is synonymous with the view that there is a unique relationship between the North and the South, that you have an artificial Border, that you have people on both sides of the Border who have a great deal in common, and also that you have a British Isles which for many years Ireland was a part of. But that is very different from saying there's going to be unification, and I don't believe that there will be.[53]

In short, when Irish Prime Ministers use Anglo-Irish summits to suggest that the machinery of unification is being put in place, they are making statements that are damaging and untrue, when they equate reconciliation of the two traditions with eventual unification they are in error, and when they assume that Britain wants to leave Northern Ireland they are incorrect.

• • •

Thus the Conservative government's policy — for, again, there is no strategy: acknowledge the existence of the Irish Dimension and the legitimacy of the pursuit of unity within a democratic framework. Accommodate this aspiration of the minority by fostering close institutional links between Belfast and Dublin, and London and Dublin. Abandon power sharing for the more fluid concept of devolved government with significant cross-community support — that is, a government that would have the participation of the minority tradition. Once again there is the hope — not a policy — that if and when such a government evolved, its members would gain confidence in each other as they worked together on common problems. Hence, they would gain the acceptance of their communities; hence Catholic support of and participation in the security forces; hence the isolation and breaking of the IRA. In time such a government would develop closer relations with Dublin because of their mutual interests. And in time an Anglo-Irish parliamentary body would provide a wider framework to discuss the totality of Anglo-Irish relations, close links between London and Dublin reinforcing close links between Dublin and Belfast. But all arrangements are subject to one caveat: without the consent of a majority in the North the constitutional position of the state is nonnegotiable. Until consent for change is forthcoming, Northern Ireland will remain a part of the United Kingdom, the legal guarantee merely reiterating the obvious. British withdrawal is unthinkable, and never in the face of an IRA campaign. And because consent is not forthcoming now, will not be in the foreseeable future, and may perhaps never be, Britain does not want out of Northern Ireland. She will want out only when Northern Ireland wants her out.

• • •

However, Britain not wanting out is different from Britain wanting to stay in. When Labour's Don Concannon says "If you're saying would [we] want to get out, yes," he is, in fact, actually saying the same thing as James Prior. Were a majority to opt for a political solution that involved some form of political association with the South, neither would stand in the way. On the contrary, both parties would facilitate the change. Meanwhile, both favor a devolved government based on a formula other than simple majority rule, and both wish for the politicians in Northern Ireland to take matters into their own hands. In sum, short of breaking the link, Westminster would like to put as much distance between itself and Belfast as possible.

• • •

The Northern Ireland Constitution Act of 1973 remains the cornerstone of British policy, no matter which government is in power. Nicholas Scott:

> The firm basis of successive British governments has been that it is the wishes of the population of Northern Ireland that must predominate, and clause one of the 1973 Act makes that very clear. There can be no change in the constitutional position of Northern Ireland without the consent of the majority of the people of that province. Implicit in

that is the corollary that were the view of the majority of people in Northern Ireland to change, no British government would stand against the wishes of the majority, because we are basing our present position on the wishes of the present majority of the population and their views, and if their views were to change it seems to me axiomatic that a change in these views would mean a change in British policy.[54]

Accordingly:

If the majority of the people in Northern Ireland in the next Border Poll were to vote to leave the United Kingdom, no British government would put an obstacle in its way. Because it could not. Of course, they could vote for all sorts of alternatives to simple membership in the United Kingdom.[55]

Questions: What if a majority of the people of Northern Ireland decided to opt out of the Union, the support for that position coming from *the* majority and opposition to it from the minority? Would Britain pass legislation to give effect to that consent? Does the right to self-determination run in two directions only, either for an association with the U.K. or for an association with the rest of Ireland? Would Britain withdraw, leaving Catholics to fend for themselves? Would the right of the minority to protection supersede the right of *the* majority to "self-determination"? But if Britain did not respect the wishes of a majority so expressed, would it not make her conditional rationale for remaining in Northern Ireland — the assertion that she is upholding the democratic rights of a majority — specious? In the absence of the minority's support for independence, would she not subordinate the rights of a majority to her own best interests? And in the absence of the South giving her benediction to negotiated independence, would Britain not, perforce, have to reject it as an option open to Northern Ireland?

Thus, the concept of consent is further constrained. It has little to do with the right of a majority to exercise their full right to choose their own future. Justifying a course of action, as the British do, on that basis is less than truthful, the consent formula itself a short-run expedient that is, perhaps, simply not capable of being translated into a long-run accommodation.

"Freely given consent" is consent that fits into Britain's strategic aims. It is inconceivable that she would simply pack her bags and go, even if a majority were to declare themselves for that action. Nor could independence be negotiated as a bilateral arrangement between Belfast and London. If the Republic withheld her consent to any arrangement that emerged, the arrangement would come to naught.

Thus, Britain's pious insistence that she will remain in Northern Ireland only so long as that is the wish of a majority is essentially self-serving. It allows her to appear wholly responsible inasmuch as she can claim a disinterested concern to see that right is done on both sides, yet it holds her less than wholly accountable, because she can excuse the failure of her political initiatives and the stringency of the security laws on grounds of the extremism of the natives rather than on the inconsistencies of her own ill-conceived policies. A more accurate statement of her position would acknowledge that though she will remain in Northern Ireland so long as that is the wish of a majority, she will not necessarily leave, even if that is the wish of a majority.

Other anomalies are at work. All — the government party and the opposition parties — pay lip service to unity with the consent of a majority. But equally, all must know that even if 51 percent gave their approval to such an arrangement, a recalcitrant 49 percent, say seven hundred fifty thousand Protestants, would be just as much an obstacle to unity as would one million. If Britain is wary of revealing her long-term perspectives on Northern Ireland for fear of arousing the ire of a million Protestants, then surely she will be just as likely to acquiesce in the face of the ire of three quarters of a million. Who would enforce the "consent of a majority"? Would Britain pass legislation expelling Northern Ireland from the U.K. if 51 percent expressed themselves in favor of joining the Republic in a 1993 Border Poll? What measures would she employ to "induce" the consent of the obdurate 49 percent? Could she induce that consent while Northern Ireland still remained within the U.K. umbrella? And if not, would she have any legal right to either enforce or enjoin anything once she had voted to expel Northern Ireland? Surely the matter would then pass to the Republic? And in such circumstances would the Republic want Britain to pass the enabling legislation once the magic number was reached?

All of which begs the question: how large a majority is necessary to give expression to the consent of a majority? The law, section one of the Northern Ireland Constitution Act of 1973, states:

> It is hereby declared that Northern Ireland remains part of her Majesty's Dominions and of the United Kingdom, and it is hereby affirmed that in no event will Northern Ireland or any part of it cease to be part of her Majesty's Dominions and of the United Kingdom without the consent of the majority of the people of Northern Ireland voting in a poll held for the purposes of this section in accordance with Schedule 1 to this Act.[56]

Thus, the guarantee contains the elements of its own ambivalence: the consent of a majority is necessary for a change in status but not sufficient. Mrs. Thatcher's agreement at the second Anglo-Irish summit in November 1981 to support legislation in the British Parliament to give effect to the consent of a majority for a change in status "if it were expressed as a result of a poll conducted in accordance with the Act"[57] is noteworthy for what it does not say. First, "support" for legislation does not guarantee passage of the legislation. Hence, the fact that a majority in Northern Ireland might opt to join a united Ireland is no guarantee that the British Parliament will pass enabling legislation, nor would she be legally bound to do so. And second, since the agreement is between the British government and the Irish government, the wishes of a majority in Northern Ireland are secondary. Presumably it would be up to the Irish government to call for enforcement of the agreement. To Protestants, Britain is saying: "So long as a majority of people in Northern Ireland want to remain in the U.K. we'll respect their wishes." And to Catholics — North and South — she is saying: "When a majority give their consent to a united Ireland we'll support legislation to help make that wish a reality when we are called on to do so by the Republic."

Thus the irony: the Protestant guarantee is supplemented by the South's right of veto over what constitutes a majority. Her veto, however, may not mean much unless it coincides with Britain's domestic interests. The agreements the two governments have entered into may be agreements a British government will be either unable or unwilling to deliver on. The historical parallel is obvious: the Home Rule Bill of 1912 passed both houses of Parliament. However, the threat of Loyalist resistance was sufficient to ensure its demise. And today, as in 1912, an unwillingness to coerce Loyalists is at the core of the British "problem": Ian Paisley knows the soft underbelly well. Nicholas Scott:

> Simple unification seems to me to be absolutely pie-in-the-sky, and I have to emphasize that even with a majority of people deciding to bring it about, the practical problems of the governments of the U.K. and the Republic of Ireland would be such that they'd actually have to sit down and work out something much more complex than just reunifying Ireland.[58]

• • •

The acknowledgment that Direct Rule is a failure is, at least, frank. Direct Rule is, of course, undemocratic. The Secretary of State for Northern Ireland is virtually a dictator, ruling his fiefdom from his castle at Stormont. When the Stormont Parliament was abolished, most executive functions of the old regime, including responsibility for economic and security matters, passed into the Secretary of State's hands. He can propose and dispose almost at will. But as a ruler he does not have to answer at the ballot box to his constituents, who come from the shires of the mainland, not the counties of Northern Ireland. Nor has the fact that six Secretaries of State have come and gone in ten years been conducive to stable government. Most of them were unfamiliar with Northern Ireland when they arrived, and some were almost as unfamiliar with it when they left.

Moreover, Direct Rule erodes a sense of responsibility among politicians, leaving them more estranged from their constituents, more alienated from the process itself, more likely to be captive to the extremes within their own parties, and more of a hostage to the actions of paramilitaries. Being powerless, the politicians become more susceptible to pointing the finger of blame at those who would deny them the power than to committing themselves fully to the arduous undertaking of developing a consensus among themselves. Ultimately, Direct Rule is colonial rule. It plants the seeds of rebellion — and not just among the nationalists.

The lack of a long-term policy, and a strategy to implement it, creates its own vicious circle, providing an incentive for the IRA to continue the battle. Inability to reach agreement on devolved government means the continuation of Direct Rule, which means more uncertainty, more violence, and more disruption of the economy, and this, in turn, makes agreement on devolved government more difficult. The admission that Direct Rule feeds a cycle of destruction and hopelessness is likely to make those who wish to see an end to Northern Ireland more intransigent: for if Direct Rule is a failure, and a devolved government impossible, surely a collapse of political will in Britain to pursue the quest for an internal settlement cannot be too far behind?

When the implementation of an Irish Dimension is added to the necessity to secure agreement on something other than a majority-rule form of devolved government, the process breaks down completely. Loyalist intransigence on one issue is finely counterbalanced by nationalist intransigence on the other: the center is the agent of the extreme.

The notion that a devolved government will result in some miraculous improvement in the economic situation is also founded on hopeful belief rather than hard pragmatism. The failure of the North's economy is due in part to structural obsolescence — the decline of the textile, shipbuilding, and engineering industries, which were at one time the wellhead of the province's prosperity. Having been in at the start of the Industrial Revolution, the province had begun to pay the penalties of the early starter before the "troubles" began in the late 1960s. Unemployment was always high — far higher than in any other region of the U.K. — and investment correspondingly low.

Of course, the violence has hurt, reducing the flow of foreign investment to a dribble. But the belief that the most peripheral, underdeveloped part of a stagnant U.K. economy may somehow reinflate itself, bringing about significant reductions in unemployment through its own efforts, is wishful thinking.

The problem has acquired a critical mass of its own. In the past decade Northern Ireland has lost one third of her industrial jobs. About one third of this loss — twenty thousand jobs — may be attributed to political instability.[59] However, the other forty thousand were lost either because of the poor competitive position of the U.K. economy in world markets or because of Northern Ireland's deteriorating competitive position within the U.K. market.[60] Higher energy and transportation costs, higher wage-per-unit-of-output costs, and lower overall levels of productivity have taken their toll. In one five-year period in the early 1970s, for example, industrial costs were 20 percent more than the price of the goods sold.[61] Even if political instability was not a consideration, there are few "good" reasons why a company should invest in Northern Ireland.

The "new" industries — which were attracted to the province in the 1960s — were unable to sustain their competitive positions in international markets; their collapse largely accounts for Northern Ireland's economic woes. And given the province's endemic structural problems — its dearth of natural resources and its virtual isolation from mainstream economic networks — few companies are likely to take up the slack. British companies have given up. They invested a meager £1.3 million sterling in the North between 1976 and 1981, compared to £57.0 million sterling in the Republic.[62] One after another they are disappearing. GEC, Courtaulds, British Enkalon, ICI, Goodyear, Carreras, British Petroleum, Pickering Foods, Metal Box, and Hoescht (U.K.) — companies synonymous with the "replacement" industries of the 1950s and 1960s — either have departed or are departing the scene for more economically advantageous and politically stable locations, often to be found south of the Border, thanks to the aggressive selling policies of the Republic's Industrial Development Authority. And then, of course, there was the spectacular collapse of the DeLorean Motor Company.*

The economic malaise may be terminal. Even the sometimes optimistic Northern Ireland Economic Council sees no real prospect of recovery for the rest of this decade. One recent report estimated unemployment among sixteen- to eighteen-year-olds at 33 percent. Given the present rate of economic deterioration and the absence of special remedial measures, it could double by the end of 1983 despite the British government's Youth Training Program.[63] And though the youth unemployment problem is not unique to Northern Ireland, it is far more severe than in the rest of the U.K., and Ulster's higher birth rate and limited avenues of emigration will ensure its debilitating persistence. Thus, the vicious circle once again perpetuates itself: the more deprived communities there are, the more successful the paramilitaries; the more successful the paramilitaries, the more deprived communities there are. A truly massive investment of resources is called for. The call, however, given the state of the public mood and public finances in Britain, is likely to go unanswered, considering the scale of subsidy in the last decade. The Westminster subvention to Northern Ireland in 1983 exceeds £1.2 billion per year, up 1500 percent since 1970.[64] Additional costs owing to the Army's presence jumped from £1.5 million in 1970 to £100 million in 1980, while the cost of military operations for the ten-year period was half a billion pounds.[65] These are distressingly large expenditures for a country itself plagued by a stagflation verging on the unmanageable, especially since there appears to be no progress toward a settlement and no prospect of progress.

• • •

* The founder of the company, John DeLorean, was arrested in Los Angeles on 20 October 1982 and charged with financing a $24 million cocaine deal. When the DeLorean Motor Company collapsed, its 350 creditors were thought to be owed £41 million sterling. The company owed the British government £21 million pounds and the government was the guarantor of another £10 million in private bank funding. The total Exchequer assistance when the company was set up in 1978 was £53 million. At its peak the DeLorean Motor Company in Belfast employed twenty-six hundred workers and produced four hundred cars per week. (See *The Times* [London], 21 and 22 October 1982.)

Withdrawal. The demands for it come in many variations and from many quarters: troop withdrawal as a precursor of total withdrawal, immediate withdrawal, phased withdrawal, a declaration of intent to withdraw that sets a specific date, a declaration of intent that does not.

Whatever the demand, the rationale is the same: Ireland is one; the British presence underwrites the intransigence of Northern Protestants who will never agree to any accommodation with the South when they don't have to. Remove the British presence and you eviscerate their intransigence. When they see the "Brits" abandoning them, they will realize that their true interests lie in striking a compromise with the rest of their countrymen. They may consider a Unilateral Declaration of Independence, but when they work through what it would take, where it would lead, and how it would turn Northern Ireland into a permanent garrison state with a permanently impoverished economy, their innate common sense will assert itself. They will not fight unification because they have too much to lose. And if they did fight, their hearts would not be it; the realization that they couldn't prevail would be a deterrent to Masada-like defiance. When the shock waves subside and the hysteria dies down, cooler heads will assert themselves: they will make their peace; and those who cannot will leave.

Of course, a troop withdrawal has already taken place. Troops from mainland Britain now make up a far lower proportion of the security forces than they have in the past. However, insofar as this policy — the RUC denies that it constitutes "Ulsterization"* — leaves behind a predominantly Protestant police force and an overwhelmingly Protestant UDR, it puts obstacles in the way of total withdrawal. But then total withdrawal, British spokesmen of every hue insist, is simply out of the question. Nicholas Scott speaks for them all:

* Interview with Sir Jack Hermon, RUC Chief Constable, at RUC Headquarters, Belfast, 21 May 1982. He said: "Normal policing is having a police service which is geared to deal with the problems of a community. That's what's happening here . . . That's what we will achieve. No Ulsterization, no artificial politically oriented idea of getting troops out at any cost, of putting Ulstermen in khaki rather than Englishmen in khaki."

It would be impossible to conceive of the British Parliament passing a law about the future constitutional status of Northern Ireland unless a majority of the people there wanted it. Self-determination is an important principle. It's one to which Britain has adhered.[66]

A unilateral withdrawal would leave Northern Ireland in the hands of a professional Protestant army and police force and a network of Protestant paramilitary organizations whose memberships could range from five thousand to fifteen thousand. UDI would almost certainly follow. Catholics in the thousands would flee across the Border, creating an immense refugee problem. The IRA would prepare to protect the Catholic enclaves, their role as protectors of the minority no longer in question; recruitment would soar, Irish-American funds skyrocket. The South at the very least would stand ready to protect the Catholic population where she could, even prepared, perhaps, to seal off predominantly Catholic enclaves in South Armagh, Fermanagh, and Tyrone. Her own claim to the Six Counties would put her on a collision course with the Protestant North.

The stage would be set for civil war. The Irish in Britain — the perhaps one million native Irish and the four million first-generation[67] — would find themselves driven to take sides, especially in traditional Irish strongholds such as Glasgow and Liverpool. The connections between Loyalist paramilitary forces and their counterparts in Scotland are well established. The fundamentalism that fuels the politico-religious conflict has its roots in Scots fundamentalism. Sectarian rioting in Belfast could trigger sectarian rioting in Liverpool and Glasgow, tribal allegiances exploding in a primitive release of irredentist nationalism. English wars were often fought on Irish soil. What grim irony if in the waning decades of the twentieth century the situation should reverse itself, and Ireland's war was fought on British soil.

Withdrawal would strengthen, perhaps irrevocably, the position of the IRA. At the very least it would undermine the Irish government. For on the day the British commenced to effect withdrawal, the IRA would claim victory. Nothing would obscure the fact that what it had fought to accomplish, it had achieved.

By insistently demanding withdrawal as a precursor to any settlement, the IRA has already shaped and defined the public's perception of a British withdrawal.

The television pictures would say it all. The cameras would roll, and in tens of millions of homes around the world, the images of Saracen trucks lining the quaysides, of silent personnel carriers slipping away, of an army dismantling the paraphernalia of war and going home, would spell out the message: a departing army is a beaten army; the IRA has won, the British have lost. The resulting propaganda possibilities for the IRA would be incalculable. Having endured the stigmata of criminality and murder, the condemnation of Church and state, the immolation of death fasts, the opprobrium of the bourgeoisie, and the contempt of the elite, they would stand vindicated: Wolfe Tone's historic objective achieved, the long, lonely, and fastidious haul against redoubtable odds a triumph of high idealism, the achievement of the end justifying the means, erasing the doubts, resolving the moral dilemmas.

Nor could an Irish state that would, perforce, have to come to the aid of Northern Catholics continue to denounce the IRA as men of violence. Of course they would be, as they are now. And they would take pride in it, as they do now. But with a unilateral British withdrawal, there would be more to the IRA than violence. There would be identity and purpose and place in the historical continuum. It would possess a new impetus to reach for its further goals, driven by the conviction that what had eluded its best efforts to accomplish for sixty years was now within grasp. And many would believe.

In a direct confrontation with Protestants it is unlikely that the Republic could prevail. She has neither the resources, the know-how, nor the stomach to forcibly bring about a united Ireland. But one thing is for sure: the catastrophic cost of an attempt to do so would destroy what is left of the Irish economy. In what would be an ironic turn of events, the Irish Army would take the place of the British Army as the army of occupation, establishing its bridgehead in Fermanagh, Tyrone, and South Armagh. The UDA would take the place of the IRA as the "fighters for freedom," with the RUC and UDR as the armed security forces of the Ulster statelet. Down and Antrim, with populations that are 80 percent Protestant, would prove impregnable. But within that impregnable garrison state, Belfast would become the graveyard battleground. Without Belfast the IRA can hardly exist; with Belfast it can hardly be eradicated. To the IRA would fall the task of protecting the community of two hundred thousand Catholics — one third of the city's total population — cut off from the outside world behind a wall of Protestant power, sealed off from assistance — even, perhaps, from resupply.

If Protestants decided to effect their own final solution, bearing down on the Catholic ghettos and rooting out, or rather exterminating, those they suspected of being IRA gunmen, the stage would be set for an apocalyptic pogrom. The scene: frenzied calls to the outside world for relief from desperate and despairing Catholics, highly charged pleas from a helpless Irish government for a U.N. peacekeeping force, worldwide headlines. Britain's responsibility to Catholics makes unilateral withdrawal unthinkable; her attention to her own long-range strategic interests makes it improbable. Her presence, especially her military presence in Northern Ireland, may make for international embarrassment on occasion, but a unilateral withdrawal could produce a plethora of disasters that would irreparably damage her prestige, making her guarantees hollow, her treaties suspect, her laws empty, her democratic system a charade.

The presence of a U.N. peacekeeping force in Ulster would add to the humiliation of both British and Irish governments. Only the paramilitaries would stand to gain. Keeping Protestant and Catholic apart is one function of the security forces at present, but of more importance is their role in preventing either side from establishing its own exclusive "no-go" areas. By the time a peacekeeping force arrived, both sides, or rather all sides, would have carved out their own power bases, partitions within Partition, which an international force would be unable to destroy or even to police. A "neutral" force, unwilling to move against either side, would be impotent. There would be no way to launch "impartial" operations against one side or the other, or of balancing an incursion against one side by an "equal" incursion against the other. Therefore, a situation likely to trigger more rather than fewer hostilities would prevail. In any event, the outcome would be stalemate, indefinite and final — and economic collapse.

Nor would Britain's problems be over. Besides the possibility — indeed, the likelihood — of all of Ireland erupting, and the threat that that would pose to her strategic interests, the possible collapse of the Irish economy would have an immediately deleterious impact on the British economy (Ireland is Britain's fourth-largest trading partner). If the conflict spread to the mainland, it could trigger large-scale rioting in the ghettos of England's own deprived and forgotten minorities; and withdrawal could have an impact on the course of nationalism in Scotland and Wales, since the message would be clear: the British will is ultimately weak; the bomb and the bullet are a lot more effective in promoting change than negotiations. The end justifies the means. Withdrawal, in short, could signal the breakup of Britain.[68]

There is, therefore, no case for unilateral withdrawal unless, of course, it is assumed that Protestants would accept that British withdrawal made unification inevitable, and that rather than fight the inevitable they would bow to it. The British are not yet willing to test that assumption, nor are the South or Northern Catholics likely to encourage them to. Nevertheless, the Protestant will to fight remains the one great imponderable, there being a remote chance that the conflict is, after all, a ghastly charade, the triumph of subterfuge — that withdrawal would bring not the apocalypse of resistance but the whimper of surrender.

Nor would a declaration of intent to withdraw, even at an unspecified date in the future, have a much different impact. Once again the IRA would appear vindicated. And the South disconcerted. Not having called for a declaration of intent to withdraw, she would now find herself in the invidious position of having to deal with the consequences. She could hardly claim credit for the event when it occurred, and yet if she were to call, even belatedly, for withdrawal, she would find herself following in the footsteps of the organization she condemned so vociferously. And were she then to continue to deny the IRA any role in the process, her actions would only strengthen the hands of the movement, since she would appear as either a reluctant or an eager convert to a policy heretofore the exclusive preserve of the IRA. Cracking down on the IRA would become more difficult.

For its part, the IRA would intensify its actions in order to turn the declaration of intent into fact. Given that withdrawal was inevitable, both sides would hunker down, stockpile arms, and wait. Rather than proving to be an incentive to negotiate, it would provide the rationale for truculence. Moreover, it could provoke Protestants to seek their independence. But if Protestants did perceive it as reason to break the Union and moved in the direction of UDI, would "mainland" troops disarm the RUC and UDR? Would the RUC and UDR take actions against Protestant paramilitary groups intent on keeping Ulster out of a united Ireland? Would Britain fight the Protestants of Ulster? The evidence of the past is that she would not. And in the absence of that resolve, she is unlikely to commit herself to withdrawal at either a specified or an unspecified date in the future.

• • •

Despite her protestations that she would never abandon a majority who wanted to remain part of the U.K. and her insistence that the guarantee is ironclad and will never be repealed, Britain's voice falls on deaf ears. She is not believed: the public posturing is taken as a camouflage for private designs. Paddy Harte, former Fine Gael spokesman on Northern Ireland, says:

> I have spoken to British politicians who are very much in favor of British withdrawal or, as they put it themselves, "getting the hell out of the place." Their next remark would be: "Now tell us how to do it." My honest belief is that if Britain could disengage from Northern Ireland without any fear of the civil war spreading to the mainland of Britain, she would. Most British politicians I've spoken to favor Irish unity — that is, some form of unity acceptable to the traditions living in Ireland.[69]

Garret FitzGerald:

In any situation which is ultimately a negotiating situation, none of the parties are likely to disclose the whole of their minds in public. And that means there can be significant disparities between publicly stated attitudes and privately stated attitudes. Secondly, apart from the fact that there is always the possibility of negotiations in the future which could be affected by publicly stated positions, you have the fact that the issues we are dealing with are ones which involve strong emotions in each of the areas — both within Northern Ireland on the Unionist and nationalist sides, in the Republic to a degree also, and in Britain perhaps sometimes to a degree greater than appreciated. And that all operates as a constraint on people stating the whole of their thought in a public forum.[70]

FitzGerald's remarks were made when he was asked to comment on James Prior's statements that reconciliation did not necessarily imply unification and that Britain did not want to get out of Northern Ireland. In many respects they are surprising, and certainly revealing. While Prior insists that the constitutional position of Northern Ireland is not up for negotiation, FitzGerald talks of a situation that is "ultimately a negotiating situation." While Prior talks of the need to allay the fears of Protestants that deals are being cut behind their backs in private meetings, FitzGerald refers to the "significant disparities between publicly stated attitudes and privately stated attitudes." Yet it was FitzGerald himself who publicly castigated Haughey for the secrecy surrounding the first Anglo-Irish summit. When he became Taoiseach, he released the text of the joint studies for the specific purpose of assuaging Protestant fears. Yet since the "strong emotions" on all sides "operate as a constraint on people stating the whole of their thought in a public forum," should not what went on at the closed meetings first between Haughey and Thatcher and then between FitzGerald and Thatcher — and the routine denials that nothing in fact went on other than what was already in the official communiqués — fuel Protestant fears? If Britain's public attitude is that the constitutional status of Northern Ireland is nonnegotiable, and that withdrawal is not therefore an option, and Ireland's position is essentially the knowing wink and the nod, implying that that is not what Britain says in private, the Unionist paranoia has a basis in fact. The problem is one of trust, without which there can be no progress.

• • •

None of the parties to the conflict trusts Britain, and with good cause. Because she will not declare herself, no one knows where she stands. Memories of duplicities in the not-too-distant past intrude upon the present, and disturb. The legerdemain of Lloyd George, conniving and intriguing to convince Unionists and Republicans alike that he stood squarely with their respective aspirations, indeed that he countenanced "with his life upon the table" the justice of their respective causes, has not been forgotten. And government actions in the last ten years, if not openly duplicitous, have had at least a sufficient appearance of being so.

Loyalists remember how close Britain came to abandoning them to a Catholic Ireland in 1914 and that it was only their threat of rebellion that stayed her hand. Little, they believe, has changed. Britain would maneuver them with all deliberate speed out of the U.K., and once again it is only their intransigence that keeps her in line. Thus, Loyalist perceptions of what Britain's ultimate intentions are make Loyalists cling to their only point of reference. Their intransigence, therefore, is inevitable.

Nationalists remember that Britain reneged on Home Rule in 1914, rather than stand up to militant Unionists. And they, too, believe little has changed. Otherwise Britain would have taken on militant Loyalists in 1974, even with force of arms, to save the power-sharing Executive. They hear Britain talking of power sharing and a fair deal for the Catholic minority, but they see the British Army invading their rights and privacy. They hear Britain talking of an Irish Dimension in the short run and overt hints of her passive support for unification in the long run, but they see no change in the status quo. Both sides, therefore, have been given to believe that they will ultimately prevail, if only they persist. If Britain is for unification but not for the coercion of Loyalists, then nationalists are encouraged to keep their aspirations alive, and Loyalists are encouraged to keep Britain reminded of the folly of coercion. Both sides have been maddened, their insanities drawing strength from the constancy of their obsessions. Hence the permanence of the sectarian divide.

No British "policy" for Northern Ireland will work unless it is part of a long-term plan. Britain owes it to herself and to both parts of Ireland to spell out how she sees the future of Ireland. And if she will not plan for the future, if she will not care enough to face up to the problem, whatever hopes she has of disengaging will perish in the mire of her own shortsightedness.

Either she accepts that Ulster will remain a part of the U.K. so long as that is the wish of a majority, or she does not. If she does, then a number of corollaries follow. First, should consent for unification emerge, a Northern Ireland government will have to give expression to it. In other words, Northern Ireland must legislate herself into an Irish state before Britain legislates her out of the U.K. Accordingly, *a devolved government in Northern Ireland is a necessary prerequisite for eventual British withdrawal.* Second, the attempt to bring into being simultaneously both a power-sharing devolved government and an Irish Dimension is a certain prescription for failure on both accounts. Much as Loyalists want "their" government back, they would rather not have one than to see it used as a means of coercing them into an institutional relationship with the South. The expression of an "Irish" Dimension should be left to governments in Belfast and Dublin to work out rather than to governments in London and Dublin to impose. Third, while institutional links between the Republic and the U.K. are a matter solely for the two sovereign governments involved, the form they take should facilitate rather than impede institutional links between North and South. Thus, Anglo-Irish summitry should be de-emphasized, and *the notion that summitry is a "process" that will ultimately lead to a "solution" must be conclusively rebutted.* Fourth, if Britain remains unwilling to coerce Loyalists, no matter what arrangements are in question, she is conceding to Loyalists the right to veto every political initiative, in which case the future will repeat the past: no arrangement will work, no devolved government will emerge, no consent will be forthcoming, and no withdrawal will be possible. Fifth, Britain must recognize that while the Emergency Provisions and the Prevention of Terrorism acts are on the books, the sweeping powers of arrest they permit will continue to be abused, thereby defeating in large measure their purpose. Better to repeal this special legislation and rely on normal legal channels to deal with political terrorism. Moreover, a devolved government must have control over security and important security portfolios must be held by members of the minority community. Sixth, Britain should leave the Republic in no doubt as to what her position is: that her full commitment is to a devolved, power-sharing government in Northern Ireland that fully protects the rights of the minority; that the constitutional status of Northern Ireland is nonnegotiable; that British withdrawal at any point in the future is predicated on there being a stable devolved government in existence; and that it is, therefore, in the long-run interests of the Republic to ensure that devolved government works.

If Britain does not accept that Northern Ireland should remain a part of the U.K. so long as that is the wish of a majority, then she must also face up to the following corollaries. First, the charge of duplicity is correct; her public pronouncements, her White Papers, her guarantees are matters of expedience to be changed, contradicted, or discarded as circumstances dictate. Second, she is willing to repeal the Northern Ireland Constitution Act and to legislate Northern Ireland out of the United Kingdom no matter what constitutional crisis or trauma the action might provoke in Britain itself and no matter how Loyalists might respond. In short, in a historic turnabout she would coerce Loyalists, even with force of arms, if necessary. Third, she would expel Northern Ireland from the U.K. and either force her consent to some arrangement with the South or abandon her to her own designs without regard to the impact in the whole of

Ireland or the U.K. In short, she would concede Ireland to the Irish, and victory to the IRA.

• • •

Of course, even if Britain would like to sever the link with Northern Ireland despite the objections of a majority there, she could not publicly acknowledge the fact. And thus her dilemma: because both Protestants and Catholics accept that she could not acknowledge such intentions, they dismiss, for their own reasons, her public statements to the contrary.

7

The Irish Republican Army: A Question of Certainty

Frenzies bewilder, reveries perturb the mind;
Monstrous familiar images swim to the mind's eye.

—W. B. Yeats
"Meditations in Time of Civil War"

THE IRA HAS A PLAN.* It has the virtue of pristine simplicity. Tenacity will pay off. Continue the armed struggle until the British get frustrated with the futility of it all and withdraw—either the cost of maintaining the Army presence will become prohibitive or the British public will get sick of the conflict or one of the political parties will break ranks. It does not seek a military victory, knowing full well there is no way to "defeat" the security forces in any military sense of the term. Rather, it seeks victory by attrition: to win it must only survive. Actions, therefore, are on a scale that does not invite a commensurate response from the security forces. The movement has shown, time and again, its capacity to survive, even when the environment in which it operates is hostile. Mao may have talked about the "water" the guerrilla fish need to sustain themselves; the

* References to the IRA are to the Provisional IRA—also called PIRA, the Provisionals, or simply the Provos. For a brief account of the split of the IRA into the Provisional wing and the Official wing see chapter 10, pp. 364–65.

IRA, however, has ably demonstrated that it can survive with very little water, and on occasion with no water at all. One expert estimates that it can function with as little as 3 percent support among the Catholic population.[1] It is almost impossible to conceive of circumstances where that level of support would not be forthcoming. The struggle of more than thirteen years, the violence visited upon the innocent, the warping of minds, the resentment and bitterness that are the legacy of countless house searches, internments, detentions, and petty harassments have built a collective consciousness in many of the working-class Catholic ghettos that ensures the movement will endure.

The breadth of house searches alone conveys the scale of possible support: more than thirty-six thousand in 1972, double that again in 1973 and 1974, thirty thousand in 1975, thirty-four thousand in 1976, twenty thousand in 1977, and fifteen thousand in 1978.[2] And in every household searched there was left behind a sense of alienation, of estrangement, of the anger felt when one's privacy is rudely and brutally invaded.

They are, of course, everyone's whipping boy, condemned routinely on all sides as "terrorists," the hard men of violence, who are responsible for perpetuating the conflict. The governments that condemn them are, often as not, hypocritical — condemnation is a function of political expediency rather than a statement of principle. The Irish government's insistence that the IRA is simply a subversive organization dismisses the past too easily. In its eagerness to have the IRA classified as one more terrorist group feeding into the network of international terrorism, it further distorts the historical continuum, undermining its own credibility and consequently its ability to make an effective case against the IRA. On the other hand, the British government's policy of treating IRA prisoners as ordinary criminals also flies in the face of its own past actions: direct talks with the IRA in 1972 and again in 1975.*

* On 7 July 1972, a party of Provisional IRA leaders, including Daithi O'Conaill, was flown secretly to London for talks with William Whitelaw, then Secretary of State for Northern Ireland. The talks were unproductive. Two days later, the truce, which the Provisionals had announced on 26 June, collapsed. It had lasted just thirteen days. After the secret talks between IRA leaders and Protes-

But condemnation is easy, even comforting. It bestows an aura of moral righteousness; reality is best dealt with by denying it, for the reality is uncomforting: the IRA exists because it has the tacit support of a significant number of people North and South who may disavow the violent means it employs but who, nevertheless, support its aspirations. And even the condemnations of violence more often than not stop well short of regarding IRA prisoners, even those who have killed or carried out the most hideous acts of mutilation, as common criminals; the deeds may be revolting but the perpetrators are not responsible: somehow it is the exalted "cause" that makes them do it. Thus, thousands of respectable, law-abiding citizens could take to the streets in support of political status for the prisoners at the Maze Prison.

• • •

Since the early 1970s the fortunes of the Provisional IRA have flowed and ebbed.[3] They flowed between 1969 and 1973, reaching perhaps their high-water mark in mid-1972 when IRA internees won recognition as political prisoners and the leadership was flown to London aboard British government aircraft for talks with British government officials, including the Secretary of State for Northern Ireland, William Whitelaw. By late 1975 they were ebbing badly: the movement had largely disintegrated, gangsterism was pervasive, internecine feuding between the Officials and Provisionals left eleven people dead in one two-week period, and informers were ubiquitous. But the IRA survived, even if the water had almost dried up, because of one simple fact: so long as the British remain in Northern Ireland, armed resistance to their presence can always be justified. Where circumstances dictate the inevitable, the inevitable will invariably

---

tant clergymen at Feakle, County Clare (10 December 1974), meetings took place between British government officials and members of Provisional Sinn Féin. See O'Conaill's remarks, p. 285. See also W. D. Flackes, *Northern Ireland: A Political Directory*, p. 116. For an account of the Feakle talks, see Eric Gallagher and Stanley Worrall, *Christians in Ulster 1969–1980*, pp. 1, 2, and 97–98. Both Gallagher and Worrall were members of the group of Protestant clergymen. They, too, assert meetings between the government and Provisional Sinn Féin; see *Christians in Ulster*, p. 100.

ensue. The tradition of violence dating back to the savage sectarian confrontations between secret agrarian societies during the late eighteenth century hardened into an ideology of violence that continues to have, even to this day, widespread support in the tightly knit, beleaguered communities on both sides of the divide. Its imperatives legitimize the use of violence in certain situations — for Catholics, situations where the forces of law and order are seen as the forces of an alien oppressor.

• • •

By 1979, Brigadier James Glover, for one, was under no illusions. Glover, who later would become the General Commanding Officer of British forces in Northern Ireland, drew up a secret report for the Army entitled "Northern Ireland: Future Terrorist Trends."[4]

Its contents were revealing. British government officials could dismiss the IRA as a ragtag collection of romantic and often bungling amateurs relying on the misled and the misfit to carry out its grisly and often inept operations. They could talk of the IRA being beaten, of the movement's imminent demise, of its lack of indigenous support, and, condescendingly, of the "Paddy Factor."* But not the Army. It saw the IRA as a symbol of implacable resistance, a hard-core professional elite, unyielding in its aims to drive out the British and to unify the country, and unrelenting in its methods. Wrote Glover:

> The Provisional leadership is deeply committed to a long campaign of attrition. The Provisional IRA (PIRA) has the dedication and sinews of war to raise violence intermittently to at least the level of early 1978, certainly for the foreseeable future. Even if "peace" is restored, the motivation for politically inspired violence will remain. Arms will be readily available and there will be many who are able and willing to use them. Any peace will be superficial and brittle. A new campaign may erupt in the years ahead.[5]

Moreover, less "active" support for the IRA would have no discernible impact on its capacity to pursue its objectives.

* The "Paddy Factor" is used derisively to explain bungled IRA activities — where IRA personnel become the victims of their own incompetence.

The Provisionals cannot attract the large number of active terrorists they had in 1972/73. But they no longer need them. PIRA's organization is now such that a small number of activists can maintain a disproportionate level of violence. There is a substantial pool of young Fianna (junior IRA) aspirants, nurtured in a climate of violence, eagerly seeking promotion to full gun-carrying terrorist status and there is a steady release from the prisons of embittered and dedicated terrorists. Thus though PIRA may be hard hit by security force attention from time to time, they will probably continue to have the manpower they need to sustain violence during the next five years.[6]

The reorganization Glover refers to took place in 1977. Up to that point the IRA was organized on a neighborhood basis. The structure was hierarchical — brigades, battalions, and companies drew their members from the neighborhoods in which they would operate. This, of course, not only made the movement susceptible to infiltration, it made it a lot easier for the authorities to identify likely suspects when a unit claimed responsibility for a particular operation. The new organization was cellular — very small active-service units with no more than two or three members, drawn from different neighborhoods. The structure was vertical, the nature of the function defining the composition of the unit. Information was disseminated on a "need to know" basis only. Only one member of a bombing unit, for example, would know in advance what the intended target was. Glover:

By reorganizing on cellular lines PIRA has become less dependent on public support than in the past and is less vulnerable to penetration by informers. The hardening segregation of the communities also operates to the terrorists' advantage. Although the Provisionals have lost much of the spontaneous backing they enjoyed early in the campaign, there is no sign of any equivalent upsurge of support for the Security Forces.[7]

And the security forces continued to be hampered in other ways: there were enclaves within the province, both rural and urban, where the IRA could base itself with little risk of betrayal; it could count on active support in emergencies, and the omnipresent fear of a return to Protestant repression ensured an immutable residue of support for the Provisionals, even under the worst of circumstances.

Nor did Glover share the official view that the IRA was made up of hoodlums, the antisocial, and the dregs of the poorer and more deprived classes. On the contrary:

> Our evidence of the caliber of the rank-and-file terrorists does not support the view that they are merely mindless hooligans drawn from the unemployed and unemployable. PIRA now trains and uses its members with some care. The Active Service Units (ASU's) are for the most part manned by terrorists tempered by up to ten years of operational experience . . . PIRA is essentially a working-class organization based in the ghetto areas of the cities and in the poor rural areas.[8]

Glover took note of other changes: there had been a movement away from the indiscriminate bombings and shootings of the early 1970s; targets were far more likely to be members of the security forces; actions "which by alienating public opinion both within the Catholic community and outside of it [were] politically damaging"[9] had been severely curtailed. This change of direction reflected a change in attitude. The movement was more keenly attuned to the nuances of effective propaganda; hence the leadership's increasing sensitivity to the need to avoid alienating support not only in Ulster itself "but also in the Republic and among those of Irish extraction overseas."[10] Ultimately the PIRA strategy rested on one simple premise: "that a campaign of attrition with its attendant costs in both lives and money will eventually persuade HMG to withdraw from Northern Ireland."[11] Hence Glover's conclusions:

> We see no prospect in the next five years of any political change which would remove PIRA's raison d'être . . . The Provisionals' campaign of violence is likely to continue while the British remain in Northern Ireland . . . We see little prospect of political development of a kind which would seriously undermine the Provisionals' position. PIRA will probably continue to recruit the men it needs. They will still be able to attract enough people with leadership talent, good education and manual skills to continue to enhance their all-around professionalism.

The movement will retain popular support sufficient to maintain secure bases in the traditional Republican areas.[12]

Glover made his sober assessment in January 1979, almost two and a half years before the hunger strikes put into motion a conveyor belt of death, traumatizing the Catholic community, unleashing a helpless rage that spilled over into the Republic and threatened the rule of government there, and polarizing the two communities in Northern Ireland as nothing else had, not even the awful events of Bloody Sunday.

• • •

The issue, ostensibly, was special-category status. In June 1972, as a result of a hunger strike in Crumlin Road Prison by Billy McKee, formerly the IRA leader in Belfast, William Whitelaw introduced "special-category" status for prisoners convicted of "political" crimes. Prisoners were not required to wear prison uniforms or to work; they were allowed more visits and food parcels, and better facilities, than ordinary prisoners; and they were housed in compounds. In short, special-category status was equivalent, at least in the eyes of the prisoners, to political status.

The situation changed in March 1976. The special-category status was abolished. Under the new policy, persons convicted of "political" crimes committed after 1 March were treated as ordinary criminals, although those convicted before that date retained their special status.

The "H-Block" protest began in September 1976 when Kieran Nugent, the first person convicted under the new regulations, refused to either wear prison clothes or do prison work as part of his demand to be treated as a political prisoner.* He went "on the blanket" — the prison blanket his only clothing. He was joined not only by incoming Republican prisoners but also by

* The H-Blocks referred to the blocks of new cells at the Maze Prison, formerly known as Long Kesh. There were eight such blocks, each shaped as the letter H, each half-upright of the letter H containing twenty-five two-prisoner cells. Each H-Block, therefore, could accommodate two hundred prisoners. And each half-upright had its own dining room–cum–recreational facility. The "line" across the H contained two classrooms and an administrative office.

Loyalists protesting that they too were not "common criminals." Loyalist prisoners were on the blanket in varying numbers, from thirty up to one hundred, until all of them dropped out of the protest in July 1978 when the issue had, in their eyes, become very much a Republican cause.[13]

The "blanket protest" became the dirty protest. Prisoners — almost four hundred at one point — smeared their excrement on the walls, floors, and ceilings of their cells. They lived in filth. It was putrid, disgusting, and repulsive. And it didn't work.[14] Hence the first hunger strikes, which began in October 1980 when seven prisoners vowed to fast to their deaths until the British government agreed to their demands for special-category status. The strike lasted fifty-three days, ending on 18 December, when it appeared that the basis of a reasonable compromise had been reached, although there was a general feeling that the prisoners had in fact backed down. Although the government did not go so far as to claim "victory," it made it clear that it had made no new concessions. Subsequent events and negotiations precipitated a tailspin. Despite what the prisoners had taken to be an understanding that their demands would be accommodated in some manner, the government would not budge.* Accordingly, on 1 March 1982, Bobby Sands, the commanding officer of the Provisional IRA within the prison, began his hunger strike.

But much more than special status was at issue. The hunger strikes were Russian roulette with an Irish twist, one last great gamble by the Provisionals to seize the initiative, to reclaim the support of Northern Catholics, to validate their claim to historical legitimacy, to arouse public opinion in the Republic, and to humanize the movement. Successful revolutionary movements need human symbols to mitigate the hard edge of their violence. The public's failure to identify more openly with the IRA was due in part to the "faceless" character of the movement — there was no one to identify with.

* The prisoners made five demands: They wanted the right to wear their own clothes, to refrain from prison work, to associate freely with one another, to organize recreational facilities and to have one letter, visit, and parcel a week, and to have lost remission time fully restored.

Bobby Sands changed all that.

"I am a political prisoner," he wrote the first day of his hunger strike. "I am a political prisoner because I am a casualty of a perennial war that is being fought between the oppressed Irish people and an alien, oppressive, unwanted regime that refuses to withdraw from our land."[15] His logic was averring the logic of Tone, Emmet, and Pearse, the historical continuum as an unchanging point in time: "I believe and stand by the God-given right of the Irish nation to sovereign independence and the right of any Irishman or woman to assert this right in armed revolution. That is why I am incarcerated, naked and tortured."[16] There was a villain — and a simple, straightforward solution. "Foremost in my tortured mind," he continued, "is the thought that there can never be peace in Ireland until the foreign, oppressive British presence is removed, leaving all the Irish people as a unit to control their own affairs and determine their own destinies as a sovereign people, free in mind and body, separate and distinct physically, culturally and economically."[17] He saw himself as part of an ennobling tradition, "another of those wretched Irishmen born of a risen generation with a deeply-rooted and unquenchable desire for freedom."[18] "I am dying," he concluded, "not just to attempt to end the barbarity of H-Block or to gain the rightful recognition of a political prisoner but primarily because what is lost in here is lost for the Republic and those wretched oppressed whom I am deeply proud to know as the 'risen people.' "[19]

He died sixty-six days later, his body having digested itself.

In the next three months, nine others followed in his death-steps. They, too, would endure by consuming themselves, like their blood brother Terence McSwiney, whose death in Brixton Prison in December 1920 after a hunger strike lasting seventy-four days resulted in a national outpouring of grief.* "It is not those who inflict the most but those who suffer the most who will conquer," the dying McSwiney had written. The myth of redemptive sacrifice hardened and held.

* McSwiney, Lord Mayor of Cork, was arrested in Cork Town Hall at an IRA conference that his captors mistakenly took to be a Republican Court. See Robert Kee, *Ourselves Alone,* pp. 122–23.

Those who suffer the most.

In this context the hunger strikes were a metaphysical ritual, a symbol: the blood-stained bond linking the failures of the past to the failures of the present; the confession of defeat transcending the blood-letting of the present, reestablishing the link with the historical past, and reaffirming the legitimacy of the cause and the movement by reaffirming the legitimacy of the means. They were atonement for the mutilations, the meaningless maimings, the innumerable futile brutalities, and the hundreds of violent and misdirected deaths sanctioned in the name of holy nationalism. They were expiation, an asking for forgiveness, an abnegation of self, a blind conviction that what could not be achieved by the murder of others could yet be achieved by the murder of self. They were an excuse for the murders of tomorrow, romantic delusion, the sublimation of reality, an aggravated assault on the national psyche, a last desperate attempt to mobilize public opinion by cheating life, an atavistic gesture of impotence to orchestrate a symphony of grief, a callous ploy to infiltrate the hidden recesses of the national consciousness, a reaching back to tribal allegiances, to the myth of martyrdom and redemption. In death the prisoners became fathers, husbands, and lovers, victims of their legends, the legacy of a generation born in fear and taught to hate. It was inevitable that some eventually would aspire to kill.

Says Nobel peace laureate Mairead Corrigan Maguire,* cofounder of the Peace People:

I watched Bobby Sands's funeral. The coffin stopped at the bottom of our garden in Andersontown. I saw at the funeral of Bobby Sands people who had been at my sister's funeral, who walked at the children's funeral, who marched in the peace rallies, walking by the coffin of

* Mairead Corrigan was the aunt of the three Maguire children who were killed in August 1976 when an out-of-control car whose driver had been shot dead by the British Army smashed into them. The children's deaths led to the peace movement and mass peace parades in late 1976 and 1977. Corrigan and Betty Williams were awarded the 1977 Nobel Peace Prize. In January 1980, the children's mother, Anne, who had never gotten over the death of her children, committed suicide. Later Corrigan married her dead sister's widower.

Bobby Sands because people are emotionally tied into the prisons. It's not that they support violence or the Provisional IRA. But they are all men from our community. We know how they have come to be there. And above all we don't want them suffering within the prisons.

When Bobby Sands died, many of us felt, it's back to square one. In fact, further back and further divided than even square one was. If you tried to call a peace rally now in Andersontown — and I'm from Andersontown, so I know it — you wouldn't get anyone to come. There is far more bitterness and a feeling of anti-Britishness in many communities. People who never even used the term *Brits out* started to use the term.[20]

Father Des Wilson, talking about the Catholic ghettos of West Belfast, echoes Maguire's sentiments:

There were people on marches against the government's treatment of the hunger strikers who had never been on a march before, people who in the past would never have gone on a march. Never was there such a determination among the mass of the people to have done with Westminster. As each death occurred, a number of things became possible which had not been possible before. It was now possible to speak respectfully of the IRA. To have done so before would have been to invite condemnation by Church and state.[21]

And the people would give short shrift to condemnations of the strikes as morally wrong. The past saw to that:

The trouble with a hunger strike is that so many honorable people in the past have used it and have been praised for it. You cannot now turn around and say a hunger strike is immoral and violent if you have said the opposite in the past. Especially not to people as politically aware as the Catholics of West Belfast.[22]

For Wilson, at least, the hunger strikes marked the beginning of the end of British rule in Northern Ireland:

In Ireland a hunger strike is something which governments ignore at their peril. There were some of us in West Belfast who said simply: "If a hunger striker dies, that is the end of British rule in Ireland." I believe that that is so. However long it may be, I believe that historians will, on looking back, point to this hunger strike in which men died as the beginning of the end of the overt political control of Ireland from Westminster.[23]

Hence the success of the hunger strikes: they allowed the IRA to reestablish itself in the heroic mold and to reaffirm its legitimacy in a historical context, thereby making it more difficult to dismiss the IRA as mere terrorists with no political constituency and representative of nothing other than the fragmented dream of a demented few. To the roster of martyrs that included Tone, Fitzgerald, Emmet, Connolly, and Pearse were now added the names of Sands, Hughes, McCreesh, O'Hara, McDonnell, Hurson, Lynch, Doherty, McElwee, and Devine.* They, too, like the men of 1916 eulogized by Yeats, would be seen as having died because of "an excess of love."

"From the beginning," says Daithi O'Conaill, "a central part of Republican strategy has been to pin the blame for what has happened in Northern Ireland on 10 Downing Street."[24] The hunger strikes presented a tailor-made opportunity for the IRA to do just that by redefining the conflict in Northern Ireland on its terms: British colonialism versus Irish nationalism, an exclusive confrontation between the strong-arm forces of oppression and the otherworldly, ethereal defiance of the forces of liberation. Even among those whose empathy for the prisoners did not turn into support for the IRA, there was a hardening of anti-British sentiment. The "Brits" were the culprits; their intransigence was deliberate provocation, their highhandedness inhumane.

But the extraordinary emotive impact of the hunger strikes also drew its intensity from another source: they were symbolic

* Bobby Sands died on 5 May 1981, the sixty-sixth day of his hunger strike; Francis Hughes on 12 May, the fifty-ninth day of his hunger strike; Raymond McCreesh and Patsy O'Hara on 21 May, the sixty-first day of their hunger strike; Joe McDonnell on 7 July, the sixty-first day of his hunger strike; Martin Hurson on 13 July, the forty-fifth day of his hunger strike; Kevin Lynch on 1 August, the seventy-first day of his hunger strike; Kieran Doherty on 2 August, the seventy-third day of his hunger strike; Tom McElwee on 8 August, the sixty-second day of his hunger strike; and Michael Devine on 20 August, the sixtieth day of his hunger strike. O'Hara, Devine, and Lynch were members of the Irish National Liberation Army (INLA).

of the prison question. Though many people were unequivocal in their condemnation of IRA terrorism, many also qualified their condemnation. There was a pervasive belief that the prisoners were in fact somehow "special," that they would not be in prison if the "troubles" did not exist. Their actions were seen as the result of the conflict, not as its cause. The prisoners, too, were victims. And they had been tried under special circumstances and in special courts.

Even Cardinal O'Fiaich subscribed to this view, thereby giving it a legitimacy it had previously lacked. "The authorities refuse to admit that these prisoners are in a different category from the ordinary, yet everything about their trials and backgrounds indicates that they are different," he said in a statement following a visit to the H-Blocks in 1978. Nor was he content to stop there. "The vast majority," his statement went on, "were convicted on allegedly voluntary confessions obtained in circumstances which are now placed under grave suspicion by the recent Report of Amnesty International. Many are very youthful and come from families which have never been in trouble with the law, though they lived in areas which suffered discrimination in housing and jobs. How can one explain the jump in the prison population of Northern Ireland from 500 to 3,000 unless a new type of prisoner has emerged?"[25]

Survey data reflected a solid base of support for the prisoners' position — one could hardly be faulted, after all, for sharing the sentiments of a Prince of the Church. The Northern Ireland Attitude Survey found that 57 percent of Catholics in the North agreed that "the British government should stop treating people convicted of crimes which they claim were politically motivated as ordinary prisoners,"[26] while the ESRI survey found that 60 percent of the public in the South took a similar view.[27] Mairead Corrigan Maguire:

> We had no prisons here fourteen years ago — we were a highly disciplined people. If we had one murder a year in Northern Ireland it was news for months. And now we've the youngest prison population in Western Europe. Why? Until the government genuinely looks at the prison question and admits these men would not be in prison if

it were not for the dangerous political situation we're in and does something genuine about that, there'll be no political dialogue . . . Even here in the peace movement in the early years we could all be together here as friends, but when we talked about Kesh the room would split, people talking on one side or the other. And it wasn't looked at as a justice or human rights issue. It was looked at simply as the prisons and the Provos and lock them up. The key issue still is the question of the prisons. Because as long as you have so many people in prisons and emotionally tied into the prisons, then you can't move forward the political dialogue to the extent that you would want to.[28]

The prisoners are different. The rate of recidivism among those convicted under the emergency laws is very low (5 percent versus 52 percent in the U.K. as a whole); the educational level prior to incarceration is relatively high, and a majority of prisoners pursue and achieve a higher educational level while inside. Two thirds of those serving long-term sentences were under fifteen when the conflict erupted in 1969, and one third were under nine.[29] They grew up in a period of endemic violence and were inevitably, albeit unfortunately, drawn into the maelstrom.

Nor do empirical data support the view that the prisoners are "criminal" in the ordinary sense of the term. A comprehensive study of the backgrounds of persons convicted under the security laws concludes that "the vast majority of those who carry out the shootings and bombings are young people, typically in their late teens or early twenties, [who] have no previous convictions for terrorist offenses . . . The bulk of IRA operations are carried out by new recruits whose background and previous records suggest that they are ordinary and fairly representative members of the working-class communities in which they live. They are not professional criminals. Nor is there any evidence that more than a handful are mentally retarded or psychologically disturbed."[30] And, of course, there is the admission of the Army itself that members of the IRA are not "merely mindless hooligans."[31]

"From talking to them," said Cardinal O'Fiaich after visiting the blanket protesters in Maze in 1978, "it is evident that they intend to continue their protest indefinitely and it seems they prefer to face death rather than submit to be classed as criminals." And, he went on, "anyone with the least knowledge of Irish history knows how deeply rooted this attitude is in our country's past. In isolation and perpetual boredom they maintain their sanity by studying Irish. It is an indication of the triumph of the human spirit over adverse material surroundings to notice Irish words, phrases and songs being shouted from cell to cell and then written on each cell wall with the remnants of toothpaste tubes."[32]

Thus the prison culture: solidarity and camaraderie, adding to the myth of continuity, isolation, and deprivation and breeding a separate community more committed, more tested, more cohesive, and more removed from the reality of Northern Ireland itself. It reinforces the motivation for resistance, the routine brutalizations distancing prisoners from the brutality of their own past actions, convincing them of the righteousness of their cause, justifying future retaliations. And for every prisoner there are mothers, fathers, brothers, sisters, wives, children, networks of friends and relatives who feed off the prison culture, adopting its values, sharing its ethos, and cultivating its resentments, their perceptions of reality mirroring and often magnifying the perceptions of the prisoners themselves. Ultimately, there is a paradox at work that makes the task of the security forces perhaps impossible to achieve, for the more successful they are in apprehending and prosecuting members of the IRA, the more the prison population swells. And the more the prison population swells, the more dominant the ethos of the prison culture, particularly in the consciousness of the minority. And the more dominant the ethos of the prison culture, the more viselike the grip of the IRA.

• • •

In one sense the IRA could only have lost on the hunger-strike issue, if Mrs. Thatcher had acceded to their demands before Sands died. The momentum generated by the strikes has provided the movement with the raw material for recruitment for years to come. It has certainly sealed the symbolic identification with the past. The fact that the hunger strikes were eventually called off might be seen as a victory for the government. But the key prisoner demands were met, although the granting of political status was never even a remote possibility. The prisoners may not have succeeded in gaining special-category status, but they did succeed in gaining a status different from that of the ordinary criminal, and for many this was the key issue, since they "could not face serving long sentences under the conditions of common convicts."[33]

Daithi O'Conaill:

> The reality was that ten men had the courage to stand by their country to the point of giving their lives for it, and that was the real victory. We demonstrated to the world that these prisoners represent a struggle which is deeply rooted in convictions and deeply rooted in history. By their moral fiber they proved the depth of their dedication which is to be found in the struggle. As a result they wiped out during the hunger strike British claims that these were mindless hooligans and so forth. The H-Block issue became a worldwide issue. In Ireland there was a massive recruitment into the Republican movement. For the first time in about five years the youth of the Twenty-Six Counties became very interested in Republican policy and in joining the Republican movement. The caliber of Bobby Sands, the fact that he had written, really got to the youth and had a very great impact on them. So over all, when one looks at it objectively, in general terms, the Republican movement gained tremendously, whether you look at it in physical terms, in the number who joined, or in terms of favorable publicity or in terms of the political climate or in terms of finance.[34]

But the hunger strikes had a far more significant impact on the IRA itself. They taught the movement invaluable lessons: that the mobilization of public opinion around a particular issue, especially an emotive issue where support for the principles involved could be exploited as support for the movement, was a powerful propaganda tool; that the contesting of elections provided a base to build an enduring political organization; that a political organization was a necessary prerequisite for taking power. The National H-Block Committee's marches and demonstrations and the media coverage they attracted created the illusion of a mass movement — the precursor of mass political action — which the Provisionals were able to manipulate to their own advantage. O'Conaill:

Republican thinking on elections was negative. There was a very strong school of thought, particularly in the North, against any participation in elections. We changed that whole outlook by involvement in the Bobby Sands by-election. It was then developed further by participation in the June '81 general elections in the South. And even those who were the strongest critics of participation in elections accepted that there were very positive gains secured. That first of all, in the Bobby Sands case, we really brought the H-Block issue to a completely new level. Had not Bobby Sands been elected M.P., his case might never have gotten the worldwide publicity which it did receive. Even the critics realized there was a very definite gain there.

Likewise in the Twenty-Six Counties. The movement acquired credibility, renewed dynamism was released within the organization, new talent came to the fore. All of these developments led to the forming of a more positive approach. There is a great consciousness now of how electoral situations can be utilized to establish a strong political organization.[35]

Hence the new strategy formally adopted at the 1981 Ard Fheis: the movement would contest local government seats in the North and take whatever seats they won. It would also contest, at its discretion, seats for Dublin, Stormont, and Westminster elections, but the seats won would not be taken, in accordance with traditional abstentionist policy. *An Phoblact,* the movement's mouthpiece, succinctly summarized the new policy with the bold headline: "By Ballot and Bullet."[36]

There are pitfalls, of course; the task ahead is formidable, to say the least. O'Conaill:

It's very difficult to reconcile the two — the constitutional and the unconstitutional. In the Northern context it is understood, and where you have good military operations it generally enhances one's prospects in elections.

In the Southern context, however, it can be the other way around, unless you have, for instance, a good strike against the British Army —

that can have a good effect. But the shooting of a few UDR men can have a negative effect, and the further South you go the greater the negative effect.

So you are caught in a bind in that sense, in that we are trying to combine two forms of action — military action and political action — which at times work against each other. It makes our task more difficult.[37]

Nevertheless, the movement fully accepts that the two lines of action are necessary: if you opt only for one or the other you are not really engaged in a "revolutionary forward movement." Danny Morrison, editor of *An Phoblact,* National Publicity Director for Provisional Sinn Féin, and considered by many to be Gerry Adams's* alter ego, further elaborates on the dichotomy:

There is a real problem. And it's whether or not one can carry out an armed struggle and contest elections successfully against all the propaganda where others can just put up the cheap call for peace. I don't think it's ever been tried before — not even Zimbabwe's winning of independence is capable of comparison. It could well be that some of the IRA's actions today might be viewed right across the electorate as unpopular actions and which could, therefore, be considered as damaging to electoral prospects in the short run, but which, in the long run, given the hindsight of victory, would make both the IRA and Sinn Féin very popular.[38] †

Moreover, you have to distinguish between the consequences of an election loss for Sinn Féin to the SDLP and the reverse — an election loss for the SDLP to Sinn Féin: Sinn Féin has a higher calling that transcends the mere winning of elections; the SDLP does not. Says Morrison:

In Sinn Féin's case, elections are only one part of the overall struggle. The main struggle, the main thrust — and this goes without saying —

* Adams is the leader of the Northern clique that dominates the movement. He is Vice President of Provisional Sinn Féin. At the moment he is the most influential member of the movement.

† Morrison gave vivid expression to the Sinn Féin policy at the party's Ard Fheis in November 1981. "Is there anyone here," he asked, "who objects to taking power in Ireland with a ballot paper in one hand and an Armalite in the other?" The answer was a resounding "No!"

is the armed struggle, because that's the only way to get the Brits out of Ireland. If every elected representative from the nationalist community was solely Sinn Féin and if the SDLP did not exist, the Brits would still refuse to get out of Ireland.

But if that is the case, what, then, is the purpose of contesting elections?

What contesting elections does do, and did, especially in the case of Bobby Sands, is that they completely undermine British propaganda, which states that Republicans have no support. They show that Republicans have popular support.

On the other hand, the position of the SDLP is far more precarious. Since it exists only to run, electoral defeat, especially at the hands of Sinn Féin, would precipitate its demise:

If the SDLP were to lose an election to Sinn Féin, that would be the end of them. They are there solely for the purpose of constitutionalism, of collaboration, and of course they represent middle-class interests, whereas in the North the Republicans have raised the question of socialism.

But if Sinn Féin loses an election, it won't be the end of the struggle, because that election will have been contested "only to advance the overall armed struggle and the image of the IRA as a revolutionary popular organization." Of course, nothing will deter opponents of the IRA from arguing that a defeat for Sinn Féin is a defeat for the IRA. And nothing, of course, could be further from the truth:

People try to make a defeat for Sinn Féin into a defeat for the IRA. But it's just not so, because Fianna Fáil, and to some extent Fine Gael, grassroots supporters support the IRA. That's how the IRA is able to exist. That's how the IRA has a base. And SDLP supporters in the North support the IRA.

Why, then, is their support, particularly in the North, not more openly apparent?

Because the nationalist community are fairly sophisticated, and they are betting on two horses. The SDLP may improve their position through political talks which we term collaboration, and the IRA could end up bringing about the defeat of the people who harass and oppress them. So they support both sides. If the nationalist people consider the SDLP to be more politically astute than Sinn Féin, then that's something we're going to have to overcome through time and through challenging the SDLP.*

Which is one reason why the movement is moving away from the policy of simple "interventionism" in elections:

Interventionism is done when one assesses that success will be relatively easy — like during the hunger strikes. But to build a political organization and a political base involves contesting elections which you are going to lose. But it's in order to advance the whole movement and build up a political machine. It is the latter we are now involved in, participating in elections in order to provide the people with alternative leadership and to build a base.

Their objective in the North: to break the grip the SDLP has on the nationalist community. O'Conaill:

Their record over twelve years has been an extremely negative one. In bargaining with the British they have been able to achieve absolutely nothing. Even in elementary things like job allocations, fair housing, education, the SDLP has made no progress. And on the major national issue the SDLP has secured absolutely nothing. The only thing they have secured is that they have exploited the suffering of the people of the North. They gained positions of prominence, but for all that,

* This interview with Danny Morrison took place on 24 May 1982. Five months later, in the October elections for the Northern Ireland Assembly, the IRA's support became more openly apparent. See chapter 13. Morrison's statement, however, is important because it indicates the process of rationalization at work: Sinn Féin's success at the polls means support in the community, but lack of success does not necessarily mean lack of support, only that "sophisticated" voters cover their bets by splitting their allegiances. The fault will lie in the stars. Thus Sinn Féin is in a no-lose situation: ultimately support will be forthcoming when victory is ensured, and since the outcome is not in doubt neither is the support it will engender.

at the moment they are left with only one publicly elected representative — John Hume.[39]

Hume, however, is a greater asset to Loyalists than to Republicans. He is among the most vocal and bitter critics of Republicans. He is a traitor. And hence the Sinn Féin Northern strategy — an electoral variation of the "shoot-and-scoot" principle:

The electoral contests we enter will be very carefully selected in the areas where we shall feel pretty confident that we can wipe out the SDLP electoral base. I think we proved that in Fermanagh–South Tyrone. We created a situation there where even the SDLP, despite all their claims that they were opposed to Owen Carron, couldn't even field a candidate. The result is history. Therefore, the policy will be one of selective contests, all designed to whittle away the claim and the standing that the SDLP have as spokespeople for the nationalist community.[40]

Their objective in the South: the large-scale politicization of the disenchanted young. Morrison:

There is a population explosion in the South. This was seen during the hunger strikes. Lots and lots of young people came out onto the streets to demonstrate their concern over the hunger strikes. Of course, the politicization they gained as a result of that has resulted in a tangible increase in support, especially in the Sinn Féin membership in the South. That will take a few years to come to fruition.

But I personally believe that the Twenty-Six Counties, that the Free State is the key to the overall struggle. I don't think the Republican movement has any problems in the North no matter what the outcome of the stress now on entering into electoral contests. It will survive in the North and go from strength to strength. In fact, because it has already broken through a generation gap — there have been twelve years of continuous fighting — where if one lad goes to jail his younger brother takes over. The structure exists in the North for the Republican movement to continue while the Brits are here and to undermine the SDLP and to politicize the nationalist community.[41]

The South, on the other hand, is different; hence the necessity for intense political action there:

Generally people aren't as politicized as the nationalist community in the North. They are much more open to Free State propaganda. Sinn Féin is banned from state radio and television. The newspapers down South all have an anti-Republican line. Anyone down South who becomes involved with the Republican movement is immediately harassed by the Gardaí. But the Twenty-Six Counties will be the key. The movement has to get into the large-scale politicization of the young, especially the young people coming out of the ghettos of the larger cities and towns. And in fact we've taken a decision to follow that exact course.[42]

And the ultimate aim of this politicization? A socialist, thirty-two-county Republic:

The aim of the Republican movement, going back sixty years, has been to establish a socialist Republic based on the 1916 Proclamation. What we want to see is a fair and equal distribution of wealth throughout the country, an end to poverty, proper schools and hospitals, an end to exploitation, everyone having the right to a home.[43]

Did this represent a move to the left? No: the movement had merely started to define itself more precisely than it had in the past.

Nevertheless, despite the suitable evasiveness of Morrison's answer, there has been a discernible move to the left in the eyes of most informed commentators. A majority of activists now come from deprived social environments rather than from traditional Republican backgrounds. Many of the old Republican shibboleths have little meaning for them, and they are viscerally more radical ideologically. Says one astute observer: "The old characterization of the Provisionals as right-wing militants could hardly be more inappropriate. For reasons of diplomacy they would abjure the characterization 'Marxist' but this is in fact what they have become. They analyze the North in terms of economic and national exploitation, their rhetoric is laced with references to class conflicts and a strong identification has grown up between them and other liberation movements throughout the world."[44]

• • •

The transformation is alien to much of the rank and file, the bulk of whom are traditional, deeply conservative Republicans. The talk of socialism, the increasing proclivity to identify with beleaguered racial minorities in Britain and with the women's movement in Ireland makes them uneasy, even bewildered. And the talk of "going political," of contesting elections, makes them still more uneasy. They remember the path Sinn Féin chose in 1969 that led to the split in the movement. Were they not, after all, the ones who said no to Marxism and no to the contesting of elections? Had they not rescued the movement and steered it back to its pristine moorings?

The tensions linger, the outcome by no means certain. Poor performance at the polls will undoubtedly aggravate matters, bringing the dilemmas into the open and making division more likely.*

• • •

They got what they wanted — a movement to the left, emphasis on radical social and economic policies, and approval of participatory politics — but the Northern radicals, who are now the vanguard of the movement and in control of the Army Council, were not assuaged. They wanted more — nothing less than a repudiation of federalism — and they got that, too, in 1981, when the Ard Fheis voted to remove it from the Éire Nua policy.†

* The poor performance by the Provisional Sinn Féin candidates in the Republic's general elections in February 1982 was seen by the more traditional elements as a vindication of their position. However, Sinn Féin's success in the October elections for the Northern Ireland Assembly more than offset that setback. (See chapter 13.) But the matter is by no means settled. According to *The Observer* (24 October 1982), police in Northern Ireland attributed the re-emergence of the INLA (it had been thought to be all but defunct after the arrest of thirty-six of its members in 1982) to the defection of a "sizeable number" of young Provos who were impatient with the IRA's preoccupation with political activity. INLA's campaign of violence in the last three months of 1982 was designed to send a message to disgruntled members of the Provisional IRA: the INLA, it said, was the "real" thing; it would have no truck with politics — the invitation was open.

† The motion to delete, however, did not secure the necessary two-thirds majority to remove Éire Nua from the movement's constitution. The necessary two-thirds vote was secured at the 1982 Ard Fheis.

Under the federal formula adopted by the Provisionals in 1972, a "new Ireland" would consist of four regional assemblies, one for each of the four historic provinces, which would enjoy a considerable measure of self-government, and a national government to deal with all-Ireland issues. Thus, in a nine-county Ulster assembly, Unionists would continue to exercise considerable, perhaps even majority, power.

The federal formula was a palliative, intended to mollify Protestant fears of being swamped in a new all-Ireland arrangement. And Sinn Féin itself acknowledged as much. The Ulster Assembly would be a parliament for the Ulster people, in which "the Unionist-oriented people of Ulster would have a working majority within the Province and would therefore have considerable control over their own affairs."[45] And that power would provide "the surest guarantee of their civil and religious liberties within a new Ireland."[46]

The spirit of accommodation is gone. Protestant fears are not a major concern of the Northern radicals, and the difference on federalism is one more difference between the Northern faction of the movement and the more traditional Southern faction.

O'Conaill, the architect of the federal concept, who is in the mainstream of the Southern faction, makes light of the differences:

> It should be borne in mind that the whole movement is committed to the principle of decentralization. But it has become obvious over the last number of years that a strong school of thought was developing in the North which opposed the concept of a nine-county assembly for Ulster. One can fully understand why. In the last number of years there has been a heightening of sectarian feeling that has produced a reaction from Republicans and nationally minded people. They have a fear that in a new Ireland the Loyalists would still dominate within a nine-county Ulster, and that they would pursue the policies of the old Stormont. One can understand the fears which have led to this rethinking.[47]

Morrison is more forthright:

> The policy on the issue of federalism is something that has been under review for several years. Many people, especially those in the North

who would be subjected to a nine-county Ulster Assembly in a federal Ireland, felt that it would be dominated by the power blocks which have traditionally held us in subjection. The opinion in the war zone was therefore totally against federalism.[48]

Which is why "war-zone" Republicans also oppose other proposals for a federal or confederal Ireland or for a condominium solution:

All these solutions are aimed at fooling the Loyalists. They're saying, "You know, it's not so bad, you're not losing so much." Whereas at the end of the day they should be told: "You're losing the link with Britain. We're all equal, so let's build the country together." I wouldn't fool them and say, "Okay, you're going to have this and that." Our own federalist policies were a sop to Loyalism. The Loyalists should be told: "We're out to break the link with Britain. This country is one country." The Loyalists are just a major idiosyncrasy. They should be told the truth: "You're entitled to no more than anyone else in the country." It's a message they have been resisting and will continue to resist, but at the end of the day it's the only just solution.[49]

And the bottom line:

The idea of a federal Ireland and a federal Ulster sounds grand and fair, but you will have as much trouble getting Loyalists to accept a nine-county parliament as you will in getting them to accept a united Ireland, so why stop short?[50]

• • •

Why, indeed?

"We don't accept the term *violence,*" says O'Conaill. "To us violence is the unlawful use of force. We maintain that the force we use is legitimate and is justified by the circumstances that prevail."[51]

Force is a means to an end, the objective "to make Northern Ireland ungovernable." When the British realize that the cost of trying to make Northern Ireland governable is prohibitive, the political will to stick it out will collapse, and withdrawal follow.

But before there can be "progress" on any front toward a solution, the British must make a declaration of intent to withdraw. Nothing else will suffice — not declarations that they favor Irish unity or that they will withdraw the guarantee. And until that declaration of intent to withdraw is forthcoming, there will be no more truces:

The feeling within the movement today [says O'Conaill] is that there were one too many truces. There is a strong feeling that the 1975 truce lasted too long and that the movement should not now enter a similar situation. The only basis for direct talks now with the British is for the British government to make a declaration of intent to withdraw. At which point the movement would be willing to enter negotiations to achieve an effective and peaceful withdrawal.

And why would a declaration by Britain that she is in favor of the long-term unification of Ireland not suffice?

Because it has been our experience that the British are absolutely notorious for double-dealing, for making a statement and then taking nine or ten different interpretations out of it. We want a clear-cut, unambiguous statement to the effect that they are leaving the country. And nothing short of that will at this point in time ever entice the Republicans into negotiations.

And why would a declaration by Britain that she is prepared to withdraw the guarantee not suffice?

Because as far as we're concerned, the principle of withdrawal is nonnegotiable. And that being such, we think it would be a mistake to enter negotiations to discuss the feasibility of withdrawal or not.

And why would a settlement evolving out of the Anglo-Irish process not suffice?

Because the summit talks are working on the basis of closer association with Britain. Fundamental to Republicanism has been the concept of a separatist identity, the breaking of the connection completely. You must sever the connection absolutely. Then you can look at the situation anew and ask what type of relationship can or should exist between an independent Ireland and Britain. To avoid that process is to ignore the lessons of eight hundred years of history. It is going to be a kind of updated Free State rule for the whole of Ireland — and that is not going to bring peace to this island.

And why would a confederal solution along the lines proposed by FitzGerald not suffice?

We are totally opposed to that. Because we believe you would have a perpetuation of partition, a perpetuation of sectarianism, and that indirectly you would still have British control. In real terms it would not be the Ireland for which so many have suffered and died.

Hence the present strategy:

Establish, not through negotiation but by putting pressure on to the point where the British will see that to break the logjam the declaration of intent to withdraw is the real important thing. Temporizing with pledges of a united Ireland or breaking the guarantee are insufficient in view of what has happened over the last twelve years.

The IRA wants to avoid a Congo-like situation. But if one emerges, responsibility for it will be entirely in the hands of the British. Morrison is unequivocal. Protestants, he says, will fight when Britain withdraws only if Britain gives them either the opportunity or encouragement to do so:

It depends on both the circumstances and the scenario of withdrawal. If the British government withdrew without resolving the issues at the center here — namely, from our point of view, the right of national self-determination for the Irish people — or if the British tried to subvert that, then that subversion would probably take the form of overt or covert support for Loyalist intransigence to enter any kind of Irish state, and there could be repartition. Of course, if the RUC and UDR remain armed, they will of course fight to keep the privileges they've traditionally had: their jobs, and their better housing. Of course they're going to fight. But how much blood is shed depends entirely on the British government. If hope is held out to the Loyalists, if they are encouraged or armed or secretly financed, then they will have something to fight for.[52]

Which means, says O'Conaill, that a declaration of intent to withdraw is not in itself sufficient. It has to be linked to two other objectives: an acknowledgment from Britain that she accepts the right of the people of all Ireland to determine their own future, and a general amnesty for all prisoners.[53] And how does the Dublin government fit into this scheme of things? O'Conaill:

It is not the policy of the Republican movement to overthrow the government of the South. What the Republican movement seeks is the abolition of both partitioned states in Ireland. It is inevitable that when the Northern state goes out of existence, the Southern Ireland state will also go out of existence.[54]

The British, to repeat the old adage, have no friends, only interests, and when they realize that their interests are no longer served by continuing to occupy Northern Ireland, they will "face the facts." O'Conaill:

The British faced the facts before in 1972 and 1975 when they sat down with representatives of the movement to discuss possible solutions. They recognized that there would not be a solution without our participation.[55]

Which is more than a Dublin government is prepared to do:

One finds a greater antipathy from the Dublin government for any participation by the IRA in fashioning the ultimate outcome. This is the historical attitude of Dublin. It is a negative one. It will not stand the test of time.[56]

Do the British want to get out of Northern Ireland? At one point, says O'Conaill, they might have, but not now:

At this stage I don't believe Britain wants to get out. The movement came to that conclusion very firmly in 1976 following the truce of 1975, which dragged on in a halfhearted way into '76. Certainly in '75 both publicly and privately the British were indicating — certainly privately indicating very strongly — that they were interested in a withdrawal. And during that period in '75 they intimated that when they nationalized the shipyards in Britain they excluded the Belfast shipyard, and that was an indication that they were cutting economic links with the North. But it's obvious that under Mrs. Thatcher that policy has been reversed, and Mrs. Thatcher is determined that the British presence remain in Northern Ireland. At this stage we accept that Britain has no intention of withdrawing. Hence the Republican concern for intensifying the war, to hit Britain harder, to make her presence more untenable.[57]

Why the change on Britain's part? O'Conaill:

The Tory obsession with a possible Russian threat to Europe has made it all the more necessary for Britain to conclude that she needs a strategic presence in Ireland to safeguard the Atlantic approaches . . . She is more concerned about her own defensive measures. She sees a presence in Ireland as vital to ensure these measures.[58]

Morrison:

Britain would probably like to get out because of the cost, but she always weighs that against the stability aspects. And there's no way either England or the EEC or the Western Alliance wants an independent Ireland at its back. Britain is acting as their agent, making sure Ireland does not go independent.[59]

Hence the justification for armed resistance:

It's obvious that the Brits won't listen to anything other than armed struggle . . . Armed struggle unleashes political embarrassment for the Brits and makes it difficult for them to politically rule Ireland. You have to use force to break chains.[60]

And to break chains you must bring it home to the British public that they are not immune from the repercussions of the conflict. O'Conaill:

There are times when priority is given to operations in England because of the political climate that obtains, and it is a higher priority with the Republican movement. That has been stated publicly, that we will strike in England and the objective is to bring it home to the English people that they can't have an army of thirty thousand operating in Ireland, and that does not leave them immune from operations in Britain. It's only when strikes are carried out in Britain that the complacency and indifference of the British people themselves becomes broken.[61]

Does the movement make a distinction between the killing of UDR men and soldiers from mainland Britain? O'Conaill:

Not really. In military terms the UDR can be a greater danger because it is made up of people who have intimate knowledge of local areas. They are the eyes and ears of the intelligence network which enables the British to continue their presence.[62]

The Protestant perception that the killing of UDR men is part of a planned campaign to kill Protestants as such rather than to kill members of the security forces is perhaps understandable, but nevertheless misconceived:

We must take the other side: that members of the UDR and RUC are members of the British Crown Forces engaged in a war of repression, and as such they're apt to be taken on. Going back to the War of Independence, one can make the point that an overwhelming number of police shot dead back then were Roman Catholics. The fact that they were Roman Catholics was immaterial. They were serving members of the RIC [Royal Irish Constabulary] and they had to be taken on. The public found it hard to accept that, although they could accept the shooting of English soldiers or Auxiliaries or Black and Tans. Anyone who wears the uniform of the British Crown engaged in a war of repression in Ireland is a legitimate target irrespective of what his religious beliefs are.[63]

Morrison, however, sees differences, especially in the media coverage of the deaths of UDR and RUC men:

The killing of British soldiers is going to affect British public opinion more than the killing of a UDR soldier from Cookstown. Also, it tends to pose the armed struggle more as a national war of liberation. On the other hand, the UDR man's death is, of course, locally presented as a bigger loss to the community — that is, the Loyalist community. When a soldier is killed in Ireland and his body taken home to England his funeral service is never heard of. But when a UDR or RUC man is killed in Ireland — it's an incredible form of war — there's a massive media intervention and analysis, and, of course, concentration of analysis on those killed by the IRA. So you've got the funeral, the dead man's circumstances — all of which are tragic of course, as are the circumstances of any man's death, but they're exploited, played up to the full, to hold the nationalist community guilty of this man's death.[64]

• • •

Time has hardened the heart. Ten years ago the IRA was prepared to cede control of an Ulster Assembly to a Loyalist majority. But not today. Loyalists are "neo-fascists, anti-nationalist and anti-democratic."[65] Either they capitulate to the inevitable or face the inevitable consequences of resistance. If they had to be taken on, it was better to get on with it. And if that meant a blood bath, well, so be it. The IRA "cannot and should not ever tolerate or compromise with Loyalism."[66] "Not an inch" would be met by "not an inch," "no surrender" by no forbearance. And since Loyalists were an elite intent on perpetuating their ill-gotten privileges who could not be trusted to behave in other than a sectarian, exclusive manner, they had to be brought under the will and the watch of the majority. Hence the necessity for a unitary state.

• • •

Thus the Provisional IRA's strategy: a long war of attrition. When the enemy itself concedes that it cannot "defeat" you, and that you will continue to flourish for as long as he maintains a presence in your land, an inescapable corollary follows: eventual war-weariness in Britain will set in, precipitating a collapse of the political will to pursue an indefinite and ultimately fruitless fight. You wear down the political will by making the cost of containing the conflict prohibitive to the British taxpayer, by sporadic bombing campaigns on the British mainland to remind the British public that the actions of their government make them legitimate targets of reprisal, and by hunting down and executing prominent British officials, for if the ruling classes are not safe, then who is? Indeed, the IRA made an invaluable discovery in 1979: in a celebrity-conscious world the assassination of one Lord Mountbatten galvanizes world opinion and excites the attention of the media far more effectively than the random deaths of a hundred nameless souls. Meanwhile, alternate periods of violence with periods of inaction, but never let the interval of inaction last too long; otherwise the public's expectations of what level of violence is acceptable might change, and therefore their reaction to it.

Making Northern Ireland ungovernable, however, is more difficult when the Army refuses to engage in excessive retaliation. Thus the need for the "help" of the Loyalists, and this the Provisionals have set out to secure. Hence the increasing emphasis on the murder of UDR and ex-UDR men. They are killed in all sets of circumstances: executioners breaking into their homes at early dawn — the infamous "five o'clock knock" — in front of wives and children, coming or going from civilian employment, on lonely roads, in open fields. When Morrison talks about the incredible impact of television, how each funeral is covered and the details of the dead man's circumstances made public, he is, perhaps even unconsciously, pinpointing the reason why wave after wave of these executions result in a frenzied, almost hysterical, reaction in the Protestant community. It is, after all, *their* people who are being murdered, and murdered only because they want to preserve *their* government and *their* state. UDR or RUC members are not thought of in the same light as the regular "mainland" Army who come from alien places and, in many respects, an alien culture. They are neighbors or the friends of neighbors, the relative propinquity magnified a hundredfold by television. Television conveys intimacy. Each death becomes a personal statement, and as the tally grows, filling living rooms each evening with the statistics of death and the rituals of burial, enveloping the consciousness with the enormity of the almost casual disregard for circumstance, and with the insult to all living things that attends each killing, the murmurings of genocide become a clamor for revenge. And revenge they get: random assassinations of Catholics; yet more paramilitary organizations plying their deadly trade out of the conviction that the British Army either cannot or will not protect the Protestant people. The urge to "go it alone" grows more insistent, the path to irrational action less resistible.

Hence the importance of Paisley as a valuable, if at times unwitting, ally of the IRA. On the one hand he acts as a catalyst, mobilizing Loyalists to take it upon themselves to look after their own interests; on the other hand, his crude behavior, vehement anti-English remarks, and disregard for the Englishman's most venerable institutions further alienate British public opinion, creating the climate for a collapse of the political will. A Protestant backlash is in the interests of the IRA not only because it makes the province more ungovernable but also because it magnifies Protestant retaliation as a purely sectarian phenomenon, thus enhancing the role of the IRA as the protector of the minority community.

The killing of the Reverend Robert Bradford, Unionist M.P. for South Belfast, is a case in point. Five days after the assassination, *An Phoblact* proudly announced that "the crisis caused by hard-hitting IRA operations last week, and in particular the execution of Loyalist extremist Robert Bradford, has sent the so-called Loyalists on a rebellious collision course with the British government which in terms of shaking and sickening British public opinion (as IRA bombs in London are successfully doing) should knock about two or three years off the British occupation of Ireland!"[67] In short, the most successful IRA operations are those that create conditions of optimal instability, maximizing the likelihood of a Protestant backlash against the Catholic community and provoking Protestants to challenge the British government in a way that is inimical to their own best interests.

The UDR or ex-UDR man is, of course, the ideal target for the IRA. Because he wears the uniform of the Crown there is always the military justification for the killing. Because he lives at home and travels openly to and from his employment, he is a more open target. He can be hit at any time and in any place. The attacker's risks of being apprehended or even of being in danger are minimal. In contrast, the "regular" Army travels in convoys, lives in barracks, can return firepower and call in assistance — all of which make it a far less inviting target, posing, in addition, far more difficult logistical and support problems. Hence the predilection for the relatively "safe" UDR or RUC target. The policy is simple: "shoot and scoot." Moreover, the IRA knows there is little the Army can do to contain such actions short of massive incursions into IRA strongholds, which are likely to prove not only unproductive but counterproductive inasmuch as they will further alienate large segments of the Catholic community. The Army is reluctant, therefore, to meet Protestant demands for large-scale retaliation because it may redound to the benefit of the IRA. In addition, since the actions are not directed at the Army per se, and are carried out in isolated, unconnected incidents, they do not coalesce into a critical mass, which would in fact impel the Army to respond forcefully, thereby crippling, temporarily at least, IRA operations and neutralizing the leadership.

And there are other practical considerations: bringing the war home to the British public is more successfully achieved through bombing campaigns on the mainland and the assassination of public figures — which merit more time and commentary on British television — than through the sporadic killing of a soldier or two or three. Indeed, the Birmingham pub bombings in November 1974, which resulted in the deaths of 19 persons and the injury of 168 others, were extensively covered by British television.* The gruesome scenes of carnage and chaos, the interviews with bemused survivors, the insistent cameras capturing the sheer suddenness of oblivion and the ostensible pointlessness of it all, catapulted Northern Ireland to the fore of Britain's consciousness to an extent unmatched either before or since.†

By ballot and bullet: the ballot to manipulate public opinion whenever a suitable issue presents itself, to chip away at the electoral strength of the SDLP in the North, and to politicize the hordes of young people pouring out of the urban ghettos in the South with nothing to do, nowhere to go, and no hope for the future; the bullet to make Northern Ireland ungovernable.

* For an account of Republican bombing campaigns in Britain in the 1970s, see Tim Pat Coogan, *The IRA,* pp. 481–90.

† Until, perhaps, the London bombings of 20 July 1982. See chapter 12, pp. 386–87.

There will be no accommodations and no compromise. Thus their "no" to a federal Ireland; "no" to a confederal Ireland; and "no" to any form of arrangement that does not meet their criteria, and only theirs: a unitary state. A socialist Republic. A Gaelic Ireland — the words shouted from cell to cell and scrawled in toothpaste on prison walls in lunatic defiance will not be forgotten.

The Provisionals have settled in for the long haul with the means and the resources to sustain the protracted campaign it entails, secure in the knowledge that a majority of Catholics, both North and South, do not regard their actions as merely criminal. So long as the Catholic ghettos exist, they will not want for recruits. So long as they have their martyrs, they will not want for a sense of historical continuity. So long as the prison culture prevails, they will not want for the propaganda of repression. And so long as the fear of a Protestant backlash lurks in the collective consciousness of the minority, they will not be abandoned.

Meanwhile they dream their dreams of an Éire Nua.

• • •

Éire Nua: the new Ireland will emerge phoenixlike when the British withdraw, having first disarmed recalcitrant Loyalists or shipped them out to distant shores, and the state to the South collapses under the weight of its own obvious irrelevance and inertia in the new order of things. Éire Nua: a socialist thirty-two-county republic for Catholic, Protestant, and Dissenter. And a Gaelic one. The conquest of centuries will be undone.

"We are opposed to personal ownership of productive property such as a large farm or a large factory," asserts the Provisionals' Éire Nua policy document.[68] "This type of ownership involves the exploitation of other people's labor for personal gain and is alien to Republican principles."[69] Accordingly, "this type of enterprise should be cooperatively owned."[70] On the other hand, "small local businesses will be permissible provided no exploitation occurs."[71] However, "there will be an upper limit to the size of any private enterprise. Anything above this limit will come under community or cooperative ownership."[72] But even when private enterprise is permitted there will be "workers' participation."[73] The language will be restored — the reconquest of Ireland beginning with the reconquest of the language. Thus, "the Irish language and Irish culture will play a basic role in the national effort and their strengthening will have special attention. Sinn Féin will strive for a situation where the Irish language will become the everyday language of the people."[74] The cultural and economic dimensions of the new state will be interwoven "in such a way that there [will be] a clear demand for native control of our resources combined with rejection of consumer pop culture which prepares the ground for capitalist and materialist exploitation."[75]

It is as though time has stood still. Once again it is a struggle between two civilizations:[76] Catholic Gaelic values — nonmaterial, spiritual, sharing, altruistic, other-directed — and Protestant English values — permissive, material, consumer-oriented, self-directed. It is a genuflection to Pearse's phantasm that "the Gael is not like other men, the spade and the loom and the sword are not for him. But a destiny more glorious than that of Rome, more glorious than that of Britain awaits him, to become the saviour of idealism in modern intellectual and social life."[77]

Pearse, of course, is the movement's revered father figure, the fountainhead of sagacity, his nine principles of nationhood the "rocks" upon which the IRA is built. Theirs is a symbiosis of convenience. The IRA, like Pearse, represents a set of myths, an idea about Ireland that satisfies the need to sublimate the past, and that compensates for the harsh, uncomforting reality of what the Irish have done to each other in the name of God and in the name of country.

The idea begins with the Easter Rising of 1916 and works itself back in time, shaping and redefining past events to conform with the requirements of the present mythology. All of history is viewed through the prism of 1916. It is refracted. What does not fit the conditions of the myth is discarded. What is left is the detritus of truth: if you are not Catholic and are not Gaelic, you are not Irish. And if you are one and not the other, you are less Irish than the real thing: the Irish-Irish. By defining nationalism in terms of language and religion, Pearse effectively excluded one quarter of the population from the nation — the partition in the heart preceded the partition on the map. By insisting on Gaelic culture as the denominator of Irishness, he denied the diversity of culture that was and continues to be at the root of Ireland's differences. By equating Catholicism with nationalism he validated religion as a political wedge.[78]

Of course, the new, twenty-six-county Irish state went to extraordinary lengths to make the Ireland of Pearse's dreams the Ireland of reality. To perpetuate the 1916 uprising as the climactic apogee of an eight hundred–year struggle against foreign oppression, it had to invent a past that conformed to the legend of heroic struggle against a hated oppressor. And it is that invention of the past which allows the IRA to continue to insist that Northern Ireland is a British problem, that the British "occupation" is the real cause of the conflict. It is a convenient belief, allowing the Irish to eschew the roots of their troubles, and obfuscating the fact that the British occupation as "cause" is cause at best only for the violence of the IRA.

• • •

The myth begins with the notion that Ireland was invaded by England eight hundred years ago and that history is linear. Thus, Ireland was subdued by superior arms and resources but not beaten; the struggle to reestablish a free and united Ireland was carried forward from generation to generation until finally, in 1921, the English capitulated and offered a compromise — independence of sorts for twenty-six counties. However, the all-Ireland elections of 1918 had mandated an all-Ireland republic. Thus, the establishment of the Irish Free State in 1921, with its dominion status and the oath of allegiance to the Crown, was an illegal act, and all subsequent Dublin governments were, therefore, illegal. The IRA was the true political and military heir of the 1918 Parliament. Its purpose: to fulfill that Parliament's mandate. It does not accept the right of the minority created at the time of the plantation of Ulster to secede from the nation. That minority was a minority of supremacists, a civilian garrison holding the bridgehead for Britain. Britain's unwillingness to surrender the bridgehead led to the artificial partition of the country in 1921. Thus, the struggle is not yet over; the British occupation of the Six Counties will be ended, the government in the South overthrown, Ireland reunited. "Our rules are taken from history," says *An Phoblact.* "We remember the famine. We remember the Fenians. We remember 1916 and the executions. We remember the Loyalist pogroms of the twenties. We remember and are most proud of the small band of Republicans who down the years carried the torch of freedom. We remember Orange Rule, 1969, the Falls curfew, internments, the Loyalist assassinations, Brit murders. We remember . . . last week."[79]

• • •

There are, of course, several things wrong with this version of history: the Ireland of the twelfth century was not a nation in any sense of the term, nor was it "united." The Ireland the Normans — not the English — "invaded" in 1170 was an Ireland of independent kingdoms constantly at odds with each other. The language the Normans brought with them was Norman-French, not English.

For the next four hundred years Irish wars were just that — wars one Irish chieftain waged against the other for local power and local control. Irish wars were tribal wars. They reflected tribal interests, not national interests. Local chieftains sided with the "invaders" whenever it suited their purposes. Most had no trouble giving allegiance to a crown in London or, for that matter, to a crown in Scotland. The invader, for his part, was easily assimilated into the native culture, often becoming "more Irish than the Irish themselves." As a result, by the early seventeenth century, Ireland was an amalgam of three different cultures — Norman, English, and Gaelic. The plantations of Ulster introduced a new variable, religion, and religion remained the barrier to assimilation. The wars of the seventeenth century were fought by the Catholic Irish on behalf of Catholic English kings. They were fought for the restoration of old rights and possessions, not for an independent Gaelic Ireland. In fact, loyalty to the monarchy was never in dispute, nor was it ever seen to be at variance with love of Ireland. The rebellion of 1798 and the uprisings of 1803, 1848, and 1867 were not "national" insurrections. Most were poorly planned and ineptly executed, pitiful exercises in futility attracting little popular support. And they were put down not by "British" troops but by local Irish Catholic militias. Some petered out because of their own lack of purpose, direction, or energy. Indeed, one of the more important aspects of the 1798 rebellion was the failure of the people to respond to the message of Republicanism, and since that failure was to be repeated in every uprising thereafter, it became in time subverted by the larger myth of heroic failure in the face of overwhelming English superiority.

This myth became an essential part of Irish identity. It held up the specter of a small nation struggling to assert itself against a malevolent and vastly superior tyrant. Failure was ennobling, strengthening. It gave sustenance to succeeding generations, inspiring the resolve to continue. Apotheosis finally came in the blood sacrifice of 1916, when failure triumphed as a ritual of redemption. In reality, the failures were neither romantic nor inspiring, but simply an expression of the fact that the cause of Irish Republicanism, as articulated and practiced by the few, had little appeal to, or support among, the many.

Wolfe Tone, whose memory is invoked to justify the words, thoughts, deeds, and actions of the Republican movement, had, according to his biographer, "little contact with the mass of the people and knew nothing of their language and culture, he disliked priests and the Papacy and he himself records his several attempts to enter the services of the British Crown."[80] Republicanism was alien to the population, its dogma in the language of the elite. To this day elitism continues to be the distinguishing hallmark of its adherents: the few taking it upon themselves to know what's best for the many, the few inflexibly intent on leading the reluctant many into the hallowed land of "Ourselves Alone."

Nor were the great mass movements of the nineteenth century movements "to break the connection" with England. Rather, they were movements either to repeal the Act of Union or for Home Rule. The struggle was for a separate and sovereign status within the British framework, not for separation and an end to the framework. The opposition in the latter part of the nineteenth century and early twentieth century did not come from Britain — indeed, the House of Commons passed Home Rule bills in 1893 and again in 1912 and 1913 — but from other Irishmen, especially the Protestants of Ulster, who would have lost much of their power and pre-eminence if Home Rule had become a reality.

Nor was a "Gaelic Ireland" a living thing. By 1841 only 50 percent of the population spoke Gaelic. The famine accelerated the decline and made it irreversible — by 1851 only 23 percent spoke Irish and a mere 5 percent spoke only Irish.[81] The concept of a Gaelic Ireland as the key to national identity did not emerge until the 1890s, by which time English was the normal language of the people. Thus, the language was endowed with a pivotal place in national identity only when it had ceased to have a pivotal place in everyday life.

And finally there is the casuistry of numbers. Says O'Conaill: "Fundamental to our philosophy is the principle of the sovereignty and integrity of the nation. As Republicans we have never accepted the right of any minority to opt out of the nation."[82] But what if Northern Ireland's population was entirely Protestant, wholly loyal in its allegiance to Britain and altogether opposed to unification? Would the concept of a thirty-two-county Irish nation-state make legal, political, or moral sense? Obviously not, and obviously the South could not assert a territorial claim to the North in such circumstances, even though a majority in the island as a whole might support the claim despite the total opposition of the North's population. Nor could an IRA, if one in fact existed, mount a military campaign for unification.

Accordingly, both the South's assertion of territorial right and the IRA's campaign owe whatever legitimacy they claim *solely* to the presence of Catholics in Northern Ireland. But once again, the South would find it difficult to assert a claim to Northern Ireland, if in addition to a majority of the North's Protestants being opposed to unity, a majority of the North's Catholics were clearly opposed to it too. Accordingly, the critical variable is the wishes of the minority in Northern Ireland. The logic: the demands of a dissenting minority in the North validate the demands of a majority in the island as a whole. The logic, of course, is wanting. It is untenable when the minority are few in number, and therefore untenable even when the minority are many in number.

• • •

Where the irredentist nationalist view of history leaves Northern Ireland's Protestants is not at all clear. On the one hand, they are Irish — if only by virtue of birth. On the other hand, they are colons, a privileged class who give their allegiance to Britain. O'Conaill:

> The reality is that they are a colon class. They are the settler class that arose out of the plantation. Republicans accept that fact, and the fact that they are of colonial breed. But they've been here for so long that they're part and parcel of the Irish nation, and we feel their place is in the body politic as such, in the nation as a whole. If they themselves could see that, it would help them come out of the siege mentality that makes them think in terms of UDI. It's not the Republican policy or part of the Republican philosophy that you would work for a situation where you would drive the colons out of the North. Our policy is based on bringing home to them that there is a place for them based on equality. They have the same rights and the same duties as any other citizen of the country. We appreciate it's going to be very difficult for all of them to accept that. There would be quite a vociferous minority who would probably never accept it, and they will be faced with the choice of either getting out or fighting.[83]

Thus the colons must be brought into line — chastised, as it were — when their actions fly in the face of the national aspiration:

> We had a resurgence of a planned campaign of assassination directed against Catholics during the hunger strikes and a policy decision was made that the architects of this sectarianism would have to be struck. It happened that the one selected and shot dead was Robert Bradford. It was a deliberate move on the part of the movement to strike at Bradford. It's the likes of the Bradfords who encourage UDA personnel to go out and shoot Catholics. Rather than get involved in a tit-for-

> tat sectarian campaign, a decision was made to strike at the very upper crust of the sectarian forces. One is pulled back to the Algerian analogy, where we saw that the colons set out to thwart the granting of independence to the Algerian people. They rebelled against the de Gaulle government and carried out some terrible atrocities. In this case the IRA had to bring it home to the Loyalists that they're not going to have a free ride in shooting down innocent people, just as the FLN had to strike hard on occasion against the colonist people in Algeria.[84]

The analogy, however, is difficult to support. The French presence in Algeria dated from 1830, a substantial Scots presence in Ulster from the sixteenth century — predating the first American settlements. There were distinct racial, ethnic, and religious differences between the French and the native Algerians — on the one hand were white European Christians; on the other were Arab and Berber ethnic groups, and Arabic and Islamic religious cultures. There are significant disparities in the numbers involved. The colon class in Algeria came to eight hundred fifty thousand — less than 8 percent of the population of Algeria. Ulster Protestants constitute 24 percent of the population of Ireland. And there are political differences: the conflict in Northern Ireland has not spread to the British mainland, the IRA bombing campaigns in Britain have no indigenous political support there, the politics of Northern Ireland do not play a significant role in British politics, nor does religion, and the Army has not become politicized over the issue.

The FLN, of course, never defeated the French Army. On the contrary, by 1960 the French Army had come very close to crushing the FLN. But the cost of getting to that point had drained political resolve in France itself and left the Algerian economy in a shambles.[85] Accordingly, the Provisionals' propensity for drawing parallels between Algeria and Northern Ireland may have little to do with the overt similarities between the two situations. Rather, it may reflect the Provisionals' nascent wish for a similar outcome: the colons in Algeria were defeated when they lost control over political will in France.

• • •

Dublin governments take the position that the IRA is an illegal, terrorist organization that seeks not only to drive the British out of Northern Ireland and unify the whole of Ireland but to overthrow the duly elected government of the Republic in the process; that the IRA does not speak for, nor have the support of, the Irish people, that the terror tactics of the IRA are abhorrent to the Irish people; and that the repeated failure of the IRA at the ballot box in the Republic clearly shows that the Irish people reject its policies and the manner in which they are pursued.

However, the state's professed repugnance at the tactics of the IRA is at best self-serving and at worst hypocritical. It was these very tactics — the clandestine bomb, assassination on the street, murder from a ditch, savage reprisals, destruction of property, random terror, and the reign of the macabre — that shaped the struggle between the IRA and the British in the years 1918 through 1921, and that led to the independence of the Twenty-Six Counties and the foundation of the state. The state honors those who ordered and carried out the gruesome and sometimes cowardly acts. They are revered as patriots, eulogized as visionaries, extolled for their self-sacrifice and selflessness. They are the National Example.

It is difficult, therefore, to dismiss the Provisionals as mere terrorists, mindless in their pursuit of violence, psychopaths bent on mayhem and murder for some obscure pathological satisfaction they derive from the bloodletting. "In Ireland," notes one scholar, "there is a historical legitimacy attributed to taking up arms in the defense of one's heritage, and explicitly in the Republican tradition a cultural exaltation of armed conflict of the guerilla type."[86] The IRA, he concludes, "has a long and in the main honorable tradition of nationalist struggle against British occupation and one would, therefore, expect to find in the Catholic population, a not inconsiderable proportion of people brought up to respect the general ideals of Irish nationalism and sympathetic to the traditional guerilla means of obtaining it."[87]

Empirical data buttress his point. The Northern Ireland Attitude Survey found that 46 percent of Catholics attribute motives of "patriotism and idealism" to the IRA and 32 percent feel that "were it not for the IRA the Northern Ireland problem would be even further from a solution."[88] In the South, the ESRI survey put the measure of support for "the motives" of the IRA at 42 percent and for the activities of the IRA at 21 percent.[89] Although the validity of these findings was hotly contested in the media, the survey authors themselves, perhaps with a premonition of the controversy that lay in store, had counseled cautious interpretation: the 21 percent support for IRA activities, they wrote, included 13 percent who were slightly supportive and only 8 percent either moderately or strongly supportive. But having said this, they went on to conclude that "opposition to IRA activities is not overwhelming and certainly does not match the strong opposition so often articulated by public figures."[90]

Another disinterested scholar is even more forthright: "PIRA," he writes, "is not simply a terrorist movement in the accepted sense of the term. Its longevity, its history and its goals suggest that it is deeply-rooted in the society in which it operates. Although it engages in acts of terror from time to time, it also fights a military campaign against what it perceives to be an alien army. Unlike the Baeder-Meinhof gang, the Brigate Rossi, and other terrorist groups, PIRA's aims are feasible, internally consistent, and find some measure of support among the wider population."[91] His conclusion: "PIRA represents the 'cutting edge' of a movement which finds roots in the frustration of relative deprivation experienced by a sector of the Catholic community in Northern Ireland."[92]

Morrison's claim that Fianna Fáil and Fine Gael voters support the IRA is corroborated by one of the leading authorities on the movement. "Throughout the seventies," he writes, "the IRA benefitted from the traditional passive support given to the movement. The bed for the night, the blind eye, the cooperation in money or services . . . The IRA is not invulnerable, bullets do wound them but one very rarely hears — in fact, in the South, never — of a doctor or a hospital reporting the fact that a wounded man is receiving treatment." However, "political support in terms of the vote continued to be withheld — or rather the type of person who might have drawn the vote continued to stand aloof from the movement."[93]

Accordingly, the Irish government's contention that the IRA's failure at the ballot box means that the IRA has no political base of support among Irish people is, therefore, not only spurious, it obfuscates reality. A paramilitary organization does not set out to win at the ballot box. It sets out to win its political aims. The one does not necessarily have anything to do with the other. Power, according to Mao's famous axiom, does indeed come out of the barrel of a gun, and the hard truth is that politics ultimately has a lot more to do with the dictates of power than with the interests of "the plain people." In the scheme of things, "winning the hearts and minds of the people" is more often the by-product than the cause of success.

But beyond that, the fact is the IRA does represent something. It is the embodiment of a concept of Irish nationalism that is largely the creation of successive Irish governments themselves. It symbolizes the holy writ of indivisible nationhood. It takes its purpose and tradition from Wolfe Tone's call, two hundred years ago, "to break the connection with England . . . to assert the independence of the country and to unite the whole people of Ireland."[94] It has pursued this aspiration relentlessly and ruthlessly. It can summon eight hundred years of what the state itself propagates as history and sixty years of its own enduring tradition to bear witness to its purpose.

It is, consequently, preposterous for Dublin governments to compare the IRA with the flotsam and jetsam of international terrorism. Such comparisons deny the present and further distort a past that successive governments have willingly subscribed to. They continue to subscribe to the same view of history as the IRA, enunciating the same goals, making the same demands, and holding out the same hopes. The IRA, therefore, is their ally, notwithstanding their protestations to the contrary. The collusion is a matter of direction, if not of degree.

Moreover, the reaction of nervous Dublin governments during the hunger strikes brought into the open once more the inconsistent attitudes they hold toward the IRA. Their attitudes vacillate depending on whether or not they see the actions of the IRA as a threat to their own positions. Thus, when it appeared that the hunger strikes would put him an in uncomfortable, perhaps even untenable, political position, Mr. Haughey called on Mrs. Thatcher to be more "flexible,"[95] and months later Dr. FitzGerald called for direct negotiations between the protesting prisoners and the British government.[96]

The Irish public make a distinction between actions taken by the authorities in the South against the IRA and actions taken by the British government. They are, of course, far less tolerant of the latter. Nor is IRA action against the British authorities seen in the same light as action against Irish authorities. The killing of a Garda will provoke outrage; the killing of a British soldier, silence. Again, survey data reflect the ambivalences. The ESRI survey found that only 46 percent of respondents in the South were in favor of the British government taking a tougher stand toward the IRA, whereas 63 percent wanted the Irish government to do so.[97] On the other hand, in the North, Catholic support for a tougher line was stronger on both counts — 55 percent of Catholic respondents, according to the Northern Ireland Attitude Survey, favored a tougher British policy toward the IRA, and 64 percent favored a tougher policy on the part of the Irish government.[98]

Taking a tougher line, however, is often more honored in the breach than in the observance by Dublin governments, especially when the IRA's Northern incursions are in question. Support for a tougher line stops well short of support for extradition. And without extradition the IRA has, in fact, a safe haven, a relatively secure staging area for launching operations against targets in the North. Brigadier Glover:

> The headquarters of the Provisionals is in the Republic. The South also provides a safe mounting base for cross-Border operations and secure training areas. PIRA's logistic support flows through the Republic where arms and ammunition are received from overseas. Improvised weapons, bombs and explosives are manufactured there. Terrorists can live there without fear of extradition for crimes committed in the North. In short, the Republic provides many of the facilities of the classic

safe haven so essential to any successful terrorist movement. And it will probably continue to do so for the foreseeable future.[99]

Dublin governments argue that the Constitution prohibits extradition in cases where political motives are a consideration. In other words, there are criminals and criminals.* The public, too, is ambivalent on the question — 46 percent support extradition, according to the ESRI survey, and 48 percent oppose it. Hardly the cutting edge of a consensus.

• • •

Ultimately, of course, the issue facing Dublin governments and the Irish public is not the IRA's popularity in the community at large, but the power it exercises and whether the best interests of the state and the people are served by making an accommodation with that power, by containing it, or by trying to eradicate it.

The IRA draws its power from its historical identity, the symbolic content of its goals, its willingness to use physical force ruthlessly and indiscriminately, its tenacity of purpose, and its capacity to disrupt the conduct of public life, thereby undermining the basis of support for the constitutional government. Accordingly, to eradicate the power of the IRA, the Dublin government must find a way to neutralize the IRA's claim to historical legitimacy, destroy its ability to endure, counter its tactics, and take away its raison d'être.

What it must avoid, at all costs, is the temptation to eradicate the movement through repression. Repression is the mainstay of paramilitary organizations, success often predicated on the ability to provoke it. If the government cracks down by suspend-

* Nor does the South subscribe to the European Convention on the Suppression of Terrorism. In April 1982 the twenty-one-nation Council of Europe Parliamentary Assembly criticized Ireland and Malta for being the only two member states not to do so. (See *Irish Times*, 30 April 1982.) And in July, members of the European Parliament in Strasbourg called on the EEC states to refuse to recognize any political asylum between member states and to start extraditing fugitives wanted for terrorist offenses who had fled across the borders of nearby states. (See *Irish Times*, 9 July 1982.)

ing constitutional rights, by setting up special courts, by denying due process, by establishing detention centers, and by increasing the powers of the security forces, it will create the very conditions that promote and perpetuate the IRA, and hasten its own demise. For these measures are a prescription for the death of democracy.

Already there should be cause for concern in the South. The Offenses Against the State Act (1939) was amended in 1972 to establish the Special Criminal Court. It consists of an uneven number of judges and no jury. The court has jurisdiction in cases where a threat to the state is involved and where there is reason to believe that a normal jury trial would be inappropriate. Except for the absence of a jury, the court's procedure is supposed to follow that of a normal court. The court did not secure many convictions against the IRA until the end of 1972, when the Dáil passed yet another amendment, placing the burden on an individual to repudiate any published allegation that he was a member of the IRA. Failure to do so is taken as evidence of membership. Moreover, a statement by a senior Garda officer that a person is a member of the IRA is also taken as evidence of membership, the onus of proof falling once again on the individual to disprove his membership in an illegal organization. The Republic's legislation, in this respect, is far more stringent than similar legislation in the North. Of further concern is the fact that the Special Criminal Court has been used for cases which are not obviously "political" in nature, although the act itself does not make a distinction between "political" and "non-political offences."[100]

Repression poses other problems. First, there is the question of time. For a revolutionary organization, and for the IRA in particular, the concept of failure does not exist. Indeed, the most remarkable attribute of the IRA is its persistence in the face of failure. When things get bad, it simply goes underground. It ceases operations. It reorganizes. As it has done in the 1920s and '30s and '40s and '50s and '60s and '70s. But it does not go away.

Second, the government that vows to stamp out a paramilitary organization must show progress toward that goal in order to justify the social, economic, and political costs that the effort entails. But how is progress measured? Indeed, how can there be victory when one well-placed bomb can make any claim of progress empty? The government, in effect, is constantly in the position of having to attain the unattainable.

The British Army has been unable to "defeat" the IRA. It would simply be wishful thinking for an Irish government to believe that it could succeed where the British — with their sophisticated counterinsurgency expertise, their experience in Malaya, Burma, and Aden, and their specialized military resources — have failed. And it would be an even more frightening miscalculation for the government to believe that it could "defeat" the IRA in a military sense while Northern Ireland remains a part of the United Kingdom.

Ultimately, there is no defense against the random bomb, and as the weaponry of terrorism becomes more sophisticated, and remote-control devices fine-tune the delivery of swift and brutal death, the task of the government becomes correspondingly more difficult. And terrorism functions best in a complex, interdependent, urban society. The opportunities to disrupt the normal flow of life and sow the seeds of alienation are more abundant; the ripple effects of a single operation are more widespread; the impact is more deadly and devastating.

Containment, of course, would rely on a judicious use of "the stick." But containment will work only if the political environment in which it operates facilitates its success. Fianna Fáil's policies have been singularly lacking in this regard. The call for the end to the guarantee, the veiled references to the desirability of a declaration by Britain of its intent to withdraw, the insistence that unification is the only solution and inevitable, imply that Fianna Fáil does not dispute the aims of the IRA, only the means it employs. Not only is the distinction lost on Northern Protestants; it is not nearly as clear-cut as some Fianna Fáil stalwarts make it out to be.

The aim of Fianna Fáil is to induce consent; the aim of the IRA, to make Northern Ireland ungovernable. The more successful the IRA is at the latter, the more susceptible Northern Protestants are to the former. Says Dr. Martin Mansergh:

> A lot of Unionists, particularly those living outside Belfast — those living in Armagh or Fermanagh or Tyrone — are perhaps skeptical in their heart of hearts about how long the present situation can be maintained. There are a lot of people who don't think that containment of the situation for twenty or thirty years while people's mentalities gradually evolve is feasible. That if nothing is done things will get worse.[101]

"Nothing," of course, is used in the context of its opposite: "something" must be done, and that something implies a loosening of the British connection. While the IRA remains a threat to security in Northern Ireland, necessitating the large-scale employment of resources to contain it, and while the conflict drags on, with its annual quotas of atrocities and crises bringing the state to the brink of disintegration time and again, a Fianna Fáil government stands to benefit from the actions of the IRA. They become a valuable tool in its campaign to induce consent by bringing about a change in political will in Britain, an objective that is, after all, the stated purpose of IRA activity.

That change in will is not likely to emerge because of Mr. Haughey's gifts of persuasion. Nor is it likely to emerge if the IRA abandons its campaign of violence — without any quid pro quo in the offing. Indeed, such a unilateral decision by the IRA would be tantamount to an admission of defeat, a clear victory for Britain, emphatic justification for her stubborn determination not to give in to terrorist demands. Political will to stay put would harden, not weaken. But if Britain decided to withdraw, she would need a rationale — under no circumstance could she appear to be beaten by the IRA. The obduracy of the Protestants and the enormous cost of waging an unwinnable war and maintaining the security for two communities who ostensibly would otherwise be at each other's throats provide the necessary mix of ingredients. If she decided to disengage, she would, of course, prefer to do so in the context of an "agreed" settlement, in which case she would be more disposed to putting pressure on Loyalists to induce their consent to an all-Ireland solution. And if that failed, then withdrawal could take place against a backdrop of the "insoluble" nature of the conflict. Having done her best and having been seen to have done her best, and having shown that the native antagonists were unreasonable to the point of lunacy, Britain would simply wash her hands of the whole unsavory mess, leaving the Irish to their own mean, and no doubt destructive, devices. *But if the IRA called a halt to its operations, there would, of course, no longer be an overt conflict, and therefore there would be a less pressing need for a "solution."* Indeed, were the IRA simply to cease and desist, the impact could be retrogressive, since there would no longer be any reason for Loyalists to make any concessions to nationalists when their "unreasonableness" no longer carried with it the threat of greater instability. It is improbable to assume that they would make concessions in the future if the IRA put the gun away, in view of their demonstrated unwillingness to make concessions in the past, no matter how menacing the IRA gun.

A decision to withdraw could not, of course, be reached simply by executive fiat. Parliament would have to pass the enabling legislation. A parliamentary debate on withdrawal, however, would be a step of last resort, carrying with it profound and uncharted constitutional implications, threatening, perhaps, the stability of the United Kingdom itself. The ethical considerations, the legal niceties, the slap to Britain's standing in the international order of world powers, since she would appear to be abandoning Northern Ireland to an uncertain fate — for Parliament could only legislate Northern Ireland out of the U.K. but not into anything else — would have a traumatizing impact on the nation and its institutions. Accordingly, if the IRA ceased operations — a "victory" for the government of the day — and if a troop withdrawal became feasible, there would be no exigent need to consider long-term disengagement, and certainly no government with an instinct for self-preservation would consider putting the matter before Parliament. Thus, withdrawal or a variant thereof — a declaration of intent to withdraw — is only likely to take place in circumstances of intractable instability caused by the unremitting persistence of the IRA campaign of violence.

Irish politicians, therefore, who use every platform to call for British withdrawal or who talk about the inevitability of unification are giving tacit support to the IRA, their condemnations of violence notwithstanding. Such condemnations, of course, are frequently qualified: although violence is not condoned, it is excused; it may be deplorable, but it has a cause — the British presence. Remove the presence and you end the violence. During the 1919–21 "War of Independence," no one gave the IRA a mandate to pursue a campaign of violence.* They simply assumed it, and out of that arrogant assumption came the state that is now the Republic. Today the state reveres "the hard men of violence" who took matters into their own hands during that struggle for "national liberation." Hence, the state's condemnation of violence in the present situation while calling for the end that the violence is intended to bring about lacks moral authority. The perpetrators of the violence are only acting out a preordained script — "Ireland unfree shall never be at peace." But the script itself is the handiwork of the founding fathers.

Moreover, when Mr. Haughey talks of Northern Ireland as "a failed political entity," that failure is due in no small measure to the IRA. It is hard to argue that the IRA did not help bring

* Although Sinn Féin overwhelmed the nationalist Home Rule Party in the December 1918 general election, Sinn Féin voters were not voting for violence. According to Robert Kee, "The one thing they [Sinn Féin voters] were certainly not voting for was an attempt to win sovereign independence by force of arms or a campaign of terrorism. This was a goal believed in only by a minority of Volunteer Activists who in the long run saw violence rather than democratic politics as the final arbiter, though they would have maintained that they were thereby expressing the national will." See *Ourselves Alone*, pp. 50–52. Nor was there public support for violence in 1919: "Throughout 1919," Kee writes, "members of popularly elected bodies, such as urban and rural district councils, often supporters of Sinn Féin, were to express condemnation or at least dislike of what was being done by the [IRA] Volunteers. It was only when condemnation and dislike for what the British Government were to do by way of retaliation began to exceed this, that popular acquiescence in what was in reality the open rebellion of a small minority materialised." Kee also notes that "throughout the so-called War of Independence from 1919–21 Cardinal Logue himself, the three Archbishops and the entire hierarchy, together with the vast majority of parish priests, condemned bloodshed by the [IRA] Volunteers as crimes and offences against the law of God." See *Ourselves Alone*, pp. 61–62.

about the fall of Stormont.* Or that it was not the catalyst resulting in internment and Bloody Sunday — events that polarized the communities to such an extent that viability ceased to have any meaning. Or that its activities did not lead to a change in attitude in London, opening the way to a recognition of the Irish Dimension. And surely it is significant that the hunger strikes brought forth a slew of proposals for an Ireland without a British presence: *The Economist*'s call for a confederal Ireland,[102] former Prime Minister James Callaghan's call for an independent Northern Ireland,[103] a similar call by the London *Sunday Times*,[104] and the Labour Party's adoption of a resolution endorsing the long-term unification of Ireland with the consent of a majority.[105] The pressures on Britain to withdraw come either directly or indirectly as a result of IRA activity. In fact, were the violence somehow miraculously to cease and a viable devolved government structure to emerge, a workable internal solution might just evolve — a prospect the irredentist elements in Fianna Fáil would find appalling.

The IRA, therefore, complements Fianna Fáil. Both subscribe to the same view of history, have the same objectives, and see British withdrawal as the key element in a settlement. The IRA ensures that Northern Ireland continues to be unstable, thereby justifying Mr. Haughey's claim that it is "a failed political entity." If the IRA abandoned its campaign of violence, that "failed political entity" might resuscitate itself. But even if it did not, the failure would not be so obvious, not being so tragic; nor so immediate, not being so destabilizing; nor so divisive, not being so lethal; nor so disruptive, not being so total; nor so irreconcilable, not being so bitter; nor so hopeless, not being so despairing.

On the other hand, the FitzGerald policy — repeal of Articles 2 and 3, and support for the evolution of stable devolved government in the North — carries with it a different set of implications. Repeal of Articles 2 and 3 is at variance with Republican ideol-

* The SDLP's withdrawal from Stormont in July 1971 precipitated, perhaps, the fall of Stormont. But this action, which followed the failure of the government to conduct an inquiry on terms set out by the SDLP into the shooting dead of two men under questionable circumstances by the British Army in Derry, reflected the SDLP's fear of being outmaneuvered by the IRA. (See D. H. Akenson, *United States and Ireland*, p. 238.)

ogy. Indeed, carried to its logical conclusion it is a repudiation of nationalism in its narrow irredentist form, an implicit attack on the myth of the past, the inescapable corollary being that unification is not about to happen in the foreseeable future and may in fact never happen.

Repeal would undermine the IRA's claim to historical legitimacy by rejecting the legality of the ends the IRA seeks to achieve. It would deny the IRA's raison d'être by denying the validity of the historical perspective the IRA calls upon to justify its actions. And it would exorcise the IRA as an idea by rejecting the idea the IRA stands for. Unification would become an aspiration, not a demand; a mutual accommodation, not an exclusive right; the outcome of a process of cooperation, not the product of duress, possible only when the Irish themselves concede that other outcomes are also possible.

But repeal is plausible only if the step has the support of a large majority in the South. It has, therefore, little chance of success without the active support of Fianna Fáil. Fianna Fáil, however, not only withholds that support, it adamantly opposes the move and is likely to do so for the foreseeable future. This impasse works in the IRA's favor, the absence of bipartisan agreement guaranteeing that any attempt to isolate the IRA will fail; the IRA's vaunted ability to endure, therefore, is as much a product of the lack of political will in the South as it is of its own indomitable sense of divine mission.

Repeal of Articles 2 and 3, however, would be only the first step. Other initiatives would be called for if a comprehensive political framework is to emerge. First, the three political parties in Britain would have to give a joint undertaking — to the extent that that is possible, since no sitting government can bind a future government — that government policy on Northern Ireland would not vary no matter which party holds the reins of government. That policy would have to assert the unequivocal commitment of Britain to remain in Northern Ireland so long as that is the wish of a majority. At present the hints of change emanating from the corridors of the political establishment, and the belief, assiduously cultivated in some quarters, that Britain wants out, encourage the nationalist constitutional parties to hold out hope for the propitious moment to arrive, and stiffen the IRA's conviction that its campaign of violence will ultimately pay off.

Second, Direct Rule would have to give way to a devolved government that has responsibility for security. A devolved government acceptable to a majority of Catholics would undercut support for the IRA in its traditional strongholds. IRA actions against security forces that are the agent of a government in which Catholics quite visibly have a share of the power, including power over security arrangements, would be viewed in a different light by the Catholic population than would IRA actions against security forces that are the agent of an occupying power. Direct Rule from Westminster simplifies the logic of the IRA's position and the rationale for its activities: it is the "pin everything on 10 Downing Street" syndrome. Rule from Stormont with Catholic participation would change the parameters of what is a defensive operation and what is a purely military one.

Third, the South would have to agree to extradition. Repeal of Articles 2 and 3 would abnegate the present rationale for avoiding the issue by removing the mantle of political protection.

Finally, Unionists would have to offer a quid pro quo — an acknowledgment that an Irish Dimension exists and that it would necessitate an institutional accommodation of some sort with the South at some point to give it full and legitimate expression.

• • •

The prisoners are different: they are ordinary. But the differences should not be exaggerated. Ultimately the IRA must be judged not on the basis of the character of its members but on the basis of its actions. Bad history, the false promises of the past, the unkept promises of the present, the pervasiveness and singularity of the myth of unity, the misguided actions of the British government, the sectarianism, the hinterlands of Loyalism, and the generations of shared deprivations make the IRA's actions understandable, but they do not justify them. The question basically is a moral one: are Northern Ireland's Catholics being politically repressed to an extent that justifies a campaign of violence to end it?

They are not. Nor is there evidence to suggest that they themselves believe they are. On the contrary, the majority are more inclined to see themselves as victims of the IRA's actions, and thus they support a tougher policy toward the IRA on the parts of both the British and the Irish governments. Moreover, the Northern Ireland Attitude Survey found, even in 1978 — despite the years of house searches, detentions, and special court procedures — that 39 percent of Northern Catholics would settle for a power-sharing devolved government within a U.K. framework.

In fact, surveys taken over the last fifteen years consistently show that a plurality of Catholics find this type of solution acceptable.[106] In short, they will accept a British framework as part of a solution when it provides a political structure that protects their rights and interests.

The banality of evil has its counterpoint in the "banality of good." When the "good" condemn the IRA as men of violence but are unwilling to confront the moral and political ramifications of their own passive and often self-serving actions, they are denying their own silent complicity in what they so earnestly protest. The IRA will not go away. But that still leaves the South with a choice. Either she can walk away from the IRA, rejecting the goals it aspires to, or she can walk behind the IRA, a few steps back, a little reluctantly perhaps, even a little shamefacedly, but nevertheless in tow, protesting all the while but not too loudly, the covert approval drowning out the overt disapproval. The former is an act of faith in renewal, the latter an act of moral and political cowardice. The choice is the South's to make, for it is there that the IRA must be confronted if it is to be contained, and in time co-opted.

Danny Morrison is right: the South is the key to the overall struggle.

8

The Ulster Defence Association: A Question of Uncertainty

Put up what flag you like, it is too late
To save your soul with bunting.

— Louis MacNeice
"Autumn Journal"

THEY DO NOT DENY THE PAST, although they do repudiate it. Yes, they were involved in sectarian killings, and yes, they were wrong. The times, they will tell you, made them do it: but they were not the only guilty ones; there was twice as much sectarian killing on the Republican side. Their Supreme Commander, Andy Tyrie, explains:

The Ulster Defence Association was born as a means of front-line defense for the Ulster people. We were actively supported by many politicians who declared, "We support you lads but we daren't say it openly or we would be ruined." These spineless jellyfish uttered catch-cries like "liquidate the enemy," "Protestant backlash," and shouted about "popish plots," and as a direct result our membership convinced themselves they were soldiers and consequently that they were entitled to use every means suitable to put down the enemy.[1]

The enemy, of course, were Catholics, *all* Catholics, it being axiomatic that to be Catholic was to be, if not a member, at the very least an active supporter of the IRA. Hence the sectarian murders:

> We had been indoctrinated for years [says Tyrie]. The Ulster people in the Protestant community had been conditioned for years to react. It was emotional and traditional. You had communities who had been conditioned to defend their areas. Protestants felt everyone in the Falls Road or nationalist areas were IRA people. Catholics thought every Shankill person belonged to the UDA or the UVF. At the time you had a Protestant community that panicked. They had no security to defend their areas. Jack Lynch was moving troops up to the Border. Haughey and Blaney were importing guns. Once again Protestants felt under siege. They were going to be wiped off the face of the earth. They weren't crimes. They were emotional acts. People reacted.[2]

Did they ever: assassination gangs striking at will and with impunity, the more defenseless the victim, the more vicious the assault; random murder on a rampage, the vicissitudes of whim the arbiter of death, the mutilation of victims intoxicating the maddened, luring the berserk. At one point up to forty-five Protestant paramilitary organizations, ranging from the very small and highly fanatical to the large and relatively well disciplined, were in the business of killing. They called themselves "defence" associations; all, other than the Ulster Volunteer Force, came into being after August 1969.

They were working class, their members drawn from Belfast and the satellite towns of Newtownabbey, Dundonald, and Lisburn; their targets: Catholic homes, pubs, churches, and recreational facilities. At first they were indigenous to their communities, often the product of imitation rather than of need. But once their lucrative potential became apparent, their number ballooned, for protection, like other goods and services in the marketplace, carried a price tag. Local shopkeepers and merchants found it more politic and less costly to meet rather than to buck the demands for what in plain parlance was extortion money. Not that the Loyalist defense associations were much different from the IRA in this regard. On both sides of the divide, internecine feuding—Loyalist against Loyalist, Republican against Republican — over territory accounted for an improvident number of deaths.

For the unemployed, the defense associations were irresistibly alluring, holding out the promise of status, money, and the power to impose. The associations, therefore, had a vested interest in continuing instability, and many, with no ideological orientation or political tradition to guide their actions, attracted their share of psychopaths: when all Catholics were the enemy — Fenian scum — all actions were justified.

The politicians gave the nod of assent. William Craig, Terence O'Neill's former Minister for Home Affairs and the leader of the Vanguard movement,* set the tone. "Let us put bluff aside," he told the Conservative Party's right-wing Monday Club in October 1972. "I am prepared to kill and those behind me have my full support. We will not surrender."[3]

• • •

The Ulster Defence Association (UDA) was founded in September 1971 to coordinate the large number of Protestant vigilante groups that had proliferated in the aftermath of the B-Specials' being disbanded.[4] It gave the Protestant working classes "their" army back, an army which would, like the B-Specials, meet ruthlessness with ruthlessness, that being the only sure-fire prescription, according to hard-line Loyalists, for putting an end to the depredations of the IRA. By the middle of 1972 the UDA probably had forty thousand members, and its military-style parades through the streets of Belfast — the thousands of "soldiers" dressed in combat fatigues, faces concealed behind the ubiquitous hood, taut with discipline and hard with purpose — made the specter of the dreaded Protestant "backlash" once more an imminent and potentially awful reality. For the next two years the UDA danced eagerly and pliantly to the tune of the politi-

* The Vanguard movement, or Ulster Vanguard, was launched by William Craig as a pressure group within the Unionist Party in early 1972. It had strong support from Loyalist paramilitary groups and organized demonstrations to protest the introduction of Direct Rule. It inspired Craig to set up the Vanguard Unionist Progressive Party, a fringe political force that ceased to exist in 1978.

cians. William Craig, Harry West (leader of the OUP between 1974 and 1979), and Ian Paisley drew on the undeniable strength of its numbers to advance their political careers.

And the UDA killed — upwards of four hundred Catholics between 1971 and 1976,[5] the chain of action and reaction a miasma of death. The IRA killed a member or former member of either the UDR or RUC, and the UDA killed a Catholic.

• • •

The turning point came in May 1974, when the Protestant working classes turned on the Unionist politicians who had negotiated a power-sharing Executive with the SDLP and the Alliance Party, and a Council of Ireland with the Republic: A power-sharing Executive at that point was perhaps tolerable, but a Council of Ireland was an anathema — a sellout, opening wide the door to unification. They moved to shut it — and fast.

The Ulster Workers' Council (UWC), with the full backing of the UDA, called for a provincewide work stoppage to take effect on 14 May, the day on which the Assembly voted to ratify the Sunningdale Agreement. Whatever reluctance there was in the Protestant community to support the strike vanished eleven days later when the British Prime Minister, Harold Wilson, contemptuously referred to the strikers as "spongers."* This was the final insult: it reduced Protestants to the level of Catholics, ignored their innumerable sacrifices on behalf of the Crown in two world wars, mocked their sense of self-reliance and self-worth, and questioned their Britishness. Ranks closed; they stood together: the stoppage was complete. Of course, once success was ensured, the politicians belatedly tried to climb on the bandwagon, but this time the grassroots would have none of it. Tyrie:

* During a BBC broadcast on 25 May 1974, Wilson said: "British taxpayers have seen the taxes they have poured out almost without regard to cost . . . going into Northern Ireland. They see property destroyed by evil violence and are asked to pick up the bill for rebuilding it. Yet people who benefit from all this now viciously defy Westminster, purporting to act as though they were an elected government; people who spend their lives sponging on Westminster and British democracy and then systematically assault democratic methods. Who do these people think they are?" See Robert Fisk, *Point of No Return*, p. 183.

> We had come to a stage where we felt that the politicians made up their minds what they wanted, but they forgot what the people had asked them to do. They knew what was better for the people than the people realized was better for themselves. And that's where the big problem came about, because we have never been allowed to think for ourselves, but we were allowed to be used.[6]

Being used: the sore rankled. "We discovered," says Tyrie, "when our members went to jail, that there were no politicians in jail. And there were very few politicians in the cemeteries."[7]

Being used: one day the politicians would encourage them onto the streets, emboldening them to undertake the actions the security forces were precluded from taking; the next, the same politicians were unctuously condemning acts of violence. Being used: they were called on to defend the Protestant way of life and all that was dear to its traditions, yet they often lived in housing as abominable and with amenities as wretched as their Catholic neighbors who were supposedly threatening their way of life.[8] Being used: they put themselves unquestioningly on the line to preserve the prerogatives of their social superiors, who wooed their support or spurned it as opportunity dictated. Being used: their "soldiers" were interned without trial, hauled before the Diplock Courts, and sentenced to long terms in jail, while their "politicians" were chauffeured to conferences, and pandered to in the media. Being used: their prisoners, like the IRA's, were victims of "the special situation," their treatment in the prisons often no better, their demands for special prison status often no different, their families often no better off. And with their sense of being used, of being neglected by their own politicians and rejected by Westminster, there came the glimmer of a new consciousness. The Protestant paramilitaries, the hard men who answered Republican violence with violence of their own, who saw themselves as engaged in a "war" with the IRA, began to advance the idea of breaking the connection with England. Before they were British they were men of Ulster, and to Ulster they gave their first loyalty.

• • •

Their first suggestions were tentative, they themselves none too sure of the putative course they were following. Glenn Barr, deputy leader of Vanguard, former Assembly member, Ulster Constitutional Convention member, and spokesman for both the UDA and the UWC, made the case for independence at the Amherst Conference* in September 1975:

> We need to create a system of government, an identity and a nationality to which both sections of the community can aspire. We must look for the common denominator. The only common denominator that the Ulster people have, whether they be Catholic or Protestant, is that they are Ulstermen. And that is the basis from which we should build the new life for the Ulster people, a new identity for them. Awaken them to their own identity. That they are different. That they're not second-class Englishmen but first-class Ulstermen. And that's where my loyalty is.[9]

In January 1978 the UDA set up the New Ulster Political Research Group (NUPRG), with Barr as chairman, "to develop a Constitutional and Political Policy on behalf of the Ulster Defence Association for presentation to the people of Northern Ireland."[10] Fifteen months later, NUPRG published a pamphlet, "Beyond the Religious Divide," presenting a plan for negotiated independence. Reviewing it in the *New Statesman,* Bernard Crick, distinguished professor of politics at the University of London, wrote: "Scepticism or dislike of such an objective [negotiated independence] has prevented British politicians and journalists

* The Amherst Conference on Northern Ireland was organized by the Committee for an Irish Forum, a committee of Irish nationals living in the United States and concerned Americans formed explicitly for that purpose. The conference was held at the University of Massachusetts from 28 August to 3 September 1975. Among those attending were forty-six participants from Northern Ireland and the Republic, including representatives of the UDA, Official Sinn Féin, the Irish Republican Socialist Party, the Orange Order, the Official Unionist Party, the SDLP, the Alliance Party, and a number of academics, journalists, labor union officials, community organizers, and Catholic and Protestant clergymen who had an intimate knowledge of what was happening in Northern Ireland. Invitees from Provisional Sinn Féin could not attend because they were denied visas. However, members of the organization most closely identified with the IRA in the United States — the Northern Ireland Aid Committee (NORAID) — did attend. The author was the founding President of the Committee for an Irish Forum.

from giving the contents of this remarkable [though] admittedly somewhat amateur document the attention it deserves . . . It is a genuine attempt to shift religious antipathy into constitutional argument and inter-community self-government."[11]

The U.S. presidential system was NUPRG's model: the emphasis on checks and balances and separation of powers. Thus, their plan calls for a Constitution and a Bill of Rights, an executive branch and a legislative branch.[12] The Chief Executive (the Prime Minister) and the Deputy would contest elections as a team and the Chief Executive would appoint his ministers from "outside of the elected representatives."[13] Politicians, therefore, would have to decide "whether they wanted to be in the legislature or whether they wanted to take a chance of being appointed to the Executive";[14] members of the legislature would, therefore, be excluded from the executive functions of government. All elections would use the Proportional Representation–Single Transferable Vote (PR-STV)* system. A Speaker of the House would be elected by two thirds of the votes of the full legislature.

* The PR-STV system is the present one used in Northern Ireland. It was introduced in the Northern Ireland Assembly elections in 1973 by the British government to give minorities a better chance of being elected. At first it was opposed by the overwhelming majority of Protestants. It has always been supported by the SDLP, Alliance, and other minority (Protestant and Catholic) parties. It is also the system of elections used in the Republic. The formula (Valid Poll ÷ Seats + 1) + 1 is applied and the number of votes obtained using this formula is called a quota. For example: A multimember constituency has cast 70,000 valid votes and it has a constituency population of 110,000, which entitles it to six representatives in the legislature. The quota is then: (70,000 ÷ 6 + 1) + 1 = 10,001. If six candidates in the first count receive 10,001 votes each, this will leave only 9994 for all other candidates. Only six quotas are, therefore, obtainable under this formula, and when they have been obtained the contest is closed because all the seats have been filled. When the voters go to the polls they vote for candidates in order of their preference, using numerical figure 1 for their first preference candidate, 2 for their second preference, and so on. All the first preferences are counted and credited to each candidate. If a candidate reaches the quota on the first count, he is elected. If he receives more than his quota, then all his surplus votes are redistributed by transferring surplus votes to continuing candidates in proportion to each such candidate's share of second preferences in the elected candidate's set of votes. There is a complicated piece of mathematics involved here, which is irrelevant in trying to point out the fairness of the system. When no candidate reaches the quota, the candidate with the fewest votes on the count board is eliminated, and his first-preference votes are transferred to continuing candidates also on the basis of second preferences.

He, in turn, would appoint the chairmen of the legislative committees, and committee members, on the basis of proportional representation. The weighted-majority requirement for the Speaker would ensure that the whole system could not even commence to operate unless minority groups participated. Overseeing both the legislative and executive branches of government would be a third branch, "a Supreme Court with an International Supreme Court Judge as President."[15] The Court would have "constitutional powers to protect the Constitution and the Bill of Rights and to overrule any law passed by the legislature which it deemed unconstitutional."[16] The independent International Supreme Court judge would come from a "friendly international government"[17] which would "supervise the transitional period in a presence that [was] not military."[18] NUPRG's preference was for the United States to serve as guarantor of the new arrangements by agreeing to nominate a Supreme Court judge to head up the new state's Supreme Court "for the first eight or twelve years."[19] Both Britain and Ireland would, of course, have to "withdraw all their claims of sovereignty over Northern Ireland,"[20] though Britain would, nevertheless, have to provide financial support "with no strings attached for a period of not less than twenty-five years."[21]

• • •

Negotiated independence: its attraction, the deceptive ease with which a rational case for it can be made. It has elegance, no loose ends, evenhandedness, symmetrical juxtapositions, balance. And it has a zero-sum impartiality, rejecting the traditional assumptions of both Republicans and Loyalists for what they really are — the stuff of fantasy.

On the Republican side is the fantasy that a majority of the people of the whole of Ireland earnestly and enthusiastically desire unification, and that unification therefore is historically inevitable. On the Loyalist side is the fantasy that Northern Ireland is an indigenous part of Great Britain and that a majority of the people of Great Britain wish to preserve the Union.

Thus, the first fantasy closes the mind to any possibility of a resolution that does not insist on a united Ireland as the final outcome, while the second brings a similar inflexibility to any alternative that does not affirm the Union with Britain as the primary consideration.

The realities, of course, are a little less absolute. Among Northern Catholics there is no overwhelming enthusiasm for a united Ireland. The prospect of losing the subsidies they receive from the British government for education and social welfare and the economic prop of the subvention further tempers their enthusiasm, while the prospect of being caught between the Irish Army, the IRA, and Protestant militants if Britain withdrew precipitately has a still more tempering effect.

Nor is there overwhelming enthusiasm in the South for unification. The public there wants it, but not yet and at no cost. The prospect of substantial increases in taxation to meet the cost of equalizing economic and social welfare benefits in the whole island further tempers their enthusiasm, while the prospect of having to fight for it has a still more tempering effect.

Britain, of course, no longer cares to conceal her own lack of enthusiasm for keeping Northern Ireland in the United Kingdom. The prospect of having to subsidize Northern Ireland indefinitely further tempers what enthusiasm remains, while the prospect of a continued political stalemate has a still more tempering effect.

What this all means is that ultimately Northern Catholics have more in common with Northern Protestants than they have with the people of the South, and Northern Protestants have more in common with Northern Catholics than they have with the people of Britain.[22] The Catholics and Protestants of Ulster have the same economic and social interests. Both are bound by the awful thread of their mutual predicament and the looming prospect of apocalypse. Both are victims of their expectations and of the mythologies of the past. And both share a common identity in many important respects, a cultural heritage dating back to the earliest of times.

Ulster was different. Cut off from the rest of Ireland "by a natural barrier of small hills (drumlins), forests, bogs, lakes and watercourses,"[23] it developed a unique set of spatial characteristics. Moreover, its primary gravitational pull was toward Scotland, which was more accessible by sea than was the rest of Ireland by land. Accordingly, Ulster was largely immune to the Anglo-Saxon influences in the rest of the country. Nor was the Scottish "pull" one way only. The noted Dutch geographer M. W. Heslinga writes: "It is frequently said that it was the Scots who made modern Ulster. There is much reason for saying that it was 'Ulstermen' who made ancient Scotland. For the colonists from east Ulster gave Scotland her name, her first kings, her Gaelic language and her faith."[24] Thus the intimacy of the relationship, each being at one time or at many times the colonizer of the other, and each in turn being colonized. And thus the inflections and idiosyncrasies of speech, manner, and accent that are indigenous to the area, and set Ulster aside from the rest of Ireland.

An independent Northern Ireland would require Catholics in Northern Ireland to give up their allegiance to the Republic, the Republic to give up her claims to a united Ireland, Protestants in Northern Ireland to give up their allegiances to the Crown, and the Crown to give up its claim to a United Kingdom of Great Britain and Northern Ireland. The corollary of independence, therefore, is that the major responsibility for resolving the conflict rests primarily with the people of Northern Ireland. It is not the responsibility of Great Britain. Nor is it the responsibility of the Republic.

More important, a solution that calls for an independent Northern Ireland would allow both Catholics and Protestants, especially the IRA and militant Loyalists, to claim victory. The IRA could legitimately claim that it had succeeded in its avowed aim to drive the British out of Northern Ireland, while the Loyalists could also legitimately claim that they had succeeded in their avowed aim never to become part of a united Ireland. Allowing both sides to claim a measure of victory could provide the framework for an accommodation that can never happen if one side is clearly seen to be the winner and the other side is clearly seen to be the loser. Thus, negotiated independence would undercut the base of support for paramilitaries on both sides by taking away their raison d'être. Moreover, by allowing the paramilitaries to claim their respective victories, independence would seek to make them part of the solution. They would be invited to participate in the negotiations leading up to the new state and encouraged to participate at a political level.

One other factor, the pattern of demographic change, strengthens the case for independence as a viable solution. Over the years the high rate of Catholic natural increase was offset somewhat by a high level of emigration, while the low rate of Protestant natural increase was mitigated by a low rate of emigration. The differential between the two net rates, however, worked in favor of Catholics. The result: a slow but persistent growth in Catholic numbers. But in recent years, a number of factors may have been contributing to a far more explosive increase in the Catholic population. First, owing to the protracted nature of the conflict, emigration from both communities has increased.[25] However, it has increased more rapidly in the Protestant community, allowing the higher Catholic birth rate to make itself felt at last.[26] In 1961, 33 percent of all Northern Ireland's marriages were Catholic; in 1977, this figure had risen to 41 percent.[27] But since the Catholic fertility rate is some 70 percent higher than the Protestant rate,[28] births to Catholics now account for some 50 percent of all births.[29] Second, the Catholic death rate has fallen because the Catholic population has become progressively younger due to its higher fertility rate.[30] Consequently, as a result of the interaction of these variables, the percentage of Catholics in Northern Ireland has increased from 33 percent to approximately 39 percent.[31] Paul Compton, a well-known Queen's University demographer, speculates that "if we assume the present natural increase differential between the two communities and no emigration, Roman Catholics will eventually form a majority of the population. Given these circumstances, calculations based on the fertility and mortality estimates for 1977 suggest a simple Roman Catholic majority by 2010–20 and a majority of the voting age population by 2025–35, about fifty years from now."[32] When account is taken of emigration, these estimates will, of course, vary, moving further away in time as the differential between Catholic and Protestant rates of emigration increases.

Preliminary results of the 1981 census, however, suggest that a fundamental demographic upheaval may be under way. An estimated 153,000 people — about 10 percent of the population — emigrated from Northern Ireland between 1971 and 1981, so that for the first time since the end of the nineteenth century the population actually declined.[33] Moreover, about one in every three young people who received a higher education left Northern Ireland.[34] Since employment opportunities abroad, especially in Britain, have been severely curtailed because of the persistent worldwide recession, only those with skills or a profession can emigrate to advantage. In Northern Ireland, of course, these emigrants are more likely to be Protestants.[35] It appears, therefore, that Protestant emigration may be substantially up, either because Protestants see no political or economic future in the province or because they have given up on the British or doubt their resolve to stay.

Catholic voting power is going to increase significantly within the next fifteen years — itself a dynamic that could set in motion an unprecedented wave of Protestant emigration accelerating the demographic chain reaction. As the voting power of the two communities approaches equality, power sharing, even under majority rule, will become a reality. Thus, in the long run majority rule may not preserve Protestant hegemony. The British guarantee, of course, extends only to the commitment that the constitutional status of Northern Ireland shall remain unchanged so long as that is the wish of a majority. But what happens if, as seems likely, Catholics ultimately obtain the majority? Would Protestants abide by the results of a referendum calling for British withdrawal? Would they be any more amenable to unification? And if not, would the Republic be any more willing to impose a united Ireland on a Protestant minority, albeit a very substantial minority, in Northern Ireland? The answers are hardly reassuring.

Protestants, therefore, might do well to sacrifice an uncertain outcome in the future for a certain though suboptimal outcome now. If their apprehension that a majority will vote in the future to join an all-Ireland state exceeds their reluctance to forego the British connection in the here and now, negotiated independence would minimize their expected losses on both counts.

And because the new state would have to have both the recognition and support of the South, Protestants would be compelled to come up with a political framework that would accommodate Catholics and safeguard their interests.

A Protestant population counterbalanced by a Catholic population of equal size would rudely expose the basic arithmetic of the impasse; namely, that the number of Catholics in Northern Ireland is too great for Protestants to impose their will unilaterally within a stable political structure in Northern Ireland, while the number of Protestants in Ireland as a whole is too great for Catholics to impose their will unilaterally within a stable political framework in Ireland as a whole. Each situation is and will continue to be subject to the tyranny of the minority, thus making an attempt to accommodate either side at the expense of the other unworkable at best, a folly at worst.

Accordingly, when the numbers in both communities begin to converge, two alternatives will come into clearer focus: on the one hand, independence, because Catholic voting power will ensure equality in the distribution of power, thus making a return to the "old Stormont days" impossible; and on the other, some form of joint administration by both Britain and the Republic to reflect the dual and equal impact of the two traditions.

In fact, joint administration is the obverse of independence. Whereas independence would call for the two communities to set aside their separate allegiances, joint administration would acknowledge and give equal weight to the legitimacy of both. Both "solutions" proceed from the premise that a settlement that attempts to accommodate one side only will fail. And both look to balance the expected gains and losses of the two communities. Thus, while independence would ensure that neither side is a "winner" in one sense of the term, joint administration would ensure that they both are in another sense.

• • •

The *Sunday Times* labeled him "a bespectacled, Zapata-moustachioed, wisecracking, nonsmoking, milk-drinking man whose appearance and manner belie his reputation."[36] The reputation, of course, is for ruthlessness, and it dies hard: in paramilitary circles, however, such a reputation has its advantages; even if undeserved, it is unlikely to be denied. Perhaps one key to Andy Tyrie's survival as leader of the Ulster Defence Association since 1973 is his ability to convey ingenuousness, his knack for making the naive sound plausible and the implausible possible. His humor blunts the hard edge. He laughs at himself, and at others, but the laughter is mostly in the eyes, its source the larynx rather than the diaphragm. Because he doesn't need to show he's in command, he appears to be, even if he is not. He has changed. The Supreme Commander is now simply the Chairman, a less ostentatious designation, though one that carries more subliminal insinuations. Eight years ago, he was taciturn, leaving the talking to others. At the Amherst Conference he said nothing, yet he was the puppeteer, his silent control a more eloquent testimony to his leadership than any presentation he could make. The late Sammy Smyth put it in perspective when called on to defend Tyrie's silence: "The qualities of leadership," he said, "are not always measured in the articulation of a policy."[37]

Today Tyrie articulates. He appears on television, gives interviews, makes himself accessible, but it is still difficult to discover what he really believes. He is more of an enigma than any other Loyalist leader; his statements of reconciliation, and of insight, are often at variance with the actions and certainly with the reputation of his organization. He is, in this sense at least, the epitome of the UDA and its unresolved tensions. On one hand, there are the fathomless darkness and some of the most gruesome sectarian murders in Northern Ireland. The hit squads of its sometimes affiliate, the Ulster Freedom Fighters (UFF), still perform their squalid deeds, though some attempt is made to see that the intended targets have a modicum of association with the Republican movement.* On the other hand, there are

* The Ulster Freedom Fighters, an illegal paramilitary group, was founded in 1973, apparently a breakaway group from the UDA. Between 1973 and 1977 it took the credit, through telephone calls, for the murder of many Catholics, often alleging that its victims had IRA connections. A "Captain White" or a "Captain Black" would make the telephone calls. At least one commentator — Jack Holland in *Too Long a Sacrifice* — claims that the UDA now commits its

the mea culpas of light and reason and the bland assertions that Catholics and Protestants share so much in common that an independent Northern Ireland built on a common Ulster identity and mutual trust is the only way forward.

What has led the UDA to come out on the side of a negotiated independence for Northern Ireland? Tyrie:

It was only a matter of sense. Everything had been tried and had failed. We have so much in common with Catholics, yet in problem situations Protestants run to Westminster to get their problems solved and nationalists run to Dublin. We feel that if we have a government of our own then we'll have to run to each other.[38]

But why should Catholics support independence, especially when agitation for it comes almost exclusively from the UDA? Because the UDA has changed, matured, shaken free of the shackles of tit-for-tat sectarianism:

Normally the UDA would have reacted to the La Mon bombing.* However, we decided not to because we felt that getting involved in indiscriminate violence would drive the ordinary decent Catholic behind the IRA.

We have proved this wasn't just a seven-day wonder. We've been saying this for the last three or four years. We have not been involved in sectarian violence.

After Bobby Sands's death, the nationalist community had been told that the UDA is going to charge into your area and bomb you and shoot you and burn you out. They were convinced this was going to happen. But it didn't and it caused great confusion in the nationalist community, who were expecting a UDA backlash.

We've come under great pressures to revert to the old standards. We are deliberately doing what we have to do. If we come into serious conflict with the Roman Catholic areas again for purely sectarian reasons, it will separate us again for another fifteen or twenty years.

---

murders under the fictitious label UFF (p. 93). Others dispute the simple claim of association. See Robert Johnstone's review of Holland's book in *Fortnight*, no. 183 (October/November 1981), pp. 23–24.

* On 17 February 1978 the Provisional IRA firebombed the La Mon House Restaurant while it was crowded with more than five hundred people. Twelve people died instantly in the blaze, and twenty-three others were badly hurt.

The IRA, of course, is trying to provoke the UDA into that type of reaction, its instrument of polarization being the hunger strikes:

The hunger strikes are now losing their propaganda value.* The conflict is only coming from one side — from the IRA and the security forces. Most countries are looking at it now as purely a terrorist-type problem with an established government trying to deal with it. And they, of course, are totally against terrorism, having experienced terrorism themselves. So they are anti-IRA. The IRA feels that there has to be a conflict brought about that involves the two communities, so that the Protestants are seen as the "bad" people again.

The rationale for independence grew out of two recognitions; first, that they — the people of Ulster — have a separate identity:

Most people are convinced that Protestants arrived here in 1607. But their ancestors arrived long before that. The Ulster people have always been here. There always has been a fight going on between the Ulster people and the rest of the Irish. Republicans call us colonists but we are not. We are not British. We are part of the British family but we are Ulster people first, both Catholic and Protestant. The problem is that if you're Catholic you're seen as Irish and if you're Protestant you're seen as British.

And second, that they, the Protestants of Ulster, are second-class citizens in their own country because of the politics of polarization:

The Catholic community felt they were second-class citizens under the British government. Little did they realize that the Protestant population were the second-class citizens and that Catholics were the third-class citizens. There has been far too much polarization of politics. Unionists always said "Vote for me and there'll be no Irish Dimension" and the SDLP said just the opposite. None of these parties ever mentioned the Ulster Dimension, and we realized that our elected representatives were sacrificing Ulster's future for the proverbial thirty pieces of silver.

* This interview with Andy Tyrie took place on 26 August 1981. Michael Devine — the last hunger striker to die — had died on 20 August. The hunger strikes were called off on 3 October 1981.

The UDA does not envisage independence as an immutable arrangement. The Constitution would be flexible enough to take account of change. Tyrie:

The Constitution could be changed if two thirds of Parliament and two thirds of the people in a referendum voted for it. If Republicans in an independent Northern Ireland could convince two thirds of the electorate to vote for unification with the rest of Ireland, that would be fine.

But even among themselves there were disagreements on how to proceed. Some were in favor of a devolved government, some were not. Tommy Lyttle, a founding member of the UDA and former public relations officer for NUPRG:

Andy Tyrie and John McMichael believe that we need a platform, that we need some sort of Assembly or a convention where our ideas can be tested and put to the people. Certainly that would test the support for independence. And that could be a bad thing. Because I don't think people here are ready yet to break away from traditional voting patterns. Any election in the near future will still be contested on Border politics. We need a period where normal politics can evolve. We've never had normal politics. We've always had the issue of the Border. If you were a Unionist you were for it, and if you were a Republican you were against it.[39]

Lyttle doesn't see an election to an Assembly getting away from that sort of thing. Continued Direct Rule could, therefore, work to the UDA's advantage:

People will get fed up with it and they'll want change. In wanting change, they may be willing to vote on the issues we're talking about. The social issues. The economic issues. The housing problem. The longer Direct Rule goes on, the more I see people coming to support the normal kind of politics we are trying to put across. From that people might evolve into thinking: we could do better on our own. I don't see where a devolved government would help us. A devolved government would call for concessions on both sides which neither side is willing to concede.[40]

In the meantime the UDA will continue the fight against the enemy — "known Republicans." Its function: to "terrorize the terrorists." Tyrie:

> The Catholic population is not our enemy. The Provos and the INLA certainly are. The UDA has always said it will support anyone who carries on a straightforward war with these organizations. But we won't support sectarian killings or anyone who carries them out.[41]

The British government refuses to acknowledge that they are in a war situation, and thus the lackluster performance of the security forces. "There's a war going on," says Tyrie, "and the sooner the British government sees it as a war the sooner they'll be able to deal with it properly."[42] But this would take an uncompromising political will to put a stop to IRA terrorism. Not only is that will in short supply, fence straddling on security issues compounds the problem:

> We don't trust the British government. They took away the B-Specials, who had dealt with the IRA, and now they are trying a more liberal model — the UDR. And they are holding them under restraint. Officers of the law are being shot dead and nothing is being done about it. Now they are struggling to put a government back in power. The turmoil in Northern Ireland is due in part to inconsistencies in British policy, which is constantly reversing itself.[43]

The UDA, therefore, has stepped into the breach: it will do whatever is necessary to put down the IRA, and if that means blood on its hands, so be it. Tyrie: "We believe we are justified in making selective attacks on known Republicans, the people who lead their campaign, give them arms, and supply them with information."[44] As for the future, he foresees the withdrawal of Britain from Ulster in his lifetime:

> The Ulster people will have to make their choice. To be thrust into a united Ireland would be an anathema to any Protestant and it would be forcibly rejected by everyone who holds their Ulster identity close to their hearts. These same Ulster people have always [seen] and will

always see themselves as a separate nation, and they are gradually recognizing that their only alternative is an independent Ulster.[45]

• • •

But the questions remain: what type of independent Ulster, and for whom? "Beyond the Religious Divide" takes studious care to avoid an explicit commitment on the constitutional question. However, since March 1979 the UDA has veered, reluctantly perhaps, but nevertheless inexorably, in the direction of a continuing, albeit tenuous, connection with Britain. First, NUPRG was disbanded. Glenn Barr, the leading spokesman for the organization and one of the prime movers behind the independence movement, "retired," ostensibly for health reasons — the official release cited a bad heart, the unofficial grapevine a broken heart. Barr, for his own good reasons, refuses comment. The UDA then founded a political party to propagate the organization's political ideation. But its name — the Ulster Loyalist Democratic Party (ULDP) — has a distinctly tribal connotation. *Loyalist,* of course, is a code word for Protestant. How a party with such overt tones of Protestant hegemony is supposed to attract Catholics begs the obvious questions.

"The aspiration of the ULDP," according to its manifesto, "is to achieve Ulster national sovereignty by the establishment of a democratic Ulster parliament, freely elected by the Ulster people whose authority will be limited only by such agreements as may be freely entered into by it with other nations, states or international organisations for the purpose of furthering international cooperation and world peace."[46] To further these ends the ULDP proposes "the introduction of an agreed written constitution for Ulster, *within* the United Kingdom."[47] (Emphasis added.)

The party's new chairman, John McMichael, a senior member of the UDA command and former secretary of NUPRG, who has emerged as the most articulate spokesman for independence since Glenn Barr's "retirement," explains:

We found that although people feel anti-Westminster and anti-English, they still have a great affection for the monarchy. So it would be independence within the EEC and the Commonwealth, which we think would be acceptable to many Roman Catholics.[48]

Perhaps, but this rationale entirely misses the point: many arrangements short of a united Ireland are almost certainly acceptable to many Catholics, but that does not make them workable. It also chooses to ignore the fact that in 1921 the IRA fought the Anglo-Irish Treaty on constitutional grounds: an Irish Free State, though independent in every conceivable sense of the term, was not acceptable so long as the tie to the Crown remained. Breaking the connection with England means breaking the connection with the Crown. An "independent" Northern Ireland under the umbrella of the British monarchy would never allow the IRA to claim a measure of victory. On the contrary, it would mock the very nature of its aspirations.

Even more damaging to the integrity of its policies is the UDA's equivocation on devolution. UDA support for a devolved government would vitiate the case the UDA itself makes for independence, since the form a devolved government should take is one of the key issues dividing the two communities. And since the UDA has already concluded that both power sharing and majority rule are unworkable, its support of either would put it in the absurd position of endorsing an arrangement it had already rejected as untenable. Moreover, no matter which side of the issue it comes down on — not that that is in doubt — it will antagonize the other community, hardly the most expeditious route to having its plans for independence win acceptance across the divide.

• • •

Unionist politicians are like children. In fact, most of the Ulster Protestants are like children who think that if they put their hands over their eyes that nobody can see them because they can't see anyone else. They know deep down in their own consciousness that they are not wanted, that they are hanging desperately onto the coattails of Britain, but that they're being shrugged off. It's going to be very difficult for them to come to grips with that — the fact that their future does not lie within the United Kingdom unless they renegotiate the Act of Union of 1801 on the terms of the Ulster people.[49]

John McMichael is articulate, but he lacks warmth. He is logical, forceful, insistent, but for all that removed: a man of passionless convictions. He is a "revisionist" Loyalist, quick to put the blame for past failures on Unionists as well as Republicans, and quick to make the case for independence at every opportunity. But always there is the quandary: renegotiating the Act of Union to accommodate a Commonwealth rather than a U.K. framework is a far cry from an independent Northern Ireland, her sovereignty secured by her sense of a collective and distinct Ulster identity.

The consent formula won't work. McMichael:

> If 49 percent of the people in Northern Ireland wanted to remain in the U.K. and 51 percent wanted to join the South, that doesn't necessarily mean that the 49 percent will accept that peacefully, because they'll look to the days when they were a majority and the minority refused to accept their wishes — even when they were a substantial majority.[50]

Yes, the ULDP is the political offshoot of the UDA, the platform for disseminating the political ideas the UDA has developed. Flexibility is the cornerstone of their proposals:

> Our aspiration is independence. But that independence is not a rigid thing in that we want a Sinn Féin Ulsterism — "Ourselves Alone," isolated from the U.K. and the South of Ireland. We believe independence means that if the vast majority of the Ulster people in both communities through their democratically elected Parliament and government decide to associate with any other nation, then we would support that. We're saying that at the end of the day all constitutional options are open so long as they are supported by the vast majority of both communities. In other words, if we want independence we're prepared to accept that you can't have it unless at least two thirds of the people — or even more, the vast majority of the people in both communities — would have to accept that independence.[51]

The Anglo-Irish talks were a ploy to recycle a warmed-over version of the Sunningdale Agreement, but the primary emphasis is now on economic rather than on political association with the South:

Instead of having political institutions like a Council of Ireland, they are trying to by-pass the Ulster people and make Northern Ireland more economically dependent on Southern Ireland than it is on Great Britain. They're shifting the economic base for the future. Eventually, if things go the way they expect them to, the people of Northern Ireland will depend on the South for their natural gas supply and will be hooked up to the European electricity grid through the South.

We will be in a position of greater economic dependence on the South. The next steps would be political frameworks emerging on an all-Ireland rather than on a U.K. basis. In short, the Anglo-Irish talks are a way to bring about the unification of Ireland in a very subtle and long-term fashion.[52]

The principle behind the new economic strategy is simple: beggars aren't in a position to be choosers. One example:

Michael O'Leary, the Tanaiste [Deputy Prime Minister of the Irish Republic], said recently in an RTE interview that the Republic would need to import more solid fuels in place of oil. Why, he asked, should the ships to carry these fuels not be built in Belfast by our "fellow" citizens rather than in Japan?

Now, the irony of the situation is that there are no more orders on the books of Harland and Wolff. They're facing closure in an industry which is symbolic of Ulster, which has epitomized the engineering skills of the Ulster people. Put in that position, how would people who constitutionally want nothing to do with Éire react when they find out their own economic future seemed to be coming from the South? Would they tell the Southern government to stick their ships? No, they wouldn't, because they need the jobs.[53]

Hence McMichael's conclusions:

In the future, when the tap is turned off from Great Britain — and it has, there's been no investment — we'll be forced to look at the Southern economic horizon rather than to the traditional network where we were just a cog in the wheel of Empire. There is no Empire, so the cog doesn't matter anymore.[54]

The cog, therefore, has to spin to the rhythms of its own revolutions. Unification, however, is not an option; the shibboleths imprison:

The fear of the Protestant population in Northern Ireland is that any constitutional linkup in any form with Southern Ireland would be the beginning of the end of the Protestant people in the North. They look at the South and see the decimation of the Protestant people that has taken place. The Protestant fear is not just of the religious power of the Catholic Church but of the international political power. Protestants really fear the international Roman Catholic Church. Ireland is probably the only place in Western Europe where the Reformation is still an issue.[55]

Traditional Unionist thinking on independence is confused. Unionists see it as an option of last resort. Their concept is negative, more of a contrivance, something they would have recourse to reluctantly if they were forced out of the U.K. rather than a viable alternative that could engage the support of the two communities. It can't work. McMichael:

If independence is to be brought about positively, it must be brought about by the will of both Ulster Protestants and Ulster Catholics, not by Ulster Protestants saying that if we don't get what we want we'll take independence. This would be suicide economically, socially, and politically.[56]

Which means that Ian Paisley is very definitely part of the problem:

With the positions he is adopting and the way he is going,* he is most likely to push us to the point where there is only a choice between accepting — humbling ourselves to accept — some sort of wishy-washy agreement to remain part of the U.K. — or independence. That type of independence would be an absolute disaster. His independence would amount to a Protestant state. It would not be independent. It would be one in which the majority would dictate to the minority.[57]

* McMichael's remarks about Paisley were made on 2 December 1981, after Paisley's Carson Trail and Day of Action. Since the Assembly elections of October 1982, Paisley has been behaving less aggressively — because, for the moment, a more moderate demeanor suits his particular purposes.

McMichael, for one, would not live in a state dominated by religious fanatics. Paisley's strength comes from his appeal in times of crisis; because he appears to do something, he assuages Protestants' sense of powerlessness:

He's the only one who's heard, because he shouts the loudest. While the vast majority of Ulster Protestants shelter under Paisley's umbrella against the rains of Republicanism during times of crisis, most of them realize when the temperature goes down that the umbrella doesn't stop the rain. They only run to Paisley because he appears to be the Superman against a united Ireland. Unfortunately, if the Ulster Protestant sees people marching about and making a lot of noise, he feels that at least something's being done.[58]

This is often impolitic. For example, following the killing of Robert Bradford, the cause of the Ulster Protestant evoked sympathy throughout the world. People were beginning to appreciate for once the real impact of Republican terrorism on Ulster Protestants. But Paisley's actions dissipated the hard-earned gains:

He's reversing the process. Now all the world again apparently sees are Protestant bigots on the march and that they're going to kill all the poor Catholics.[59]

And thus the reason why the UDA did not support the Day of Action:

If we had come out and supported the Day of Action, which was seen to be Paisley's Day of Action, that would have associated us with Paisleyism and would have frightened the life out of every Catholic in Northern Ireland.

The conjunction of Ian Paisley plus the UDA would have driven Catholics right back into their tribal camps. We took a lot of short-term hassle because we hadn't supported Paisley as if he were our leader. It's very important that no particular party in Northern Ireland creates another monolith, in that there wouldn't be any possibility of reconciliation if you have circumstances where there is one majority and one minority. We feel we scored a great victory over both the

IRA and the INLA when we didn't throw our support behind Paisley's Day of Action or behind the Third Force.[60]

Paisley aids and abets the IRA, time and again playing into its hands:

There's no way the Provisional IRA or INLA would shoot Paisley because he is the bogeyman who is thrown up against Catholics. If the Catholic population wants to be free of the Provos, the Provos wave Ian Paisley in front of them to frighten them. It used to be that they'd wave the UDA, and they still probably do to a certain extent.[61]

Which made it all the more imperative, especially after the Bradford killing, for the UDA not only to dissociate itself from Paisley but to be seen to have done so:

Most of the Catholic population and some of the Protestant population believed that the UDA was Paisley's army. We took the opportunity to show them that we were not Ian Paisley's army. It has gained us some ground with the Roman Catholic community . . . The Catholic population may be beginning to understand that perhaps the Loyalist paramilitary organizations are far more rational than the politicians.[62]

The Provisionals, of course, saw this as an extremely counterproductive development. Hence their strategy after the hunger strikes:

We knew for quite a while — and we were expecting it during the hunger strikes — that the Republican movements, particularly the INLA, had drawn up lists of leading Loyalists — and the emphasis wasn't really on politicians — that could be used to draw the Loyalist paramilitaries and then the Loyalist people into the conflict. Hopefully, from their point of view, the UDA and others would get involved in sectarian killings which would drive the Catholic people behind the Provisionals and INLA. We always appreciate that widespread violence from the Loyalist side would magnify Catholic fears and drive Catholics into the arms of the Provos.[63]

As regards basic philosophic tone, the UDA finds itself identifying more with Official Unionism than with Paisley's unorthodoxy:

Originally the UDA would have been seen as being more in tune with the Democratic Unionist Party. But now we're moving more into line with the conservative Official Unionist position. The UDA are more and more coming out in favor of people like Harold McCusker . . .[64] Many of the grassroots members of the OUP, and district councilors and even M.P.s at Westminster, are completely disillusioned with the leadership. They see nothing constructive happening. They see there is no room in the future for what they believed in traditionally — and they're looking for new ideas. Many are interested in the ideas we are putting forward.[65]

The UDA knows that many will be skeptical of its new-found concern. Nevertheless, despite whatever obstacles may lie ahead, its commitment to achieving its goals is complete:

The UDA has settled down and developed its own political philosophy. We are determined that we will push on in this lane. This year we tested two candidates at the polls — they didn't get elected but we weren't disappointed. We put them up for election to show the world that we were a genuine political party and not just a political front for a violent organization. We will continue to contest elections. We understand it will be years before people understand what we're trying to do politically, moving towards an Ulsterization policy and then hopefully independence. It's going to take a fairly long time to sink in. Also we understand that people are still reluctant to vote for people involved in paramilitary organizations. We accept that. We accept that it's a long struggle, but we are going to continue.[66]

Of course, the perception of the UDA as a paramilitary organization is a handicap, "a great difficulty and a cross we have to bear."[67] And the past shackles them in other ways too:

The UDA can't change as fast as it would like because it has the weight of the responsibility of the prisoners of the past and their dependents to look after. It shackles the UDA to be in a political organization so long as those prisoners exist.[68]

Yes, the leadership is in front of its rank and file — five years in front, perhaps, but confident nevertheless that it will carry the day:

We're more and more confident that over the next three to five years more and more people will turn their backs on traditional politicians. They'll be looking for something new. For a new form of leadership that concerns itself with the Ulster people, not sections of the Ulster people. The DUP, for instance, has no interest in winning Catholics over or in crossing the religious divide.[69]

The UDA does. And how do they intend to woo Catholics to their position?

We'll just continue what we've been doing during the past year. It will become more and more obvious that the UDA is taking a very steady line, that we're not willing to fall into line behind sectarian politicians. It will take time. What people forget is that we also have to sell the idea to Protestants.[70]

• • •

Thus, the UDA's policy, or rather, its aspiration: independence, but independence within a Commonwealth framework; a separate state but not necessarily a permanent one. Of course, Catholic support for independence will have to be overwhelming — a formidable task but not an impossible one. It will begin to emerge when the UDA's "restraint" is seen for what it is — a gesture of conciliation. "Ulster" people must look to themselves and their history to forge a common identity. They must come to see Northern Ireland not as an Irish problem but as an Ulster problem. They must recognize that neither the Republic nor Britain is doing right by Ulster, that neither can guarantee the position of her client community. To redress their wrongs, therefore, the two communities must address each other. Meanwhile, the UDA will take the fight to the IRA. "Known Republicans" are the enemy and will be dealt with accordingly. The UDA, needless to say, reserves to itself the right to identify "known Republicans."

And this, of course, is the problem. For just as Protestants look on the killing of a UDR member by the IRA as the killing of a Protestant per se, so too do Catholics look on the killing of a Republican by the UDA — even when he is a member of the IRA — as the killing of a Catholic per se. Accordingly, although the UDA may have abandoned its ferocious murder campaign of the early 1970s, the results of its actions today are often distressingly the same. The UDA is not a monolith. The ruling eight-man "inner council" has the inevitable divisions between the hard-liners, who want to mount a more aggressive retaliatory campaign against the IRA, and the more moderate — between those who think purely in paramilitary terms and those who want to move in a political direction. McMichael himself, unconsciously perhaps, may have been projecting the dilemma of the UDA when he speculated on the reasons for the upsurge in IRA violence in November and December 1981:

You must look at the confusion at the end of the hunger strikes and the takeover from the Southern command. The Northern leadership has emerged supreme. They decided to drop their abstentionist policies. Danny Morrison said — and this is important — that they weren't going totally political because they're afraid of the INLA taking over the whole political role and leaving them in the position in which they left the Officials — and that's why Danny Morrison said that if they got engaged in politics there would be a ballot box in one hand and an Armalite in the other. I think the recent violence was to show first that they weren't defeated by the hunger strikes and also to show that they hadn't gone soft because they were putting more emphasis on politics.[71]

Not going soft: for the UDA this presents a special predicament, because its power has come from the barrel of a gun, because it is a force to be reckoned with only while it can mobilize large numbers of armed members to give muscle to the myth of a Protestant backlash, only while policymakers have to take into account its possible reactions to their proposals. Turning the other cheek on every occasion means members turning to other paramilitary organizations eager to usurp its position of pre-eminence. Hence the selective campaign against "Republican targets" — killings often enough to reassure its own members that it has not lost its hard edge, yet not sufficient enough to reestablish it as an indiscriminate sectarian murder machine. It is a fine balance.

Increasingly, targets tend to be better-known members of the Catholic community because it is easier to identify better-known figures with particular Republican organizations or causes, thus facilitating quasi justifications for the deeds. Moreover, when victims are relatively well known in their local communities there are fewer ripple effects in the Catholic community at large. The actions appear prearranged, not random, aimed at "somebodies" rather than "nobodies," and this lessens the fears of the "ordinary" Catholic that people like himself might become random targets. Thus, the UDA is credited with the killings of, among others, Miriam Daly and Noel Little, both prominent nationalists, and both highly regarded in their communities. It does not deny the responsibility. And of course, two members of the UDA attempted to murder Bernadette (née Devlin) McAliskey and her husband.

The contamination of the violence is complete, and the consequences are ineluctable. The UDA may now heap scorn on Paisley, yet it is bound fast to him, a reluctant accomplice, perhaps, but nevertheless an ally. Whenever he uses the threat of violence to intimidate his opponents, the UDA implicitly becomes a part of that threat even when it tries to dissociate itself from his actions, because ultimately they corroborate each other, each iterating the sentiments of the other, the language of righteousness a substitute for the language of violence. He will fight unification, they will fight unification; he calls Republicans enemies of the state, they call Republicans enemies of the state. He forms a "defense" association and justifies the killing of his enemies in "self-defense"; they kill their enemies in the name of "self-defense." Accordingly, not only is there an explicit convergence of interests between Paisley and the UDA, there is also an implicit convergence of methods.

• • •

"We must sell the idea to Protestants," says John McMichael, but not much selling has been done. *Ulster* is the UDA's monthly mouthpiece. But it does not spread the word of toleration, or emphasize the need for reconciliation, or look at problems as the common concern of the two communities, although it does periodically remind its readers that an independent Northern Ireland is the only just solution for the put-upon people of Ulster.

In the context of the magazine *Ulster,* however, "the people of Ulster" means the Protestant people. As either pabulum or propaganda it preaches the politics of divisiveness, putting religious differences before intercommunity needs, political allegiances before common identity.

It, too, must have its enemies. Thus, the SDLP are rascals, traitors, and worse. "The Ulster Defence Association," it reported in 1980, "is preparing a dossier concerning the SDLP's involvement with Irish terrorist organizations for submission to the Secretary of State."[72] This document would "cite meetings which took place between the SDLP, a foreign government [the Irish government] and terrorist organisations to plot the downfall of the Northern Ireland parliament."[73] Less than a year later the publication took it upon itself to expose the skullduggery behind the Haughey/Thatcher talks: the focus of the "negotiations" was "the constitutional future of Northern Ireland";[74] the tradeoff, the South to abandon her neutrality in return for a united Ireland. And, of course, there was the ominous shadow of conspiracy: "Éire" would not yield to American pressure to join NATO while the Anglo-Irish question was unsettled. Hence the American pressure on Britain and Britain's willingness to betray Ulster. Readers were reminded that "Winston Churchill offered Northern Ireland to DeValera during World War II under similar circumstances,"[75] and that "DeValera refused the offer only because he couldn't bring himself to trust the British to deliver the goods."[76] *

The South, according to *Ulster,* is "a wasteland of backwardness" that continues to receive "massive financial aid from the U.K."[77] Without this aid it could not keep itself above "the swamp waters of Irish Republican myth, legend and revolution."[78] Over the years the aid has flowed in "through laundered international bank accounts in merchant bank accounts such as J. P. Morgan of New York and Warburgs of London."[79] Nevertheless, under Republican rule the country stagnated, "unable to keep the mother tongue alive never mind

* For the lengths to which Churchill was prepared to go, see Robert Fisk, *In Time of War: Ireland, Ulster and the Price of Neutrality* (London: André Deutsch, 1983).

the economy."[80] Whatever success she has had in recent years is due entirely to the subsidy she receives from the EEC: "This aid," *Ulster* calculates, "amounts to two pounds per week for every Irish man, woman and child, compared to a contribution from the U.K. of six pounds per week for every man, woman and child."[81] Conclusion: "We . . . the people of Ulster and mainland Britain have contributed to Southern Ireland's economic boom . . . We have literally emptied our pockets to fill theirs and as a result our industry and agriculture have suffered."[82]

The Ulsterman's claim to self-determination is based on the fact "that Southern Ireland is a foreign state with whom we can find nothing of importance in common. Our heritage, history and culture are separate and different."[83] The Ulster people are Protestant people, their will to survive impervious to the tenacity of opposition. Thus, "for four centuries by murder, boycott, bombing and every means possible with no holds barred the Gaelic Irish have endeavored to oust from Ireland those who favored a broader outlook with political, religious and economic ties with the outside world — the Ulster people."[84] And when the gunmen who shot McAliskey* were sentenced to long terms of imprisonment, the UDA's "voice" reported that it was "probably the first time that the majority of people in Ulster were sorry that a victim of violence did not die." Moreover, while her likes were around, "young men [would] always seek to destroy them."[85]

And so on: the Army turned a blind eye to the activities of the IRA; Catholics got more than their fair share of public housing; Catholics bred too much and were rewarded for it; the Catholic Church was intolerant, one Catholic bishop being "a tailor-made example of Catholic bigotry and intolerance" for threatening "to excommunicate the parents of [Catholic] school children who desired to attend a Protestant school for reasons of convenience."[86] And, of course, at the heart of things was the collusion between the Catholic Church and the IRA. "The sinister role of the Roman Catholic Church in Ulster's troubles,"

* The UDA refers to McAliskey as Ulster's "wicked witch."

the magazine reports, "has left Protestants in no doubt that the IRA's terror campaign is being aided and abetted by certain influential members of the cloth who see the removal of the Protestants from 'Catholic' soil as a means to an end."[87]

The themes reiterate themselves, a chorus of complaints ulcerating the hate-sores. Ulster Protestants are betrayed by both Westminster and their "own" politicians. They are abused by Westminster and the IRA. They are under siege from Dublin and the IRA. Rather than being the colonizer, they are colonized. Rather than being subsidized by their "friends," they subsidize their tormenters. Rather than being lauded for their patience in the face of extreme provocation, they are condemned for defending their basic rights. They are alone in a friendless world, the victims of a conspiracy not only between Westminster and Dublin but also between Catholicism and Republicanism. Even international bankers covet their meager possessions. Ulster is a synonym for Loyalist, for Protestant, for opposition to unity. The aspiration of the people of Ulster to run their affairs free from the meddling of outsiders is synonymous with the aspiration of Protestants to run things their way, and their way only.

• • •

In one sense the UDA's concept of independence is tautological, since the precondition for the outcome mandates the outcome. Of course independence would follow if two thirds of the people in both communities agreed to it, for neither Britain nor the Republic could sustain a legitimate claim against the arrangement. And likewise, of course some form of unification would follow if two thirds of the people in both communities agreed to it, for even diehard Loyalists would be hard put to mount a sustainable opposition.

The two-thirds consent stipulation, therefore, is a variant of the obvious: namely, that any constitutional settlement will have to have the support of an overwhelming number in both communities. Negotiated independence presupposes trust, but the problem is the lack of trust. If two thirds of the people in both communities trusted each other to the point where they could agree to independence, they probably could agree to any number of alternative arrangements. Trust must precede the framework of the arrangement rather than the converse. Reconciliation will determine the form of the settlement rather than the settlement the form of reconciliation — a set of constitutional arrangements does not a nation make.

Nor is the forging of a common identity as simple a matter as it is made out to be. Both communities may feel abandoned by their putative reference groups, the Republic and Great Britain, but a common sense of apartness does not provide the impetus for developing a common sense of purpose, especially when both communities have an unequal sense of who they are in the first place. The Protestants of Ulster may be in search of an identity, but Catholics are not; Protestants may have only a disparate — even confused — sense of who they are, but Catholics have a very unambiguous sense.

The UDA attempts to solve the question of identity by attaching itself to the Cruthin. According to its view of history, the Picts (or Cruthin) were the original settlers of Ireland.[88] Driven North by the invading Gaels, they carved out an enclave in what today are counties Down and Antrim. But even when they were finally conquered by the marauding Gaels and assimilated into Gaelic culture, they did not vanish. Rather, their settlements in Scotland continued to thrive, and their descendants, now lowland Scots, returned in the seventeenth century to reclaim their ancient land, their lineage more pristine than the Gaels they allegedly displaced.

This version of history may have perfectly sound antecedents. It may even make the Scots-Irish the equals of the Gaelic-Irish in terms of entitlement, and provide them with the stuff of identity. But this is not sufficient, because it does nothing to establish a common Ulster identity: an identity for the Protestants of Ulster is not an identity for the people of Ulster. Nor, strictly speaking, is Ulster the proper frame of reference, for although all of Northern Ireland is part of Ulster, all of Ulster is not part of Northern Ireland.

There is no common history, other than the history of conflict. The "new" Ulster identity propagated by the UDA simply extends the source of the conflict back in time, validating "their" side without invalidating "the other" side.

Nor is there a common myth to transcend the myths of division. And if one were to emerge, it would have to be powerful enough to prevail over the Gaelic Catholic myths of 1601, 1798, 1803, 1848, 1867, and 1916, and the Protestant myths of 1641, 1690, 1912, and 1916.

The Protestant myth of 1916 has a special significance. Like its Catholic counterpart, it too is a myth of sacrifice. Protestant Ulster paid her dues on 1 July 1916 at the Somme, when fifty-five hundred soldiers of the Thirty-sixth Ulster Division drawn almost to a man from the Ulster Volunteer Force perished in a heroic but futile advance: the price had been exacted, the loyalty proved, the right earned. And it was Loyalist insistence on the prerogatives of this right that led William Craig to assert in 1968 that Northern Ireland's Constitution "was more than an agreed Act of Parliament," that it was in fact nothing less than "a settlement made when our grandfathers and fathers made their heroic stand."[89]

Nor is a common identity likely to emerge, let alone prevail, when the proposed constitution makes provision for abolishing the state. A stipulation that Protestants would accept unification when two thirds of the people in both communities voted for it would only encourage nationalists not to give up their old aspirations, thus preventing whatever "Ulster" identity they might have superimposed on their Irish identity from taking hold. When the conditions for unification are spelled out in advance, they encourage action to meet them. At best many nationalists would give only a conditional allegiance to the new state while they worked assiduously to abolish it — an outcome that would hardly be much different from the present situation.

Northern Ireland's instability comes in part from the fact that she is perceived as being impermanent. Ending the uncertainty that impermanence gives rise to is an argument for independence. But for independence to work it would have to be seen as a final solution, not an interim one. The future would have to look out for itself. And if some form of association with the rest of Ireland was desired, it would have to develop in circumstances similar to the way in which individual nation-states decide to apply for EEC membership. The process would have to evolve, consensus an end in itself, not a means to an end.

• • •

Although the arguments for independence are persuasive, the arguments against it may be overwhelming.

Protestants would see Catholic agreement to independence as a ploy to get the British out. Furthermore, if the IRA agreed to it, Protestant distrust would only intensify, for what, they would ask, would prevent the IRA from resuming its campaign for unification once the British had cut Northern Ireland loose. On the other hand, if the IRA did not agree to independence, the new state would come into existence as a garrison state, the primary emphasis remaining on security, every Catholic still suspect, a situation that would make independence unworkable.

The IRA, of course, will not agree to independence — the enemy now is as much Loyalism as British imperialism, the objective not only to effect a British withdrawal but to smash the Northern state. Daithi O'Conaill:

> We are totally opposed to the idea of an independent Northern Ireland. We have had the hard, bitter experience of over sixty years of Unionist rule in the Six Counties. For all intents and purposes Northern Ireland was an independent state until the abolition of Stormont in 1972. In no way could we see an independent Northern Ireland being anything different from what it had been prior to 1972. The belief that an independent six-county state would overcome sectarian politics is both naive and dishonest and flies in the face of the unsavory record of Stormont for fifty years.[90]

Once Protestants took the step toward independence, it would be irreversible. Once out of the U.K., there would be no way back in. If an independent Northern Ireland did not work, what options would they have? If they could not manage on their own, would they not have to look South?

On the other hand, Catholics would see Protestant agreement to independence as a ploy to reestablish a Protestant state. What guarantees would they have, once the new state was founded, that Protestants would not revert to their pre-1969 behavior? Had Protestants not had their "independence" for sixty years and had they not abused it? Would an independent Northern Ireland merely institutionalize the framework for future abuse? Who would guarantee the rights of the minority? And if there were abuses, how would the guarantors redress the situation?

An independent Northern Ireland state could not, of course, exist outside the European Economic Community. Since every member of the EEC, however, has the right to veto a new state's application for membership, the Republic could veto the entry of a new Northern Ireland state, thereby destroying the viability of the state itself. Accordingly, negotiated independence is an option only if the Republic is amenable to it: Dublin, therefore, would have to be included among the "negotiators." And since Dublin would also be called upon to remove Articles 2 and 3, to face down the IRA, and to subscribe to an extradition treaty with the new state, its influence on the form of the final arrangements could be formidable. The question, of course, is whether a Dublin government could live up to its end of the arrangements, even under the best of circumstances.

Moreover, even if there were agreement between Britain, the Republic, and the two communities in Northern Ireland on the form of an independent Northern Ireland state, it would not guarantee the state's coming into being. All other members of the EEC would have to give their consent to the arrangement; all would have to be amenable to there being two Irelands, with twice the voting power of other states in the Council of Ministers. Would nations like West Germany with sixty-two million people or France with fifty-three million people give twice the voting power on matters of crucial concern to their interests to a two-nation island of five million people? It seems highly unlikely. But this does not mean that the EEC would necessarily be unreceptive to the idea of an independent Northern Ireland. It might concur to some arrangement that was the precursor of a future all-Ireland association, or it could insist on the two states speaking with a single voice in the chambers of Europe (an "Irish Dimension"?).

Other problems: What if the predominantly Catholic areas — Fermanagh, Tyrone, and South Armagh — decided to secede? Would a Northern Ireland Army try to win back part of its "national" territory? Would the South interfere? How many, North or South, would find a Northern Ireland state with Rev. Ian Paisley the head of government acceptable? How would members of the security forces be selected, and in what proportions? What kind of Northern state would be envisaged? Socialist? Capitalist? Marxist? Would it be a progressive state? A backward state? A stable state? Who would guarantee the arrangements? How? And would an independent state require so many guarantees that it would in fact no longer be independent?

No constitutional proposal can obscure the fact that there are two traditions in Northern Ireland, two separate societies, two distinct and diverse value systems. Somehow independence would have to accommodate the differences. Given the degree of voluntary segregation that exists, however, the chasm between the two communities seems difficult, perhaps even impossible, to bridge.

There is no popular support for independence. Invariably it shows up in opinion polls as a marginal choice in both communities — acceptable to less than 10 percent of both Catholics and Protestants as a "best solution," according to the most optimistic surveys. Moreover, so long as the IRA continues its military campaign it is difficult to see how old antagonisms can be set aside and new alliances forged.

Ironically, the appalling state of the economy may provide the only basis for forging a new alliance between the two communities. Both communities suffer the ravages of high unemployment and endemic stagnation, and both agree that extraordinary measures are required to forestall total collapse. Independence could either precipitate the final collapse or avert it. Since it is ludicrous to talk of Northern Ireland as being economically viable at the moment, it is ludicrous to argue that an independent Northern Ireland would not be economically viable. Of course, special trading arrangements with Britain and Ireland would be necessary. And of course Britain or the EEC would have to provide a subsidy for a number of years. A stable Northern Ireland, however, would be well worth the cost.

Not that the extent of the long-run economic difficulties should be underestimated. Northern Ireland probably has the most open economy in Western Europe. Imports and exports account for 90 percent of Gross Domestic Income compared to 25 percent in the U.K. as a whole;[91] the economy is excessively dependent on public expenditure; the average level of unemployment has always been exceptionally high; she has no natural resources, her energy base is tied to oil refining,[92] investment opportunities are poor, costs are often prohibitive, and competitiveness is lacking. Undoubtedly these drawbacks are formidable, and in some instances insuperable, but they are not absolute barriers to independence unless they come to be regarded as such by the people themselves. But if all they can look forward to is a repetition of the dismal past, an independent Northern Ireland, even with an uncertain economic future, may yet recommend itself.

• • •

The UDA's call for an independent Northern Ireland, though ambiguous on some points and lacking a clear sense of direction, nevertheless accommodates the SDLP's short-term objectives, since it acknowledges that the future of Northern Ireland lies in breaking the link with Britain. John Hume:

> The UDA's political development is very helpful. We want them to come to the conference table asking for their independence. It's their bargaining chip . . .[93] In fact, sometimes it seems to me that the only people who understand the realpolitik of what's going on are the Protestant paramilitary groups — and that's quite extraordinary in a sense.[94]

No less extraordinary, however, has been the UDA's success at modifying, indeed transmogrifying, the perceptions many leading politicians had of the organization. Garret FitzGerald:

> There are obviously people in it who feel this [that the IRA wanted to draw them into a sectarian conflict], and they have held back others

who would have entered into a violent campaign of revenge earlier. And it is good that there should be that restraining force there. Everybody must be glad it exists.[95]

Harold McCusker:

They've learned what a lot of people in Northern Ireland haven't — the lessons of marching about and wearing uniforms and getting people worked up to a frenzy and then going over the top and getting involved in criminal activity. Of course, they themselves openly admit their own past involvement in a lot of criminal activity. But the leadership generally appears to have learned a lot of lessons from those times, and they still have the responsibility for the men they have in jail. They've tried to go political and they've tried very hard. They've even got one or two councilors elected. I would like to see them emerging as the Republican Clubs have emerged — into a full-blown political organization which has foresworn violence and sees the ballot box as the way forward. It's important that they do have success. Because if you go through the democratic process, and the democratic process rejects you, there's a tendency to fall back on the bullet again.[96]

Robert McCartney is more equivocal, a little wary as to the final direction of the organization, but nevertheless sympathetic:

It seems the UDA has totally involved itself in drinking-club activities, taxis, discos, and gaming machines. I do not see it — with certain exceptions — transforming its energy into political activity. In recent times John McMichael has spoken out on a number of issues very sensibly.[97]

On the plus side, for McCartney, is the UDA's refusal to support Paisley's Day of Action, or to be the willing instrument of "ambitious politicians who were willing to use them, and in certain circumstances their violence, and then when it was politic to do so to disown them."[98] He insists, however, that if the UDA is to become either serious or respectable it must discard many of its fund-raising activities and put its house in order.

I now feel there is a genuine desire within the UDA organization or certain sections of it to make a positive political contribution. But they are, of course, victims of the circumstances in which they came into being—and of their past activities. I think they would benefit from an increase in positive Unionist leadership.[99]

James Molyneaux, on the other hand, is not impressed:

They fight Council by-elections as democrats and all that, and they conceal very carefully their ambitions about independence. But underneath they have some very sinister figures and there's reason to believe they have linkages with bodies outside of the U.K. which wouldn't be to your liking or mine.[100]

He attributes the UDA's unwillingness to support Paisley's Day of Action to pragmatism:

What they were scared of was that if they aligned themselves too closely with Paisley's antics on that occasion, and then that some of the wilder adolescent members of Paisley's Third Force, which was in the making at that time, were quite capable of doing something absolutely stupid—and the Protestant paramilitaries were aware that if that happened and if they were in any way remotely connected with Paisley in the Day of Action, it would have been they who would have got "the chopper" and not Paisley's irresponsibles.[101]

For all that, however, Molyneaux believes there is a natural political alignment between Paisley and the UDA insofar as both want independence. The problem: "They don't trust each other."[102]

Seamus Lynch, on the other hand, attaches great significance to the UDA's emerging political maturity:

From my point of view as a socialist Republican, we must go back to the father of Republicanism, Wolfe Tone, who said we must break the connection with England, and here we have for the first time the NUPRG talking about breaking the connection with England. To us this is very significant. We, as a party, welcome that breakthrough. The UDA must be encouraged into the political arena—as must all groups who have participated in violence. Elements within the UDA have learned that people who have been in politics have gained their power politically on the backs of young people in the Loyalist community who were engaged in paramilitarism . . . The only good thing that has come out of the violence of the last twelve or thirteen years is the growing level of political awareness from the Loyalist population — and the UDA has been to the fore in that.[103]

But O'Conaill, not surprisingly, is skeptical. The leopard, he says, doesn't change its spots:

> The sectarian campaign of the UDA has hindered a dialogue. The UDA has been responsible for killing between six hundred and seven hundred Catholics. Even when we were talking with them, there were attempts on Republicans and a number of our people were shot. When we queried the Loyalists with whom we were talking about this, the response was, "Oh, that's a maverick element within the UDA." We do not believe in dealing with people who on the one hand claim to have support and credibility and on the other can claim lack of control.[104]

On one point, however, he will make a concession, though it is a concession of degree rather than of kind:

> We believe the UDA is still carrying out and is committed to a policy of assassination of Republicans. We accept there has been a noticeable falloff in the assassination of ordinary Catholics and we welcome that. To an extent one can understand the UDA shooting IRA volunteers. However, overall, the track record of the UDA makes them difficult to trust.[105]

• • •

Thus the UDA's metamorphosis from ruthless sectarian paramilitary organization to struggling political neophyte. Although its political forays have not brought a stampede of public support for its positions, they have won it a measure of respectability, which pays a handsome dividend: its past transgressions, if not forgotten, are for the most part largely forgiven; and its current lapses, if not forgiven, are for the most part largely excused. Indeed, one of the anomalies of the conflict is the fact that neither the UDA's violence in particular nor Protestant paramilitary violence in general has been put on an equal footing with the IRA's. Although condemnations of all violence are prolix, prolific, and earnestly predictable, the most inspired denunciations are directed at the IRA. One reason, perhaps, is that Protestant paramilitarism is fragmented. It is not always clear who carries out the "military actions" and, therefore, not always clear who is to blame. The more broad-based the rebuke, the more unfocused the message. It is difficult to refute the "maverick element" explanation and correspondingly easy for the UDA to take refuge in it: "sick" individuals do not draw on themselves the opprobrium reserved for "sick" organizations.

The IRA, on the other hand, is regarded as a well-disciplined, highly motivated movement, hardly a haven for the capricious freelance operator. Thus, IRA violence appears to be organized, the Loyalists' sporadic; the IRA's calculated, the Loyalists' retaliatory; the IRA's part of a master plan, the Loyalists' part of a mindless folly. In addition, the IRA's acts are often more visibly atrocious and thus more likely to provoke outrage, more intentionally offensive and thus more likely to invite excoriation, more consistently spectacular and thus more likely to attract television coverage. Besides, there is also a conventional belief that all violence would cease if only the IRA were to call a halt to its military campaign. The corollary of this, of course, is that Protestant paramilitary violence is inherently reactive in character, a conclusion the UDA itself carefully cultivates.

9

Frameworks

Many talk about a solution to Ulster's political problem but few are prepared to say what the problem is. The reason is simple. The problem is that there is no solution.

— Richard Rose[1]

NOR SHOULD THERE BE a search for a "solution" as such, but rather for a framework that will accommodate a range of alternative settlements. Ultimately, the form of settlement will depend on the shape of the framework. And the shape of the framework will depend, in turn, on how the building blocks supporting it are chosen and put in place.

The paradoxes are ironic: in 1920 Loyalists rejected majority rule for Ireland as a whole and insisted on the right of the minority to secede. Today they insist on majority rule for Northern Ireland and reject the right of the minority to secede. On the other hand, in 1920 Republicans rejected the right of the minority to secede and insisted on majority rule for Ireland as a whole. Today they reject majority rule for Northern Ireland and insist on the right of the minority to secede. The only consensus, therefore, is not to have a consensus.

But the numbers — the size of the Catholic minority in Northern Ireland and of the Protestant minority in Ireland as a whole — establish the outer bounds of the differences. They insist on the unavoidable: first, a solution involving Dublin only is unacceptable to Loyalists, and, therefore, unworkable, because Loyalists have the numbers to make it unworkable; and second, a solution involving Westminster only is unacceptable to nationalists, and, therefore, unworkable, because nationalists have the numbers to make it unworkable.

If the protagonists could accept these two simple and perhaps rather obvious facts, they might be able to agree at least on what is *not* possible, acceptable, or workable. For ultimately their choices are limited: they can either recognize the legitimacy of both traditions or reject the claims of both. Indeed, the two options converge when the latter, in the form of negotiated independence where the guarantors are the Republic and Great Britain, becomes a special case of the former. Thus, the first building block: the two sovereign governments must acknowledge that a settlement involving either one exclusively is unworkable.

The second building block is a chip off the first: Articles 2 and 3 of the Republic's Constitution must go. They corroborate the myth of inevitability — the pervasive nationalist myth that a united Ireland is somehow preordained — and establish a corrupting affinity between the constitutional and the unconstitutional. Their repeal would be symbolic — not in the sense of either assuaging the fears of Protestants or attenuating their siege mentality, but in the sense of indicating to nationalists in the North that the South is abandoning her commitment to unification as *the* compelling national aspiration. It would constitute the first step toward taking the gun out of Irish politics, separating the course of the nation not only from the means but from the ends of the violence by making the ends as illegitimate as the means. Catholics in the North would have to confront the new situation and adjust to its reality, a process that might not prove difficult for some, given their own less than preponderant support for an all-Ireland solution.

The South is the key to the problem. Only the South can pronounce the dream of unification false and step away from it. Only the South can confront her own reality — the absence of a consensus there for unification — and make it part of a larger reality. Only the South can take away the raison d'être of the IRA by rejecting the ideas it stands for. Only the South can take away the raison d'être of political Protestantism by ensuring that unification will not happen. Only the South can articulate the precept that the full recognition of the tradition of the minority in Northern Ireland can take place in a framework that doesn't necessarily involve unification. Only the South can repudiate the tradition of violence endemic to Irish political life, and only by addressing the causes of this violence can the South face up to the consequences. And only the South can abjure the brutal sentimentality permeating Irish society that condones, if not a cult of death, then at least a cult of indifference to life in the name of higher callings and exalted causes. Mark Patrick Hederman writes:

> We [the editors of *The Crane Bag*] have reached the point where we feel that violence — such as we are experiencing in Northern Ireland at the moment — is now almost a feature of our temperament as Irish people . . . The attempt to cover it up — as bees try to cover over with wax any unwelcome visitor to the hive — and to pretend that it does not exist, is doomed to failure. The disease will continue to fester and to break out again in other places and in other ways.[2]

Hence the third building block: Britain must declare her long-term intentions; Britain must care enough to make painful decisions, to understand that *the absence of change in the face of IRA violence precludes change in the absence of IRA violence,* thus ensuring that the disease will continue to fester; Britain must acknowledge that her attempts to guarantee a Northern Ireland state make her responsible for the acts of political Protestantism; and Britain must assert her political will, especially the will to coerce Loyalists, for unless she does so the future will remain as dismal as the past.

The fourth block: both Britain and the Republic must acknowledge the obvious — namely, that the concept of the consent of a majority in Northern Ireland has no meaning, and that formulae that invoke it, or processes designed to bring it about, add another dimension to the problem because they raise false expectations, encourage the pursuit of outcomes that can't live up to their promise, and abet strategies that will only make a settlement more difficult.

And the final blocks: both nationalists and Unionists in Northern Ireland, insofar as they represent the "centers" of their traditions, must address the inconsistencies that undermine their respective positions. For nationalists, this means facing up to the following suppositions: that Unionists would follow an irrational act (calling for independence) with a rational act (negotiating for it); that Unionists would accept a guarantee of their position in a new Ireland from those who want to take away the present guarantee of their position in the U.K.; that an autonomous Northern Ireland with a federal link to the Republic and an institutional link to the U.K. would somehow satisfy what is important to Unionists — their "Britishness" and their Protestantism — but that the obverse, an autonomous, power-sharing Northern Ireland with a federal link to the U.K. and an institutional link to the Republic, would not satisfy what is important to nationalists — their "Irishness" and their Catholicism.

And for Unionists, it means acknowledging an Irish Dimension and that a settlement other than in the context of a U.K. association alone is possible. In fact, only when they admit to the possibility of a settlement in an all-Ireland context does a non–all-Ireland solution become feasible, because the admission tolls the knell of exclusivity, giving recognition to the fact that the minority are their equals in every respect. And since the fourth block — the rejection by the two governments of majority consent for unification as a formula for a change in the external status quo — would work to their benefit, they must accept its corollary, and reject majority consent as a formula for an internal arrangement. In short, the preconditions for a nonunity settlement are also the conditions for power sharing.

There are other building blocks: in Northern Ireland, the painstaking process of building coalitions; in Britain, bipartisan agreement and repeal of repressive legislation; and in the South, a bipartisan policy, an extradition treaty, and broad constitutional reform accommodating pluralism. But even as the South moves to discard the myths of the past she must encourage ways in which to bring the IRA into the process, for not to do so will ensure that it will remain part of the problem. Hence the importance of a national consensus.

"The crack"* is over, but few, even yet, seem to realize it — and perhaps can't, until they call the "enemies" by their real names.

* "The crack" is a phrase used by people in the South to describe the fun derived from some activity. Often an activity is undertaken solely for the sake of "the crack."

Part II

10

The South: New Elections

Things don't always happen as politicians want them to — as I know myself.

— Garret FitzGerald, Taoiseach
24 December 1981[1]

HE WAS TO KNOW AGAIN.

Six months after Garret FitzGerald first took office, his government fell, the victim of his own seemingly inimitable political ineptitude. He had been determined to have the country face up to the harsh economic realities; the first order of business, therefore, was the elimination of the budget deficit. His budget reflected his determination. It called for draconian measures, including substantial increases in the value-added tax (VAT) on clothing and footwear. Nothing would escape the tax dragnet — even children's shoes were not exempted.* But FitzGerald fine-tuned his proposals without regard to the hard political realities: his coalition's survival depended upon the support of a number of independent deputies, including Jim Kemmey, an independent socialist, and when Kemmey could not prevail upon FitzGerald to modify the more regressive proposals, Kemmey

* FitzGerald's rationale for not exempting children's shoes: women with small feet would buy children's shoes and thereby evade the tax.

took the honorable course and the government went down to defeat.

The February 1982 general election was fought entirely on economic issues: who would cut inflation, reduce the deficit, eliminate the reliance on foreign borrowing, stimulate exports, and most important, create jobs. The electorate weighed the certain costs of FitzGerald's proposed budget — he had meant the medicine to be painful, for he would cure the sickness in one massive treatment rather than have it linger and poison — against the uncertain costs of Charles Haughey's proposals, for he would have the public believe that even if the economic circumstances were dire there was a less painful way out of the pit. The electorate balanced FitzGerald's promise of austerity against Haughey's past profligacy and gave its verdict. And once again it was inconclusive.

Fianna Fáil secured eighty-one seats; Fine Gael, sixty-one; Labour, fifteen; Sinn Féin, the Workers' Party, three; and independents, four. The seven Provisional Sinn Féin candidates failed to make an impact. Whatever electoral support had been forthcoming during the hunger strikes had evaporated. Sinn Féin, the Workers' Party, on the other hand, cut into Labour's traditional support and emerged as the new party of the left, in the enviable position of possibly holding the balance of power in a new government.

The Workers' Party, of course, had undergone a metamorphosis. It had its antecedents in Sinn Féin, the political wing of the IRA. When the IRA decided in 1969 to give recognition to the Westminster, Dublin, and Stormont parliaments with a view to contesting elections on a broadly Marxist platform, the change in policy split the movement.[2] The faction opposing the change formed the "Provisional" IRA and its political counterpart, "Provisional" Sinn Féin, and those upholding it became the "Official" IRA and "Official" Sinn Féin. For a period in the early 1970s the Provisionals and the Officials battled the British security forces and each other in bitter and often deadly disputes over territory. But in May 1972, after one of their military reprisals drew the wrath of many in the Bogside, the Officials announced a cease-fire: henceforth, they declared, they would use force only to defend areas attacked by Protestants or by the British military. They coalesced, for the most part, with the Republican Clubs — the Northern Ireland equivalent of Official Sinn Féin in the South — and concentrated on community politics. "Official" Sinn Féin became Sinn Féin, the Workers' Party.

The horse trading began: the price of power would come high. FitzGerald, in a volte-face that only served to raise more questions about his political competence, dropped from his budget proposals the items that had brought down his government in the first place. But it would not suffice, for Mr. Haughey would be neither outbid nor outdone. He needed just two votes to secure a majority. One — Neil Blaney's — he could count on, for Blaney was the former Fianna Fáil minister arrested along with Haughey during the Arms Crisis in 1970. The other — Tony Gregory's — he would buy with a promise to meet forty-two separate demands Gregory made, which would cost taxpayers hundreds of millions of pounds. Gregory, in fact, was pushing the proverbial open door.*

The spectacle of the two leaders currying favor demeaned the process. FitzGerald's special aura faded.

On 9 March 1982, Charles Haughey once again became Taoiseach, and once again he went on the offensive. The first priority of his new government, he told Dáil Éireann, would be to find "a solution for the tragic problems of Northern Ireland."[3] And though he would welcome "any political progress that might be made between the two communities in Northern Ireland,"[4] he reiterated his contention that "overall responsibility for satisfactorily resolving the problem lies with the two sovereign Governments and must be exercised by them."[5] He looked forward to the day "when the rights of self-determination of all the people of Ireland will again be exercised in common, and when the final withdrawal of the British military and political presence takes place."[6]

* Tony Gregory, the newly elected T.D. for Dublin Central, was a young political activist and community organizer whose constituency included some of the poorest parts of Dublin. His agreement to support a Fianna Fáil government was conditional on the commitment of the government to fund a number of inner-city projects on Gregory's list of priorities. Haughey gave that commitment. See Vincent Browne, "Squandermania."

James Prior dismissed Haughey's remarks about British withdrawal as being "totally unrealistic,"[7] and Haughey in turn took the unprecedented step of joining with John Hume in a statement rejecting, in advance of their finalization and official publication, Prior's proposals for a devolved government in Northern Ireland. The proposals, they said, were "deficient" because "they concentrated on the details of an Administration for Northern Ireland without due regard for the broader dimensions of the problem."[8] Nor did Haughey leave it at that. A few days later, he insisted that only a British announcement of intention to withdraw would open the way to an eventual agreement.[9]

The six months in opposition had hardened the rhetoric. Ending the guarantee was only an interim measure. Haughey wanted to proceed directly to the end game: Britain out of Ireland. The calls were now more insistent, the tone more discordant.

11

The North: "Rolling" Devolution

> In a way I have rather a fatalistic approach. I doubt if I can make a much bigger bloody mess of the thing than it's in right now, so I may as well have a go. I might fail, but I reckon trying and failing isn't going to make things much worse.
>
> —James Prior, Secretary of State for Northern Ireland
> 3 April 1982[1]

APRIL. At last Jim Prior had a plan. After six months of free-wheeling discussions with all and sundry, of consultations and cajoleries, of gentle arm-twisting and not-so-gentle hand-holding, of discarding the impossible, defining the plausible, and calculating the probable, Prior went public with a plan for devolved government in Northern Ireland that was immediately either rejected outright or criticized severely by every major constitutional political party North and South.[2]

"The difference in identity and aspiration lies at the heart of the 'problem' of Northern Ireland,"[3] the government's White Paper acknowledged. This difference could not be "ignored or wished away." It recognized that "the sense of two different identities" would continue to be "an important and continuing reality of social and political life in Northern Ireland," and that "the application of simple majority rule would (as in the past) leave the minority in perpetual and ineffectual opposition" where they could become "prey to those who seek change by violent means." Accordingly, any new structures of government would have to be "acceptable to both sides of the community."

The plan called for a seventy-eight-member Assembly that would determine how power should be exercised, the "crucial" requirement being that the Assembly's recommendations would have to command "widespread acceptance throughout the community." To ensure this, no less than 70 percent of the members would have to agree on how devolved power should be exercised. But the 70 percent formula would not be an absolute prerequisite. When fewer than 70 percent of the members agreed to an arrangement, the Secretary of State could recommend parliamentary acceptance if he was convinced that the arrangement was acceptable to both communities. Devolution could be either total, or partial — that is, on a department-by-department basis — and it could be revoked; hence the appellation "rolling devolution." But even if devolution failed to "roll," the Assembly would not be without function. It would have powers to "debate, vote and report" on impending legislation and other matters, and to have its reports laid before Westminster. It would also have a system of committees that would "monitor and scrutinize the work of the departments," thereby allowing it "to influence the development of policy from the onset of the Assembly's life."

The White Paper was less forthcoming on the question of an Irish Dimension. It referred to the Anglo-Irish Intergovernmental Council, noting that it gave "institutional expression to the unique relationship between the two governments without affecting national sovereignty." It was up to the two Parliaments, it said, "to consider whether the governmental meetings of the Council should be complemented by an Anglo-Irish body at Parliamentary level in which members of the Parliaments of the United Kingdom and the Republic of Ireland could take part." And, if they decided that it should, then "the government would expect the arrangements to enable members of the Northern Ireland Assembly to participate if they so wished."

Thus the Prior plan: Northern Ireland would have an election for an Assembly. This Assembly would have "scrutinizing, deliberative and consultative functions" from the start. However, its primary function would be to arrive at a set of arrangements for either full or partial devolution. If these arrangements met certain criteria and were approved by the Secretary of State, the government would recommend them to Parliament for acceptance. The Anglo-Irish process would take care of the Irish Dimension.

• • •

The SDLP was outraged. "Given our analysis of this insulting document," John Hume told the media, "it is difficult for us to avoid the unkind conclusion that Mr. Prior's so-called initiative has more to do with his own political future than with the future of the people of Northern Ireland."[4] In 1973 Britain had offered real power sharing and an Irish Dimension. Now power sharing was offered not as a right "but only on the basis of it being granted by Unionists."[5] And that simply wasn't on.

Seamus Mallon, the SDLP's deputy leader, spelled out their objections:

> The basic objection is that it is almost totally Unionist-oriented. It excludes in concrete terms an expression of the Irish Dimension. It is geared towards creating what we would regard as a majority-rule situation with the edges softened by the committee system, and we also view the mechanics of the proposals as being unworkable insofar as it seems that it would be absolutely impossible ever to arrive at a position of full devolution because the Unionist parties themselves have already said they're not going to contemplate power sharing in any shape or form. We also think that the way in which interparty haggling would have to take place at every stage of devolution would make it almost impossible to work.[6]

The total exclusion of an Irish Dimension, however, was the final straw: "After acknowledging that the question of identity was the essence of the problem and that it could not be ignored, the White Paper blithely proceeded to do just that."[7] Devolution of itself would not bring about a lasting solution. There had to be "a very strong and positive and concrete expression of the Irish identity."[8] The SDLP would support devolution as a means only if it was part of a more comprehensive Anglo-Irish process.

In Dublin, government reaction was sparingly caustic. The proposals were "unworkable," their focus "mistaken." They ignored "the broader dimensions of the problem." Only policies "designed to promote peace, stability and reconciliation between the two major Irish traditions," which would "develop the totality of relations within these islands," could contribute to a "true solution." The framework: the Anglo-Irish Intergovernmental Council, and in particular "an Anglo-Irish Parliamentary Institution in which Northern Ireland representatives" would participate. How Northern Unionists would be made to participate was left unstated — they simply would be deprived of the option not to.[9]

Haughey's own reaction was unsparingly caustic. "The Prior initiative," he said in the course of a radio interview, "will be regarded in history as one of the most disastrous things that has ever happened in Anglo-Irish relations"[10] because "insofar as they sidestep, and therefore downgrade the Anglo-Irish process and the Parliamentary Council, they have set back the process of Anglo-Irish relations."[11] His objections were total, and not just with the form of the proposals: you did not resuscitate failed political entities.

FitzGerald's objections, on the other hand, were with the form of the proposals rather than the substance. Some were technical: it was "unclear as to how the proposed system might work apart from doubts as to whether it would work."[12] And though some of the ambiguities were perhaps intentional, "to leave room for negotiations," others reflected perhaps that "the British government hadn't fully thought out how it was supposed to operate."

As regards the "Irish Dimension," or rather the recognition of the Irish identity of the minority and their right to express it, FitzGerald said:

> That's given a very clear expression in the White Paper philosophically — clearer expression perhaps than it had been given previously, but this is towards the end of the White Paper and nothing follows from it. There's no operational consequence. In fact it's expressed in a curious way, backwards — that what is proposed above reflects this

identity when all that is proposed above is that any Executive would need to command the support of both communities. This is not [only] what was envisaged during discussions. Other aspects of the Irish identity of the people of Northern Ireland were discussed along with means of expressing them, and considerable encouragement was given to the idea that expression could be given to these aspects and that obstacles to the expression of the Irish identity might be removed. None of this is featured in the White Paper, which suggests that in its preparation there was some change in thinking on the British side for reasons that are not clear at this point.

What actually emerged was disappointing, therefore, in the light of what seemed likely to emerge at one point. The fact that the White Paper didn't call for the abolition of the Flags and Emblems Act, which was "a legal prohibition inhibiting the expression of the Irish identity of the minority," was a letdown.* And then, of course, there were the doubts as to whether it would be possible, assuming you had an Assembly, "to move towards a power-sharing Executive given that the initiative was being left to the parties and that it was not an initiative to be taken by the British government." FitzGerald:

There are genuine fears on both sides that the parties themselves may be unwilling to create an Executive on a power-sharing basis by their own voluntary action, and you may then be left with an Assembly in which they will be shouting at each other — and none of them want to get back to that . . . So, the shift away from an idea canvassed at one stage on the British side of a separate Executive which they would nominate or draw from the Assembly headed by the Secretary of State, to a situation where the initiative has to come from the parties, was a very serious weakening of the whole thing, which makes it less likely to succeed.

* The Flags and Emblems (Display) Act (Northern Ireland) of 1954 "gives special protection to the occupiers of land or premises who wish to display a Union Jack. It is an offence to prevent or threaten forcibly to interfere with such display. In respect of other emblems any police officer may, if he apprehends a breach of the peace, require the person displaying the emblem to remove it, and in the event of failure to comply may enter the premises to remove and detain it. Failure to remove such emblems on police request constitutes an offence." Quoted in Tim Pat Coogan, *The IRA*, p. 441. The "other emblems" referred to invariably meant the Tricolour of the Irish Republic.

But FitzGerald would not damn the proposals out of hand: it was for the parties in Northern Ireland to try to improve upon them.

Unionist objections were familiar. They would not budge; majority rule was democratic rule. James Molyneaux:

> Our main objection is that it is something very far removed from straightforward democracy. It's inherently unworkable because it has two fatal provisions built in. One which says that things can only be done with a weighted majority of 70 percent, which has the effect of giving a veto to perhaps a tiny cranky body getting not more than 7 percent or 8 percent in an election, and that could be a party on either side of the political divide. The second big weakness is, of course, what's called cross-community consent, which isn't the requirement that Protestants and Catholics must consent — that would be comparatively simple — but that Unionist and Republican Catholics must agree, and that makes the thing completely unworkable right from the start.[13]

Harold McCusker took a somewhat more sanguine view:

> I'm one of the few who say if Charlie Haughey rejected it, if the SDLP rejected it, if Sinn Féin rejected it, if the Provisional IRA rejected it, if the Irish Independence Party rejected it, then there must be something in it for the Unionists to find encouraging, and I've tried to convince some of my colleagues of that. I think some of them are slowly moving round. I think fundamentally what we object to is the prospect of the illusion of power and the talking-shop syndrome and all the difficulties that spring from that. There's also an underlying rejection of the idea that we should be expected to get 70 percent agreement when in most other places 51 percent and sometimes even less is enough for people to govern. My view about these proposals — and it's the view, I think, of more people than is realized — is that they should be given a try. I don't think we should once again be seen as the wreckers.[14]

And McCusker had a plan of sorts, or at least the inkling of a strategy:

> The task facing Unionism is to try and hammer out an agreement with the Alliance Party so that in fact one would establish an Executive in

Northern Ireland which would have members in it who are elected Roman Catholics . . . And then the ball would be in the British government's court, because if you produced 70 percent support encompassing three parties, with maybe the acquiescence of one or two other minor parties — for example, the Republican Clubs may be happy to acquiesce in a system without necessarily voting for it — Jim Prior might have a lot of trouble saying "I'm not going to accept this."[15]

The Democratic Unionist Party wanted an Assembly, but not, of course, the Assembly Mr. Prior had in mind. "For all of the evils, and they are many, in the Prior Bill," Ian Paisley told a meeting of the party faithful, "Unionists must not lose sight of the fact that the quite distinct first part of the package whereby Ulster people are allowed to freely elect their own Assembly and to begin to bring Direct Rule to account through the much needed scrutiny committees has much to commend itself."[16] But that was all. Power sharing? Never. "Through its inequitable 70 percent mechanism and its 'cross-community' prerequisite," he declared, "the Prior Bill affords Republicans an intolerable guarantee of absolute veto on the government of Northern Ireland."[17] The DUP would go into the Assembly "to kybosh power-sharing and an Irish Dimension."[18]

On the Loyalist side, only the Ulster Defence Association was not heard from. More immediate matters occupied its attentions. In mid-April, four senior members, including Andy Tyrie and John McMichael, were arrested on charges of conspiring to possess firearms and ammunition, and documents "which could be useful to terrorists."[19] Among the items confiscated from UDA headquarters by the RUC: "The Terrorist and Assassin's Bible."[20] A month later Tyrie and McMichael were released on bail when three leading Protestant churchmen intervened on their behalf, arguing that Tyrie was "a moderating influence on the more extreme elements in the UDA."[21] For the moment, however, the emphasis on politics had gone. The hard line was asserting itself again.

• • •

They were an unlikely pair to find themselves political bedfellows — the staid, middle-of-the-road, distinctly nonideological Unionist Alliance Party and the radical left-of-center, distinctly ideological Republican Workers' Party — but at first it seemed that only they would contest the Assembly elections.

Founded in 1970 as a nonsectarian party, the Alliance is studiously "moderate" on the constitutional question. It supports power sharing and the constitutional position of Northern Ireland within the U.K. It nominates candidates of both religious persuasions and campaigns vigorously in both communities. Moderation, however, is not a virtue in Northern Ireland politics, as the party's electoral record shows. The high-water mark of its fortunes came in 1974 when it won 14 percent of the first-preference votes and seventy seats in the district council elections. Eight years later it was the victim of the increasing polarization between the two communities resulting from the deaths of the IRA hunger strikers. Its share of the vote fell by 40 percent and the number of council seats it held to just thirty-eight.

Party leader Oliver Napier described the Alliance's position on the Prior plan:

> The issue is how power is to be exercised. If you will not face that head-on, then rolling devolution of the general pattern set out by Mr. Prior is the only way to make any movement forward. On the question of power sharing, I actually think it would have been better to have faced the issue head-on, and to have said, "We're going to have elections to an Assembly in Northern Ireland, power will only be transferred on a power-sharing basis. We can't force you to share power but unless you do so you're not getting any." I would have preferred that to be the line of the Secretary of State and the British government. Having said that, the reality of the situation — and this is something very few of the Unionist politicians are prepared to accept — is that in practice no power will ever be transferred by any British government unless there is at least some reasonable semblance of cross-community politics, because the implications within Northern Ireland would be serious, but more important the implications within Britain would be serious. Because the electorate would see this as handing power back to a one-party government. The relationships between Britain and the Irish Re-

public would be very much affected. And internationally Britain would have trouble.[22]

But he, too, had his criticisms: the 70 percent trigger mechanism "was a load of nonsense"; if the 70 percent voting for the return of power consisted only of the Unionist parties, "it would go before Parliament with a government recommendation to reject the transfer of power."

On the question of cross-community support, the Alliance would insist on the inclusion of the SDLP in a power-sharing coalition, provided, of course, that the SDLP contested the elections and took their seats. Napier:

> If the SDLP fight the election and sit in the Assembly and are not demanding some major extraneous things for the right to share power, then my party will totally support their right to be involved in power sharing. If the Unionists say, "We're not going to share power with these people because they want a united Ireland," then we will not support a call for a return of power which excludes the SDLP on these conditions . . . Power sharing doesn't mean that you have the luxury of picking and choosing those elected representatives with whom you share power.

However, if the SDLP fought the election but either abstained from the Assembly or made ludicrous demands, that would create "a new situation that would have to be looked at in the light of that situation."

Nor was the Alliance opposed to participation in a parliamentary tier of the Anglo-Irish Intergovernmental Council, provided that it was clearly seen to be an institutional forum only:

> We would have to know what the parliamentary tier is going to do. If the parliamentary tier had any right to interfere in the internal affairs of Northern Ireland, then I would question whether one should go along with it. But if, as I suspect is more likely, the parliamentary tier is a kind of club which is a forum for getting to know people and for discussion of common problems but without political overtones, then I can see no danger to it. In fact it could have benefits.

The Workers' Party,* on the other hand, calls for a devolved government in Northern Ireland, but without enforced power sharing, which it views as an instrument for perpetuating sectarianism. The unity of the working classes is seen as a precondition for the unity of the country. Hence the evolution of democracy in Northern Ireland takes precedence over the national question. It wants a strong Bill of Rights guaranteed by the Westminster government and lodged with the European Court of Human Rights, and in the long run a thirty-two-county workers' republic. Its support for devolved government, and absence of support for guaranteed power sharing, leads Republicans of the Provisional ilk to refer to it derisively as "Sinn Féin, the Unionist Party."

It, too, found much to criticize in Prior's proposals: the 70 percent formula was sectarian in its approach; the limited powers of the Assembly would preclude its tackling the province's economic problems; there were no provisions for repealing repressive legislation, no provisions for a Bill of Rights. Nevertheless, they would contest the elections, and take their seats. Thomas MacGiolla, president of the party:

> The Prior proposal must be taken in the context of previous proposals to replace Direct Rule. We are completely opposed to Direct Rule. Whatever lack of democracy there was in the old Stormont there is less in Direct Rule. In fact, a military dictatorship has existed in Northern Ireland for the last ten years. The previous effort to replace Direct Rule was on the basis of agreement between the parties and the British government negotiating this agreement, and of course it collapsed within a few months, because power sharing wasn't acceptable to the Unionist people. This is the first real effort to begin the process of replacing Direct Rule. We would favor nearly anything to replace Direct Rule as a beginning. But despite all our criticism, we make the point that it is in an Assembly such as this where these criticisms could be made. The SDLP have different reasons for opposing it because it doesn't contain power sharing. But they could argue out their criticisms in the Assembly. The Unionist parties — both the DUP and the OUP —

* At its Annual Conference on 25 April 1982, Sinn Féin, the Workers' Party voted to call itself simply the Workers' Party.

have their criticisms because they want simple majority rule. They could put those forward in the Assembly. And all of this could create political debate for the first time. Because without any political forum there's just an open field for the British military dictatorship on the one hand, and the Provos, the UDA, and the UVF on the other. So it's paramilitary and military rule, and Prior's proposals give the opportunity for opening up political debate, and through that we could endeavor to get greater powers for the Assembly. We are interested particularly in greater powers in regard to the economy because the economic situation is disastrous. So, reluctant as we were, we said, "Right, let's have this Assembly and let's argue out there what type of future we see for Northern Ireland."[23]

• • •

If the politicians found fault with Prior's proposals on almost every count, the public did not appear to follow suit. An *Irish Times* poll of opinion in Northern Ireland found that 60 percent of respondents were at least "somewhat in favor" of a new Assembly, while 55 percent were in favor of power sharing, including, surprisingly, 45 percent of Protestants.[24] At the extremes, only 13 percent of Catholics were unreservedly opposed to the idea of a new Assembly, and only 21 percent of Protestants were unreservedly opposed to power sharing.[25] The pundits took due note of the survey's findings, but the politicians scoffed, for there was no place in which the timeworn adage "The only poll that counts is the poll on election day" was more pertinent than in Northern Ireland. In the privacy of the ballot box people remember their madnesses, and vote their pasts.

Prior himself took the criticism of his proposals in stride. His purpose was not to please but to prevail. He would fail only if one of the major parties went beyond criticism to an actual boycott of the election.

The purpose of the 70 percent weighted formula? It was only a procedural mechanism. Prior:

If there is 70 percent support for a particular transfer of powers, it is discussed by the House of Commons. It has to be laid before the House of Commons. That's all [the 70 percent requirement] does. Beyond that we have said quite clearly that even if there is 70 percent and it doesn't contain a sufficient element of cross-community support, then no government would ask Parliament to support it, because unless you have cross-community support you will not have political stability, and therefore there's no purpose in the government trying to put it forward.[26]

How would he define cross-community support? He wouldn't really. The SDLP's participation in an arrangement would be sufficient to ensure it, but in some circumstances not, perhaps, necessary:

Is it just the odd Catholic? The answer is that it must be more than the odd Catholic. The next question is, is it the SDLP, and the answer is that I don't know. I have told the SDLP that as far as I'm concerned, while I would hope and expect them to play a role in any devolved administration, I can't guarantee it to them. It may well be that Parliament would decide that there was a formula which gave an adequate degree of cross-community support but which didn't necessarily include the SDLP. It seems that it would be unlikely, but one can't by any means be certain. It can be cross-community support without the SDLP, but it's unlikely to be — but we shall just have to see.

As regards the SDLP's criticism of the proposals:

The SDLP feels that they haven't got enough help from the government on the Irish Dimension, but they know perfectly well that were the government to be more specific on the Irish Dimension, this would make Unionists even more suspicious of the plan. I've never sought the agreement of any of the parties. What I'm trying to do is to narrow down the differences and the fact of the matter is that the Unionists and the DUP on the one hand, and the SDLP on the other, have found fault with what I'm proposing. But what I've been trying to do is to make it possible, first of all, for an Assembly to be set up with certain scrutinizing powers and so on. Then I'm making it possible to move towards a transfer of powers to self-government. But in those circumstances there would have to be a positive element of cross-community support. I don't believe I can go further, but if I wait until I have sufficient agreement from one side or the other, I'll wait a generation before they're ever going to agree.

As regards the Irish Dimension:

There are a minority of the population in Northern Ireland who seek unity but who recognize that unity is not going to come, and we are seeking therefore to see whether or not there are ways by which you can, as it were, give credibility to their Irishness, and when I was having consultations with Dr. FitzGerald we were trying to see how this could be accomplished consistent with the guarantees about consent, which Dr. FitzGerald himself has always stated.

After FitzGerald's government had fallen, FitzGerald had written him asking that he not make any irrevocable decisions during the election campaign. Nor did he. Nevertheless, "there were certain misconceptions" about his policies that he would have sorted out had FitzGerald been returned to office. He gave a full explanation to the new government's Minister for Foreign Affairs, Mr. Gerry Collins, and although he didn't satisfy the new government, he thought he had at least "enlightened" Mr. Collins's understanding. Prior: "We recognize the importance of the Irishness of the minority and desire to see that it is properly recognized within the context of the government of Northern Ireland."

• • •

Thus the rationale behind rolling devolution: Britain could not impose a solution; she could not impose either majority rule on the nationalists or an Irish Dimension on the Unionists. The two communities would have to come up with their own settlements. But Britain could impose a framework establishing the reference points for a satisfactory agreement.

At the same time, the framework itself had to remain sufficiently tenuous so as to induce both communities into the process. The structure of the framework was, therefore, subordinated to the one overriding imperative: there had to be an election.

Since all parties had rigid positions, a framework that fully met the conditions of any one party would necessarily be rejected by the others. Prior, therefore, had to create a set of arrangements that met no one party's positions yet was not sufficiently removed from them so as to result in the party's refusing to contest the elections. Consequently, the anticipated intensity of response became the barometer of whether to move toward or away from a party's positions. Thus the balancing acts, and the ordering of priorities. If a proposal was objectionable to one party on all counts, Prior had to calculate whether the severity of the objection would translate itself into a decision to boycott the elections. And thus Prior's calculations: a strong Irish Dimension was more likely to result in a Unionist boycott than a weak Irish Dimension was in a nationalist boycott. Moreover, before there could be an Anglo-Irish Dimension there had to be an Assembly.

There were, of course, other constraints. The need to minimize defections on the Tory right, the timetable calling for a fall election, and Prior's own uncertain relations with Mrs. Thatcher sometimes ruled out the most preferred options.

And there were, of course, other considerations. Even if the Assembly failed to agree on how to devolve power, it would democratize Direct Rule to some extent and give the political parties some responsibility for Northern Ireland's affairs. It was hard to see how they could fail to agree on everything within the Assembly's purview, especially in light of the dire state of the economy. Moreover, even if they failed to agree on how to devolve power, Dublin and Westminster could go ahead and establish the Anglo-Irish parliamentary body and appoint members of the Assembly to it. And this, of course, would put the SDLP in a quandary if they contested the elections but boycotted the Assembly, since they would be unable to take their places in an Anglo-Irish parliamentary body unless they took their seats in the Assembly. Thus the SDLP might be induced into participating in the Assembly. On the other hand, Unionist appointees could be counted on not to take their seats in an Anglo-Irish parliamentary body at first — indeed, they might even boycott the Assembly itself at that point. But their paranoia would get the better of them. Their fears that an Anglo-Irish parliamentary body might start tinkering with the constitutional position would drive them to participate, if only as observers, to safeguard their position. Moreover, if they boycotted the Assembly, they would leave Northern Ireland's affairs in the hands of the non-Loyalist parties in the Assembly and a London-Dublin parliamentary body, hardly a situation that would recommend itself to hard-nosed Unionists. Thus the Unionists might be induced to participate in an Anglo-Irish parliamentary body.

If the Assembly got off the ground, it would provide a framework for tradeoffs. For example, in exchange for meeting the 70 percent weighted formula for power sharing, Unionists could demand an equivalence: making the consent of 70 percent necessary for a change in the constitutional status. Or they could trade off their participation in an Anglo-Irish parliamentary body for a less restrictive power-sharing formula.

In short, members of the SDLP were being told that power sharing was not a preordained right, that they would have to find ways to trade for it; and Unionists were being told that since majority rule was not democratic rule, it too was not a preordained right and they too would have to find ways to trade for a partnership arrangement. Both sides were being given a veto: Britain would not hand back power to the majority without the consent of the minority. Nor would she give a share of power to the minority without the consent of the majority. Accordingly, unless they accommodated each other, neither would have its way. The absence of a proposed North-South link effectively pre-empted the grounds on which Unionists could boycott the election, while the lure of an Anglo-Irish interparliamentary body would ultimately make it difficult for nationalists to continue a boycott of the Assembly. Or at least that was the theory.

Of course, Unionist partnership with the Alliance and the odd Republican would not constitute broad cross-community support representative of the other tradition. The traditions were political, not religious, and support would have to reflect political aspirations, not religious affiliations. The fact, however, that some Unionists were thinking in terms of a coalition with the Alliance while the Alliance was insisting on the inclusion of the SDLP appeared to create a framework for future tradeoffs.

• • •

One by one, the other parties decided to contest the elections: the DUP because it wanted to take on the OUP and consolidate its successes of 1979, because elections would provide an opportunity for Ian Paisley's party to establish itself as the Protestant party of Northern Ireland, because an Assembly would give Paisley a wider range of options and a springboard to independence, if necessary; the OUP because it couldn't afford not to,* because ground conceded in one election would be hard to make up in the next, because support would fragment and drift to the DUP; and Provisional Sinn Féin because it wanted to undermine the SDLP. Only the SDLP equivocated, the party split between the "Greens," those who had given up any hope of an acceptable internal settlement, and the rest, those who had not. Ultimately, in the last week of August, they reached a compromise. They would contest the elections but boycott the Assembly.† Once again, abstentionism was the preferred route in nationalist politics, the choice now between abstentionists with an Armalite in one hand and abstentionists who had upheld parliamentary participation for twelve years as the way forward. The SDLP umbrella had all but folded, the perspective narrowed, and the main question was no longer power sharing or even alternative systems of devolution, but unification, leaving only the when and the how to be determined.

Meanwhile, James Prior would have his elections.

* The OUP election manifesto pledged to turn the Assembly into a majority-rule body, to oppose power sharing with nationalists under all circumstances, and to fight every suggestion of an Irish Dimension. (*Irish Times*, 29 September 1982.)

† The SDLP election manifesto, entitled "Stand Firm," pledged to bring the Assembly to a quick end, and called for the creation in its place of a Council for a New Ireland whose membership would be open to "elected Democratic parties" in the Dáil and the Assembly who believed in what the manifesto called "a new Ireland." At the time, Hume indicated that this would exclude members of Sinn Féin who might be elected to the Assembly. The council would have a limited life and have the specific task of examining the obstacles to the creation of a new Ireland. Out of its deliberation would come a "blueprint" so that a debate on real alternatives could begin. (*Irish Times*, 2 October 1982.) An Irish forum, which had a frame of reference broadly in keeping with what the SDLP had called for, was set up in March 1983. See chapter 14, p. 413n.

12

The South: Political and Economic Malaise

Ireland's stand on the Falklands has led to a greater degree of anti-Irish feeling in Britain than at the time of the Birmingham bombings.

— Gerry Fitt, independent M.P. for West Belfast
29 April 1982[1]

APRIL 1982, of course, will be remembered for the Falklands/ Malvinas crisis, which quickly escalated into war, claiming among its casualties Anglo-Irish relations.

Argentina's invasion of the islands eight thousand miles away in the distant reaches of the Atlantic triggered an emotional response among the British public not evident since the days of Suez. But unlike Suez, the Falklands united all segments of public and political opinion, and this time Britain had the weight of world opinion firmly on her side. The notorious right-wing junta in Argentina was almost universally despised, the fate of thousands of the *desaparecidos* testimony to its totalitarian fascism. A country that devoured its own could hardly assert a moral claim to sovereignty over eighteen hundred people resolutely demanding to retain their British connection, to the point of being, if anything, more British than the British themselves. Jingoism would have its day again; the Imperial Power would assert herself to defend her people no matter where they were: honor demanded no less.

The dispute evoked an immediate response in both parts of Ireland, but especially in Northern Ireland. Indeed, the all-too-obvious parallels between the situations in Northern Ireland and the Falklands obscured the far more important differences. Atavism, however, is not persuaded by mere distinctions.

Embattled Unionists embraced the cause of the embattled Falklanders, their identity of interests complete. They, too, wanted only to maintain their link with Britain despite the claims to sovereignty of a belligerent neighbor. They, too, asserted the right of a majority to determine their own future. And they, too, saw themselves as victims of Foreign Office machinations. The Foreign Office was the villain. For had it not admonished the islanders for years to recognize the "Argentinian Dimension"? Had it not wanted to abandon the islands? And had it not sought to do so by making the islands more economically dependent on Argentina? In everything, Unionists saw the sinister hand of the Whitehall establishment conspiring to get rid of the Falkland Islands, and many went further, maintaining that the Foreign Office had implicitly encouraged an Argentinian invasion in the belief that the government would not dispatch a military force to retrieve the islands. Unionists, therefore, would not rest until the islands were resecured. Talk of diplomatic settlement with an Argentinian presence perhaps remaining on the islands unnerved them, for if Britain would not honor the wishes of a majority in the Falklands today, she might not honor the wishes of a majority in Northern Ireland tomorrow. And if the Argentinian invasion was not repulsed, might not the Republican state to the South, sensing the weakness of the British will, attempt to "reclaim" Northern Ireland? "If Britain [does] not establish full control over the Falklands," said John Taylor, a Unionist and member of the European Parliament, "there is a danger that the Irish Army would be ordered to invade Northern Ireland."[2] Of course, the suggestion was preposterous, but many believed the Falklands were not a test of British will in some far-off corner of the

Southern Hemisphere but of British intentions in Northern Ireland.

Nationalists, on the other hand, took a jaundiced view of the Imperial reawakening. Neil Blaney, now an independent member of the Dáil on whose support Haughey's government's survival depended, was unequivocal: "We should support Argentina," he declared, "for both political and economic reasons — politically because of the continued British occupation of the Six Counties of Northern Ireland, and economically because Argentina is one of the few countries with which we have a credit trade balance."[3] Support for Britain's position in the South Atlantic dispute was equated with support for her position in Northern Ireland, and support for the islanders with support for the Unionists of Ulster.

Haughey's government went along with the EEC sanctions against Argentina, but the sinking of the *General Belgrano,* with the loss of hundreds of lives, changed things. The government was "appalled"; Mr. Paddy Power, the Minister for Defence, declared that Britain was now the aggressor, and though Mr. Haughey quickly disavowed the remark, his subsequent actions left few in doubt as to what he felt. The *Belgrano* incident, he announced, compromised Irish neutrality. He moved to reassert it: hence the government's call for a meeting of the United Nations Security Council, which in Britain's eyes would have severely undermined her position if it had been successful, and hence the government's refusal to back continuing EEC sanctions against Argentina.[4]

Haughey justified his actions. "Once it became clear that they [the sanctions] could be seen to support military activity," he said, "we had as a neutral state no alternative but to withdraw from the sanctions position."[5] "Nonsense," snapped FitzGerald, Irish neutrality was "a complete red herring":[6] the government's moves were "clumsy and unnecessarily damaging to our relationship with Britain."[7]

Also unnecessarily damaging was the government's heavy-handed opposition to Britain during the EEC impasse over Britain's veto of farm price increases. Ultimately, the veto was overridden when the EEC discarded the Luxembourg compromise by making a majority rather than a unanimous decision, but not before the relations between Britain and Ireland had soured some more.

The British government, for its part, had no misgivings about Haughey's intention: once again it was a question of England's difficulty being Ireland's opportunity. His actions were seen as mean, vindictive, and aimed at embarrassing Britain at every turn. They would not be forgotten. The "special relationship" between Haughey and Thatcher had become no relationship — Mr. Haughey, for his own good reasons, had seen to that. And the "good" reasons were many: the need to alleviate the pressure on Blaney to ensure Blaney's continuing support, and the need to secure his own position within Fianna Fáil. His own standing with the grassroots would rise the more he appeared to be the target of official British disapproval: asserting Ireland's sovereignty against Britain's interests never did a good Republican harm. Besides, he could attribute the failure of the Anglo-Irish process to deliver what he tenaciously insisted had been agreed upon to Britain's arrogant refusal to acknowledge the legitimate interests of Ireland's sovereign neutrality rather than to the reality of the actual arrangements, and thus avoid having to admit that the claims he had made on its behalf following his December 1980 meeting with Mrs. Thatcher were, if not wholly inaccurate, at least wholly exaggerated. Once again, he would not be called to account. He would stall the process rather than have it expose him.

Anti-Irish sentiment in Britain was quick to surface. Irish export orders were canceled; British tabloids called for a boycott of Irish goods; tourism slowed; the summer summit between Mr. Haughey and Mrs. Thatcher was postponed indefinitely; and Lord Gowrie, Minister of State for Northern Ireland, hinted that the Anglo-Irish parliamentary body would probably be delayed. At every level the cycle of deterioration fed on itself. And then came the bombings.

On 20 July, six British soldiers and two civilians were killed and fifty others maimed or injured when two bombs exploded in Central London.* The soldiers were involved in ceremonial duties, one group a company in full regalia on horseback making their daily journey from their barracks to Whitehall; the other, members of a band playing to a lunchtime audience. Both bombs went off without warning and both were primed for maximum impact — the shrapnel and six-inch nails embedded in the bombs would see to that. That soldiers would die was certain, but who else and how many was left to chance.

And then, of course, there were the horses: the spectacle of the splendid animals reduced to a bloodied pulp moved the public as much, if not more, than the human dead. The attention given to the horses was due, perhaps, to the British public's special affection for animals. Or perhaps in a world grown accustomed to the horrors man visits on man, common humanity implying guilt by association, they felt that innocent animals, at least, should not be held accountable for man's condition. Once again television brought home the macabre scenes of slaughter, the mess of men and animals testimony to the madness of men. The IRA had had its day. And, it vowed, there would be many more such.

Eight days later, following a speech in the Dáil by the Minister for Foreign Affairs, Mr. Gerry Collins, in which he criticized Prior's initiative, calling the proposed Assembly "misguided," the Irish Ambassador to the United Kingdom, Eamonn Kennedy, was summoned to the Foreign Office and told that Britain considered herself under no obligation to consult the Dublin government about matters affecting Northern Ireland.[8] The following day, Mrs. Thatcher reiterated her government's position in the Commons. "No commitment exists," she said, "for Her Majesty's Government to consult the Irish government on matters affecting Northern Ireland."[9] The Irish government, in turn, tersely rejected her position on the grounds that it was contrary to the December 1980 agreement between Mr. Haughey and Mrs. Thatcher reflected in their joint communiqué. "In the light of this agreed statement and many other similar ones," the govern-

* Three more people died later.

ment said, "it is difficult to find any justification for the recent British claims that there was no commitment on the part of the U.K. government to consult with the Irish government on matters affecting Northern Ireland."[10] But the government did not stop there. It attacked Dr. FitzGerald for his intention "to put down the motion in Dáil Éireann to establish a watered down Anglo-Irish parliamentary tier." It implied that FitzGerald was doing so at the behest of British Ministers, "a matter of grave concern." It reiterated the Haughey refrains: "the parliamentary tier should be set up by the two governments"; FitzGerald's agreement to leave this to the two parliaments "was to be deplored"; a parliamentary tier not established by the two governments "as a forum for consultation on political and constitutional matters" would be "very limited and of little more value than a social club for parliamentarians." And it questioned meetings FitzGerald had had with Prior, concluding that "the activities of the opposition leader must become a cause of concern not merely to the Irish government but to the entire nationalist community in Ireland whose well-founded opposition to the Prior proposals is being undermined by him." Dr. FitzGerald attacked Mr. Haughey for seeking "to cover his own ineptitude in handling Irish-British relations by the use of innuendos and untruths of a kind happily rare in Irish politics."

The antagonisms were raw, the differences real, exchanges marred by personal antipathies and mean insinuations, debate absent. Haughey had alienated the British government, the Northern Ireland Office, and the South's major opposition party. The result: stalemate and acrimony; the rhetoric of innuendo and snide opportunism once again became a substitute for vision and action.

• • •

Anglo-Irish relations were not the only thing to deteriorate: the decline of the Republic's economy kept pace. By the fall of 1982, one hundred sixty thousand people were unemployed — an increase of 77 percent over the 1979 figure — no prospect of relief was in sight, and still more would join their ranks, according to the experts. Some seventy thousand young people, accounting for 21 percent of the labor force aged twenty-five or under, were out of work,[11] while the labor force itself was increasing by twenty-one thousand persons per year.[12] Unemployment among males under twenty-five had increased by 122 percent since the beginning of 1980, among males over twenty-five by 60 percent, among females under twenty-five by 149 percent, and among females over twenty-five by 47 percent.[13] According to an Organization for Economic Cooperation and Development review of youth unemployment policies in the Republic, the population might increase by one half million people between 1979 and 1989.[14] The most optimistic estimates of the fiscal 1982 budget deficit put it at £900 million — at least 33 percent higher than projected.[15] Inflation slowed but at 17 percent remained intolerably high.[16] The one optimistic note: the balance-of-trade deficit was likely to fall from 17 percent of GNP in 1981 to 10 percent in 1982.[17] However, because of the increase in interest payments on the government's foreign borrowing, the balance-of-payments deficit would only fall from 15 percent of GNP in 1981 to 10 percent in 1982.[18] Indeed, interest payments on foreign borrowing would absorb over 4 percent of GNP in 1982 and principal repayments a further 4 percent.[19] The cost of meeting current payments on the government's foreign borrowing was ensuring that the recession would not end. Moreover, the government's penchant for borrowing showed no signs of letting up. For the second year in a row, overall state and semistate borrowing would amount to at least 22 percent of GNP[20] and for the first six months of 1982, the government's foreign borrowing came to £750 million — 6.3 percent of GNP and almost 60 percent of the previous year's record total of £1285 million.[21] The national debt had tripled in five years.[22] Approximately one fourth of current government spending went to service the public debt — interest payments were the largest single line item in the budget.

The problems ran deep. The public sector employed one fourth of the labor force and spent two thirds of the national income.[23] The marginal tax rate on average industrial earnings was 52 percent, indicating both the narrowness of the tax base and the high level of taxation needed to finance the high level of public expenditure. But exorbitant as it was, the tax rate was simply not high enough to sustain the level of public expenditure. Between 1977 and 1981 the extraordinary increase in government spending was financed by borrowing, especially foreign borrowing. Both the increase in the numbers employed in the public sector (up 13 percent between 1977 and 1981 compared to a 1 percent net increase in manufacturing industry jobs) and the increase in public-sector average real income levels (up 27 percent in the same period compared to a 9 percent increase in industry and a 37 percent decrease in real farm incomes) would have put intolerable strains on the non–public-sector segments of the economy if they had been financed by taxation alone.[24]

But the strains existed, with the inability of the economy to generate lasting jobs in the private sector to stem, let alone reduce, the level of unemployment exposing the shifting foundations. Given the structure of employment and the excessive level of public expenditure, there was no way the public sector itself could either reduce unemployment or absorb a significant number of those coming into the labor market in the foreseeable future.

A few figures illustrate the dimensions of the problem. Between 1977 and 1981, jobs in manufacturing industry increased by 2500 (roughly 625 per year), jobs in the private service sector by 37,000 (9250 per year), and jobs in the public sector by 36,178 (9035 per year).[25] Thus, the average annual increase in the number of jobs was 18,910, of which 48 percent came from the public sector. By 1982, however, the public sector could no longer play the role of even a limited absorbent. Meanwhile, up to twenty-one thousand people would come on to the labor market each year for the rest of the decade. Even if the private sector found a way to absorb half — something it had spectacularly failed to do in the past except briefly in the heydays of the late 1970s — at least one quarter of a million people would be unemployed by 1990. The government itself finally acknowledged the seriousness of the situation in late September: according to its own best estimates, if current trends in both the balance-of-payments deficit and the budget deficit were to go unchecked, unemployment would approach three hundred thousand by 1987.[26]

Jobs. How are they to be created? And where? More public-sector jobs mean higher taxation to support them, since large-scale foreign borrowing is no longer an option. Would an already overtaxed non–public-service sector be willing to assume the burden? How much would the public sacrifice in order to create new jobs?

Not much, if past behavior was a guide to future intentions. Unions demanded payments of "disturbance" money when employees were moved from one location to another, even when the locations were within walking distance of each other, and of "inconvenience" money when their members had to stand in bank lines to cash their checks, even when they were paid to do so; the logic: aggravation demanded extra compensation. In 1982, unit wage costs were expected to increase eight times faster than in the U.K. — a shocking commentary on the country's lack of competitiveness.[27] And when Haughey finally decided to postpone the 5 percent pay increases due to three hundred thousand public-sector employees, the unions promised to fight the move and the minority support that kept his government in power indicated it would desert him in the Dáil. The Irish Congress of Trade Unions called for a one-day national work stoppage on 26 October — the day on which the Dáil reconvened — and Fine Gael, the paradigm of fiscal rectitude in January 1983, came out in opposition to the freeze.

In the past, of course, no sacrifices were called for. The safety chute of emigration disposed of the surplus labor..But the years of tight labor markets in Britain were gone. The unemployed stayed put, their numbers relentlessly increasing, their resentments smoldering, the young more disposed toward the radical — and the violent. One opinion poll of young unemployed people indicated that, nationally, 16 percent rated the Provisional IRA as a good organization; the corresponding figure for Dublin respondents was 23 percent.[28]

For the first time there is a generation of young people adrift on the "filthy tide" of modern culture, contaminated at one remove by the political violence in Northern Ireland. It is easy for the young to make common cause with their counterparts in the ghettos of Belfast, and easy too for them, given the ambiance of violence that has enveloped their socialization, to embrace the culture of violence at their doorsteps.

The telltale signs are abundant. Crime doubled in the years from 1971 to 1981, increasing annually at an exponential rate.[29] The 1980 level was 14 percent above the 1979 level, the 1981 level was 22 percent above the 1980 level,[30] and in some Dublin suburbs it is now rising by more than 50 percent a year.[31] The increase in armed robberies — up 58 percent in 1981 over the previous year's level — has become particularly disturbing, an ominous harbinger of what may lie ahead unless the country moves to put its house in order.[32]

Indeed, unless the Republic gives its full attention to providing jobs for the thousands of young people coming into the labor force each year in the decades ahead, a two-class society will undoubtedly emerge. One — the middle and professional classes, the public servants and the private entrepreneurs — will covet their comparatively affluent lifestyles and their established political clout. The other — the underclass of the unemployed and the deprived, separate and unequal — will pour out of the urban ghettos that ring the cities and towns.

The IRA will have its sea.

• • •

Nor was the government's ability to deal with the formidable economic problems it confronted made easier by the instability of successive governments: two general elections in seven months and a third in the offing had subordinated government to the demands of electioneering. The 1981–82 coalition government of Garret FitzGerald was a minority government, and therefore weak. The Fianna Fáil government of Charles Haughey was a minority government and therefore weak. It governed either with a view to holding on to its precarious position or with a view to positioning itself for the next general election. Unfortunately, neither had much to do with ameliorating the public welfare.

When elections prove to be inconclusive, the temptation to

barter with minority parties for their support is irresistible. Fine Gael's willingness after the February 1982 election to abandon those aspects of its platform that had brought down its coalition government in the first place only made it look inept and insincere, while Fianna Fáil's preposterous arrangements with Tony Gregory managed to make even the cynical wince: the price of power had no upper bound.

And the temptation to use crucial by-elections as opportunities to spread the Exchequer's largess is also irresistible. Haughey gambled on having a by-election in Dublin West in May 1981, in order to secure an overall majority. Not only did the gamble fail, but the economic cost in terms of election "strokes" — the tax sanctions, mortgage subsidies, and advance payments of welfare allowances — severely added to the budget deficit, compromising both the government's integrity and its economic plans. Moreover, the fact that the government could fall at any moment made the temptation to engineer its fall more irresistible. Thus, a less than responsible government faced a less than responsible opposition. Government was irresolute and was seen to be irresolute. Politicians manipulated and were seen to manipulate. They urged restraint and practiced abandon. They sounded the warning and turned off the alarm, their actions a travesty of their words. In one move of astonishing political cynicism, the government decided to increase Parliament allowances by up to 50 percent the same week it imposed a pay pause on the public sector.* Little wonder, perhaps, that an EEC poll showed that faith in democracy was on the decline in Ireland.[33] And less wonder that so few seemed ready to sacrifice for the future.

And then, of course, there was the Haughey factor. He led a badly divided party. He was held in low public esteem. No rumor about him — and they were many — suspended disbelief. Opinion polls showed that he was a liability to his party in the 1982 elections. And the liability persisted. Although he withstood a challenge to his leadership after the general election, he did not emerge secure. Scandals dogged him and their impact was cumulative, bringing into question his judgment, his integ-

* *Irish Times,* 7 August 1982. The increases were subsequently rescinded.

rity, and his style of governance.* There were many within his own party who wanted to oust him. Thus he led with one eye on his government's precarious balance in Parliament, and with the other on his own precarious position in Fianna Fáil. One weakness reinforced the other.

The seemingly pivotal position of the Workers' Party in the emerging scheme of things also raised questions that have yet to be answered satisfactorily. Does the Official IRA still exist? Of course it does, says Daithi O'Conaill: "They [the Workers' Party] have an armed wing. There's no doubt about that. They have maintained elements who have control of weapons and who utilize weapons. They engage in very strong-arm tactics. Anyone living in Belfast is very much aware of the fact that there is an armed section."[34] Of course it doesn't have an armed wing, says Thomas MacGiolla, or if it does, he has no knowledge of it and the Workers' Party has no connection with it. "I certainly have no knowledge of them [the Official IRA]. All I know is that I am convinced and I am aware that there is no question of any military organization in any way associated with us at the present," he said in the course of an interview on RTE.[35] He went on, "I have no reason to think that [the Official IRA] still exists. Certainly it doesn't exist in any way down here [in

* Haughey's election agent, Pat O'Connor, was accused of voting twice in the February elections. Although the charge was dismissed, the grounds were technical, leaving the issue unresolved. The former Fine Gael–Labour coalition Minister for Justice, Mr. Jim Mitchell, T.D., revealed that while Haughey was Taoiseach he had installed a telephone system in his office that would have allowed him to listen in to the conversations of Dáil deputies. Again, although no one accused Haughey of using the system improperly, the insinuation that he had done so hurt. Malcolm McArthur, wanted for the murder of two people, was arrested in the home of Patrick Connolly, the Attorney General. Not only did Haughey fail to demand Connolly's immediate resignation, he allowed him to go to the United States on vacation before eventually recalling him and accepting his resignation. A brother-in-law of Sean Doherty, the Minister for Justice, was charged in an assault case. A witness in the case was unaccountably detained by the RUC in Fermanagh, thereby precluding his appearance in court. Despite Doherty's denial that he was involved in or knew of the arrest, rumors of his frequent interference in police matters persisted. When Haughey characterized the events surrounding the arrest of McArthur as "grotesque, unprecedented, bizarre, and unbelievable," Conor Cruise O'Brien coined the acronym GUBU to describe the performance of Haughey himself in office. The GUBU factor entered the vernacular overnight. See Vincent Browne, "The GUBU Factor."

the South]. There was for some years a suggestion that it may have existed in the North, and I pursued that there for quite a number of years to see any evidence of its existence and I am satisfied that it certainly doesn't exist in any association with us."[36] However, *Magill* magazine asserted a continuing link between the two,[37] and the Workers' Party response — accusing *Magill* of irresponsible gutter journalism and the like — did not adequately rebut *Magill*'s charges. *Magill* concluded that: "The Official IRA is alive and active and almost all of its operators are members of SFWP [Sinn Féin, the Workers' Party]." And that "the Official IRA has been involved in robberies, murders, kneecappings, intimidation and racketeering right up to the present day."[38]

It was perhaps a measure of the national drift that a small party (at the time, the Workers' Party had three representatives in the Dáil) with known past associations with the Official IRA could hold the balance of power in government, and yet few seemed intent on determining whether it continued a clandestine association with the Official IRA — an illegal organization — and, if so, for what purpose. One obvious question: how does the Workers' Party finance its activities? For a small party — the best estimates put membership around one thousand — it has a full-time staff of twenty, mortgage and upkeep costs on at least ten premises it owns in both the North and South, and publishing costs for five periodicals and innumerable political pamphlets. Membership fees, even if they are augmented by "special" collections, simply cannot meet the bill.

• • •

The proposed abortion referendum symbolized the political malaise. Abortion, of course, is illegal in the Republic. And there is no lobby to amend the existing legislation to make abortion any more readily available. None of the churches supports more liberal legislation. Yet a small pressure group — the Pro-Life Amendment Campaign (PLAC) — secured a promise, from both Dr. FitzGerald when he was Taoiseach and Mr. Haughey when he was Leader of the Opposition, to hold a constitutional referendum to prohibit abortion. The Protestant churches — the

Presbyterian Church of Ireland, the Church of Ireland, the Methodist Church, and the Irish Council of Churches — voiced their strong opposition. A "copper-clad" constitutional prohibition in such a complex moral matter was more than they "in Christian conscience" could willingly accept.[39] They felt the issue should be dealt with through the legislation already on the books rather than through a constitutional prohibition that would reflect the teachings of one church — the Catholic Church — that abortion is wrong under all circumstances. Nor was there a groundswell of public support for the amendment — only 41 percent of the public favored a referendum, according to one survey.[40] Nevertheless, the government pressed ahead with its plans to put the issue on the ballot before the end of 1982. And it became a political issue with accusations from elements in Fianna Fáil that FitzGerald had gone "soft" on the issue. The question was no longer abortion but the "traditional values of the Irish people."[41] The struggle, it must never be forgotten, was between two civilizations, and the Gael once again was being called on to "become the saviour of idealism in modern intellectual and social life."[42]

Passage would further damage North-South relations. The referendum itself had the appearance of being confessional, putting the Protestant churches on one side of the issue and the Catholic hierarchy on the other. It would be a movement away from pluralism, powerful ammunition for Northern Unionists to buttress their arguments as to the power and influence of the Catholic Church in the South, proof beyond dispute that Home Rule was indeed Rome Rule. And of course, it would compromise, perhaps irrevocably, FitzGerald's proposed "Constitutional Crusade."*

* For a further discussion of the abortion amendment, see page 406 n.

13

The North: New Elections

> This time last year and right through most of last year I thought that however the IRA had arrived at using their hunger strikes to further their own ends, we would have had a setback for a number of years. In fact the very opposite has occurred. The manipulation, and I say this seriously, the manipulation of the hunger strikes for ulterior, quite mercenary purposes which transcended the morality of death, causing death, has done the IRA more harm and dealt them such a grievous blow as they must regret ever having embarked on that hunger strike.
>
> — Sir Jack Hermon
> Chief Constable, Royal Ulster Constabulary
> 21 May 1982[1]

THE FIRST REACTIONS to the results of the Assembly elections were, like much of what happens in Northern Ireland, wildly exaggerated. Provisional Sinn Féin won five seats — two more than it had been expected to — taking 10 percent of the first-preference votes. The pundits rushed to judgment: extremism was having its day, paramilitarism had triumphed. The beleaguered SDLP won fourteen seats and 20 percent of the first-preference votes, the latter a slight improvement, in fact, over its showing in the 1981 local elections. Again the pundits rushed to judgment: a weary, dispirited, and divided party was on its way to being eclipsed; constitutionalism had collapsed. On the Unionist side, the OUP emerged with twenty-six seats and 30 percent of the first-preference votes, and the DUP with twenty-one seats and 23 percent of the first-preference votes. For the moment, at least, Paisley's juggernaut had been halted — in part, ironically, because of the disarray on the nationalist side and the abominable state of Anglo-Irish relations; for once the bogeymen were suspect, with the specter of sellout less salient and, therefore, less salable. Most surprising, and certainly most overlooked, was the showing of the Alliance Party, which captured ten seats in the Assembly with 9 percent of the first-preference votes. In Northern Ireland, moderation, in whatever guise, when it does express itself, tends to be ignored — somehow it is equated with dullness, not sense.

Also overlooked: only 60 percent of the electorate chose to cast a ballot. Which means that even assuming an equal turnout in the two communities (traditionally, Protestants turn out in considerably larger numbers), at best just one Catholic in five eligible to vote voted for Sinn Féin — hardly the stuff of which revolutionary mandates are made.

Nevertheless, Sinn Féin was perceived to have won, and this perhaps was inevitable since, in the process world, the perceptions of reality are a far more important determinant of attitudes than actual facts. Facts are important only to the extent that they reinforce perceptions. Facts, however, of themselves rarely alter perceptions. Thus, once again in Northern Ireland, what appeared to have happened was more important than what had actually happened. Not that Sinn Féin's success should be disputed: it should not. It should, however, be put in its proper perspective.

The success of Sinn Féin was due to several factors, some fortuitous, some the product of careful planning, and some in the nature of the process itself. First, its successes came early in the counting, and given the slowness with which the proportional representation counting system works, they became the most discussed. In the absence of other results, the only results became the most significant results. The initial impression that Sinn Féin was running neck and neck with the SDLP became an ingrained perception, which even the final results were never quite able to dispel. Second, the vote for Sinn Féin came in areas in which hard-core Republican support was historically strongest. These were the carefully selected areas in which Sinn Féin had chosen to take on the SDLP, in which electoral "shoot and scoot" was most likely to succeed. And it did. Third, since Sinn Féin had not chosen to take on the SDLP in every constituency but only in those in which the SDLP was most vulnerable, its strategic planning optimized its chances of success. Its successes would be clearly perceived to be successes; its failures, given the backdrop, would go unnoticed. Fourth, Sinn Féin brought out its own voters, those who had abstained in the past: the young, the jobless, the ghetto-wise for whom the IRA was not only a symbol of resistance but also a symbol of hope. To this extent Sinn Féin's success was due to Britain's arrogance and in particular to Mrs. Thatcher's intransigent, disdainful position during the hunger strikes. Had she not "won" that round, putting the IRA in its proper place, and gone on to more heraldic triumphs in the Falklands? She had, however, forgotten that some mythologies are real: that it is those who suffer the most who do in fact conquer. She forgot about internment, the rubber bullets and the plastic bullets, the house searches and the indiscriminate screenings, the prisons and the repressive security laws, manifestly more repressive when violations by the security forces were allowed to go unpunished. She forgot about the joblessness and the fierce sectarian nationalism in Fermanagh and South Tyrone and mid-Ulster. She forgot that some things do not change, that the "integrity" of the quarrel is immutable. But the hard-core Republican supporters did not. Because they had not put candidates forward in the past, they had not been heard from. Because they had not been heard from, they were assumed not to exist. Because Britain would not face up to the situation in Northern Ireland, she could not face up to the facts: that hard-core Republican support exists; that hard-core anti-Britishness exists. For the British themselves have seen to that. Thus Provisional Sinn Féin mobilized the neglected, the young with the long memories and the old with the short ones, and they made themselves heard. What they said, however, was neither new nor even frightening, only obvious. What may yet be more frightening is how Loyalists ultimately respond to what they see as confirmation of their worst fears.

The SDLP, on the other hand, was in a no-win situation almost from the beginning. The divisions within the party were real, and other factors were at work, adding to its dilemmas. First, the apathy of SDLP supporters: a survey prior to the election found that 49 percent of SDLP supporters were opposed to the policy of abstentionism.[2] The Alliance Party's surprising showing indicates, perhaps, the extent of the SDLP's misjudgment of voter sentiment on the issue. Second, abstentionism reduced the SDLP to Sinn Féin's level: the differential became the question of violence, which was, in the context of the "targeted" constituencies, more of a consideration to those who did not live in areas of violence than to those who did. Third, the failure to contest Fermanagh–South Tyrone in 1981 had undermined not only the SDLP's credibility but also its raison d'être: the contesting of elections and the settlement of differences in a parliamentary tradition. Once the electoral yardstick is conceded even in principle, it is difficult to redeem in the brutality of practice. Once the political lines on abstentionism were blurred, the unblinkered became the more committed. Fact: hard-core Republicans have no blinkers. Fourth, John Hume had no lifeline. James Prior's statements that there could be no parliamentary tier to the Anglo-Irish Council without the establishment of a Northern Ireland Assembly,[3] that "recent events"—the deterioration of relations between the Republic and Britain, owing in part to the Republic's position on the Falklands and Haughey's dismissive, antagonistic attitude toward Prior's initiatives—would delay a parliamentary tier, and finally his observation, in September, that Anglo-Irish talks should be shelved for a period to allow both sides "a period of reflection"[4] put the SDLP in an untenable position. For Prior either could not or would not hold out to Hume what Hume needed most—the promise of an Anglo-Irish parliamentary body—if abstentionism was to be seen as a positive act to bring about a positive result rather than a negative reaction in the absence of a coherent strategy.

Nor would Haughey come to Hume's aid. His insistence that his government would not consider an Anglo-Irish parliamentary body until the Northern Assembly was dead and buried put Hume in a double bind:[5] the chess player had no chess board. Prior would not offer and Haughey would not give. Nor would Haughey even endorse the SDLP in the election itself. In an interview with the Belfast Catholic paper the *Irish News* on 19 October, during which he was asked what advice he had to offer nationalist voters, he conspicuously avoided referring to the SDLP, committing himself instead only to the vague statement that "it is important that the view of the nationalist community should be clearly registered so that they cannot be underestimated or misrepresented subsequently."[6] The *Irish Times* noted, wryly, that "the absence of any direct or indirect criticism of candidates supporting violence such as Sinn Féin was regarded in some quarters as significant."[7] The understatement must have made John Hume wince.

• • •

Despite formidable obstacles, the SDLP did not fail. Sinn Féin, however, did win. In politics, reality, of course, is subordinated to expectations. Winners become losers when the margin of winning is less than conventional expectations. And losers become winners when the margin of loss is less than conventional expectations. By doing better than expected, winning five rather than three seats, Sinn Féin appeared to make the SDLP do worse. Indeed, had the SDLP won one more seat it would have been lauded for holding its own.

The impact, therefore, was psychological and on the side of Sinn Féin. Propaganda would have its day.

The tragic irony, of course, is that the IRA once again had to fine-tune its military campaign; the targets: RUC and UDR personnel. While the political campaign was under way, the military campaign was held in check. Now the balance had to be redressed. Within the movement the hard men wanted their day, too, particularly since there were indications that the movement's more militant members were deserting it for the INLA, which practiced a far more indiscriminate ruthlessness and had no predilection for politics. And of course the IRA attempted to use the election results as a "mandate" for their actions, and of course the Loyalists believed them. And now that the Loyalists had "their" parliament, perhaps they could be nudged to take the final, fateful, step.

Ian Paisley, too, would want his day.

• • •

Ultimately Prior's cleverness worked against him. His calculations that the SDLP would contest the elections were correct. But his calculation that only the SDLP would speak for the nationalist community was incorrect. His failure to take account of Sinn Féin — to realize that Sinn Féin was out to undermine the SDLP as the voice of nationalism in Northern Ireland, and to appreciate Sinn Féin's relative strength, given the circumstances of the preceding year — undermined a central tenet of his thinking: that he could postpone his inducements to the SDLP until after the Assembly elections, when the SDLP had emerged once again as the dominant, indeed the only, voice of the "other tradition." And thus he played into the hands of Sinn Féin, allowing it to assert that the SDLP had achieved nothing after twelve years of "collaboration," making its own abstentionism meaningful in the context of its politics and the SDLP's meaningless in the context of its past behavior. The arrogance of Prior's rationality mocked the rationality of Sinn Féin's arrogance. And the latter won.

In that sense the election results confirmed the obvious: the IRA does represent something, and that something has a cohesive and potent constituency. It represents a minority of the minority in Northern Ireland, its maniacal determination giving it a political importance that exceeds its actual support.

Ultimately the IRA cannot be left out of the process. But neither can it be given in to. Northern Ireland cannot resolve that intractable impasse. Nor can Britain. Only the South can. And if she does not face up to that responsibility, there will continue to be no alternatives in the North. And there will continue to be murder.

James Prior gave John Hume no rope. But James Prior may have hanged himself. He got his election, a short-term goal, but once again it was not part of a long-term plan. Once again Britain would not coerce the Loyalists. Nor would she spell out her long-term intentions. And once again the short-term results would impede, perhaps preclude, long-term alternatives.

14

The Uncivil Wars

There is no point in having a bipartisan approach [toward Northern Ireland] if it is the wrong one.

— Charles J. Haughey
27 February 1983[1]

IN EARLY OCTOBER, Haughey's opponents within the party moved against him when they put a motion of no confidence in his leadership to a meeting of the Fianna Fáil Parliamentary Party. Although the motion was defeated, 58–22, the debate was acrimonious and the dissidents were openly unrepentant, exuberantly, even defiantly, recalcitrant. The charges and countercharges, the intensive lobbying, the complaints of strong-arm tactics and suggestions of harassment and intimidation, left the impression of a party in deep and bitter disarray, the divisions palpable, ugly, and unbridgeable. Once again Haughey had persevered, yet the prevailing view was that his days as party leader were numbered, that he had lost the moral authority to go on. But Haughey refused to accept what appeared to be so obvious to others. Confidence in him both in the country at large and in his own party may have been severely wanting, but his confidence in his own ability to survive was unshakable. He would not stand down. Nor would he be pushed, cajoled, or gently reasoned out of office. For the moment he could appeal over the heads of his parliamentary colleagues to their grassroots constituencies. And for the moment that control was sufficient.

But there were some events he could not control: the sudden death of Dr. Bill Loughnane, T.D. for Clare, on 18 October, and the severe heart attack suffered by Jim Gibbons, T.D. for Carlow–Kilkenny, two days later, undermined his government's precarious position in the Dáil. To survive it would need not only the support of the independents Gregory and Blaney, but of the Workers' Party, and that, it turned out, was not forthcoming.

The ostensible reason for the Workers' Party decision to put the country to its third general election in fifteen months was its opposition to the cuts in public expenditure called for in "The Way Forward," the government's new economic plan, which was published on 21 October and taken up for debate when Dáil Éireann resumed on 26 October.

"The Way Forward" was Fianna Fáil's belated attempt to deal with the interminable economic crisis. The budget deficit would be eliminated in four years. Sharp reductions in government spending, especially in health and social welfare benefits, a ceiling on civil service numbers, and increasing tax revenues as a result of a projected 5 percent annual increase in economic growth would bring about the desired results. However, achieving a 5 percent rate of expansion depended on what the *Irish Times* called a series of "heroic assumptions" about the behavior of the country's trading partners that led to the comforting—and convenient—conclusion that Ireland would increase her exports dramatically by cutting deeply into foreign markets. Somehow she would miraculously improve her competitive position, despite the fact that the plan itself estimated that inflation would increase 13 percent in 1983 and between 8 percent and 9 percent thereafter.

Yet even the most heroic assumptions could not disguise the realities behind the employment situation: if all the plan's targets were met—and some were unrealistic to the point of being merely wishful—unemployment would still increase in both 1983 and 1984, and almost a hundred thousand people would be out of work in 1986.

On 4 November the Workers' Party voted with Fine Gael to bring down the government, a decision greatly facilitated by divisions within the Labour Party. For the Labour Party, too, was in disarray, following the resignation of party leader Michael O'Leary and his defection to Fine Gael after a disagreement with his party colleagues on the question of a future coalition with Fine Gael. The Workers' Party seized the moment to capitalize on Labour's divisions and cut into Labour's share of the vote, thereby consolidating its claims to being the workingman's party.

• • •

The issue of the election was Haughey. Not that he did not try to distract attention from himself. First, he tried to make abortion the issue. The day before his government fell, it submitted the wording for the constitutional amendment to the Dáil. "The state," the new amendment would read, "acknowledges the right of the unborn, and with due regard to the equal right of the mother, guarantees in its laws to respect, and as far as practicable, by its laws to defend and vindicate that right." Fine Gael, Haughey charged, "could not be trusted" to put the amendment to the people.[2] On the contrary, FitzGerald immediately replied, Fine Gael would, if elected, put the amendment to the people no later than 31 March 1983.[3] FitzGerald, it appeared, had learned something about power, and if the price of power was his imprimatur on a piece of sectarian legislation, he would pay, not gladly, perhaps, but nevertheless in hard currency. For the moment at least, he was deaf to the opposition of the Presbyterian Church, the Methodist Church, the Church of Ireland, and the Irish Council of Churches.*

* Ultimately, the abortion issue proved to be a matter of acute embarrassment to FitzGerald. In February 1983, the Attorney General advised FitzGerald that the proposed amendment was unworkable, that it might, in fact, legalize abortion. FitzGerald's government, after some vacillation, came up with new wording, to wit: "That nothing in [the] Constitution shall be invoked to invalidate any provision of a law on the grounds that it prohibits abortion." The Protestant churches indicated that they found the new wording less unacceptable. But the Catholic bishops and Fianna Fáil would have none of it. The hierarchy openly

Although the abortion issue fizzled, Haughey was unfazed: if not abortion, perhaps Northern Ireland. FitzGerald, he charged, could not be trusted on the "National Question": FitzGerald was the tool of a British government actively working on his behalf, interfering once again in Irish affairs. Fianna Fáil leaflets were unabashedly unsubtle: "Thatcher wants Garret. Do you?" they asked. But the public wouldn't buy it: only 5 percent thought of Northern Ireland as an issue.[4] Ironically, it was FitzGerald himself who gave Fianna Fáil an issue when he called for an all-Ireland court and an all-Ireland police force to combat terrorism. The public was decidedly unreceptive, fearful that such a step would inevitably lead to a spillover of the violence. It could lead to worse, Fianna Fáil charged — indeed, to nothing less than RUC patrols in the streets of Dublin.[5] For the first time in the campaign Fianna Fáil had the initiative. But it hardly mattered; the overriding issue was Haughey's own credibility.

Provisional Sinn Féin did not contest the elections, a clear indication of its developing political sense. It had decided to nominate candidates for elections in the South only when they could make an "unanswerable case" that they would be elected. None could make that case in November 1982, and therefore none would stand. The impression created by the Assembly elections would not be dissipated. Failure to make an impact in

---

intervened on behalf of the Fianna Fáil wording, despite the bitter opposition of the other churches. John Cooney, News Focus Editor of the *Irish Times,* wrote, "In siding with the pro-amendment lobbyists, a pressure group, the bishops have given an unexpected belt of the crozier to Dr. FitzGerald, the Dáil, the Protestant Churches, and some Catholic theologians and laity. They have demoted legislative democracy by endeavouring to inject a theocratic dimension to the 1937 Constitution." The Church of Ireland Primate, Dr. Armstrong, said that the two wordings embodied the theological position of the Catholic Church. "This is the Mother and Child Act all over again," he said in an interview on RTE on 3 April. "Can you argue and can you force a moral theology on a whole people which is symptomatic of only one church?" (*Irish Times,* 4 April 1983). On 27 April the government's proposed wording was defeated by 87 votes to 65, with eight of Dr. FitzGerald's own backbenchers voting against him. The Fianna Fáil wording was then accepted by 87 votes to 13, and that wording became the amendment that would be put to the electorate in the referendum. It was, said Church of Ireland Dean Victor Griffin, "a bad day's work."

the South could only undermine the impact Sinn Féin had made in the North. Uncertain returns were not worth certain risks, and thus the policy of "electoral scoot."

On 24 November, the South went to the polls once again. Perhaps the major surprise was not that Fianna Fáil lost out to the combined opposition but that it managed to do so well under the circumstances, testimony to the enduring strength of the party at the grassroots level. It commanded 45 percent of the first-preference votes, down only 2 percent since February, but it lost six seats, down from eighty-one to seventy-five. Fine Gael took seventy seats, Labour sixteen, and the Workers' Party just two. A coalition government of Fine Gael and Labour was back, and with it, for the moment, a semblance of stability, although a significant element within the Labour Party was not overly enthusiastic with the new arrangement. The new government's position on Northern Ireland was conspicuously at odds with Fianna Fáil's. It called for "the establishment of effective devolved political institutions in Northern Ireland with participation of both communities there" and the "full recognition of the Irish identity of the nationalist section of the population there on a par with existing recognition of the British/Irish identity of the Unionist section of the population."[6]

• • •

The Northern Ireland Assembly struggled into existence when elected members from the Alliance, the DUP, and the OUP met at Stormont on 11 November. The DUP and the Alliance teamed up to elect Jim Kilfedder, an independent Unionist, as Presiding Officer. Kilfedder had left the OUP in 1979 because he felt that the leadership had succumbed to the thinking of Enoch Powell on integration. The maneuverings that attended his election exposed the divisions between the DUP and OUP, and more significantly, perhaps, within the OUP itself — between the Molyneaux stalwarts who continued to favor integration, their public positions to the contrary, and the McCusker stalwarts who saw devolution as the way forward.

Within days, the Assembly had moved from being a "talking shop" to being a squabbling one. The OUP fought with Kilfedder over the allocation of scrutiny committee assignments, the Alliance fought with the OUP over the appointment of a Catholic as chairman of the Committee on Education, and everyone fought with Jim Prior over security.

At one time or another in the opening months, every party threatened to boycott the proceedings. Procedures broke down; petty bickering held up progress on the most trivial of matters. The Assembly sputtered and stalled, unsure of its direction, unable to agree on anything other than the need for more stringent security measures. Some members seemed determined to make it fail, and for obvious reasons: if an Assembly could not carry out the minimal functions within its jurisdiction, even in the absence of the SDLP's participation, Britain would have no option but to continue Direct Rule indefinitely, and the indefinite had a way of becoming permanent.

Meanwhile, murder had acquired its own momentum. Between the Assembly elections, which took place on 21 October, and 16 November, sixteen people were either gunned down or blown to bits. The pattern was familiar: the IRA or the Irish National Liberation Army would kill a policeman or a member or former member of the UDR; and the Protestant paramilitaries would kill a Catholic. The INLA, frenetically active, was convinced that it could at last wrest the military initiative from the IRA. The climax of its campaign came on 6 December when it detonated a bomb at the Droppin' Well pub-cum-disco at Ballykelly, County Derry, which was frequented by off-duty British soldiers. Sixteen people — twelve soldiers and four civilians — died on the spot; another civilian died later and sixty-six others were injured, some seriously and permanently. Within the week, two INLA members were shot dead by the RUC at a checkpoint on the outskirts of Armagh; and shortly afterwards, amid mounting allegations that the security forces had been given shoot-to-kill orders, Prior confirmed the existence of special antiterrorist squads within the police force but denied that they had been given orders to kill suspects. The statistics did not support him: security forces had gunned down seven people — all but one of whom were members of the IRA or INLA — in the ten weeks following the Assembly elections.[7] John Hume was outraged. The British, he thundered, had abandoned the rule of law.[8] Within the SDLP, disillusionment ran deeper. The SDLP had come full circle: they were almost all Green now.

And Harold McCusker talked of the secret thoughts that came to him in the dead of night. The two communities, he said, were "mutually hostile." They didn't live together, few worked together; there was little cultural interaction, no educational contact. Protestants, he said, had "a simple choice." Either they gave in to the Provos and let them have what they wanted or they made a decision "to put them out of business for good by using whatever methods and all methods" they could.[9] Did he mean civil war? Yes, he said, he did.

• • •

There were other secrets. And they almost tore Fianna Fáil asunder. Although Haughey had lost the election, he appeared to have consolidated his own position as leader of the party. Many of the leading members of the "gang of twenty-two" had fared poorly at the polls. Five lost their seats. Others, though reelected, saw their margins shrink. The Parliamentary Party endorsed his leadership, and for the moment he appeared to have gained a respite. The dissidents were willing to wait, for they had no obvious course of action and no acceptable alternative to Haughey was available. Haughey took up his duties as Leader of the Opposition with relish and vigor, wasting no time in drawing attention to the divisions between the Coalition partners as they scrambled to put together their fiscal 1983 budget.

And then the bugging scandal broke. First came the government's announcement that the telephones of two prominent journalists had been tapped at the behest of the former Minister for Justice, Sean Doherty. Although no laws had been broken, the circumstances of the tapping were questionable. The government sought and received the resignations of the Garda Commissioner and the Deputy Commissioner in charge of security, who was a close personal friend of Haughey's. At first, the Fianna Fáil front bench took an aggressive stand, deploring "the damaging efforts of [the] government to exploit the security services which provide a vital and essential function, for political purposes."[10] But it quickly became clear that it was Doherty either alone or with the knowledge of others who had done the exploiting. Both journalists had written extensively and knowledgeably of the infighting within Fianna Fáil. The wiretaps, it was obvious, were intended to flush out the source of Fianna Fáil leaks, even though the leadership struggles of the party were hardly the stuff of national security. And then came the government's second bombshell: in the course of its investigation into the wiretapping, it had discovered that Ray McSharry, the former Tanaiste (Deputy Prime Minister), and Haughey's closest colleague in Fianna Fáil, had bugged a conversation with Dr. Martin O'Donoghue, a leading dissident who had resigned from the Cabinet rather than support Haughey during the October leadership struggle. The recording equipment had been supplied by the Deputy Garda Commissioner in charge of security, who later arranged for the tape's transcription. Both McSharry and Doherty immediately resigned from the Opposition front bench, and calls on Haughey to step down became a groundswell. But he would not budge, despite the fact that he himself had agreed, before the full details were available, that he would have to share the responsibility if wiretapping had occurred, since "any Head of Government must take responsibility for anything that happens during his Administration."[11] Now he denied knowledge of both goings-on, the inference being that without knowledge he had no responsibility. But the damage appeared to be insurmountable, and the questions were eerily familiar: what did he know and when did he know it? On both counts the answers were far from unequivocal.

Those who had stood with him in October turned against him. First the parliamentary members, and then the party's National Executive. The message was uniform and brutal: he must go. Contamination had befouled the party. The intrigues, the abuses of power, the unctuously phrased inquiries into who might be financially compromised if they failed to support Haughey, and the hints of possible financial support for those who might be persuaded to change their minds had dirtied the once proud party of the austere and frugal de Valera. Still, Haughey would not go. He was beyond consideration of party or country, perhaps even of self, stranded on the outer edge of a dark, abysmal consciousness. For him, too, only the enemies were real.

Once again, he reached out to the constituencies over the heads of the parliamentary deputies, charging that "the selective revelations by the present government of security information of a kind never before disclosed by any previous administration was now being exploited to damage Fianna Fáil."[12] And that "if the forces hostile to Fianna Fáil and everything it stands for were ever to taste the triumph of bringing down one Fianna Fáil leader by these tactics, no future leader could ever again hope to withstand them successfully." Fianna Fáil was heir to "the true Republican tradition," it was a party neither of the left nor of the right but rather "the party of the nation." The people of Ireland, he said, "must cherish and enhance their own way of life, their separate identity, their values and their cultures," and "Fianna Fáil's purpose must always be to uphold the cause of the unity of Ireland, her national independence, and her right to decide her place and her role in international affairs." In short, for Haughey and his partisans, his struggle for political survival was one more engagement in the battle between two civilizations. Some things served a ubiquitous purpose.

He prevailed: against all odds and despite the confident predictions of the media, of his political opponents, and even of some of his own supporters. At a climactic meeting on 7 February the Parliamentary Party voted 40–33 to endorse his leadership. For the moment the leadership struggle was over, and the party's direction set.

But the divisions will not go away. They may in fact be terminal. Perhaps, like the once monolithic Unionist Party, Fianna Fáil will disintegrate under the weight of an internal dissension whose fires it cannot smother, and form itself into two mutually hostile parties — Official Fianna Fáil and Provisional Fianna Fáil, as it were — each claiming to be the true voice of constitutional Republicanism. But even if this does not happen, Fianna Fáil may find in the near future that for the first time since 1932, it is no longer the largest political party in the state. In recent years Fine Gael's electoral performance has been nothing short of spectacular. In 1977 it held 43 of the 148 parliamentary seats, and in 1983 it held 70 of 166. It has succeeded brilliantly in capturing the urban vote, and if it continues to do so, a Fine Gael ascendancy may shortly become a reality.

Haughey's continued leadership will make Fianna Fáil even more stridently nationalistic. Unable to deal with the present, the party takes refuge in the past, substituting atavism for purpose. While he stays on, it will be difficult to achieve rapprochement between Fianna Fáil and Fine Gael on Northern Ireland, and there will be little prospect of bipartisanship, despite the agreement of the two parties to sit with the SDLP in an all-Ireland forum to draw up a blueprint for a "new Ireland."*

* The looming prospects for a general election in Britain put pressure on both Fine Gael and Fianna Fáil to respond in some positive way to John Hume's call for a Council for a New Ireland (see p. 382n). If Hume had not been able to secure the Southern parties' agreement to some kind of forum, Provisional Sinn Féin, which was set to target SDLP candidates in the Westminster election, would have had powerful political ammunition to show that Hume was politically impotent and that his policies were politically bankrupt. If they had been able to point out that Hume could not persuade anyone — even the supposedly nationalist Southern politicians — to back his proposals, then they could ask just who would. Hume, on the other hand, was in a position of being able to forcibly point out to both Haughey and FitzGerald that if they were not prepared to bury their differences for the moment, there might well be no SDLP around to accommodate after the Westminster elections, unless they gave him the semblance of a campaign platform to counter Provisional Sinn Féin. Sometimes "blue smoke and mirrors" are the substance of politics — the appearance of agreement is as important as agreement itself. The *Irish Times* in an editorial on 14 March noted, perhaps a little skeptically, that "we will have to wait and see just how far the cooperation of Fianna Fáil goes."

Some weeks later, the leaders of the four parties (Fianna Fáil, Fine Gael, Labour, and the SDLP) agreed on the forum's make-up. Fianna Fáil would appoint nine members, Fine Gael eight, Labour five, and the SDLP five. In addition, each party could nominate a number of alternates: Fianna Fáil four, Fine Gael three, Labour two, and the SDLP five. Forum meetings would take place at Dublin Castle under the chairmanship of Colm Ó'hEocha, President of University College, Galway. The first session — and the only one that would be conducted in public — was scheduled for 30 May. Three weeks before that, Dr. FitzGerald said in the Dáil, in response to a question, that he felt it was appropriate "to leave the question of a Constitutional Review to one side during the relatively brief life of the Forum." (*Irish Times*, 11 May 1983.) Meanwhile, the British Prime Minister, Mrs. Thatcher, called for a general election to take place on 9 June.

Captive to the past, Fianna Fáil will ransom the future. Nor is there any reason to believe that a new leader could move Fianna Fáil off its present irredentist course. For a new leader, if he were to hold the party together, would have to emphasize traditional party values and aspirations — a change in direction, even if only symbolic, would deepen the divisions, perhaps to the point of schism.

• • •

Not that division is the exclusive preserve of Fianna Fáil. Indeed, the story of Ireland today — North and South — is the story of endemic division, symptomatic of the larger illness, a creeping paralysis of will choking off political dialogue at every turn, its debilitating contagiousness more pervasive because of the seemingly irreconcilable divisions between the two parts of Ireland and within Northern Ireland. Only Fianna Fáil's is so obvious because it is so public. But for others, the divisions are no less real even if they are less manifestly self-destructive. They exist: within Labour over coalition, especially when the harsh economic measures necessary to straighten out the South's fiscal affairs hurt the constituencies Labour represents, once again posing for the party fundamental questions of identity and direction; between the Coalition partners over strategies to pursue, and tradeoffs to make, in order to achieve economic and social harmony; between Fianna Fáil and the Coalition over almost every issue of substance; within the Official Unionist Party over devolution; between the Official Unionist Party and the Democratic Unionist Party for leadership of the Protestant community in Northern Ireland; within the Social Democratic and Labour Party over a course of action to follow; between the Social Democratic and Labour Party and Provisional Sinn Féin for leadership of the Catholic community in Northern Ireland; within Provisional Sinn Féin between the traditional nationalists and the radical socialists; between the IRA and the INLA in the struggle for military leadership; within the Ulster Defence Association between those who would pursue a political course and those who will not; between the Ulster Defence Association and fringe Protestant paramilitary organizations for the position of paramilitary pre-eminence; between the "haves" — the working — and the "have-nots," the 15 percent of the work force in the South and the 20 percent in the North who are out of work; between the Catholic Church and the Protestant churches over mixed marriages and the abortion referendum; and between every party, constitutional or unconstitutional, North or South, Republican or Loyalist, Catholic or Protestant, and the British government. Ireland is indeed "an island of comfortless noises."

Thus the opening months of 1983. For Ireland it was very definitely not the best of times.

Notes
Bibliography
Index

Notes

When author and short title alone are given herein, full references will be found in the Bibliography.

The Players

1. Ken Heskin, *Northern Ireland: A Psychological Analysis*, p. 38.
2. W. D. Flackes, *Northern Ireland: A Political Directory*, p. 48.

Introduction

1. Morris Frazer, *Children in Conflict*, dust jacket.
2. Seamus Heaney. "Triptych: II Sibyl." In *Field Work* (New York: Farrar, Straus & Giroux, 1979), p. 13.
3. Robert Kee, *The Most Distressful Country*, pp. 7, 8.
4. F.S.L. Lyons, "The Burden of Our History," p. 22.
5. Ibid.
6. Desmond Fennell, "The Northern Ireland Problem," pp. 2–3.
7. John Hunter, "An Analysis of the Conflict in Northern Ireland," p. 15.
8. Ibid.
9. Winston Churchill, quoted in A.T.Q. Stewart, *The Narrow Ground*, p. 14.
10. J. Bowyer Bell, "The Chroniclers of Violence in Northern Ireland," p. 510.
11. Ibid., p. 513.
12. Ibid.

1. The Anglo-Irish Process: A Question of Consent

1. John Hume, quoted in *Irish Times*, 16 November 1981.
2. These and remarks following are taken from address by the Taoiseach, Dr. Garret FitzGerald, T.D., to the Sandymount Branch of Fine Gael, 9 December 1981.
3. Material for the profile of Charles Haughey is drawn from Vincent Browne (ed.), *Magill Book of Irish Politics*.

4. See Vincent Browne, "The Making of a Taoiseach."
5. Remarks taken from the presidential address by the Taoiseach, Mr. Charles J. Haughey, T.D., at the Forty-ninth Fianna Fáil Ard Fheis, Royal Dublin Society, Dublin, 16 February 1980.
6. Meeting between Mr. Haughey and Mrs. Thatcher, Joint Communiqué, 21 May 1981. Reported in *Irish Times*, 22 May 1981.
7. Ibid.
8. Address by the Taoiseach, Mr. Charles J. Haughey, to members of the Fianna Fáil organization in the Metropole Hotel, Cork, Sunday, 27 July 1980.
9. From Charles Haughey's press conference following 8 December 1980 Dublin summit. Quoted in *Irish Times*, 9 December 1980.
10. Ibid. See also Bruce Arnold, "Political Constraints: Dublin," for a thorough analysis of the first Anglo-Irish summit—an analysis that is none too favorable to Mr. Haughey.
11. Meeting between Mr. Haughey and Mrs. Thatcher, Joint Communiqué, 8 December 1980.
12. Press conference following 8 December 1980 Dublin summit. Quoted by Bruce Arnold in "Political Constraints: Dublin," p. 153.
13. Press conference following 8 December 1980 Dublin summit.
14. Address by the Taoiseach, Mr. Charles J. Haughey, to Dáil Éireann. See Dáil Éireann: *Parliamentary Debates*, 11 December 1980, col. 971.
15. These and statements following taken from Joint Communiqué, 8 December 1980.
16. Material for the profile of Garret FitzGerald is drawn from Vincent Browne (ed.), *Magill Book of Irish Politics*.
17. FitzGerald's remarks in this paragraph taken from interview on Radio Telefís Éireann (RTE) program *This Week*, with Gerald Barry, 27 September 1981.
18. Address by the Taoiseach, Dr. Garret FitzGerald, to Seanad Éireann. See Seanad Éireann: *Parliamentary Debates*, 9 October 1981, col. 185.
19. Address by the Taoiseach, Dr. Garret FitzGerald, to the Sandymount Branch of Fine Gael, 9 December 1981.
20. Address by the Taoiseach, Dr. Garret FitzGerald, to Seanad Éireann. See Seanad Éireann: *Parliamentary Debates*, 9 October 1981, col. 182.
21. Address by Professor James Dooge, Minister for Foreign Affairs, to Seanad Éireann. See Seanad Éireann: *Parliamentary Debates*, 8 October 1981, cols. 54–55.

22. Address by the Taoiseach, Dr. Garret FitzGerald, to Seanad Éireann. See Seanad Éireann: *Parliamentary Debates,* 9 October 1981, col. 182.
23. These and remarks following taken from address by Mr. Charles J. Haughey, President, Fianna Fáil, at the unveiling of the Eamon de Valera memorial, Ennis, County Clare, 11 October 1981.
24. Address by Mr. Charles J. Haughey, President, Fianna Fáil, to a conference on Northern Ireland organized by Ogra (Young) Fianna Fáil, 17 October 1981.
25. Ibid.
26. In reply to questions at a lunch given by the Association of European Journalists in Dublin on 20 November 1981. Reported in *Irish Times,* 21 November 1981.
27. Remarks by Dr. FitzGerald at a news conference in the Irish Embassy, London, following the summit, 6 November 1981.
28. Remarks by Mrs. Thatcher at her news conference following the summit, 6 November 1981. Reported in *Irish Times,* 7 November 1981.
29. Meeting between FitzGerald and Thatcher, Joint Communiqué, 6 November 1981.
30. These and remarks following taken from Joint Communiqué, 6 November 1981.
31. These and remarks following taken from Dr. FitzGerald's press conference, London, 6 November 1981.
32. Mrs. Thatcher's press conference, London, 6 November 1981. Reported in *Irish Times,* 7 November 1981.
33. Mr. Haughey's press conference. Burlington Hotel, Dublin, 7 November 1981. Reported in *Irish Times, Irish Independent,* and *Irish Press,* 9 November 1981.
34. Ibid.
35. These and remarks following taken from address by Mr. Charles Haughey to Dáil Éireann. See Dáil Éireann: *Parliamentary Debates,* 10 November 1981, cols. 1580–1602.
36. *Anglo-Irish Joint Studies,* published 11 November 1981.
37. Interview with the then Taoiseach, Dr. Garret FitzGerald, Department of the Taoiseach, Merrion Street, Dublin, 24 December 1981.
38. Interview with Robert McCartney, Europa Hotel, Belfast, 28 December 1981.
39. Interview with James Molyneaux at residence of Rev. Martin Smyth, Belfast, 29 December 1981.

40. Interview with Harold McCusker at his residence, Portadown, County Armagh, 29 December 1981.
41. Interview with John McMichael, UDA Headquarters, Newtownards Road, Belfast, 30 December 1981.
42. Interview with Rev. Ian Paisley, Ravenhill Road, Belfast, 30 December 1981.
43. Meeting with Charles Haughey, Leinster House, Kildare Street, Dublin, 21 December 1981.
44. These and remarks following taken from interview with Dr. Martin Mansergh, Leinster House, Kildare Street, Dublin, 21 December 1981.
45. Remarks from radio interview on BBC 4. Reported in *Irish Times* on 31 October 1981. Mr. Haughey repeated the sentiments in an RTE radio interview on 9 February 1982. Reported in *Irish Times,* 10 February 1982.
46. These and remarks following taken from interview with the then Taoiseach, Dr. Garret FitzGerald, 24 December 1981.

2. The South: A Question of Commitment

1. See Tom Garvin, "Nationalist Elites, Irish Voters and Irish Political Development."
2. See F. S. L. Lyons, *Culture and Anarchy,* pp. 147–77.
3. Conor Cruise O'Brien, *States of Ireland,* p. 121.
4. For definitive treatment of Church-state relations in Ireland see J. H. Whyte, *Church and State in Modern Ireland.* For an account of the mother-and-child-health-scheme crisis, see chapter 7, pp. 196–228; chapter 8, pp. 239–73; and appendices A, B, and C, pp. 377–432; and D. H. Akenson, *United States and Ireland,* chapter 8, pp. 130–67.
5. D. H. Akenson, *United States and Ireland,* pp. 140–41.
6. Ibid.
7. Ibid.
8. Ibid., p. 148.
9. Rev. Felim O'Briain, quoted in Paul Blanshard, *The Irish and Catholic Power,* p. 201.
10. Archbishop Sheehan, quoted in Blanshard, op. cit., p. 127.
11. J. H. Whyte, "Church-State Relations in the Republic of Ireland," paper delivered 30 August 1975, at the Amherst Conference on Northern Ireland. See chapter 8, page 319n, for details of the Amherst Conference.
12. Terence Brown, *Ireland: A Social and Cultural History,* pp. 301–11.

13. Ibid., p. 306.
14. Charles Haughey, quoted by John Henahan in "The Storm over Birth Control Laws," *Boston Sunday Globe,* 15 March 1981.
15. Jack White, *Minority Report,* p. 9.
16. Ibid., pp. 10–12.
17. Ibid., p. 16.
18. Ibid., p. 12.
19. Ibid.
20. Ibid., p. 14. See also Brendan Walsh, "Religion and Demographic Behaviour in Ireland."
21. F.S.L. Lyons, *Culture and Anarchy,* p. 148.
22. Thomas E. Hackey, "One People or Two?" p. 238.
23. Quoted in Hackey, op. cit., pp. 238–39.
24. Ian McAllister, "Political Opposition in Northern Ireland," p. 356.
25. Richard Rose, Ian McAllister, and Peter Mair (hereinafter cited as Rose et al.), "Is There a Concurring Majority About Northern Ireland?"
26. Conor Cruise O'Brien, *States of Ireland,* p. 198. Lynch made his remarks in the course of a nationwide broadcast on Wednesday, 13 August 1969.
27. Quoted in O'Brien, op. cit., p. 256.
28. Rose et al., "Is There a Concurring Majority About Northern Ireland?"
29. Keith Kyle, "Panorama Survey of Irish Opinion."
30. E. E. Davis and R. Sinnott, "Attitudes in the Republic of Ireland Relevant to the Northern Ireland Problem."
31. Ibid., p. 33.
32. Ibid., pp. 44–45.
33. Ibid., p. 51.
34. Ibid. From cross-tabulation supplied by the authors.
35. Ibid.
36. Ibid., p. 97.
37. Economic and Social Research Institute, "Some Issues in the Methodology of Attitude Research," p. 46.
38. See, for example, the results of the Northern Ireland Attitude Survey (Autumn 1978) and the Opinion Research Center Survey (July 1979) reported in *Fortnight,* no. 173 (October/November 1979), p. 6; Rose et al., "Is There a Concurring Majority About Northern Ireland?"; Richard Rose, "Opinion Over Ulster at Sword's Point"; and the Market Research Bureau of Ireland Survey for the *Irish Times* published in the *Irish Times* on 25 May 1982.

39. Ibid.
40. National Opinion Poll, November 1981. Results quoted in *Sunday Independent*, 22 November 1981.
41. Rose et al., "Is There a Concurring Majority About Northern Ireland?"; Market Research Bureau of Ireland/*Sunday Independent* Survey published in the *Sunday Independent*, 7 February 1982.
42. Fine Gael, "Ireland: Our Future Together," p. 10.
43. Ibid.
44. Ibid., p. 11.
45. Brendan Walsh, "Population, Employment and Economic Growth in Ireland."
46. See *Irish Times Annual Review*, 1980.
47. *The Economist*, 24 January 1981, p. 51.
48. *Irish Times* editorial, "The Monster," 30 January 1982.
49. "Quarterly Bulletin," Central Bank of Ireland, Autumn 1982, Statistical Appendix, p. 8.
50. P. Bacon, J. Durkan, J. O'Leary, and S. Scott (hereinafter cited as Bacon et al.), "Quarterly Economic Commentary," December 1982, p. 35.
51. Ibid.
52. Bacon et al., "Quarterly Economic Commentary," May 1982, p. 27.
53. "Quarterly Bulletin," Central Bank of Ireland, Autumn 1982, p. 12.
54. Bacon et al., "Quarterly Economic Commentary," December 1982, pp. 20 and 34.
55. "Quarterly Bulletin," Central Bank of Ireland, Autumn 1982, p. 17.
56. Ibid., p. 9.
57. Derived from data in Bacon et al., "Quarterly Economic Commentary," February 1982, p. 23, and December 1982, p. 34.
58. *Irish Times* editorial, "8000 Casualties," 13 January 1982. In February 1983 the level had already reached 14.5 percent.
59. Vincent Browne, "Economy: The High Road to Disaster."
60. A. Foley and P. Walbridge, "The Socio-Economic Position of Ireland Within the European Economic Community."
61. Data refer to 1977. See J. Sheehan and R. W. Hutchinson, *Demographic and Labour Force Structure.*
62. Ibid., p. 48.
63. Ibid., p. 7.

64. Fine Gael, "Ireland: Our Future Together," p. 15.
65. J. Sheehan and R. W. Hutchinson, *Demographic and Labor Force Structure,* p. 10.
66. R. W. Hutchinson and J. Sheehan, *A Review of Selected Indicators,* p. 47. Data refer to 1978–79.
67. Ibid., p. 45.
68. Ibid., p. 43.
69. Fine Gael, "Ireland: Our Future Together," pp. 30–31. Appendix A, Tables 3 and 4.
70. Brendan Dowling, "Some Implications of a Federal Ireland."
71. John A. Bristow, "All-Ireland Perspectives," p. 150.
72. Rose et al., "Is There a Concurring Majority About Northern Ireland?"
73. E. E. Davis and R. Sinnott, "Attitudes in the Republic of Ireland Relevant to the Northern Ireland Problem." From cross-tabulation supplied by the authors. Overall, 51 percent of respondents were unwilling to pay higher taxes for a united Ireland (p. 53). The Gallup poll for the BBC made a similar finding in 1978. See Keith Kyle, "Panorama Survey of Irish Opinion," p. 32.
74. Keith Kyle, op. cit., p. 32.
75. See, for example, Rose et al., "Is There a Concurring Majority About Northern Ireland?"
76. E. E. Davis and R. Sinnott, "Attitudes in the Republic of Ireland Relevant to the Northern Ireland Problem," p. 52.
77. E. E. Davis and R. Sinnott, "Attitudes in the Republic of Ireland Relevant to the Northern Ireland Problem." From cross-tabulations supplied by the authors. The differences are not significant, but they are suggestive, especially in light of the question's wording. Of those who agreed that Loyalist paramilitary violence would be more of a problem, 65 percent opted for some form of an all-Ireland solution, whereas 74 percent of those who disagreed with the statement opted for an all-Ireland solution. (Overall, 68 percent opted for some form of all-Ireland solution.) On the other hand, of those choosing a unitary state, 34 percent disagreed with the statement that Loyalist paramilitaries would be more of a problem, and 58 percent agreed; of those choosing a federal solution, 38 percent disagreed and 58 percent agreed; of those choosing a devolved power-sharing government, 27 percent disagreed and 70 percent agreed; of those choosing Direct Rule, 32 percent disagreed and 64 percent agreed; of those choosing independence, 23 percent

disagreed and 73 percent agreed; and of those who opted for joint control, 32 percent disagreed and 66 percent agreed. Overall, 33 percent disagreed and 60 percent agreed.

78. Ibid.
79. Ibid., p. 61. See also Rose et al., "Is There a Concurring Majority About Northern Ireland?"
80. E. E. Davis and R. Sinnott, "Attitudes in the Republic of Ireland Relevant to the Northern Ireland Problem," p. 86.
81. Ibid., p. 69.
82. Ibid., p. 74.
83. Ibid.
84. Ibid., p. 76.
85. Keith Kyle, "Panorama Survey of Irish Opinion," p. 29.
86. Computation made from data in Keith Kyle, "Panorama Survey of Irish Opinion," p. 29.
87. Keith Kyle, "Panorama Survey of Irish Opinion," p. 24.
88. Remarks by Mr. Lynch before political correspondents, 15 June 1978, reported in *Irish Times,* 16 June 1978.
89. Ibid.
90. E. E. Davis and R. Sinnott, "Attitudes in the Republic of Ireland Relevant to the Northern Ireland Problem," pp. 64–66.
91. Economic and Social Research Institute, "Some Issues in the Methodology of Attitude Research," p. 48.
92. Ibid., p. 46. Sixty-eight percent agreed with the statement that "the major cause of the problem in Northern Ireland is British interference in Irish affairs."

3. The Social Democratic and Labour Party: A Question of Guarantees

1. For an account of the origins of the SDLP, its role in Northern Ireland politics, and the internal politics and tensions it has had to withstand, see Ian McAllister, *The Northern Ireland Social Democratic and Labour Party.*
2. Ciaran McKeown, "The New Europa Style SDLP."
3. Quoted in *Fortnight,* no. 177 (July/August 1980), p. 11.
4. Interview in *Irish Times,* 31 December 1980. Hume's most comprehensive analysis of the guarantee appears in his "Irish Question:A British Problem"; see also Seamus Deane and Barre Fitzpatrick, "Interview with John Hume." The case against withdrawing the guarantee is made by Michael McDowell in "Removing the British Guarantee."

5. Interview with John Hume at his residence, Londonderry, 28 August 1981.
6. Ibid.
7. These and remarks following taken from interview with John Hume at his residence, Londonderry, 2 December 1981.
8. Interview with John Hume at his residence, Londonderry, 30 December 1981.
9. Interview with John Hume, 2 December 1981.
10. Ibid.
11. Interview with John Hume, 30 December 1981.
12. Interview with John Hume, 2 December 1981.
13. Ibid.
14. Interview with John Hume, 30 December 1981.
15. Ibid.
16. Interview with Robert McCartney, Europa Hotel, Belfast, 28 December 1981.
17. Address by John Hume to SDLP Annual Conference, Newcastle, County Down, 15 November 1981. Reported in *Irish Times,* 16 November 1981.
18. Ibid.
19. Interview with John Hume, 28 August 1981.
20. Interview with James Molyneaux at the residence of Rev. Martin Smyth, Belfast, 29 December 1981.
21. Interview with John Hume, 2 December 1981.
22. Ibid.
23. Interview with Robert McCartney, 28 December 1981.
24. Interview with Paddy Harte, Department of Posts and Telegraphs, General Post Office, Dublin, 2 September 1981.
25. Interview with John Hume, 30 December 1981.
26. Ibid.
27. Interview with John Hume, 2 December 1981.
28. Interview with John Hume, 30 December 1981. Hume's full remarks on that occasion were: "The same objectives [he was referring to Garret FitzGerald's Constitutional Crusade] can be obtained by a solemn declaration from the Dáil guaranteeing the position of Protestantism in any new Ireland, even going so far as to lodge that declaration with the U.N."
29. Presidential address by the Taoiseach, Mr. Charles J. Haughey, T.D., at the Forty-ninth Fianna Fáil Ard Fheis, Royal Dublin Society, Dublin, 16 February 1980.
30. Ibid.

31. Interview with John Hume, 2 December 1981.
32. Ibid.
33. Ian McAllister, "Political Opposition in Northern Ireland," p. 355.
34. Ibid.
35. Ibid., pp. 355–56.
36. See D. H. Akenson, *United States and Ireland,* p. 221.
37. Interview with Harold McCusker at his residence, Portadown, County Armagh, 29 December 1981. The previous interview he refers to took place at the Europa Hotel, Belfast, 25 August 1981.
38. Address by John Hume to SDLP Annual Conference, 15 November 1981. Reported in *Irish Times,* 16 November 1981.
39. Interview with Harold McCusker, 29 December 1981.
40. John Devine, "Polling Time Again in the North's Valley of Hate."
41. Interview with John Hume, 28 August 1981.
42. Ibid.
43. Ibid.
44. Interview with Harold McCusker, 25 August 1981.
45. Interview with Robert McCartney, 28 December 1981.
46. Interview with Jim Allister, Ravenhill Road, Belfast, 27 August 1981.
47. Interview with Ian Paisley, Ravenhill Road, Belfast, 30 December 1981.
48. Interview with James Molyneaux, 29 December 1981.
49. Ibid.
50. Interview with Seamus Lynch, Republican Clubs Headquarters, Springfield Road, Belfast, 26 August 1981.
51. Interview with Oliver Napier, Europa Hotel, Belfast, 14 August 1981.
52. Interview with Paddy Harte, 2 September 1981.
53. Interview with John McMichael, UDA Headquarters, Newtownards Road, Belfast, 30 December 1981.
54. Ibid.
55. John Hume's address to SDLP Annual Conference, 15 November 1981. Reported in *Irish Times,* 16 November 1981.
56. Ibid.
57. Ibid.

4. Official Unionism: A Question of Consistency

1. R. L. McCartney, "The Case for the Unionists."
2. Ibid.
3. Ibid., Foreword.

4. Ibid.
5. Remarks to Seanad Éireann. See Seanad Éireann: *Parliamentary Debates,* 9 October 1981, col. 186.
6. Editorial, *Irish Independent,* 9 October 1981.
7. For a history of the Ulster Unionist Party from its inception in the 1880s to its collapse in the early 1970s, see John F. Harbison, *Ulster Unionist Party.*
8. This statement and those following taken from R. L. McCartney, "The Case for the Unionists," pp. 1–7.
9. For a discussion of the dual minority theory, see H. Jackson, *The Two Irelands.*
10. Interview with Rev. Martin Smyth, Official Unionist Party Headquarters, Glengall Street, Belfast, 17 August 1981.
11. Interview with Robert McCartney, Europa Hotel, Belfast, 28 December 1981.
12. Ibid.
13. Ibid.
14. Interview with James Molyneaux at the residence of Rev. Martin Smyth, 29 December 1981.
15. Ibid.
16. Ibid.
17. See, for example, the survey for *Sunday Times* (London), by Market and Opinion Research International (MORI). The poll indicated that 50 percent of respondents were against the Union, 29 percent were for it, and 21 percent didn't know what they would do. After adjustment for the "don't knows," the poll's findings showed 63 percent against the Union and 37 percent for it. See *Sunday Times,* 21 December 1980. The results were similar to a poll taken in 1975.
18. See, for example, Rose et al., "Is There a Concurring Majority About Northern Ireland?" and Richard Rose, "Opinion Over Ulster at Sword's Point." E. E. Davis and R. Sinnott, in "Attitudes in the Republic of Ireland Relevant to the Northern Ireland Problem," quote a 1978 Gallup poll in which only 25 percent of British respondents thought that the most "workable or acceptable" solution was for Northern Ireland to remain part of the U.K. Twenty-one percent saw unification as the "best" solution; 24 percent thought an independent Northern Ireland was, and 13 percent thought that joint control of Northern Ireland by the British government and the Irish government would be either most acceptable or workable. See p. 61.

19. Interview with James Molyneaux, 29 December 1981.
20. Patrick Buckland, *History of Northern Ireland,* pp. 56–57.
21. John Austin Baker, "Ireland and Northern Ireland," p. 14.
22. Interview with Robert McCartney, 28 December 1981.
23. R. L. McCartney, "The Case for the Unionists," p. 5.
24. *Northern Ireland Hansard,* vol. 16, col. 1090, quoted by G. Bell in *Protestants of Ulster,* p. 40.
25. *Northern Ireland Hansard,* vol. 16, col. 1070, also quoted in Bell, op. cit., p. 40.
26. Quoted in Richard Rose, *Governing Without Consensus,* p. 301. O'Neill made these remarks a few days after resigning as Prime Minister on 28 April 1969.
27. Interview with Robert McCartney, 28 December 1981.
28. Ibid.
29. See Ken Heskin, *Northern Ireland: A Psychological Analysis,* p. 26. According to Rose, 46 percent of Protestants report attendance at church at least once a week, and another 18 percent at least monthly. See Richard Rose, *Governing Without Consensus,* p. 264.
30. Ken Heskin, in *Northern Ireland: A Psychological Analysis* (p. 26), elucidates upon this point.
31. Ibid.
32. For a succinct account of how partition emerged, see J. C. Beckett, "Northern Ireland."
33. See p. 32 for the wording of Articles 2 and 3 of the Constitution.
34. J. C. Beckett, "Northern Ireland," p. 124.
35. Ibid., p. 129.
36. Ian McAllister, "Political Opposition in Northern Ireland," pp. 354–57.
37. See M. W. Heslinga, *The Irish Border as a Cultural Divide,* p. 65, footnote (b).
38. For a survey of the literature on discrimination see J. H. Whyte, "Interpretations of the Northern Ireland Problem." He concludes that "the real question for examination is not whether discrimination has occurred but how much" (p. 260). He cites two comprehensive studies which use 1971 census data. The first concludes that "being a Catholic will, in itself, tend to be a disadvantage, the disadvantage increasingly cumulative throughout the individual's occupational career." (See Joseph Boyle, "Educational Attainment, Occupational Achievement and Religion in Northern Ireland," p. 99.) The second also concludes that there is a striking pattern of cumula-

tive disadvantage. Catholics are much more likely than Protestants to be unemployed. And among the employed, they are more likely than Protestants to be manual workers, in the lower-status, unskilled occupations. (See Edmund Aunger, "Religion and Occupational Class in Northern Ireland.") For an opposite point of view, however, see Christopher Hewitt, "Catholic Grievances, Catholic Nationalism and Violence in Northern Ireland." He concludes that while it "is undeniable that Protestants did on occasion discriminate against Catholics . . . [and that] the Unionist regime was sectarian, making no attempt to recruit Catholics as party members or candidates . . . [nevertheless] an examination of the evidence suggests that Catholic grievances have been exaggerated considerably" (p. 364). See also D. H. Akenson, *United States and Ireland,* pp. 218–22.

39. D. H. Akenson, *United States and Ireland,* p. 222.
40. For a survey of the literature on self-segregation, see J. H. Whyte, "Interpretations of the Northern Ireland Problem," pp. 271–73. See also Gary Easthope, "Religious War in Northern Ireland."
41. For a comprehensive examination of the origins of conditional allegiance, see David W. Miller, *Queen's Rebels: Ulster Loyalism in Historical Perspective.*
42. Richard Rose, *Governing Without Consensus,* p. 205.
43. Ibid., p. 208.
44. Ibid., pp. 209–17.
45. See Arend Lijphart, "Review Article: The Northern Ireland Problem," p. 86.
46. Ken Heskin, *Northern Ireland: A Psychological Analysis,* p. 49.
47. R. L. McCartney, "The Case for the Unionists," p. 5.
48. Richard Rose, *Governing Without Consensus,* p. 214.
49. These and remarks following taken from interview with Harold McCusker, Europa Hotel, Belfast, 25 August 1981.
50. These and remarks following taken from interview with Harold McCusker at his residence, Portadown, County Armagh, 29 December 1981.
51. Interview with Harold McCusker, 25 August 1981.
52. These and remarks following taken from interview with James Molyneaux, 29 December 1981.
53. See W. D. Flackes, *Northern Ireland: A Political Directory,* p. 135.
54. Interview with Robert McCartney, 28 December 1981.
55. Ibid.

5. Paisleyism: A Question of Intent

1. For accounts of Paisley's early activities, see Patrick Marrinan, *Paisley: Man of Wrath,* and David Boulton, *The UVF, 1966–73,* pp. 23–61.
2. Interview with Ian Paisley, Ravenhill Road, Belfast, 30 December 1981. The Carson he refers to is Sir Edward Carson (1854–1935), the Dublin-born attorney who commanded the political opposition to Home Rule.
3. Ibid.
4. M. Perceval-Maxwell, "The Ulster Rising of 1641."
5. Robert Kee, *The Most Distressful Country,* pp. 118 and 121.
6. For a comprehensive exposition of Protestant ideology and the political/religious basis of Loyalism, see Frank Wright, "Protestant Ideology and Politics in Ulster." See also David Roberts, "The Orange Order in Ireland."
7. See Ken Heskin, *Northern Ireland: A Psychological Analysis,* pp. 28–30. Also see Richard Rose, *Governing Without Consensus,* especially pp. 247–74.
8. Extracts from the *Protestant Telegraph* quoted by David Boulton in *The UVF, 1966–73,* p. 63.
9. Ibid.
10. Ibid.
11. *Protestant Telegraph,* 24 November 1981, p. 11.
12. Ibid.
13. Ibid.
14. Ibid.
15. Richard Rose, *Governing Without Consensus,* p. 263.
16. Interview with Ian Paisley, 30 December 1981.
17. The biographical sketch of Paisley is drawn from Patrick Marrinan, *Paisley: Man of Wrath,* pp. 1–22. Other pertinent materials appear in David Boulton, *The UVF, 1966–73,* especially with regard to the early association between Paisley and Protestant paramilitary organizations; and in G. Bell, *Protestants of Ulster* (pp. 46–47). Bell makes the telling observation that "he is not just one of the leaders of the Protestant lower classes, he [Paisley] is a product and manifestation of a large section of them. Unlike Edward Carson, James Craig or Basil Brooke, Paisley is of the people in whose name he speaks,which is one reason he will be there at the end, whatever that is." See also Ed Moloney, "Paisley," and Ken Heskin, *Northern Ireland: A Psychological Analysis,* pp. 111–25.

18. Ken Heskin, op. cit., p. 118.
19. See Richard Rose, *Governing Without Consensus,* p. 254. "He [Paisley] does this [maintains the connection between religion and politics] not only in terms of traditional political values but also in terms of Protestant fundamentalist values that he would argue are as relevant today as they were when Martin Luther nailed his 95 theses to the church door in Wittenberg in 1517."
20. See Frank Wright, "Protestant Ideology and Politics in Ulster," especially pp. 224–32.
21. Interview with Ian Paisley, 30 December 1981. The Protestant population of the Republic, according to the 1971 census, was 4.28 percent.
22. See Richard Rose, *Governing Without Consensus,* pp. 216–17. "Protestants tend to see their regime [Rose was writing before the fall of Stormont] as a bulwark of religious faith against Catholics within the six counties, against the more Catholic Irish outside their Provincial pale, and against the forces of error and darkness everywhere growing stronger in a threatening and increasingly ecumenical world."
23. Ian Paisley, "A Call to the Protestants of Ulster," *Protestant Telegraph,* 9 January 1982, pp. 6–9.
24. Interview with Ian Paisley, 30 December 1981.
25. See Rosemary Harris, *Prejudice and Tolerance in Ulster,* p. 187. "The basic political problem of the poorer Protestant was that to secure his independence from the Irish Republic he had to support politically those whom he neither liked nor trusted." For a review of the literature on intra-ethnic tensions, see J. H. Whyte, "Interpretations of the Northern Ireland Problem," pp. 276–77.
26. See J. H. Whyte, "Interpretations of the Northern Ireland Problem," pp. 274–75.
27. Richard Rose, *Governing Without Consensus,* p. 256.
28. See Frank Wright, "Protestant Ideology and Politics in Ulster," p. 237–38.
29. See Richard Rose, *Governing Without Consensus,* p. 156: "The civil rights demonstrations begun in 1968 posed a novel challenge to the regime, substantively and in tactics. The civil rights groups reversed the tactics of Sinn Féin. Instead of trying to change the regime by refusing recognition of British sovereignty, they sought to change it by claiming full rights as British citizens . . . within a Northern Ireland context . . . The civil rights programme was

revolutionary, i.e. an attempt to transform the regime by sharing political power among Catholics and Protestants within Northern Ireland."

30. See Liam de Paor, *Divided Ulster,* pp. 60–61. Also J. H. Whyte, "Interpretations of the Northern Ireland Problem," p. 266, and F.S.L. Lyons, *Culture and Anarchy,* pp. 137–41.
31. See Russell Murray, "Political Violence in Northern Ireland," pp. 326–29.
32. Interview with Ian Paisley, 30 December 1981.
33. Ibid.
34. Ian Paisley in the *Protestant Telegraph,* 8 August 1981.
35. Ian Paisley quoted in *Irish Times,* 18 January 1982.
36. Ian Paisley, *No Pope Here.*
37. Interview with Ian Paisley, 30 December 1981.
38. Ian Paisley, "A Call to the Protestants of Ulster," *Protestant Telegraph,* 9 January 1982, p. 7.
39. Ibid., p. 8.
40. Ibid., p. 9. Dr. John Girvan was moderator of the General Assembly of the Presbyterian Church.
41. Ian Paisley, quoted in David W. Miller, *Queen's Rebels: Ulster Loyalism in Historical Perspective,* p. 2.
42. Miller (see note 41) first developed this "no nation" theory, as J. H. Whyte ("Interpretations of the Northern Ireland Problem") calls it.
43. Interview with Jim Allister, Ravenhill Road, Belfast, 27 August 1981.
44. See Richard Rose, *Governing Without Consensus,* p. 87, for the full text of the "Ulster Covenant."
45. See "Ulster's Declaration" in the *Protestant Telegraph,* 28 March 1981, p. 16.
46. A.T.Q. Stewart, *The Narrow Ground,* p. 185.
47. Ian Paisley in the *Protestant Telegraph,* 24 November 1981, p. 5.
48. Interview with Ian Paisley, 30 December 1981.
49. Ibid.
50. These and remarks following taken from interview with Jim Allister, 27 August 1981.
51. Ian Paisley in the *Protestant Telegraph,* 3 August 1968, quoted in G. Bell, *Protestants of Ulster,* p. 43.
52. Ian Paisley, "A Call to the Protestants of Ulster," *Protestant Telegraph,* 9 January 1982, p. 7.
53. Ibid.

54. Ian Paisley in the *Irish Times*, 27 November 1971. Quoted in G. Bell, *Protestants of Ulster*, p. 45.
55. David Boulton, *The UVF, 1966–73*, p. 51.
56. Interview with Daithi O'Conaill, Provisional Sinn Féin Headquarters, Parnell Square, Dublin, 4 December 1981.
57. Ibid.
58. Ibid.
59. Interview with John McMichael, UDA Headquarters, Newtownards Road, Belfast, 2 December 1981.
60. Interview with Ian Paisley, 30 December 1981.
61. Interview with James Molyneaux at the residence of Rev. Martin Smyth, 29 December 1981.
62. Ibid.
63. These and remarks following taken from interview with Ian Paisley, 30 December 1981.
64. I am grateful to Hugh Munroe's "The Northern Ireland Question — A Diagnosis" (an unpublished paper) for some of the thoughts expressed here. Munroe's conclusion: ". . . a united Ireland arrived at in a way in which its creation can be seen as an accommodation to the genuine Unionist feelings of many Northern Irish people offers the most honourable . . . solution . . ." This would involve ". . . a new view of Irish nationalism which is open to the idea of permanent links between a united Ireland and Britain . . ."

6. Britain: A Question of Inconsistency

1. See Tom Hadden, "Why Everyone Distrusts British Intentions." Nicholas Mansergh convincingly makes the point in "The Government of Ireland Act, 1920."
2. Quoted by Thomas Jones, *Whitehall Diary*, vol. 3, p. 131.
3. See John Cole, "Security Constraints," p. 127. The strike lasted five years. Withholdings came to £5 million sterling. Arrears are still being paid off.
4. See John McGuffin, *The Guinea Pigs*, for an account of in-depth interrogation practices used.
5. See Kevin Boyle, Tom Hadden, and Paddy Hillyard, "The Facts on Internment."
6. Ibid.
7. For an analysis of security policy between 1968 and 1981, see John Cole, "Security Constraints," and Richard Clutterbuck, "Comment on Chapter Seven: Security Constraints."

8. United Kingdom, Parliament, *Report of the Commission to Consider Legal Procedures to Deal with Terrorist Activities in Northern Ireland* (the Diplock Report).
9. Diplock quoted in John Cole, "Security Constraints," pp. 128–29.
10. See Kevin Boyle, Tom Hadden, and Paddy Hillyard, "Emergency Powers: Ten Years On."
11. Ibid., p. 6.
12. Ibid., p. 7.
13. Amnesty International, *Report of the Amnesty International Mission to Northern Ireland.*
14. United Kingdom, Parliament, *Report of the Committee of Inquiry into Police Interrogation Procedures in Northern Ireland* (the Bennett Report). See also Peter Taylor, *Beating the Terrorists?,* for case histories of abuses in police interrogation in 1977 and 1978 at the Castlereagh, Gough, and Omagh interrogation centers. Taylor points out that "no police officer has ever been successfully convicted of ill-treatment, despite successful civil claims against the RUC and out-of-court settlements." The Director of Public Prosecution chose not to prosecute in 97 percent of the cases brought to his attention, but the decision not to prosecute was not a determination that no assault had occurred.
15. See p. 209n.
16. Paul Johnson, *Ireland: A Concise History,* p. 232.
17. Information on plastic bullets comes from *Fortnight,* no. 182 (July/August 1981), pp. 4–5.
18. Data for security forces refer to February 1983. Data supplied by the Northern Ireland Office, Belfast, 21 February 1983.
19. See *Fortnight,* no. 182 (July/August 1981), p. 6.
20. Data for RUC refer to February 1983. Data supplied by the Northern Ireland Office, Belfast, 21 February 1983.
21. Northern Ireland Attitude Survey, quoted by E. E. Davis and R. Sinnott, "Attitudes in the Republic of Ireland Relevant to the Northern Ireland Problem," p. 86.
22. Ibid.
23. For firearm statistics, see Barry White, "Political Constraints: Belfast," p. 169.
24. Labour Party, *Northern Ireland,* p. 7.
25. Ibid.
26. These and remarks following taken from interview with Don Concannon, House of Commons, Westminster, London, 19 May 1982.
27. Labour Party, *Northern Ireland,* pp. 22–23.

28. Ibid., p. 23.
29. See John Simpson, "Economic Alternatives." About one third of the economic decline is attributed to the violence.
30. These and remarks following taken from interview with James Dunn, House of Commons, Westminster, London, 19 May 1982.
31. See Rose et al., "Is There a Concurring Majority About Northern Ireland?"
32. Ibid.
33. Ibid.
34. Ibid.
35. Ibid.
36. Ibid.
37. Ibid.
38. United Kingdom, Parliament, *Northern Ireland: Constitutional Proposals.*
39. United Kingdom, Parliament, *The Government of Northern Ireland: Proposals for Further Discussion.*
40. *Fortnight,* no. 184 (December 1981/January 1982), p. 15.
41. Ibid., p. 16.
42. *Irish Times,* 14 November 1981.
43. See Conservative Central Office news release, 16 February 1982.
44. Ibid.
45. Ibid.
46. Ibid.
47. Ibid.
48. Ibid.
49. Ibid.
50. These and remarks following taken from interview with James Prior, Stormont Castle, 25 May 1982.
51. Interview with Nicholas Scott, Northern Ireland Office, Great George Street, London, 19 May 1982.
52. Quoted in *Irish Times,* 1 January 1982.
53. Interview with James Prior, 25 May 1982.
54. Interview with Nicholas Scott, 19 May 1982.
55. Ibid.
56. Section One, Northern Ireland Constitution Act, 1973, Chapter 36, Part I, Preliminary, Article 1.
57. See Joint Communiqué of FitzGerald/Thatcher meeting, 6 November 1981.
58. Interview with Nicholas Scott, 25 May 1982.
59. See John Simpson, "Economic Alternatives."

60. Ibid.
61. See John Simpson, "A Review of Economic and Industrial Strategy."
62. Ed Moloney, "British Investment Withdrawal."
63. Ed Moloney, "Depressing Outlook for Unemployed Youngsters."
64. Source for subvention data: Northern Ireland Office, Belfast, 21 February 1983.
65. See *Hansard,* 24 May 1979, for "Additional Costs of the British Army in Northern Ireland." Figures for 1969–80 reproduced in Ed Moloney, "The IRA," p. 16.
66. Interview with Nicholas Scott, 19 May 1982.
67. See Kevin O'Connor, *The Irish in Britain,* pp. 151–52. According to Brendan Walsh, however, "There were 684,000 persons born in the Republic of Ireland recorded as resident in Britain in the 1971 census compared with a 1977 total of 563,000, according to the results of the Labour Force Survey." See Brendan Walsh, "Population, Employment and Economic Growth in Ireland," p. 17.
68. See Tom Nairn, *The Break-up of Britain,* for a left perspective on how the emergence of more radical nationalism in Scotland and Wales will trigger the breakup of Britain because of the near-emergency economic and political conditions of the 1980s.
69. Interview with Paddy Harte, Department of Posts and Telegraphs, General Post Office, Dublin, 2 September 1981.
70. Interview with Dr. Garret FitzGerald, Leinster House, Dublin, 27 May 1982.

7. The IRA: A Question of Certainty

1. Richard Clutterbuck, "Comment on Chapter Seven: Security Constraints," p. 141.
2. Tim Pat Coogan, *The IRA,* p. 478.
3. For an account of IRA activities in the 1970s, see Jack Holland, *Too Long a Sacrifice,* pp. 37–62, 120–51. For a history of the IRA, see J. Bowyer Bell, *The Secret Army 1916–79,* and Tim Pat Coogan, *The IRA.* For IRA strategies, tactics, actions, and prospects see: Mark Patrick Hederman, "Interview with Seamus Twomey"; Vincent Browne, "Interview with a Senior Member of the IRA Leadership," "The New Provo Strategy," and "The IRA's Twenty-Year War"; Ed Moloney, "The IRA"; Richard Kearney, "The IRA's Strategy of Failure"; Paul Wilkinson, "The Provisional IRA: An Assessment in the Wake of the 1981 Hunger Strike"; "The Provos

Have Second Thoughts," *Fortnight*, no. 187 (July/August 1982), pp. 4–5; and Danny Morrison, "The Provos Will Not Lay Down Their Arms."

4. "Northern Ireland: Future Terrorist Trends" is quoted in full in Sean Cronin, *Irish Nationalism*, pp. 339–57.
5. Quoted in Sean Cronin, *Irish Nationalism*, p. 339.
6. Ibid., p. 342.
7. Ibid.
8. Ibid.
9. Ibid., p. 347.
10. Ibid.
11. Ibid.
12. Ibid., p. 356.
13. Irish Council of Churches, Board of Community Affairs, "The H-Block Issue," p. 6.
14. For a full and sympathetic account of the "blanket protest," see Tim Pat Coogan, *On the Blanket*.
15. *The Diary of Bobby Sands*, p. 7.
16. Ibid.
17. Ibid.
18. Ibid.
19. Ibid., pp. 7–8. The allusion to the "risen people" comes from Patrick Pearse's poem "The Rebel":

    And I say to my people's masters: Beware,
    Beware of the thing that is coming, beware of the risen people
    Who shall take what you would not give. Did ye think to conquer the people,
    Or that law is stronger than life or man's desire to be free?
    We shall try it out with ye, ye that have harried and held,
    Ye that have bullied and bribed, tyrants, hypocrites, liars.
20. Interview with Mairead Corrigan Maguire, Peace House, Lisburn Road, Belfast, 29 December 1981.
21. *Fortnight*, no. 183 (October/November 1981), p. 6.
22. Ibid.
23. Ibid.
24. Interview with Daithi O'Conaill, Provisional Sinn Féin Headquarters, Parnell Square, Dublin, 21 August 1981.
25. Cardinal O'Fiaich's statement was issued after his visit to the Maze Prison on 30 July 1978. The full text and the British government's response appear in U.S. Congress, *Northern Ireland: A Role for the United States?*, pp. 93–95.

26. See E. Moxon-Browne, "The Water and the Fish," p. 66.
27. E. E. Davis and R. Sinnott, "Attitudes in the Republic of Ireland Relevant to the Northern Ireland Problem," p. 81.
28. Interview with Mairead Corrigan Maguire, 29 December 1981.
29. *The H. Block: The Hunger Strike in the Maze Prison* (Belfast: The Peace People), p. 7.
30. Kevin Boyle, Tom Hadden, and Paddy Hillyard, "Emergency Powers: Ten Years On," p. 4.
31. See page 263.
32. Cardinal O'Fiaich quoted in U.S. Congress, *Northern Ireland: A Role for the United States?*, p. 94.
33. Gerry Foley, "Bernadette and the Politics of H Block," p. 13.
34. Interview with Daithi O'Conaill at Provisional Sinn Féin Headquarters, Parnell Square, Dublin, 4 December 1981.
35. Ibid.
36. *An Phoblact* (Provisional Sinn Féin's newspaper), 5 November 1981.
37. Interview with Daithi O'Conaill, 4 December 1981.
38. These and remarks following taken from interview with Danny Morrison, Provisional Sinn Féin Headquarters, Falls Road, Belfast, 24 May 1982.
39. Interview with Daithi O'Conaill at Provisional Sinn Féin Headquarters, Parnell Square, Dublin, 2 January 1982.
40. Ibid.
41. Interview with Danny Morrison, 24 May 1982.
42. Ibid.
43. Ibid.
44. Vincent Browne, "The New Provo Strategy."
45. Provisional IRA, *Freedom Struggle*, p. 95.
46. Ibid.
47. Interview with Daithi O'Conaill, 4 December 1981.
48. Interview with Danny Morrison, 24 May 1982.
49. Ibid.
50. Ibid.
51. These and remarks following from interview with Daithi O'Conaill, 4 December 1981.
52. Interview with Danny Morrison, 24 May 1982.
53. Interview with Daithi O'Conaill, 2 January 1982.
54. Ibid.
55. Ibid.

56. Ibid.
57. Interview with Daithi O'Conaill at Provisional Sinn Féin Headquarters, Parnell Square, Dublin, 26 May 1982.
58. Interview with Daithi O'Conaill, 2 January 1982.
59. Interview with Danny Morrison, 24 May 1982.
60. Ibid.
61. Interview with Daithi O'Conaill, 2 January 1982.
62. Interview with Daithi O'Conaill, 26 May 1982.
63. Ibid.
64. Interview with Danny Morrison, 24 May 1982.
65. *An Phoblact,* 5 November 1981.
66. Ibid.
67. *An Phoblact,* 19 November 1981.
68. Sinn Féin, "Éire Nua: The Sinn Féin Policy," p. 4.
69. Ibid.
70. Ibid.
71. Ibid., p. 5.
72. Ibid.
73. Ibid.
74. Ibid.
75. Ibid., p. 11.
76. See F.S.L. Lyons, *Culture and Anarchy,* p. 61.
77. Patrick Pearse, quoted in F.S.L. Lyons, op. cit., p. 87.
78. See John Newsinger, " 'I Bring Not Peace but a Sword.' " He concludes that "the rebels of Easter Week and after saw themselves as fighting in a holy cause that was sanctified by God and were prepared to die for it. John Devoy, Padraic Pearse, Terence McSwiney, Eamon de Valera and the thousands of rank and file Republicans were fighting for both Faith and Fatherland. For them the identification between Catholic and Irish nationalism was absolute" (p. 625).
79. Quoted in Tim Pat Coogan, *The IRA,* p. 593.
80. Frank MacDermot, *Tone and His Times,* Introduction.
81. F.S.L. Lyons, *Culture and Anarchy,* p. 8.
82. Interview with Daithi O'Conaill, 21 August 1981.
83. Interview with Daithi O'Conaill, 4 December 1981.
84. Ibid.
85. See John Dunn, *Modern Revolutions,* pp. 146–72.
86. Ken Heskin, *Northern Ireland: A Psychological Analysis,* p. 85.
87. Ibid.

88. E. Moxon-Browne, "The Water and the Fish," p. 58.
89. E. E. Davis and R. Sinnott, "Attitudes in the Republic of Ireland Relevant to the Northern Ireland Problem," p. 149.
90. Ibid.
91. E. Moxon-Browne, "The Water and the Fish," p. 69.
92. Ibid.
93. Tim Pat Coogan, *The IRA,* p. 473.
94. Tone quoted in Frank MacDermot, *Tone and His Times,* p. 182.
95. See *Fortnight,* no. 180 (March/April 1981), p. 9.
96. See *Fortnight,* no. 183 (October/November 1981), p. 14.
97. E. E. Davis and R. Sinnott, "Attitudes in the Republic of Ireland Relevant to the Northern Ireland Problem," p. 78.
98. E. Moxon-Browne, "The Water and the Fish," p. 61.
99. Sean Cronin, *Irish Nationalism,* p. 345.
100. See E. Moxon-Browne, "The Water and the Fish," pp. 54, 58.
101. Interview with Dr. Martin Mansergh, Leinster House, Kildare Street, Dublin, 21 December 1981.
102. *The Economist,* 23 May 1981, p. 11.
103. Callaghan first publicly advocated an independent Northern Ireland on 2 July 1981. See *Hansard,* vol. 7, no. 133, cols. 1046–53.
104. *Sunday Times,* 16 August 1981.
105. The Labour Party passed the resolution at its annual conference in Brighton on 29 September 1981.
106. See chapter 2, note 38, for references.

8. The Ulster Defence Association: A Question of Uncertainty

1. *Ulster,* vol. 1, no. 3, 1978.
2. Interview with Andy Tyrie, UDA Headquarters, Newtownards Road, Belfast, 26 August 1981.
3. William Craig, quoted in "The Ulster Independence Debate—Again," prepared by a coalition of community workers on behalf of the New Ulster Political Research Group. Belfast: October 1980.
4. See W. D. Flackes, *Northern Ireland: A Political Directory,* pp. 138–41, for a brief account of the UDA's history. See also Jack Holland, *Too Long a Sacrifice,* pp. 84–119.
5. This is the figure used by Holland, an unsympathetic observer (see *Too Long a Sacrifice,* p. 86). However, all figures are estimates. Michael McKeown, in "Chronicles: A Register of Northern Ire-

land's Casualties 1969–80," estimates that Loyalist organizations were responsible for 574 of the 2000 deaths that had occurredup to January 6, 1980. The security forces were responsible for 220 deaths, Republican groups for 1024, and 182 deaths could not be classified (p. 5). See also Martin Dillon and Denis Lehane, *Political Murder in Northern Ireland,* for an examination of murders committed up to mid-1973.

6. Quoted by John Kearns in "Ulster Workers' Council Strike."
7. Interview with Andy Tyrie at La Mon House Restaurant, Comber, County Down, 30 December 1980.
8. In 1961, 44 percent of all dwellings in Northern Ireland had no bath and 23 percent had no inside toilet. Even in 1969, 22 percent of all dwellings — one hundred thousand homes — were officially classified as unfit for habitation, and half the houses were over fifty years old. See G. Bell, *Protestants of Ulster,* pp. 26–27. Ten years later, 14 percent of dwellings were statutorily unfit, compared with 5 percent in England (see Labour Party, *Northern Ireland,* p. 22).
9. Glenn Barr, "Presentation on Behalf of the Ulster Defence Association."
10. New Ulster Political Research Group (NUPRG), *Beyond the Religious Divide,* p. 1.
11. Quoted in *Ulster,* vol. 2, no. 4 (1979).
12. NUPRG, "Beyond the Religious Divide," pp. 5–9.
13. NUPRG, *Supplementary Introduction to Documents for Discussion,* p. 10.
14. Ibid.
15. Ibid., p. 8.
16. Ibid.
17. Ibid., p. 9.
18. Ibid.
19. Glenn Barr quoted in U.S. Congress, *Northern Ireland: A Role for the United States?,* p. 50.
20. NUPRG, *Supplementary Introduction to Documents for Discussion,* p. 8.
21. Ibid.
22. See Richard Rose, *Governing Without Consensus,* pp. 214–15.
23. F. S. L. Lyons, *Culture and Anarchy,* pp. 115–16.
24. M. W. Heslinga, *The Irish Border as a Cultural Divide,* p. 118.
25. See *Irish Times,* 9 July 1982.
26. B. Browne, in "Emigration Shifts Balance in North," makes the case for Protestants accounting for a substantially higher proportion of emigrants in the 1970s than in previous decades. Paul

Compton, in "The Demographic Background," is reluctant to agree (p. 87). However, see *Irish Times,* 9 July 1982. The Catholic birth rate was approximately 49 percent higher than the Protestant rate in 1976–77. See Paul Compton, op. cit., p. 85, for annual average rates for the period 1961–77, and his "Contemporary Population of Northern Ireland," p. 16, for other pertinent data.

27. See *The Crane Bag,* vol. 4, no. 2 (1980), p. (*ii*).
28. Paul Compton, in "Fertility Differentials," p. 1405, estimates that in 1971 the Catholic marital fertility rate per 1000 married women aged fifteen to forty-nine was 188, and that the Protestant rate was 109 per 1000.
29. Paul Compton, "The Demographic Background," p. 85.
30. Ibid.
31. A preliminary analysis of the 1981 census estimated that the Catholic population in January 1981 accounted for somewhere between 38.5 percent and 39.2 percent of the total population. See *Irish Times,* 25 February 1983. See also note 33 (below) for the impact of emigration.
32. Paul Compton, "The Demographic Background," p. 88.
33. The enormous differences between estimates and actual facts were revealed when the 1981 census figures were released (see *Irish Times,* 9 July 1982). Paul Compton, in "The Demographic Background," pp. 86–87, bases his population projections and the denominational changes in the population on the estimates of the Registrar General, which suggested that from mid-1972 to mid-1979, "the total net outflow from the Province was 83,800." Elsewhere (in "Contemporary Population of Northern Ireland," p. 9), he estimates net migration from June 1971 to June 1979 to have been 93,500. Actual net outflow from 1971 to 1981 was, as indicated, 153,000. Net outflows for other periods were 92,228 (1951–61) and just 24,000 (1966–71).
34. *Irish Times,* 9 July 1982.
35. Ibid.
36. See *Fortnight,* no. 123 (March 1976), p. 6.
37. Sam Smyth, "Presentation on Behalf of the Ulster Defence Association."
38. These and remarks following from interview with Andy Tyrie, 26 August 1981.
39. Interview with Tommy Lyttle, UDA Headquarters, Newtownards Road, Belfast, 26 August 1981.
40. Ibid.

41. Interview with Andy Tyrie, 26 August 1981.
42. Ibid.
43. Ibid.
44. Ibid.
45. Andy Tyrie, "Independence Is the Only Alternative," in Guardian Newspapers, *The Guardian, Ulster 1980,* p. 4. This booklet reprints articles on Northern Ireland appearing in *The Guardian,* 18–23 February 1980.
46. Statement issued by Ulster Loyalist Democratic Party, UDA Headquarters, Newtownards Road, Belfast.
47. Ibid.
48. John McMichael quoted in Barry White, "The Changing Face of the UDA."
49. Interview with John McMichael, UDA Headquarters, Newtownards Road, Belfast, 2 December 1981.
50. Ibid.
51. Ibid.
52. Ibid.
53. Ibid.
54. Interview with John McMichael, 26 August 1981.
55. Ibid.
56. Interview with John McMichael, 2 December 1981.
57. Ibid.
58. Ibid.
59. Ibid.
60. Ibid.
61. Interview with John McMichael, 30 December 1981.
62. Ibid.
63. Interview with John McMichael, 2 December 1981.
64. Ibid.
65. Interview with John McMichael, 30 December 1981.
66. Ibid.
67. Ibid.
68. Ibid.
69. Ibid.
70. Ibid.
71. Interview with John McMichael, 2 December 1981.
72. *Ulster,* December 1980, p. 1.
73. Ibid.
74. *Ulster,* August 1981, p. 10.
75. Ibid., p. 11.

76. Ibid.
77. Ibid., p. 12.
78. Ibid.
79. Ibid., pp. 12–13.
80. Ibid., p. 13.
81. Ibid.
82. Ibid., p. 14.
83. Ibid., p. 15.
84. Ibid., p. 21.
85. *Ulster,* February 1982, p. 18.
86. *Ulster,* December 1981, p. 21.
87. *Ulster,* September 1981, p. 12.
88. Ian Adamson, *The Cruthin.*
89. William Craig, quoted in David W. Miller, *Queen's Rebels: Ulster Loyalism in Historical Perspective,* p. 123.
90. Interview with Daithi O'Conaill, Provisional Sinn Féin Headquarters, Parnell Square, Dublin, 21 August 1981.
91. John Simpson, "A Critical Look at the Economics of an Autonomous Northern Ireland."
92. About 87 percent of Northern Ireland's plants are oil-fired, compared with 22 percent in Great Britain. See *Belfast Telegraph,* 6 March 1981.
93. Interview with John Hume, 28 August 1981.
94. Interview with John Hume, 2 December 1981.
95. Interview with Garret FitzGerald, 24 December 1981.
96. Interview with Harold McCusker, 29 December 1981.
97. Interview with Robert McCartney, 28 December 1981.
98. Ibid.
99. Ibid.
100. Interview with James Molyneaux, 29 December 1981.
101. Ibid.
102. Ibid.
103. Interview with Seamus Lynch, 26 August 1981.
104. Interview with Daithi O'Conaill, 21 August 1981.
105. Ibid.

9. Frameworks

1. Richard Rose, *Northern Ireland: Time of Choice,* p. 139.
2. Mark Patrick Hederman, " 'The Crane Bag' and the North of Ireland," *The Crane Bag,* vol. 4, no. 2 (1980), p. 99.

10. The South: New Elections

1. Interview with Dr. Garret FitzGerald, 24 December 1981.
2. For accounts of the "split," see J. Bowyer Bell, *The Secret Army*, pp. 355–72, and Tim Pat Coogan, *The IRA*, pp. 419–30.
3. Statement by the Taoiseach, Mr. Charles J. Haughey, in Dáil Éireann, 9 March 1982.
4. Ibid.
5. Ibid.
6. Ibid.
7. See *Fortnight*, no. 186 (May/June 1982), p. 15.
8. Joint statement issued following a meeting between the Irish government and representatives of the SDLP, Monday, 22 March 1982.
9. See *Fortnight*, no. 186 (May/June 1982), p. 16.

11. The North: "Rolling" Devolution

1. David McKittrick, "How the Prior Plan for the North Was Born."
2. United Kingdom, Parliament, *Northern Ireland: A Framework for Devolution.*
3. This statement and those following taken from *Northern Ireland: A Framework for Devolution*, pp. 5–11.
4. *Irish Times*, 1 May 1982.
5. *Sunday Independent*, 10 September 1982.
6. Interview with Seamus Mallon, Leinster House, Kildare Street, Dublin, 13 May 1982.
7. Ibid.
8. Ibid.
9. Quotations in this paragraph from a government statement issued by the Government Information Service, 5 April 1982.
10. Charles Haughey interviewed on *This Week*, RTE radio, 23 May 1982.
11. Ibid.
12. These and following remarks taken from interview with Garret FitzGerald, Leinster House, Kildare Street, Dublin, 26 May 1982.
13. Interview with James Molyneaux, House of Commons, Westminster, 18 May 1982.
14. Interview with Harold McCusker, OUP Headquarters, Glengall Street, Belfast, 14 May 1982.
15. Ibid.
16. *The Voice of Ulster*, July 1982, p. 3.
17. Ibid.

18. See *Fortnight*, no. 187 (July/August 1982), p. 13.
19. *Belfast Newsletter*, 15 May 1982.
20. Ibid.
21. *Irish Times*, 15 May 1982.
22. These and following remarks taken from interview with Oliver Napier, Europa Hotel, Belfast, 14 May 1982.
23. Interview with Thomas MacGiolla, Workers' Party Headquarters, Gardner Street, Dublin, 22 October 1982.
24. *Irish Times*, 25 May 1982.
25. Ibid.
26. These and following remarks taken from interview with James Prior, Stormont Castle, 24 May 1982.

12. The South: Political and Economic Malaise

1. Gerry Fitt quoted in *Irish Times*, 29 April 1982.
2. John Taylor quoted in *Irish Times*, 24 May 1982.
3. Neil Blaney quoted in *Irish Times*, 24 April 1982.
4. RTE interview with Charles Haughey, 23 May 1982. Reported in *Irish Independent*, 24 May 1982.
5. Ibid.
6. RTE interview with Garret FitzGerald, 23 May 1982. Reported in *Irish Independent*, 24 May 1982.
7. Ibid.
8. See *Irish Times*, 28 July 1982.
9. Margaret Thatcher quoted in *Irish Times*, 30 July 1982.
10. This quote and others in this paragraph from Irish government statement quoted in *Irish Times*, 30 July 1982.
11. *Irish Independent*, 19 October 1982.
12. Dr. Kieran Kennedy, Director, Economic and Social Research Institute, supplied the estimate (interview, 22 October 1982).
13. Professor Brendan Walsh, *Sunday Independent*, 17 October 1982.
14. *Irish Times*, 3 September 1982.
15. See *Irish Times*, 1 October 1982.
16. Central Bank of Ireland, *Quarterly Bulletin*, p. 9.
17. Ibid., p. 17.
18. Ibid.
19. Central Bank of Ireland, *Quarterly Bulletin*, Statistical Appendix, p. 9.
20. Bacon et al., "Quarterly Economic Analysis," December 1982, p. 35.
21. *Irish Times*, 2 July 1982.

22. *Irish Times,* 9 July 1982.
23. See *Sunday Independent,* 25 April 1982.
24. Ibid.
25. Data from *The Way Forward,* Government Publications, The Stationery Office, Dublin, October 1982.
26. Ibid., p. 14.
27. Ibid., p. 13.
28. See "Aspect Opinion Poll," *Aspect,* 13–26 May 1982, pp. 8–9.
29. *Report on Crime 1980* (Report for the year ended 31 December 1982, from the Commissioner of the Gárda Síochána to the Minister for Justice), June 1981, and *Report on Crime 1981,* June 1982.
30. *Report on Crime 1980,* p. 1, and *Report on Crime 1981,* p. 1.
31. *Irish Times,* 5 June 1982.
32. *Report on Crime 1981,* p. 1.
33. *Irish Times,* 3 July 1982.
34. Interview with Daithi O'Conaill at Provisional Sinn Féin Headquarters, Parnell Square, Dublin, 26 May 1982.
35. Thomas MacGiolla quoted in *Magill,* April 1982, pp. 7 and 9.
36. Ibid.
37. *Magill,* April 1982.
38. Ibid., cover.
39. The Church of Ireland Bishop of Limerick, Killaloe, and Ardfert, Dr. Walton Empey, quoted in *Irish Times,* 27 September 1982.
40. IMS Survey quoted in *Irish Times,* 20 September 1982.
41. Remarks of the Fianna Fáil Minister for the Gaeltacht quoted in *Irish Times,* 27 September 1982.
42. See pp. 293.

13. The North: New Elections

1. Interview with Sir Jack Hermon at RUC Headquarters, Belfast, 21 May 1982.
2. Survey results quoted in *Irish Times,* 16 October 1982.
3. See *Fortnight,* no. 188 (October 1982), p. 19.
4. James Prior quoted in *Irish Times,* 13 September 1982.
5. Mary Holland in *Sunday Tribune,* 17 October 1982.
6. Charles Haughey quoted in *Irish News,* 19 October 1982.
7. *Irish Times,* 19 October 1982.

14. The Uncivil Wars

1. From RTE interview with Charles Haughey on 27 February 1983, reported in *Irish Times,* 28 February 1983.

2. *Irish Times,* 6 November 1982.
3. Ibid.
4. *Irish Times*/MRBI Poll published in *Irish Times,* 15 November 1982.
5. *Irish Times,* 22 November 1982.
6. Fine Gael–Labour "Program for Government." Published in *Irish Times,* 13 December 1982.
7. *Irish Times,* 15 January 1983.
8. *Irish Times,* 31 December 1982.
9. *Irish Times,* 18 December 1982.
10. Fianna Fáil statement quoted in *Sunday Independent,* 23 January 1983.
11. Charles Haughey quoted in *Sunday Independent,* 23 January 1983.
12. This and remarks following taken from Charles Haughey's statement to the Fianna Fáil party organization published in *Irish Times,* 4 February 1983.

Bibliography

Adamson, Ian. *The Cruthin.* Bangor, County Down, Northern Ireland: Donard Publishing Co., 1974.

Akenson, D. H. *The United States and Ireland.* Cambridge, Mass.: Harvard University Press, 1973.

Amnesty International. *Report of the Amnesty International Mission to Northern Ireland, 28th November to 6th December 1977.* London: Amnesty International, 1978. AI Index No.: EUR 45/01/78.

Arendt, Hannah. *Eichmann in Jerusalem: A Report on the Banality of Evil.* Harmondsworth, Mddx., Eng.: Penguin Books, 1977.

Arnold, Bruce. "Political Constraints: Dublin." In *The Constitution of Northern Ireland,* edited by David Watt, 146–56. London: Heinemann, 1981.

Arthur, Paul. *Government and Politics in Northern Ireland.* Harlow, Essex, Eng.: Longman, 1980.

Aunger, Edmund. "Religion and Occupational Class in Northern Ireland." *Economic and Social Review* 7, no. 1 (1975), 1–18.

Bacon, P.; J. Durkan; J. O'Leary; and S. Scott. "Quarterly Economic Commentary." Dublin: Economic and Social Research Institute, February, May, August, and December 1982.

Baker, John Austin. "Ireland and Northern Ireland." *The Furrow* (January 1982), 13–21.

Barr, Glenn. "Presentation on Behalf of the Ulster Defence Association." Paper read at the Amherst Conference on Northern Ireland. Amherst: University of Massachusetts, August–September 1975.

Barritt, D. P., and C. F. Carter. *The Northern Ireland Problem: A Study in Group Relations.* Oxford: Oxford University Press, 1962.

Beckett, J. C. "Northern Ireland." *Journal of Contemporary History* 6, no. 1 (1971), 121–34.

Bell, G. *The Protestants of Ulster.* London: Pluto Press, 1976.

Bell, J. Bowyer. "The Chroniclers of Violence in Northern Ireland: A Tragedy in Endless Acts." *Review of Politics* 38, no. 4 (October 1976), 510–33.

———. *A Time of Terror: How Democratic Societies Respond to Revolutionary Violence.* New York: Basic Books, 1978.
———. *The Secret Army 1916–1979.* Dublin: Academy Press, 1979.
Blanshard, Paul. *The Irish and Catholic Power.* Boston: Beacon Press, 1953.
Boal, Frederick W., and J. Neville H. Douglas, eds. *Integration and Division: Geographical Perspectives on the Northern Ireland Problem.* London: Academic Press, 1982.
Boulton, David. *The UVF, 1966–73: An Anatomy of Loyalist Rebellion.* Dublin: Torc Books, Gill & Macmillan, 1973.
Boyd, Andrew. *Holy War in Belfast.* Tralee, Republic of Ireland: Anvil Books, 1969.
Boyle, Joseph. "Educational Attainment, Occupational Achievement and Religion in Northern Ireland." *Economic and Social Review* 8, no. 2 (1976), 79–100.
Boyle, Kevin; Tom Hadden; and Paddy Hillyard. "Emergency Powers: Ten Years On." *Fortnight,* no. 179 (December 1979/January 1980), 4–8.
———. "The Facts on Internment." *Fortnight,* no. 94 (November 1974), 9–12.
Bristow, John A. "All-Ireland Perspectives." In *Political Cooperation in Divided Societies,* edited by Desmond Rea, 137–55. Dublin: Gill & Macmillan, 1982.
Brown, Terence. *Ireland: A Social and Cultural History 1922–1979.* London: Fontana, 1981.
Browne, B. "Emigration Shifts Balance in North." *Hibernia* 42, no. 16 (1978).
Browne, Vincent. "Interview with a Senior Member of the IRA Leadership." *Magill,* August 1978, 14–27.
———. "The Making of a Taoiseach." *Magill,* January 1980, 22–37.
———. "The Arms Crisis 1970." *Magill,* May 1980, 17–28.
———. "The Berry File." *Magill,* June 1980, 39–73.
———. "The Misconduct of the Arms Trial." *Magill,* July 1980, 17–28.
———. "The New Provo Strategy." *Magill,* November 1981, 4–5.
———. "Economy: The High Road to Disaster." *Magill,* January 1982, 21–38.
———. "Squandermania." *Magill,* March 1982, 10–13.
———. "The IRA's Twenty-Year War." *Magill,* August 1982, 8–10.
———. "The GUBU Factor." *Magill,* November 1982, 15–16.

Browne, Vincent, ed. *The Magill Book of Irish Politics.* Dublin: Magill Publications, 1982.

Buckland, Patrick. *The Factory of Grievances: Devolved Government in Northern Ireland.* Dublin: Gill & Macmillan, 1979.

———. *A History of Northern Ireland.* Dublin: Gill & Macmillan, 1981.

Budge, I., and C. O'Leary. *Belfast: Approach to Crisis 1613–1970.* London: Macmillan, 1973.

Burton, F. *The Politics of Legitimacy.* London: Routledge & Kegan Paul, 1978.

Central Bank of Ireland. *Quarterly Bulletin.* Dublin: Central Bank of Ireland, Autumn 1982.

Clutterbuck, Richard. "Comment on Chapter Seven: Security Constraints." In *The Constitution of Northern Ireland,* edited by David Watt, 140–45. London: Heinemann, 1981.

———. *Protest and the Urban Guerilla.* New York: Abelard-Schuman, 1973.

Cohan, A. S. "The Question of a United Ireland: Perspectives of the Irish Political Elite." *International Affairs* 3, no. 2 (April 1977), 232–54.

Cole, John. "Security Constraints." In *The Constitution of Northern Ireland,* edited by David Watt, 122–39. London: Heinemann, 1981.

Community of the Peace People. "The H Block: The Hunger Strike in the Maze Prison." Lisburn Road, Belfast: Peace People, October 1980.

Compton, Paul A. "Fertility Differentials and Their Impact on Population Distribution and Composition in Northern Ireland." *Environment and Planning A* 10 (1978), 1397–1411.

———. "The Contemporary Population of Northern Ireland and Population-Related Issues." Belfast: Institute of Irish Studies, The Queen's University, 1981.

———. "The Demographic Background." In *The Constitution of Northern Ireland,* edited by David Watt, 74–92. London: Heinemann, 1981.

Coogan, Tim Pat. *The IRA.* London: Fontana, 1971.

———. *On the Blanket: The H Block Story.* Dublin: Ward River Press, 1980.

Cronin, Sean. *Irish Nationalism, A History of Its Roots and Ideology.* Dublin: Academy Press, 1980.

Darby, J. *Conflict in Northern Ireland: The Development of a Polarized Community.* Dublin: Gill & Macmillan, 1976.

Dash, Samuel. "Justice Denied." New York: International League for the Rights of Man, 1972.

Davis, E. E., and R. Sinott. "Attitudes in the Republic of Ireland Relevant to the Northern Ireland Problem: Vol. 1." Dublin: Economic and Social Research Institute, Paper No. 97 (September 1979).

Deane, Seamus, and Barre Fitzpatrick. "Interview with John Hume." *The Crane Bag* 4, no. 2 (1980), 39–43.

de Paor, Liam. *Divided Ulster.* Harmondsworth, Mddx., Eng.: Penguin Books, 1970.

Deutsch, Richard, and Vivien Magowan. *Northern Ireland 1968–1973: A Chronology of Events. Vol. 1: 1968–1971.* Belfast, Blackstaff Press, 1973.

Devine, J. "Polling Time Again in the North's Valley of Hate." *Sunday Independent,* 16 August 1981.

Devlin, Bernadette. *The Price of My Soul.* London: André Deutsch, 1969.

Dillon, Martin, and Denis Lehane. *Political Murder in Northern Ireland.* Harmondsworth, Mddx., Eng.: Penguin Books, 1973.

Doob, Leonard W., and William J. Foltz. "The Belfast Workshop: An Application of Group Techniques to a Destructive Conflict." *Journal of Conflict Resolution* 17, no. 3 (1973), 489–512.

———. "The Impact of a Workshop upon Grass Roots Leaders in Belfast." *Journal of Conflict Resolution* 18, no. 2 (1974), 237–56.

Dowling, Brendan. "Some Implications of a Federal Ireland." Dublin: Economic and Social Research Institute, Memorandum Series No. 97. Presented at the University of Ulster, Coleraine, November 1974.

Dunn, John. *Modern Revolutions: An Introduction to the Analysis of a Political Phenomenon.* Cambridge: Cambridge University Press, 1972.

Easthope, Gary. "Religious War in Northern Ireland." *Sociology* 10, no. 3 (September 1976) 427–49.

Economic and Social Research Institute. "Some Issues in the Methodology of Attitude Research." Dublin: Economic and Social Research Institute, Policy Research Series No. 3 (November 1980).

Edwards, Owen Dudley. *The Sins of Our Fathers: Roots of Conflict in Northern Ireland.* Dublin: Gill & Macmillan, 1970.

Farrell, Michael. *Northern Ireland: The Orange State.* London: Pluto Press, 1976.

Faul, Fr. Dennis, and Fr. Raymond Murray. *The Birmingham Framework.* Dungannon, County Tyrone, 1977.

Fennell, Desmond. "The Northern Ireland Problem: Basic Data and Terminology." Galway: University College, 1981.

Fine Gael. "Ireland: Our Future Together." Dublin: Fine Gael, February 1979.

Fisk, Robert. *The Point of No Return.* London: André Deutsch, 1975.
FitzGerald, Garret. *Towards a New Ireland.* London: Charles Knight, 1972.
Flackes, W. D. *Northern Ireland, A Political Directory 1968–1979.* Dublin: Gill & Macmillan, 1980.
Foley, A., and P. Walbridge. "The Socio-Economic Position of Ireland Within the European Economic Community." Dublin: National Economic and Social Council, May 1981.
Foley, Gerry. "Bernadette and the Politics of H Block." *Magill,* April 1981, pp. 9–21.
Fortnight magazine (Belfast).
Frazer, Morris. *Children in Conflict: Growing Up in Northern Ireland.* New York: Basic Books, 1977.
Gallagher, Eric, and Stanley Worrall. *Christians in Ulster 1969–1980.* Oxford: Oxford University Press, 1982.
Gallagher, Frank. *The Invisible Island: The Story of the Partition of Ireland.* London: Victor Gollancz, 1957.
Garvin, Tom. "Nationalist Elites, Irish Voters and Irish Political Development: A Comparative Perspective." *Economic and Social Review* 8, no. 3 (1977), 161–86.
———. *The Evolution of Irish Nationalist Politics.* Dublin: Gill & Macmillan, 1981.
Greaves, C. Desmond. *The Irish Crisis.* London: Lawrence & Wishart, 1972.
Guardian Newspapers. *The Guardian, Ulster 1980, Reprint of Articles Appearing in The Guardian, Feb. 18–23, 1980.* Manchester, Eng.: Guardian Newspapers, 1980.
Hackey, Thomas E. "One People or Two? The Origins of Partition and the Prospects for Unification in Ireland." *Journal of International Affairs* 27, no. 2 (1975), 232–46.
Hadden, Tom. "Why Everyone Distrusts British Intentions." *Fortnight,* no. 111 (September 1975), 8–11.
Harbison, John F. *The Ulster Unionist Party 1882–1973: Its Development and Organisation.* Belfast: Blackstaff Press, 1974.
Harris, Rosemary. *Prejudice and Tolerance in Ulster: A Study of Neighbors and Strangers in a Border Community.* Manchester, Eng.: Manchester University Press, 1972.
Hederman, Mark Patrick. "Interview with Seamus Twomey." *The Crane Bag* 1, no. 2 (1977), 107–12.
Hepburn, A. C., ed. *The Conflict of Nationality in Northern Ireland.* London: Edward Arnold, 1980.

Heskin, Ken. *Northern Ireland: A Psychological Analysis.* New York: Columbia University Press, 1980.

Heslinga, M. W. *The Irish Border as a Cultural Divide.* Assen, The Netherlands: Van Gorcum, 1979.

Hewitt, Christopher. "Catholic Grievances, Catholic Nationalism, and Violence in Northern Ireland During the Civil Rights Period: A Reconsideration." *British Journal of Sociology* 33, no. 3 (September 1981), 362–80.

Hewitt, John. "A Question of Identity." Paper read at the Conference on Independence. Corrymeala, Ballycastle, County Antrim, 1976.

Holland, Jack. *Too Long a Sacrifice: Life and Death in Northern Ireland Since 1969.* New York: Dodd, Mead & Co., 1981.

Hume, John. "The Irish Question: A British Problem." *Foreign Affairs,* Winter 1979/80, 300–13.

Hutchinson, R. W., and J. Sheehan. *A Review of Selected Indicators of Economic Performance in Northern Ireland and the Republic of Ireland During the 1970's.* Belfast and Dublin: Cooperation North, December 1980.

Hunter, John. "An Analysis of the Conflict in Northern Ireland." In *Political Co-operation in Divided Societies,* edited by Desmond Rea, 9–59. Dublin: Gill & Macmillan, 1982.

Irish Council of Churches, Board of Community Affairs. "The H. Block Issue." Belfast: Irish Council of Churches, 1980.

Irish Government Publications. *Reports on Crime 1980 and 1981: Report of the Commissioner, Gárda Síochána, to the Minister for Justice.* Dublin: The Stationery Office, July 1981 and June 1982.

Irish Government Publications. *The Way Forward: National Economic Plan 1983–1987.* Dublin: The Stationery Office, October 1982.

Jackson, H. *The Two Irelands — The Problem of the Double Minority: A Dual Study of Inter-Group Tensions,* Minority Rights Group Report No. 2, Revised Edition. London: Minority Rights Group, 1972.

Johnson, Paul. *Ireland: A Concise History from the Twelfth Century to the Present Day.* London: Panther Books, 1981.

Jones, Thomas. *Ireland 1918–1925* (volume 3 of *Whitehall Diary,* edited by K. Middlemas). Oxford: Oxford University Press, 1971.

Kearney, Richard. "The IRA's Strategy of Failure." *The Crane Bag* 4, no. 2 (1980), 62–70.

Kearns, John. "Ulster Workers' Council Strike, May 1974" (unpublished paper). Belfast, 1976.

Kee, Robert. *The Most Distressful Country* (volume 1 of *The Green Flag*) and *Ourselves Alone* (volume 3 of *The Green Flag*). London: Quartet Books, 1976.

Kyle, Keith. "The Panorama Survey of Irish Opinion." *The Political Quarterly* 50, no. 1 (January/March 1979), 24–35.

Labour Party. "Northern Ireland: Statement by the National Executive Committee." London: Labour Party, 1981.

Lijphart, Arend. "Review Article: The Northern Ireland Problem; Cases, Theories and Solutions." *British Journal of Political Science* 5, part 1 (January 1975), 83–106.

Lyons, F.S.L. *Ireland Since the Famine.* London: Fontana, 1973.

———. "The Burden of Our History," the W. B. Rankin Memorial Lecture. Belfast: The Queen's University, 1978.

———. *Culture and Anarchy in Ireland 1890–1939.* Oxford: Oxford University Press, 1979.

McAllister, Ian. *The Northern Ireland Social Democratic and Labour Party: Political Opposition in a Divided Society.* London: Macmillan, 1977.

———. "Political Opposition in Northern Ireland: The National Democratic Party 1965–70." *Economic and Social Review* 6, no. 3 (April 1975), 353–66.

McCann, Eamonn. *War and an Irish Town.* Harmondsworth, Mddx., Eng.: Penguin Books, 1974.

McCartney, R. L. "The Case for the Unionists." Belfast, 1981.

McCracken, J. L. "The Political Scene in Northern Ireland 1926–1937." In *The Years of the Great Test,* edited by Francis MacManus. Cork: Mercier Press, 1967.

MacDermott, Frank. *Tone and His Times.* Dublin: Anvil Books, 1980.

McDowell, Michael, "Removing the British Guarantee." *The Crane Bag* 4, no. 2 (1980), 34–38.

MacGreil, M. *Prejudice and Tolerance in Ireland.* Dublin: College of Industrial Relations, 1947.

McGuffin, John. *The Guinea Pigs.* Harmondsworth, Mddx., Eng.: Penguin Books, 1974.

McKeown, Ciaran. "The New Europa Style SDLP." *Fortnight,* no. 97 (January 1975), 8.

McKeown, Michael. "Chronicles: A Register of Northern Ireland's Casualties 1969–80." *The Crane Bag* 4, no. 2 (1980), 1–5.

McKittrick, David. "How the Prior Plan for the North Was Born." *Irish Times,* 3 April 1982.

MacManus, Francis, ed. *The Years of the Great Test.* Cork: Mercier Press, 1967.

Magill magazine (Dublin).
Mansergh, Nicholas. "The Government of Ireland Act, 1920: Its Origins and Purposes." In *Historical Studies (IX): Papers Read Before the Irish Conference of Historians,* edited by John Barry. Belfast: Blackstaff Press, 1974.
Marrinan, Patrick. *Paisley: Man of Wrath.* Tralee: Anvil Books, 1973.
Miller, David W. *Queen's Rebels: Ulster Loyalism in Historical Perspective.* Dublin: Gill & Macmillan, 1978.
Moloney, Ed. "Paisley." *The Crane Bag* 4, no. 2 (1980), 23–27.
———. "The IRA." *Magill,* September 1980, 13–28.
———. "British Investment Withdrawal." *Irish Times,* 14 August 1982.
———. "Depressing Outlook for Unemployed Youngsters." *Irish Times,* 20 March 1982.
Morrison, Danny. "The Provos Will Not Lay Down Their Arms." *Fortnight,* no. 182 (December 1982), 4–5.
Moxon-Browne, E. "The Water and the Fish: Public Opinion and the Provisional IRA in Northern Ireland." In *British Perspectives on Terrorism,* edited by Paul Wilkinson. London: George Allen & Unwin, 1981.
Murphy, John A. *Ireland in the Twentieth Century.* Dublin: Gill & Macmillan, 1975.
Murray, Russell. "Political Violence in Northern Ireland 1969–1977." In *Integration and Division: Geographical Perspectives on the Northern Ireland Problem,* edited by F. W. Boal and J. N. H. Douglas, 309–11. London: Academic Press, 1982.
Nairn, Tom. *The Break-up of Britain.* London: Verso Editions, 1981.
Newsinger, John. " 'I Bring Not Peace but a Sword': the Religious Motif in the Irish War of Independence." *Journal of Contemporary History* 13, no. 3 (July 1978), 609–28.
New Ulster Political Research Group (NUPRG). "Beyond the Religious Divide." Belfast: NUPRG, March 1979.
———. *Supplementary Introduction to Documents for Discussion: Beyond the Political Divide.* Belfast: NUPRG, September 1980.
O'Brien, Conor Cruise. *States of Ireland.* New York: Pantheon Books, 1972.
———. *Neighbours: The Ewart-Biggs Memorial Lectures 1978–79.* London: Faber & Faber, 1980.
O'Connor, Kevin. *The Irish in Britain.* Dublin: Torc Books, Gill & Macmillan, 1974.
O'Donnell, E. E. *Northern Ireland Stereotypes.* Dublin: College of Industrial Relations, 1977.

Paisley, Ian. "No Pope Here." Belfast: Martyr Memorial Publications, April 1982.

Perceval-Maxwell, M. "The Ulster Rising of 1641 and the Depositions." *Irish Historical Studies* 21, no. 82 (September 1978), 144–67.

Provisional IRA. "Freedom Struggle: The Provisional IRA." (This document was banned in the Republic.)

Rea, Desmond, ed. *Political Cooperation in Divided Societies.* Dublin: Gill & Macmillan, 1982.

Roberts, David. "The Orange Order in Ireland: A Religious Institution." *British Journal of Sociology* 14, no. 2 (1973), 213–80.

Rose, Richard. *Governing Without Consensus: An Irish Perspective.* Boston: Beacon Press, 1971.

———. *Northern Ireland: Time of Choice.* Washington, D.C.: American Enterprise Institute for Public Policy Research, 1976.

———. "Opinion Over Ulster at Sword's Point," *Public Opinion,* October/November 1979, 48–49.

———; I. McAllister; and P. Mair. "Is There a Concurring Majority About Northern Ireland?" Studies in Public Policy No. 22. Glasgow: Center for the Study of Public Policy, University of Strathclyde, 1978.

Sands, Bobby. *The Diary of Bobby Sands.* Dublin: Sinn Féin Publicity Department, June 1981.

Sheehan, J., and R. W. Hutchinson. *Demographic and Labour Force Structure in the Republic of Ireland.* Belfast and Dublin: Cooperation North, November 1980.

Simpson, John. "A Review of Economic and Industrial Strategy." *Fortnight,* no. 135 (October 1976), 4.

———. "A Critical Look at the Economics of an Autonomous Northern Ireland." Paper read at the Conference on Independence, Corrymeala, Ballycastle, County Antrim, 1976.

———. "Economic Alternatives." *Fortnight,* no. 187 (July/August 1982), 8.

Sinn Féin. "Éire Nua: The Sinn Féin Policy—The Social, Economic, and Political Dimensions" (as adapted and approved by the Ard Fheis of 1979). Dublin: Sinn Féin, 1979.

Smyth, Sam. "Presentation on Behalf of the Ulster Defence Association." Paper read at the Amherst Conference on Northern Ireland. Amherst: University of Massachusetts, August–September 1975.

Stewart, A.T.Q. *The Ulster Crisis: Resistance to Home Rule 1912–14.* London: Faber & Faber, 1967.

———. *The Narrow Ground: Aspects of Ulster 1609–1969.* London: Faber & Faber, 1977.

Sunday Times Insight Team. *Ulster.* Harmondsworth, Mddx., Eng.: Penguin Books, 1972.

Taylor, Peter. *Beating the Terrorists?* Harmondsworth, Mddx., Eng.: Penguin Books, 1980.

Terchek, Ronald J. "Conflict and Cleavage in Northern Ireland." *American Academy of Political and Social Science Annals* 433 (September 1977), 47–58.

United Kingdom, Parliament. *Report of the Tribunal Appointed to Inquire into the Events of Sunday, 30 January 1972, Which Led to Loss of Life in Connection with the Procession in Londonderry on That Day,* chaired by Lord Widgery. H.L.101, H.C.220. London: Her Majesty's Stationery Office, April 1972.

———. *Report of the Commission to Consider Legal Procedures to Deal with Terrorist Activities in Northern Ireland,* chaired by Lord Diplock. Cmnd. 5185. London: Her Majesty's Stationery Office, December 1972.

———. *Northern Ireland: Constitutional Proposals.* Cmnd. 5259. London: Her Majesty's Stationery Office, March 1973.

———. *Report of the Committee of Inquiry into Police Interrogation Procedures in Northern Ireland,* chaired by Judge Bennett. Cmnd. 7497. London: Her Majesty's Stationery Office, March 1979.

———. *The Government of Northern Ireland: Proposals for Further Discussion.* Cmnd. 7950. London: Her Majesty's Stationery Office, July 1980.

———. *Northern Ireland: A Framework for Devolution.* Cmnd. 8541. London: Her Majesty's Stationery Office, April 1982.

U.S. Congress. Report by two members of the Committee on the Judiciary, 95th Congress. *Northern Ireland: A Role for the United States?* Washington, D.C.: U.S. Government Printing Office, December 1978.

Walsh, Brendan. "Population, Employment and Economic Growth in Ireland." *The Irish Banking Review,* June 1981, 17–23.

———. "Religion and Demographic Behaviour in Ireland." Dublin: Economic and Social Research Institute, Paper No. 55 (1970).

Walsh, Dermot. *Arrest, Interrogation and Diplock Courts.* Belfast: Cobden Trust, 1983.

Watt, David, ed. *The Constitution of Northern Ireland: Problems and Prospects.* London: Heinemann, 1981.

White, Barry. "The Changing Face of the UDA." *Belfast Telegraph,* 26 August 1981.

———. "Political Constraints: Belfast." In *The Constitution of Northern Ireland,* edited by David Watt. London: Heinemann, 1981.

White, Jack. *Minority Report: The Anatomy of the Southern Irish Protestant.* Dublin: Gill & Macmillan, 1975.

Whyte, J. H. *Church and State in Modern Ireland.* Dublin: Gill & Macmillan, 1971.

———. "Church-State Relations in the Republic of Ireland." Paper read at the Amherst Conference on Northern Ireland. Amherst: University of Massachusetts, August–September 1975.

———. "Interpretations of the Northern Ireland Problem: An Appraisal." *Economic and Social Review* 9, no. 4 (1978), 257–82.

Wilkinson, Paul, ed. *British Perspectives on Terrorism.* London: George Allen & Unwin, 1981.

———. "The Provisional IRA: An Assessment in the Wake of the 1981 Hunger Strike." *Government and Opposition* 17, no. 2 (1982), 140–56.

Wilson, Sam. *The Carson Trail.* Belfast: Crown Publications, 1982.

Wright, Frank, "Protestant Ideology and Politics in Ulster." *European Journal of Sociology* 5, no. 14 (1973), 213–80.

Index